EGYPT
Under The
Pharaohs

PORTRAIT HEAD OF A WOODEN STATUE OF AN ANCIENT EGYPTIAN, CALLED THE SHEIKH-EL-BELLED, PROBABLY OF THE TIME OF THE IVTH DYNASTY (ABOUT 3700 B.C.), FOUND AT SAQQARAH, AND NOW IN THE MUSEUM AT GÎZEH. (*See p.* 37.)

Height about 3 feet 8 inches.   Engraved from a Photograph.

EGYPT
Under The
Pharaohs

Heinrich Brugsch-Bey

BRACKEN BOOKS

LONDON

Egypt Under the Pharaohs

First published in 1902 by John Murray, London

This edition first published in 1996 by Bracken Books,
an imprint of Random House UK Ltd, Random House,
20 Vauxhall Bridge Road, London SW1V 2SA

Copyright © Heinrich Brugsch-Bey & M. Brodrick 1902

ISBN 0 09 185049 5

Printed and bound in Guernsey by
The Guernsey Press Co. Ltd

PREFACE

THE estimation in which Brugsch-Bey's 'History of Egypt under the Pharaohs' is held, and the continuously increasing demand for it, have induced the publisher to bring out a cheaper and more convenient edition. While presenting this to the public in one volume instead of two, the greatest care has been taken that, in condensing the Author's style, all the original information should be retained.

The only omissions made in this edition have been that of the essay on 'The Exodus and the Egyptian Monuments,' the discovery of the site of Pithom having proved the Author's theory to be no longer tenable, and the transcription of the Tablet of Usertsen III., which is not given because a transliteration without the hieroglyphs would be absolutely useless.

The much-vexed question of the nationality of the Bubastites has, so far as possible, been accommodated

to Brugsch-Bey's present views without altering the
tenor of the chapter.   It is a well-known fact that the
learned Author has, since writing his History, considerably modified his opinion concerning their Assyrian
origin.

At the same time the whole text has been subjected
to a thorough revision, and, where necessary, has
been corrected in conformity with the most recent discoveries in Egyptological science.   A special notice of
the 'Royal Mummies of Deir-el-Bahari,' and also of
the 'find' in February of this present year, has been
added, as well as new Maps and a complete list of the
Pharaonic Kings, with their Cartouches.

With regard to the transliteration of the Egyptian
names, I have adopted that which appears to me to be
most in accordance with our English alphabet, and
which receives the sanction of such authorities as
Lepsius, Brugsch, and Renouf.   The system of dotted
letters—*e.g.* à, ḥ, ḳ, ṭ, ṣ —though useful for those who are
able to read hieroglyphs, is liable to mislead the general
reader; it has therefore not been considered advisable
to use such letters in this work.   The only exception is
in the case of the *t'*, which is always pronounced like
ch in chip, *e.g.*

> T'efab = Chefab;
> Pai-net'em = Pai-nechem.

Most gratefully do I acknowledge the generous assistance of Mr. LE PAGE RENOUF, the Keeper of Egyptian and Assyrian Antiquities in the British Museum. While preparing the manuscript of this edition he has given me the benefit of his constant help and advice, and, though ill able to spare the time, has kindly read the whole work as it passed through the press.

M. BRODRICK.

LONDON: 1891

CONTENTS

CHAPTER I.

INTRODUCTORY.

CHAPTER II.

DYNASTIES I.–IV.

CHAPTER III.

DYNASTIES V.–XI

PAGE

CHAPTER IV.

DYNASTY XII.

CHAPTER V.

DYNASTIES XIII.–XVII.

CHAPTER VI.

THE HYKSOS.

CHAPTER VII.

AAHMES — HATSHEPSU.

CHAPTER VIII.

TEHUTI-MES III.

CHAPTER IX.

AMEN-HOTEP II.—TEHUTI-MES IV.—AMEN-HOTEP III.

CHAPTER X.

THE HERETIC KINGS.

CHAPTER XI.

RAMSES I. AND SETI I.

CHAPTER XII.

RAMSES II.

CHAPTER XIII.

RAMSES II. (*continued*) AND HIS SUCCESSORS.

CHAPTER XIV.

DYNASTY XX.

CHAPTER XV.

DYNASTIES XXI.–XXIV.

CHAPTER XVI.

DYNASTY XXV.

CHAPTER XVII.

DYNASTIES XXVI.–XXX.

GENEALOGICAL TABLES.

PLANS AND ILLUSTRATIONS.

MAPS.

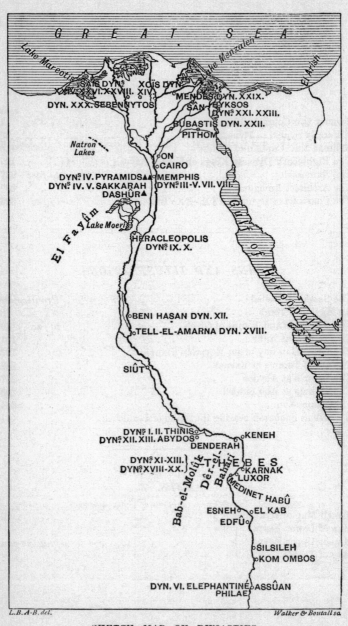

GREAT SEA

Lake Mareotis
The Manzaleh
El Arish

SAIS DYN.
XXIV. XXVI. XXVIII. XIV.
XCIS DYN.

MENDES DYN. XXIX.
DYN. XXX. SEBENNYTOS
SAN. HYKSOS
DYNS XXI. XXIII.

BUBASTIS DYN. XXII.
PITHOM

Natron
Lakes

ON
CAIRO
DYNS IV. PYRAMIDS MEMPHIS
DYNS IV. V. SAKKARAH DYNS III-V. VII. VIII.
DASHÛR

El Fayûm
Lake Moeris

Gulf of Heroöpolis

HERACLEOPOLIS
DYNS IX. X.

BENI HASAN DYN. XII.

TELL-EL-AMARNA DYN. XVIII.

SIÛT

DYNS I. II. THINIS
DYNS XII. XIII. ABYDOS
KENEH
DENDERAH

DYNS XI-XIII. THEBES
DYNS XVIII-XX. KARNAK
LUXOR
MEDINET HABÛ

Bab-el-Molûk
Dêr-el-Baharî

ESNEH EL KAB
EDFÛ

SILSILEH
KOM OMBOS

DYN. VI. ELEPHANTINÉ ASSÛAN
PHILAE

L.B.A.B.del.
Walker & Boutalls.

SKETCH MAP OF DYNASTIES.

TABLE OF THE PRINCIPAL KINGS OF ANCIENT EGYPT, WITH THEIR CARTOUCHES.

DYNASTY I.—THINITE.

			B.C.				B.C.
1	Mena	. . .	4400	5	Hesep-ti	. .	4266
2	Teta	. . . .	4366	6	Mer-ba-pen	. .	4233
3	Atet	. . .	4333	7	Semen-Ptah	. .	4200
4	Ata	. . . .	4300	8	Qebh	. . .	4166

DYNASTY II.—THINITE.

			B.C.				B.C.
9	Neter-baiu	. .	4133	11	Ba-en-neter	. .	4066
10	Ka-kau	. . .	4100	12	Uat'-nes	. .	4033

			B.C.
13	Senta	. . . .	4000

DYNASTY III.—MEMPHITE.

		B.C.				B.C.
14	T'at'ai . . .	3966	17	Teta . . .		3866
15	Neb-ka . . .	3933	18	*Set'es . . .		3833
16	Ser . . .	3900	19	1 Nefer-ka-Ra } 2 Huni		3800
			20	Sneferu . .	3766	

DYNASTY IV.—MEMPHITE.

		B.C.			B.C.
21	Khufu . . .	3733	23	Khaf-Ra . .	3666
22	Tat-f-Ra . .	3700	24	Men-kau-Ra . .	3633
	25	Shepses-ka-f . .	3600		

DYNASTY V.—ELEPHANTINÉ.

		B.C.			B.C.
26	User-ka-f . .	3566	30	1 User-en-Ra } 2 An	3433
27	Sahu-Ra . .	3533	31	Men-kau-Hor .	3400
28	Kakaa . .	3500	32	1 Tat-ka-Ra } 2 Assa	3366
29	1 Nefer-f-Ra } 2 Shepses-ka-Ra	3466	33	Unas . .	3333

DYNASTY VI.—MEMPHITE.

		B.C.			B.C.
34	Teta	3300	38	Nefer-ka-Ra (Pepi II.) .	3166
35	1 User-ka-Ra 2 Ati	3266	39	Mer-en-se (?)-em-sa-f .	3133
36	1 Meri-Ra 2 Pepi I.	3233	40	Neter-ka-Ra . . .	3100
37	1 Mer-en-Ra 2 Hor-em-sa-f	3200	41	1 Men-ka-Ra 2 Nit-aqert (*Queen Nitocris.*)	3066

DYNASTIES VII.–XI.

		B.C.			B.C.
42	Nefer-ka-Ra . .	3033	50	Nefer-ka-Hor . .	2766
43	Nefer-ka-Ra-nebi .	3000	51	Nefer-ka-Ra-Pepi-senb	2733
44	Tat-ka-Ra-Maat . .	2966	52	Nefer-ka-Ra-annu .	2700
45	Nefer-ka-Ra-khentu	2933	53	Nefer-kau-Ra . .	2666
46	Mer-en-Hor . . .	2900	54	Nefer-kau-Hor . .	2600
47	Se-nefer-ka-Ra . .	2866	55	Nefer-ari-ka-Ra . .	2566
48	Ka-en-Ra . . .	2833	56	1 Neb-kher-Ra 2 Mentu-hotep (V.)	2533
49	Nefer-ka-Ra-terer .	2800	57	Se-ankh-ka-Ra . .	2500

DYNASTY XII.—THEBAN.

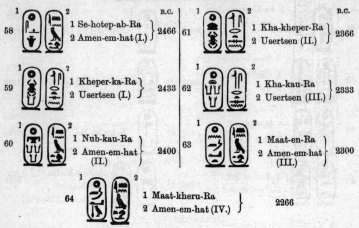

	B.C.		B.C.
58 — 1 Se-hotep-ab-Ra / 2 Amen-em-hat (I.) } 2466	61 — 1 Kha-kheper-Ra / 2 Usertsen (II.) } 2366
59 — 1 Kheper-ka-Ra / 2 Usertsen (I.) } 2433	62 — 1 Kha-kau-Ra / 2 Usertsen (III.) } 2333
60 — 1 Nub-kau-Ra / 2 Amen-em-hat (II.) } 2400	63 — 1 Maat-en-Ra / 2 Amen-em-hat (III.) } 2300

64   1 Maat-kheru-Ra / 2 Amen-em-hat (IV.) }   2266

A gap which comprises more than 500 years, and during which the time of the Hyksos falls. In all Dynasties XIII.-XVII., B.C. 2233-1733, circa.

DYNASTY XVIII.—THEBAN.

65   1 Neb-peh-tet-Ra / 2 Aahmes (I.) (*Amosis or Amasis I.*) } 1700

66   1 Ser-ka-Ra / 2 Amen-hotep (I.) } 1666

67   1 Aa-kheper-ka-Ra / 2 Tehuti-mes (I.) } 1633

68   1 Aa-kheper-en-Ra / 2 Tehuti-mes (II.) } 1600

69   1 Maat-ka-Ra / 2 Hat-shepset-khnem-Amen. (*Queen Hathepsu*) } . . —

70   1 Men-kheper-Ra / 2 Tehuti-mes (III.) } . . . . . . —

B.C.

71 1 Aa-kheperu-Ra
    2 Amen-hotep-neter-haq-Annu (II.) } 1566

72 1 Men-kheperu-Ra
    2 Tehuti-mes (IV.) } 1533

73 1 Maat-neb-Ra
    2 Amen-hotep-haq-Uast. (*Amen-hotep III.*) } . . . 1500

74 1 Nefer-kheperu-Ra-ua-en-Ra
    2 Amen-hotep-haq-Uast
    3 Khu-n-Aten. (*Amen-hotep IV.*) } . . . 1466

    1 Ser-kheperu-Ra-sotep-en-Ra
    2 Amen-meri-en-Hor-em-heb. (*Horus*) } . . . 1433

One generation of heretic kings.

DYNASTY XIX.—THEBAN.

75 1 Men-pehtet-Ra
    2 Ra-messu. (*Ramses I.*) } 1400

76 1 Men-Maat-Ra
    2 Amen-meri-en-Seti
    3 Meri-en-Ptah. (*Seti I.   Meneptah I.*) } . . . 1366

77 1 User-Maat-Ra-sotep-en-Ra
    2 Ra-messu-meri-Amen. (*Ramses II.*) } . . . 1333

78 1 Ba-en-Ra-meri-en-Amen
    2 Ptah-meri-en-hotep-her-Maat. (*Meneptah II.*) } . . 1300

79 1 Khu-en-Ra-sotep-en-Ra
    2 Ptah-meri-en-se-Ptah. (*Meneptah III.*) } . . . 1266

80 1 User-khau-Ra-meri-Amen
    2 Ra-meri-Amen-merer-Set-nekht. (*Setnekht*) } . . 1233

DYNASTY XX.—THEBAN.

			B.C.
81	1 User-Maat-Ra-meri-Amen 2 Ra-meses-haq Annu. (*Ramses III.*) } · · · ·		1200
82	1 User-Ra-sotep-en-Amen 2 Ra-meses-meri-Amen-Ra-haq-Maat. (*Ramses IV.*) }		· 1166
83	1 User-Maat-Ra-sotep-en-kheper-Ra 2 Ra-mes-meri-Amen-Amen suten-f. (*Ramses V.*) }		· —
84	1 Ra-Amen-Maat-meri-neb 2 Ra-Amen-meses-neter Annu. (*Ramses VI.*) } · · ·		—
85	1 Ra-user-Amen-meri-sotep-en-Ra 2 Ra-Amen-meses-ta-neter-haq-Annu. (*Ramses VII.*) } ·		—
86	1 Ra-user-Maat-khu-en-Amen 2 Ra-Amen-meses-meri-Amen. (*Ramses VIII.*) } ·		—
87	1 Se-kha-en-Ra Meri-Amen 2 Ra-meses-se-Ptah. (*Ramses IX.*) } · · ·		—
88	1 Nefer-kau-Ra-sotep-en-Ra 2 Ra-meses-merer-Amen-kha-Uast. (?) (*Ramses X.*) }		—
89	1 Ra-kheper-Maat-sotep-en-Ra 2 Ra-mes-suten Amen. (*Ramses XI.*) } · · ·		—
90	1 User-Maat-Ra-sotep-nu-Ra 2 Amen-mer-Ra-meses. (*Ramses XII.*) } · · ·		—
91	1 Men-Maat-Ra-sotep-en-Ra 2 Ra-meses-merer-Amen-kha Uast neter haq Annu. } (*Ramses XIII.*)		· 1133

DYNASTY XXI.—THEBAN.

B.C.

92   1 Neter-hen-hotep-en-Amen
      2 Her-Hor-se-Amen. (*Her-Hor*)   ·   ·   ·   ·   ·   1100

93   Pai-net'em I.   ·   ·   ·   ·   ·   ·   ·   ·   ·   —

94   1 Kheper-kha-Ra-sotep-en-Amen
      2 Amen-meri-Pai-net'em (II.)   ·   ·   ·   ·   —

DYNASTY XXII.—BUBASTITE.

95   1 Kheper-sekhet-Ra-sotep-en-Ra
      2 Amen-meri-Shashanq (I.)   ·   ·   ·   ·   966

96   1 Kherp-kheper-Ra-sotep-en-Ra
      2 Amen-meri-Uasarken. (*Osorkon I.*)   ·   ·   ·   —

97   1 Het'-kheper-Ra-sotep-en-Ra
      2 Amen-meri-Auset-meri-thakeleth.   (*Takeleth I.*)   ·   ·   —

98   1 User-Maat-Ra-sotep-en-Amen
      2 Amen-meri-Uasarken.   (*Osorkon II.*)   ·   ·   ·   —

99   1 Kheper-sekhem-Ra-sotep-en-Amen
      2 Amen-meri-Shash[anq] (II.)   ·   ·   ·   —

100   Takeleth II.   ·   ·   ·   ·   ·   ·   ·   ·   —

101   1 User-Maat-Ra-sotep-en-Amen
      2 Amen-meri-se Bast-Shashanq (III.)   ·   ·   ·   —

B.C.

102
1 User-Maat-Ra-sotep-en-Amen }
2 Amen-meri-Pa-mai } . . . . —

103
1 Aa-kheper-Ra }
2 Shash[an]q IV. } . . . . —

DYNASTY XXIII.—TANITE.

104 Amen-meri-Peta-se-Bast 766

105
1 Aa-kheper-Ra-sotep-en-Amen
2 Ra-Amen-meri-Uasarkena. (*Osorkon III.*) } . . . —

DYNASTY XXIV.—SAÏTE.

106 Bakenranf. (*Bocchoris*) 733

DYNASTY XXV.— ETHIOPIAN.

107 Pa-ankhi. (*Piankhi*) . . . . —

108
1 Nefer-ka-Ra
2 Shabaka. (*Sabaco*) } 700

109
1 Tat-kau-Ra }
2 Shabataka } . . . . —

110
1 Ra-nefer-tem-khu
2 Taharaqa. (*Tirhakah*) } . . . . . —

DYNASTY XXVI.—SAÏTE.

B.C.

111   1 Uah-ab-Ra
2 Psamthek. (*Psammetichus I.*)   666

112   1 Nem-ab-Ra
2 Nekau. (*Necho*)   612

113   1 Nefer-ab-Ra
2 Psamthek. (*Psammetichus II.*)   .   .   .   596

114   1 Haa-ab-Ra
2 Uah-ab-Ra. (*Apries*)   591

115   1 Khnem-ab-Ra
2 Aahmes-se-Nit. (*Amasis II.*)   .   .   .   572

116   1 Ankh-ka-en-Ra
2 Psamthek. (*Psammetichus III.*)   .   .   .   528

DYNASTY XXVII.—PERSIAN.

117   Kambathet. (*Cambyses*)   .   .   .   :   .   .   .   527

118   Khshaiarsha. (*Xerxes the Great*)   486

119   Artakhshashas. (*Artaxerxes*)   465

120   1 Ra-meri-Amen
2 Antherirutsha. (*Darius Xerxes*)   .   .   521

Dynasty XXVIII.—SAÏTE.

121　　Amen-rut.　(*Amyrtæus*)　.　.　.　.　.　.　—

B.C.

Dynasty XXIX.—MENDESIAN.

122　　Niafaaurut　.　.　.　.　.　.　.　.　.　.　399

123　　1 Khnem-Maat-Ra ⎫
　　　　2 Haker　　　　　 ⎭　.　.　.　.　.　.　393

124　　1 User-Ra-sotep-en-Ptah ⎫
　　　　2 Psamut　　　　　　　　⎭　.　.　.　.　.　380

Dynasty XXX.—SEBENNYTUS.

125　　1 S-net'em-ab-Ra-sotep-en-Amen
　　　　2 Nekht-Hor-hebt-meri-Amen.　(*Nectanebo I.*) ⎫
　　　　　　　　　　　　　　　　　　　　　　　　　⎭　.　.　.　37,

126　　1 Kheper-ka-Ra
　　　　2 Nekht-neb-f.　(*Nectanebo II.*) ⎫
　　　　　　　　　　　　　　　　　　　　⎭　.　.　.　.　—

THE

HISTORY OF EGYPT.

CHAPTER I.

INTRODUCTORY.

It is the purpose of this work to collect what the
monuments and books tell of the history of that most
remarkable land and people on the favoured banks of
the Nile, beginning with the first native king, Mena. In
spite of all that has perished, never to be recovered,
the last thirty years have brought to light an extraordinary and almost unexpected wealth of new discoveries. A walk through the rooms of the Egyptian
Museum at Gîzeh brings us at each step to monuments
of the most remote ages, and there, there may be seen an
unbroken series of new witnesses of the old time, raised
out of the earth into the light of day, to give information about the long-vanished past, whose starting-point
can no longer be reached even by the remotest stages
in the ordinary historical measurement of time.

The Tablets of Saqqarah and Abydos, both containing a selection of Egyptian monarchs from the first
Pharaoh Mena onwards, give the most authentic evidence, now no longer to be doubted, that the primeval

ancestors of the Egyptian dynasties, the Pharaohs of Memphis, must be recognised as real historical personages, and that King Ramses II. (about 1350 B.C.), the Sesostris of the Greek fabulous history, was preceded by at least seventy-six authentic sovereigns. What conquests the growing knowledge of the old Egyptian language and writing has won for historical research is best shown by the numerous writings of distinguished men of science, amongst which are the works of real genius by the Viscount E. de Rougé on the irruption of the Mediterranean peoples into Egypt in the times of the Nineteenth and Twentieth Dynasties, and the invaluable contributions which M. Chabas, of Chalons, has made towards a knowledge of the same reigns. In sixty centuries the old Egyptian race has undergone but little change; it still preserves those distinctive features of physiognomy, and those peculiarities of manners and customs, which have been handed down to us by the united testimony of the monuments and the accounts of classical writers, as the hereditary characteristics of this people.

Historical researches concerning a race of mankind are inseparably connected with the momentous enquiry after their primeval home. The sciences of ethnology and comparative philology must be taken into consideration to determine, even though it be but approximately, the origin of nations and the directions in which they have migrated. Suffice it to say, however, that, according to ethnology, the Egyptians appear to form a third branch of the Caucasian race, the family called Cushite; and this much may be regarded as certain, that in the earliest ages of humanity, far beyond all historical remembrance, the Egyptians, for reasons unknown to us, left the soil of their early home, took their way towards the setting sun, and finally crossed that bridge of nations the Isthmus of Suez, to find a new fatherland on the banks of the Nile.

Comparative philology, in its turn, gives powerful support to this hypothesis, for the primitive roots and the essential elements of the Egyptian grammar point to such an intimate connection with the Indo-Germanic and Semitic languages, that it is almost impossible to mistake the close relations which formerly prevailed between them. According to Greek tradition the primitive abode of the Egyptian people is to be sought in Ethiopia, and the honour of founding their civilisation should be given to a band of priests from Meroë. Descending the Nile, they are supposed to have settled near the later city of Thebes, and to have established the first State with a theocratic form of government.

But it is not to Ethiopian priests that the Egyptian empire owes its origin, its form of government, and its high civilisation ; much rather was it the Egyptians themselves that first ascended the river to found in Ethiopia temples, cities, and fortified places, and to diffuse the blessings of a civilised state among the rude dark-coloured population.

Supposing, for a moment, that Egypt had owed her civil and social development to Ethiopia, nothing would be more probable than the presumption of our finding monuments of the greatest antiquity in that primitive home of the Egyptians, while in going down the river we ought to light only upon monuments of a later age. Strange to say, the whole number of the buildings in stone, as yet known and examined, which were erected on both sides of the river by Egyptian and Ethiopian kings, furnish the incontrovertible proof, that the long series of temples, cities, sepulchres, and monuments in general, exhibit a distinct chronological order, of which the starting-point is found in the Pyramids, at the apex of the Delta.

The Egyptians themselves held the belief that they were the original inhabitants of the land. The fertile valley of the Nile formed in their opinion the heart and centre of the whole world. To the west of it dwelt the groups of tribes which bore the general name of Ribu or Libu, the ancestors of those Libyans who, inhabiting the northern coasts of Africa, extended their abodes eastward as far as the Canopic branch of the Nile. From the evidence of the monuments they belonged to a light-coloured race, with blue eyes and blond or red hair. It is a noteworthy phenomenon that as early as the Fourth Dynasty members of this race wandered into Egypt to display their dexterity as dancers, combatants, and gymnasts in the public games.

The great mixture of tribes who had their homes in the wide regions of the Upper Nile—near Syene—have on the monuments the common name of Nahasu. From the representations of them we recognise the ancestors of the negro race. Eastwards, across the Isthmus of Suez, were the people of that great nation which the Egyptians designated by the name of Aamu. These were the Pagans, the Kaffirs, or ' infidels ' of their time. In the coloured representations they are distinguished chiefly by their yellow or yellowish-brown complexion, while their dress has sometimes a great simplicity, but sometimes shows a taste for splendour and richness in the choiceness of cut and the variegated patterns woven into the fabric. In these Aamu scientific research has since perceived the representatives of the great Semitic family of nations. Moreover it is a fact established beyond dispute, that even in the most glorious times of the Egyptian monarchy the Aamu were settled as permanent inhabitants in the neighbourhood of the present lake Menzaleh, where many places formerly bore unmistakably Semitic names.

The most remarkable nations among them who appear in the course of Egyptian history as commanding respect by their character and their deeds are the Kheta, the Khar (or Khal), and the Ruten (or Luten).

Egypt is designated in the old inscriptions, and by the later Christian Egyptians, by a word signifying 'the black land,' and which is read in the Egyptian language *Kamit*. The ancients had early remarked that the soil was distinguished by its very dark colour, and certainly this peculiarity suggested to the old Egyptians the name of the black land. This receives a further corroboration from the fact that the neighbouring region of the Arabian desert bore the name of *Tesherit*, or 'the red land.' On countless occasions the king is mentioned as 'the lord of the black country and of the red country,' in order to show that his rule extended over cultivated and uncultivated Egypt in the wider sense of the word. The Egyptians called themselves simply the people of the black land (Kamit), and the inscriptions have handed down to us no further distinctive appellation.

But a number of other names recorded on the monuments designate this same land of Egypt in special manners. Amongst the oldest is unquestionably Tamera, which seems to have meant 'the country of the inundation.' Others alluded to Egypt poetically. Among these are the following: the land of the sycomore; the land of the olive; the land of the Holy Eye; the land of the sixth day of the moon (intercalary day). The explanation of many of these names can only be sought in those writings of the ancient Egyptians which relate to the doctrine of divine things and to the legends of the gods. The Hebrews gave the land the name of *Mizraim*; the Assyrians, *Muzur*; the Persians, *Mudraya*. At the basis of all these designations there lies an original form, which consisted of the three letters M—z—r.

Ancient Egypt, commonly called 'the double land,' consisted of two great divisions, the land of the South and the land of the North. The first corresponds to that part of Egypt which we now know as Upper Egypt, and which the Arabs down to the present day call Sahid. Upper Egypt began on the south at the ivory-island city of Elephantiné, which lay opposite to Syene, the modern trading town of Aswân. Its northern boundary reached to the neighbourhood of Memphis. Lower Egypt comprehended the remainder: the Bahari of the Arabs, the Delta of the Greeks. The chief division of Egypt, which, according to sacred tradition, was referred back to the time of the god-kings, explains the name of 'double country,' especially in the title of the kings, and enables us to see clearly the grounds of the opposition by which the sovereignty of the south was committed to the god Set, and that of the north to Horus, the son of Osiris.

Following tradition, every king, on the day of his solemn coronation—which was distinct from the day of his receiving the kingdom in his father's lifetime or on the death of his predecessor—received as his chief insignia two crowns, of which the white upper one symbolised his sovereignty over the South, the red lower one his dominion over the North.

The land of Egypt resembles a narrow girdle, divided in the midst by a stream of water, and hemmed in on both sides by long chains of mountains. On the right side of the river the Arabian hills accompany the stream for its whole length; on the western side, the low hills of the Libyan desert extend in the same direction with the river from south to north up to the shore of the Mediterranean Sea. The river itself was designated by the Greeks and Romans by the name of Neilos (ὁ Νεῖλος) or Nilus. Although this word is still retained in the Arabic language as Nil, with the special meaning of ' inundation,' its origin is not to be sought in the old Egyptian language ; but, as has been lately suggested with great probability, it should be derived from the Semitic word Nahar or Nahal, which has the general signification of ' river.' From its bifurcation south of the ancient city of Memphis, the river parted into three great arms, which watered the Lower Egyptian flat lands which spread out in the shape of the Greek letter Δ (Delta), and, with four smaller arms, formed the seven famous mouths of the Nile.

The land on both sides of the river was divided from the earliest times into districts called Nomes. This division is to be found on the monuments of the Fourth Dynasty, where some are mentioned by name with their chief towns. Thirty centuries later the same districts appear on Ptolemaic and Roman monuments arranged in regular and detailed tables, which separate the upper and lower country by a clear division. Upper Egypt contained 22, Lower Egypt 20, and these the native language designated sometimes by the word Sep or Hesep, sometimes by the word Tash. According to the account given in a papyrus, the older division into 36 districts rests on a particular view, which connected the terrestrial partition into nomes with the 36 ruling houses of the heavens in astrology. Each district had its own capital, which was the seat of the governor for the time being, whose office and dignity passed by inheritance, according to the old Egyptian laws, from the father to the eldest grandson on the mother's side, and formed likewise the central point of the particular cult of the district.

From the sacred lists of the nomes we learn the names of the temple of the chief deity, of the priests and priestesses, of the sacred trees, and also the names of the town-harbour of the holy canal, the cultivated land and the land which was only fruitful during the inundation, and much other information. Thus we can form the most exact picture of Egyptian agricultural life in all its details. The several districts were separated from each other by boundary stones, and the authorities took the greatest pains in attending to the measurement of the lands, to the making of canals, and the inspection of the dikes. It happened very often that the inhabitants of one district threatened an attack on the occupants of another, which not infrequently broke out into a violent struggle, requiring the whole armed power of the king to extinguish.

The disastrous results of such feuds sometimes affected even the whole dynasty, the reigning family being displaced by the conqueror. Hence arose those changes of dynasty and different names of the capitals of nomes which we find in Manetho's ' Book of the Kings.' Three districts, however, throughout the course of Egyptian history maintained the reputation of being the seats of national government: in Lower Egypt, Memphis and Heliopolis; in Upper Egypt, Thebes. The ancient inhabitants, like their descendants, were chiefly an agricultural people. The walls of the sepulchral chapels are covered with thousands of bas-reliefs and their explanatory inscriptions, which preserve the most abundant disclosures respecting the labours of the field and the rearing of cattle as practised by them. On festivals the Pharaohs themselves sailed along the sacred river in their gorgeous royal ship, to perform mystic rites in special honour of agriculture. The priests regarded the plough as a most sacred imple- ment, and held that the highest happiness of man, after the completion of his pilgrimage here below, would consist in tilling the Elysian fields, in feeding and tend- ing his cattle, and navigating the breezy water of the other world in slender skiffs.

The husbandman, the shepherd, and the boatman were, in fact, the first founders of that advanced civilisation which flourished in the Nile valley.

Some writers regard the Egyptians as a reflective, serious, and reserved people, very religious, occupied only with the other world, and caring nothing or very little about this lower life. But is it possible that such a country and such a climate could have produced a race of living mummies and of sad philosophers, a people who only regarded this life as a burthen to be thrown off as soon as possible ? No ! No people could be gayer, more lively, of more childlike simplicity, than those old Egyptians, who loved life with all their hearts, and found the deepest joy in their very existence. Far from longing for death, they addressed to the host of the holy gods the prayer to preserve and lengthen life, if possible, to the 'most perfect old age of 110 years.' The song and dance and flowing cup, cheerful excursions to the meadows and papyrus marshes—to hunt with bow and arrow or throw-stick, or to fish with spear and hook—were the recreation of the nobler classes after work was done.

In connection with this merry disposition, hu- morous jests and lively sallies of wit, often passing the bounds of decorum, characterised the people from age to age.

From a very early period stone was wrought ac- cording to the rules of an advanced skill ; and metals

—gold, silver, copper, and iron—were melted and wrought into works of art or tools; wood, leather, glass, flax, and even rushes were all in daily use, and on the potter's wheel vessels were formed from the Nile mud and baked in the furnace. Sculptors and painters too found profitable work among the wealthy patrons of art at the court of the Pharaohs.

The noble class (suten rekh) of the Egyptian people derived their origin chiefly from the royal house; to them were committed the offices of the court. They held as their hereditary possessions villages and tracts of land, with the labouring people thereto belonging, bands of servants, and numerous herds of cattle. To their memory, after their decease, were dedicated those splendid tombs the remains of which are on the Libyan desert or in the caverns of the Egyptian hills.

Ambition and arrogant pride formed a remarkable feature in the spirit of the old dwellers on the Nile; yet in the schools the poor scribe's child sat on the same bench beside the offspring of the rich, and the masters knew how by timely words to goad on the laggards by holding out to them the rewards which awaited rich and poor alike. Many a monument consecrated to the memory of some nobleman gone to his long home, who during life had held high rank at the court of Pharaoh, is decorated with the simple but laudatory inscription, 'His ancestors were unknown people.' Above all things they esteemed justice, and virtue had the highest value in their eyes. The law which ordered them— 'to pray to the gods, to honour the dead; to give bread to the hungry, water to the thirsty, clothing to the naked'—reveals to us one of the finest qualities of old Egyptian character—pity towards the unfortunate. The forty-two commandments of their religion, which are contained in the 'Book of the Dead,' are not inferior to the precepts of Christianity; and in reading the old inscriptions concerning morality we are tempted to believe that Moses modelled his teachings on the patterns given by those old sages.

They were not free, however, from vices and failings. Hatred, envy, cunning, intrigue, combined with an overweening sentiment of pride, contradiction, and perversity, added to avarice and cruelty—such is the long series of those hereditary faults which history reveals to us among the Egyptians by innumerable examples.

Nor did the rule of the Pharaohs open to the inhabitants of the land the gates of a terrestrial paradise. The people suffered and endured under the blows of their oppressors, and the stick quickened the despatch of business between the peasant and the tax-gatherer. We need but glance at the gigantic masses of the Pyramids; they tell more emphatically than living speech or written words of the miseries of a whole population, which was condemned to erect these everlasting monuments of Pharaonic vanity: and when, thirty centuries later, Herodotus visited the Pyramids of Gîzeh, the Egyptians told him of the imprecations wrung from their unhappy forefathers during the erection of those monuments.

The Egyptians were as enquiring as ourselves about prehistoric times, but with this difference, that for them primeval history was concerned but little with the people and much more with the fame of their kings. Their enquiries were directed to the names and genealogies of the princes who ruled the land before the first authentic king, Mena. As they could not discover from their monuments any records of their land before the Pharaoh Mena mounted the throne, their imagina-

tion supposed three ages which followed one another,
till Mena placed the double crown upon his head.
During the first a dynasty of the gods reigned in the
land, followed by the age of the demi-gods, while the
dynasty of the mysterious Manes closed the prehistoric
time.

The theology of their priests filled up these ages
with heavenly persons and names. The calculations
of the courses of the stars, based on the cycle of the
risings of Sothis (the Dog Star), gave the numbers
which were added as regnal years to the names of
these imaginary sovereigns. As the priests of various
cities differed in their doctrines concerning the nature
of the gods and their connection with earthly things it
is not surprising that the lists of the prehistoric dynasties contained different names and numbers, according
to the respective origin of each.

Subjoined are the names of the divine kings of the
first age, first in the Theban order and then according
to the Memphite.

The Dynasty of the Gods.

I. *According to the Theban Doctrine.*

1. Amen-Ra, ' the King of the Gods ' .   Zeus
2. Mentu, his son   .   .   .   .   Mars
3. Shu, son of Ra   .   .   .   .   Agathodæmon
4. Seb, son of Shu   .   .   .   .   Saturn
5. Osiris, son of Seb   .   .   .   .   Dionysos
6. Horus, son of Osiris   .   .   .   Hermes

II. *According to the Memphite Doctrine.*

1. Ptah, ' the Father of the Gods ' (the
    Architect of the World)   .   .   .   Hephaistos
2. Ra, son of Ptah (Fire—Existent Being
    —the Present)   .   .   .   .   .   Sol (the Sun)
3. Shu, his son (the Air)   .   .   .   .   Agathodæmon
4. Seb, his son (the Earth)   .   .   .   .   Saturn

5. Osiris, his son (Water—Being that has
    existed—the Past) . . . . Dionysos
6. Set, son of Seb (the Annihilation of
    Being) . . . . . . Typhon
7. Horus, son of Osiris (the Coming into
    Being—the Future) . . . . Hermes

Thus Ptah of Memphis, whom the inscriptions
honour with the title of 'father of the gods,' is the
Architect, in the highest sense of the word. This is at
once indicated by his name, for Ptah, in the Egyptian
language, signifies ' architect.' There are inscriptions
which throw light on the sacred attributes of this
Architect of the Universe. The following texts, on the
walls of the temple of Denderah, call the god 'the
chief of the society of the gods, who created all Being.'
'All things came into existence after he existed.' ' He is
the lord of truth and king of the gods.' At Philæ it is
said ' he who created all being, who formed men and
gods with his own hands;' and again, 'he is the father
of beginnings, who created the egg of the sun and
of the moon,' and is 'the father of all the gods,
the first existing.' He is 'God the creator, who was
before the creation of the universe, his own exclusive
work.'

Ra, the Sun, his successor, according to the
Memphite doctrine, is invoked in several sacred hymns
as 'the son of Ptah.' In different localities he bears
the double names of Khnem-Ra, Amen-Ra, and in
another deeply mystic sense he is the divine form of
existence. He is 'that which is to-day—the present;'
his son and successor, Shu, is identical with wind or
air. The divine Seb, who in the temple of Esneh is
called the son of Shu, represents the earth, and is identical with the Greek Kronos.

To his son Osiris—the divinity adored in nearly all

parts of the land—the Egyptian priests assigned the particular meaning of Water. According to a deeper conception they believed that they recognised in him the symbol of completed existence ; for he is that which was yesterday—the past. There is no need to dwell here upon the hostile divinity, his brother Set. Next to him comes the god of light, Horus, the son of Osiris and his divine wife, Isis. He symbolises the return of the new life, that which will be to-morrow—the future —the being born again in the eternal cycle of earthly phenomena. Such is Horus, the primeval form and type of every royal successor of the Pharaohs, just as Ra represented the reigning, Osiris the deceased king. A myth spun out to great length about Horus, whom Isis by her mysterious magical arts awakens to life from the dead Osiris in the form of a child, tells of the combat of the youth and his companions with Set, the brother and murderer of his father, of the final victory of the god of light over Set, the prince of darkness and of eternal conflict and annihilation, and of the exaltation of the young king Horus on the undivided throne of his father Osiris.

Frequent mention is made in the old records of the royal gods, as of real personages. Besides the name of their dynasty they have a second name of honour, and, just like the Pharaohs, they bear respectively the authentic title under which the god Tehuti, the sacred scribe of the gods, registered each of them in the ' Book of the Kings,' at the command of the Sun god, Ra. They have their individual history, which the scribes wrote down in the temple books ; they married royal brides, and begat a very numerous posterity.

The monuments say little about those monarchs designated by Manetho as the Dynasties of the Demigods and Manes, nor is there in the Turin Papyrus the

slightest intelligible information about them, though
it is possible that they are all included under the general
name of Hor-Shesu. It must, however, be granted
that Egypt had really a life before the historic age, but
that the monuments—apart from the myths—contain
nothing about the condition of the land in those primeval times. All that can be allowed is that Egypt's prehistoric age must of necessity correspond to the time
of the first development of society and the dawn of
the arts and sciences. German Egyptologists have
attempted to fix the era when Mena, the first Pharaoh,
mounted the throne, with the following results :—

	B.C.			B.C.
Boeckh	, 5702	Lauth	.	4157
Unger	. 5613	Lepsius	.	3892
Brugsch	. 4455	Bunsen	.	3623

The difference between the extreme dates is enormous, amounting to no less than 2,097 years ! It is as
if one should hesitate whether to fix the date of the
accession of Augustus at B.C. 207 or A.D. 1872.

The calculations in question are based on the
extracts from a work on the history of Egypt by the
Egyptian priest Manetho. His book, which is now lost,
contained a general review of the kings, divided into
Thirty Dynasties, arranged in the order of their names,
with the length of their reigns, and the total duration
of each Dynasty. Though this invaluable work was
little known and certainly but little regarded by the
historians of the old classical age, large extracts were
made from it by some of the ecclesiastical writers; but
in process of time the copyists, either by error or
designedly, corrupted the names and the numbers.

The deciphering of the Egyptian writing has, however, proved that much of the original work was both
valuable and authentic. And so the Manethonian list

of the kings served, and still serves, in spite of its corrupted state, as a guide for assigning to the royal names read on the monuments their place in the Dynasties. The pedigree of twenty-four court architects, as given in the opposite Table, the last mentioned of whom, Khnum-ab-Ra, was alive in the twenty-seventh and thirtieth years of the reign of Darius I., has given rise to the new method of fixing the dates of the Pharaohs anterior to the Twenty-sixth Dynasty, with the help of existing series of genealogies.

The credit of this is due to a Swedish scholar, M. Lieblein.

The importance of his standard for all measurements of Egyptian chronology is incontestable. Assuming the round number of a century for three consecutive human lives, we possess the means of determining approximately the time which has elapsed from King Mena to the end of the Twelfth Dynasty, and again from the beginning of the Eighteenth Dynasty to the end of the Twenty-sixth.

As far as present discoveries go there is no possible means of doing so more exactly. The Tablet of Abydos, in a corridor of the temple of Seti I. at Harabat-el-Madfûneh, gives a succession of sixty-five kings from Mena, the founder of the line, down to the last reign of the Twelfth Dynasty. To these sovereigns, therefore, would be assigned a period of $\frac{65}{3} \times 100 = 2166$ years.

It appears certain that the long series of the kings, which the Turin Papyrus once contained, was arranged by the author according to his own ideas and views; for he gives carefully, besides the names of the Pharaohs, the years, months, and days of their reigns, but he forgets to give any account of the contemporary reigns of two kings, which have been proved beyond

TABLE OF THE CHIEF ARCHITECTS.

Epoch Year	Chief Architects of Pharaoh	High Priests of Amen in Thebes
1200	Bek-en-Khonsu	
1166	Ut'a-Khonsu	
1133	Nefer-mennu	
1100	Mi	King Her-Hor
1066	Si-uer-nenen-heb	King Pi-ankhi
1033	Pepi	King Pai-net'em I.
1000	Amen-her-pa-mesha	Men-kheper-Ra
965	Hor-em-saf I.	King Pai-net'em II.
933	Mermer	Prince Auputh
900	Hor-em-saf II.	Prince Shashanq
866	T'a-heb I.	
833	Nas-shunu I.	Nimrod
800	T'a-heb II	
766	Nas-shunu II.	King Uasarken
733	T'a-heb III.	Shashanq
700	Nas-shunu III.	
666	T'a-n-hebu	
633	Nas-shunu IV.	
600	Uah-ab-Ra-ran-uer	
566	Ankh-Psamthek	
533	Aah-mes se-Nit	
500	Khnum-ab Ra	

all doubt by the inscriptions, and which was a very usual custom in the succession of a son to his father.

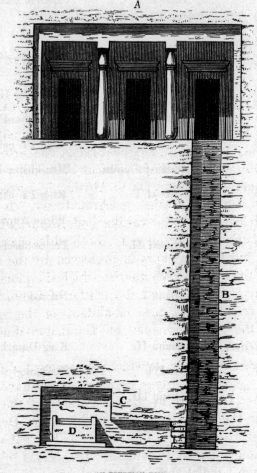

AN EGYPTIAN TOMB.

A, the exterior building, containing one or more chambers, generally with painted scenes of life, and inscriptions. B, the vertical pit. C, the vault, with the sarcophagus (D) containing the body.

CHAPTER II.

DYNASTIES I.-IV.[1]

THE PHARAOHS OF THE FIRST THREE DYNASTIES.

IN Upper Egypt, west of the river, stood a small town
called Tini, a name which the Greeks converted into
This or Thinis. It was the ancient metropolis of the
eighth nome, and lying near to Abydos, it formed only
a separate quarter of that celebrated city. It chose
for its tutelary deity the warlike god Anhur, while at
Abydos Osiris was worshipped. Both cities have now
vanished, but their memory is preserved by the necropolis and the splendid sanctuaries which the pious faith
of the Egyptians raised on the border of the desert at
the place which the modern inhabitants of the country
call by the Arabic name of Harabat-el-Madfûneh
(Harabat the sunken).

Tini, which in the Roman times enjoyed a certain
repute for its purple dyes, must anciently have been
held in special honour by the inhabitants of the land,
for, under the sovereigns of the Nineteenth Dynasty,
the highest servants of the state, of Pharaoh's own
race, were denoted by the title of 'King's son of Tini,'
a distinction which elsewhere occurs only in the titles
'King's son of Cush,' or of the land of the Ethiopians,
and 'King's son of Hineb,' that is, the city of the Moon,
Eileithyiapolis.

The high fame of this town rested, beyond doubt, on

[1] For Table of Kings see pp. xix, xx.

the received tradition that it had been the cradle of
the first Egyptian king, and the hereditary seat of his
successors for two dynasties. The name of this first
sovereign of ancient Egypt was MENA, 'the
steadfast.'

Mena. Our only knowledge of him is confined to a
few statements of doubtful credit, found in classical
writings. He is said to have been the first lawgiver of
Egypt, but to have corrupted the simple manners of the
olden time, in that he replaced the frugal mode of life
by royal pomp and sumptuous expense. To him also is
ascribed the foundation of Memphis, the splendid capital
of the Old Empire, after he had first diverted the Nile,
in order to gain a wide space for building the new city.
By the construction of an enormous dike, the previous
course of the river, along the Libyan hills, was cut off,
and the bed thus left empty was for ever filled up.

Linant-Bey, one of the most active improvers of
modern Egypt, is convinced that the great dike of
Cocheiche is in all probability the same which Mena
caused to be constructed 6,000 years ago. The
Egyptians, like the other nations of antiquity, began
the work of founding a city by building the temple,
which formed the centre of the future town. New
sanctuaries, erected later, occasioned the building of
new quarters, which surrounded the oldest temple, and
finally formed with it a single great city. The names
given to the several temples embraced likewise the
dwelling-places of the inhabitants which adjoined and
belonged to it, and thus is explained the fact that the
monuments mention the same town under the most
different designations.

The chief name of Mena's city was also that of the
nome, Anbu-hat, or the 'white wall;' in general it
bore the title Men-nefer, the 'good place,' which the

Greeks altered to Memphis, the Copts to Memphi, and
the cuneiform inscriptions render Mimpi. The last
trace of the old name is preserved in Tell-el-Monf, the
modern designation of a heap of ruins close to the former royal residence of the first Pharaohs. More rarely
it was called Kha-nefer, the 'good appearance,' or
Makhata, the 'land of the scales,' and frequently by the
sacred appellation of Ha-kha-Ptah, 'house of worship
of Ptah,' who often bears the additional title of Seker
or Sekari, traces of which seem to be preserved in the
name of the modern village Saqqarah, near the ancient
city of Memphis. The wife of the god, a lion-headed
goddess adorned with the sun's disk, bore the name of
Sekhet, whose son, Nefer-atmu, or Im-hotep, was the
Asclepios of Egyptian mythology.

All that now remains of this celebrated city consists of heaps of overthrown and shattered columns,
altars, and sculptures which once belonged to the
temples of Memphis, and of a far-extended line of
mounds of *débris*.

The temple of Ptah lay on the south side of the
salt-encrusted plain which stretches between the
'Swine's Hill,' Kum-el-Khanzir, on the east, and the
little Arab village of El-Qassarîeh on the west. Its
length lies from north to south, and the mighty statue of
Ramses II. shows where the splendid gate of the temple
once stood. The former existence of the sacred lake to
the north is proved by the inscription upon the statue.

In the immediate neighbourhood of the village of
El-Qassarîeh (which means 'wash-pot') are shown the
broken remains and columns of a temple, the inscriptions on which declare Ramses II. to be its founder
and builder. The chief axis was from east to west,
and it was built of polished blocks of granite and
alabaster, in honour of the divine Ptah.

Judging from the writings of Abd-el-Latîf, an Arab physician of the thirteenth century, it would seem that in the Middle Ages the remains of the once great city of Memphis were still so well preserved that their materials and the perfection of their workmanship excited the admiration of Arab visitors.[1]

The repeated excavations which have been undertaken in our day on the site of Memphis have given results hardly worth naming, for the immense masses of stone used in the building of the temples have been in the course of time transported to Cairo, to supply the materials needed for the mosques, palaces, and houses of the city of the Khalifs.

The high priests of Ptah appear to have distinguished themselves by their authority and influence, and even princes of the blood royal did not find it beneath their dignity to hold that office at Memphis, for example, Khamuas, the favourite son of Ramses II., who died early, and ' gave many gifts to the gods of the temple, and fulfilled the rules of the divine service.' It was not until the decline and fall of the kingdom, and until Memphis and Thebes ceased to be the famous residences of the Pharaohs, that the authority of the high priests came gradually to an end.

Along the margin of the desert, extending from Abû Roâsh as far as Meidûm, lay the necropolis of Memphis, where were buried the contemporaries of the Third, Fourth, and Fifth Dynasties. Their memories have been kept alive by pictures and writings on the walls of the sacrificial chambers built over their tombs. In that obscure age, when the symmetrical building of the Pyramids and the well-executed design of the sepulchral chambers demanded skill and intelligence, the office of architect was the occupation of the noblest

---

[1] *Relation de l'Égypte*, translated by S. de Sacy.

men at court, many of whom were either sons or
grandsons of the king.   Great dignity also belonged to
the nobleman who was honoured with the office of ' a
prophet of the Pyramid of Pharaoh.'   His duty was to
praise the memory of the deceased king, and to devote
the god-like image of the sovereign to enduring remembrance.   The honour of the office was mentioned in·
the prophet's own tomb, and was associated with the
name of his deified king.

The Memphite tombs tell much concerning the
customs of Pharaoh and his court.   The sovereign
bears the official title of ' King of the Upper and Lower
Country;' he is also called Per-ao, ' the great house,'
better known, perhaps, under the Hebrew equivalent of
Pharaoh.   The people honoured him as 'lord' (neb)
and 'god' (neter).   At sight of him every native prostrated himself and touched the ground with his nose, and
it was an especial favour if the command of his lord
permitted him only to kiss his knee.   He was spoken
of as ' His Majesty,' and briefly, but not less respectfully, by a word·equivalent to the German *man*.

At the court of Pharaoh, with regard to attendance
on the sovereign, order, rank, and time were exactly
defined, as well for nobles of the purest descent as for
the mass of busy servants.   Not only did the splendour
of his birth secure for the nobleman dignity and
authority in the eyes of the people, but far greater
weight was given to prudent wisdom, noble culture,
and the brightness of virtue.   Good service was rewarded with honours and gifts, the noblemen receiving
such titles as ' hereditary highness' (erpa) or 'intimate
friend' (semer-uat).

The management and service of the court, as well as
the administration of the country, was conducted under
Pharaoh's direction by the governor and bailiff and a

countless host of scribes, while the duties of personal attendance upon the king were performed by inferior officials controlled by the high steward. The boy distinguished by early intelligence, and who gave good promise for the future, was associated with the king's children as their companion in play and lessons, while a guardian of noble family superintended the ' house of the king's children,' on whom devolved heavy responsibility for the bodily health, for the education and discipline of the royal children.

The queen and the other ladies of the royal familv were for the most part honoured with the sacred dignity of ' prophetess of the goddesses Hathor and Nit;' they lived in the ' women's houses,' guarded by free men chosen by the king, and it was permitted to the princesses to ally themselves in marriage with some of the great nobles.

The duty of attending to the buildings and all kinds of work in stone belonged to skilled persons of the noble class. In the caverns of the mountain of Tûrah, opposite to Memphis, they quarried limestone for building the royal pyramids and tombs, and for the artistic work of the sarcophagi and columns; or they resorted to the southern region, to hew out the hard granite from the Red Mountain, behind the city of Aswân, and constructed rafts for the conveyance of the vast masses of stone to the lower country in the favourable season of the inundation. The dreaded band of taskmasters was set over the wretched people, who were urged to speedy work more by the punishment of the stick than by words of warning.

The inhabitants of the country in the extensive environs of the towns, or in the villages of the open plain, were kept in order by governors of nomes. The judges enforced strict obedience to the written law, and

administered justice to the oppressed, whose complaints
it was the duty of the king's deputies to hear.

The warlike hosts of young soldiers (Mesha), consisting of infantry, whom the master of the armoury
equipped with clubs and axes, spears, and bows and
arrows, were commanded by experienced generals. It
was the duty of the commander-in-chief to plan the
campaign, dispose the troops, and go out to war with
his soldiers. Of a more peaceful kind was the celebrated office of the 'teachers of mysteries' (Herseshta),
for they were the possessors of all hidden wisdom in
those ancient times. 'The mystery-teachers of heaven'
looked upwards, and, as wise astronomers, explained
the ever-changing course of the stars. 'The mystery-
teachers of all lands' contemplated the nature of earthly
things, and appear to have been the geographers of the
ancient world. 'The mystery-teachers of the depth,'
if we are not mistaken, were the possessors of knowledge of that which the earth conceals in its depths and
were initiated into the peculiar nature of the soil.

Others, 'mystery-teachers of the secret word,' wrote
books on subjects of deep thought, whilst the 'mystery-
teachers of the sacred language' devoted themselves to
the special knowledge of the Egyptian tongue. Most
frequently of all we meet with the 'mystery-teachers of
Pharaoh,' or 'of all the commands of Pharaoh,' wise
men who held the position of private secretaries to
their master. Next to them we read of 'mystery-
teachers who examine words,' without doubt either
learned men of letters or judges who listened to complaints and compared the evidence of the witnesses.

The scribes were divided into many branches, according to their position and business. In obedience to the
commands of their master, they either wrote the events
of his domestic life or accurately recorded his income

and expenditure, and kept his books in good order.
For a scribe of talent the way was open to the highest
honours. The mass of servants and skilled workmen
were also divided into fixed orders and gradations.

In this way the welfare of the court and country
was secured by the adjustment of the individual
members. Everyone maintained his place according
to his own worth; and the machinery of the state ran
in the regular course, being set in motion by the all-
powerful will of Pharaoh. Blind obedience was the oil
which caused the harmonious working of the whole.

And this great world, buried in its deep desert grave
for more than 6,000 years, is now beginning to wake up
out of its long sleep, like the briar rose in the legend,
and to relate in childishly simple language its long past
history in home and state.

To return to King Mena. After conducting a campaign against the Libyans he was seized and devoured
by a crocodile. Such is the story of the ancients.
Was Set, the lord of the horrid water-monsters, embittered
with envious hatred against the founder of the most
ancient state?

The names alone of the successors of the first
Pharaoh are preserved in the Tablets of Saqqarah and
Abydos, and harmonise to some extent with the Turin
Papyrus, which when complete contained the names of
the same kings, together with the length of their reigns
in a similar order. From a merely superficial examination [1] it is clear that, with the exception of two or three
names towards the end of the Third Dynasty, they are
radically different from those of the Pharaohs who
succeeded them. For the most part the older ones
suggest the ideas of strength and terror. Thus Mena is
'the constant;' Teta, 'the smiter;' Ka-kau, 'the bull of

[1] See Table of Kings, p. xix. *et seq.*

bulls;' Senta, 'the terrible;' Huni, 'the hewer.' It is not until the 22nd name on the monumental list that the gods Amen, Sebek, or Tehuti become incorporated into the royal cartouche, while from henceforth the sign of the god-king Ra is paraded in a suitable place of honour in the upper space.

Among the rulers of the most ancient kingdom Nefer-ka-Sekari ('perfect through Sekari') is the only one whose name plainly preserves the remembrance of a deity. But then the question naturally arises, How was it that a king of Tini, the capital of Upper Egypt, gave himself a name which, by the presence of the divine Sekari at Men-nefer (Memphis), suggests the capital of Lower Egypt? However this may be, one thing is certain, that Mena laid the foundation of this future metropolis, and that the descendants of his house held their court at Men-nefer, not at Tini.

Unfortunately the monuments are silent until the time of Sneferu (Dyn. III.), and our information concerning the most ancient rulers of Egypt comes only from the fragments of Manetho and from Greek stories of doubtful veracity.

Mena's son and successor, TETA, built the royal palace in Memphis, and wrote, wonderful as it may sound, a work on anatomy, 'for he was a physician.' The monuments are silent concerning this physician-king; but a papyrus roll of the most remote age, bought in Thebes by Ebers, tells in archaic language that, when King Teta sat on the throne, a prescription for making the hair grow was much commended. More important than this information is the testimony that the writings of the Pharaohs on medical subjects reach back as far as the First Dynasty.

To mention one only, the long medical papyrus
found in the necropolis of Memphis, and now in the
Berlin Museum, contains prescriptions for the cure
of malignant leprosy and many other kinds of illness,
treats of fractures, and teaches, although in a simple,
childish way, of the construction and mechanism of
the body. Though composed in the reign of Ramses II.,
there is a passage in it which throws back the origin
of one part of the work to the fifth king of the Tablet
of Abydos. It runs thus :—

This is the beginning of the sum of all methods for the cure of
bad leprosy. It was discovered in a writing of very ancient origin
in a writing-case underneath the feet of the divine Anpu, in the
town of Sekhem, at the time when the deceased Sapti[1] was king.
After his death the writing was brought to the sanctuary of the
blessed king Senta, on account of its miraculous power of healing.

When UENEPHES (Ata) ascended the throne the
land of Egypt suffered from a great famine. In spite
of it the people were employed in building pyramids
on the site called Ka-kam ('black bull'), where the
bodies of the sacred Apis-bulls reposed in the Serapēum
in the desert. The place is near the modern village of
Saqqarah, and it is probable that the building with
steps called the 'pyramid of degrees,' whose hollow
chamber contained the bones of bulls and inscriptions
relating to the royal names of Apis, was a common
sepulchre, consecrated by Ata to this animal.

[This pyramid, unlike all the others, does not face
the points of the compass; it is oblong, not square, and
instead of containing one chamber has many of unique
form in the interior. These were explored, in 1821,
by Minutoli, an Italian officer, and in one of them he
found a skull and the soles of feet, both of which were
carefully gilded. Two of the chambers were inlaid

[1] Dyn. I., No. 5.

with a kind of mosaic, consisting of green faïence and stucco.]

When SEMEN-PTAH inherited the crown a great number of miracles were displayed, and a violent plague raged in the country. When BA-EN-NETER ascended the throne the earth opened at Bubastis and swallowed up many people. When KA-KAU (' bull of bulls') succeeded to the kingdom the worship of Apis was instituted in the city of Memphis, and that of Mnevis at On. A sanctuary and priesthood were founded to the honour of the sacred ram Mendes at the town of that name. Pure men served the sacred Apis-bull, whose death was deeply lamented; his body, adorned with decorations, was exposed on a high bier, and even his name, Hapi, was borne as an honour by many distinguished persons.

With regard to the laws of the kingdom, Ba-en-neter, who had apparently no sons, enacted as a standing rule for ever that women should inherit the throne. The working of this new custom had important consequences in the establishment of many a dynasty, either when the queen, after the death of her husband, took the reins of government or stepped into the place of her youthful son, or when the daughter and heiress of a deceased Pharaoh, who had no sons, gave her hand to a foreign husband. According to the ancient custom the mother's pedigree had great weight in the order of inheritance, because it gave an unconditional claim of right to the son as the true heir of ' the father of his mother.' The husband of a royal heiress appeared as king in name only, but it devolved on the son of such a marriage to maintain his full right to the throne and sceptre by virtue of his maternal descent. If a Pharaoh married the daughter of a noble family, not of royal race, the offspring of the union, as appears from many occurrences in the history of the kingdom, had not equal rights with the true royal children.

The father of the new Pharaoh was honoured by the title of 'father of the divine one' (*Atef-neter*), while the mother was called 'mother of the king' (*Mut-suten*). In the majority of cases the succession of the dynasties was determined by the union of new suitors with heiresses of the blood royal, whether the chosen husbands could trace their pedigree back to royal ancestors or not.

Under the rule of NEFER-KA-RA tradition relates that the waters of the Nile suddenly assumed for eleven days the taste of honey.

We know nothing of SEKER but the strange tradition which says he was 5 cubits in height and 3 in breadth!

Under NECHEROPHES, the first king of the Third Dynasty, the tribes of Libya revolted against their Egyptian masters, and Pharaoh only succeeded in sub-duing them when, by the help of the gods, the moon appeared to grow of a gigantic size, which threw terror into the ranks of the enemy.

The heir of this king, TOSORTHROS, was skilled in the art of healing sickness and injuries to the body, and on account of this wisdom the title of 'god of healing' was given him. He was also diligent in other matters, and was skilled in the art of erecting solid masses of building in well-hewn stone. Also he gave instruction in the painting of the written characters for the benefit of people expert in writing.

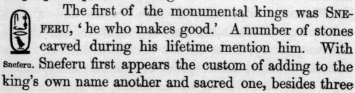

The first of the monumental kings was SNE-FERU, 'he who makes good.' A number of stones carved during his lifetime mention him. With Sneferu. Sneferu first appears the custom of adding to the king's own name another and sacred one, besides three

high-sounding titles. Without distinguishing the individual the first title was that of Horus, who dispenses
life and prosperity ; the second, ' lord of the double
diadem ; ' and the third, ' the image of the golden Horus,
conqueror of his opponent.' After each king's name
was placed that of his pyramid to distinguish him, and
as a pledge of lasting fame. It was a pious custom
whenever the king or a great noble was mentioned to
add immediately after his name, 'Life, health, and
strength be to him.'

On the steep wall of rock in the Wady-Magharah,
where, in the very ancient caverns, the traces of the
miner may easily be recognised, Sneferu appears as a
warrior, with a mighty club striking a vanquished
enemy to the ground. The inscription engraved beside
the picture mentions him clearly by name, with the
title of ' vanquisher of a foreign people.' The land,
which formerly yielded copper ore, and blue and green
precious stones, seems to have been a possession much
coveted by the rulers of Kamit,[1] and it was without
doubt Sneferu who gained possession of this mountainous peninsula. By a short sea passage from Egypt,
or by a longer journey on the backs of asses, the
soldiers of the king and the troops of miners, with the
steward and overseer, reached the valley of the mines.
Even at this day the traveller can see and read on the
half-defaced stone a number of pictures and writings.
Standing on a high rock, which commands the entrance
to the Wady-Magharah, his eye discovers without
difficulty the ruins of the strong fortress whose well-
built walls once enclosed huts beside a deep well,
and protected the Egyptian troops from sudden attack.
There were also temples there dedicated to Hathor,
whom the Egyptians worshipped as the protectress of

[1] See p. 5.

the land of Mafkat,[1] and to the sparrow-hawk of Sopt, the ' lord of the east.'

The princes of the Fourth and Fifth Dynasties maintained with a powerful hand the inheritance that Sneferu left them. The mines were permanently worked, the enemy conquered, and the gods worshipped. Sneferu bethought himself in good time of the end of his life, and of a worthy monument. The royal edifice of the pyramid that stands near Meidûm contained, we doubt not, his body. The name of the building is in good Egyptian Kha, ⋆ ⬔, a word which served to denote sometimes ' the rising ' (of the sun), sometimes ' the festival,' sometimes ' the crown.'

Here it was, in close proximity to the pyramid, that some natives discovered the entrance to some tombs of ancient time, and brought to light, amongst other things, two statues remarkable for their antiquity and their admirable art. They are portrait statues of a man and his wife, sitting side by side in a dignified attitude on a die-shaped seat. The man, who was called Ra-hotep, was the son of a king, and had filled many important offices during his life. He led the warriors in the service of the monarch, and in On, the town of the god Ra, he bore the sacred office of chief priest. His wife, Nefert ('the beautiful' or ' the good'), was the grand-daughter of a king who is not named.

An old papyrus obtained by De Prisse in Thebes speaks thus of Sneferu : ' Then died the holiness of King Huni. Then was raised up the holiness of King Sneferu as a good king over the whole country. Then was Kakem appointed governor of the city.'

---

[1] In the Sinaitic peninsula.

DYNASTY IV.

To restore as completely as possible the names and order of the Pharaohs of the Fourth and Fifth Dynasties, the Tablets of Abydos and Saqqarah (p. xx. *et seq.*) and the Turin Papyrus may together be considered as approximating to the truth.

According to the testimony of the Tablets the successor of the good king Sneferu was KHUFU, the Cheops of Herodotus. With him begin the memorable traditions of Egyptian history, as recorded by the Greek and Roman authors.

Khufu.

No one who has once set foot on the black soil of Egypt ever turns on his homeward journey till his eyes have looked upon that wonder of antiquity the threefold mass of the Pyramids on the edge of the desert, which is reached after an hour's ride over the long causeway from the village of Gîzeh, on the left bank of the Nile. From the far distance are clearly seen their giant forms, looking as if they were mountains; yet they are but tombs built by the hands of men, and which, raised by Khufu and two other kings of the same family and dynasty, have been the admiration and astonishment alike of the ancient and modern world. Perfectly adjusted to the cardinal points of the horizon, they differ from each other both in breadth and height, as is shown by the measurements of Colonel Howard Vyse :—

		Height.	Breadth.
1.	Pyramid of Khufu	450·75 feet	746 feet
2.	Pyramid of Khaf-Ra	447·5 „	690·75 „
3.	Pyramid of Men-kau-Ra	203 „	352·87 „

The mode of construction of these enormous masses was for long an almost insoluble enigma to even experts in engineering.

According to their ancient custom the Egyptians,

while they lived in health and vigour, were ever
mindful to turn their looks westward to where the door
of the grave would one day close on the body, which
should rise to a new existence after an appointed
number of years; while the soul, though bound to the
body, was free to leave and return to the grave each
day.

In such a belief it was their custom betimes to dig
their graves in the form of a deep shaft in the rock,
and, as a superstructure to this 'eternal dwelling,' to
raise sometimes only a hall, sometimes several apart-
ments, and to adorn these richly with coloured writing
and painted sculptures, as if it were meant for a house
of pleasure and joy. Not seldom did death snatch
away the builder before his work was finished. In
such a case the visitor finds pictures which the
draughtsman's skilful hand had sketched in outline
with a red crayon on the polished surface of the stone
wall, but time had not been left for the painter to fill
in the picture with bright and varied colours.

The Pharaoh, therefore, as soon as he mounted
the throne, immediately began building his tomb
The kernel of the future edifice was raised on the
limestone soil of the desert, in the form of a small
pyramid built in steps, of which the carefully constructed and well-finished interior formed the king's
eternal dwelling. A covering was added to the outside of the kernel, followed by a second, and sometimes even a third and fourth; and when, at last, it
became almost impossible to extend the area of the
pyramid farther, a casing of hard stone, polished like
glass, and fitted accurately to the angles of the steps,
completely covered the gigantic building.

A special name was assigned to each pyramid, to
distinguish it from its neighbours. Thus the sepul-

chral monument of Khufu bore the title of 'Khut,' i.e. 'the Lights.'

The stones for the building of it were chosen from three different places. The inner material—a spongy limestone without consistence—was found close at hand. The better sort of stone, chosen for the steps and the successive layers, was brought from Tûrah upon rollers along the causeway (above half a mile long) which reached from the left bank of the river, immediately opposite to that mountain, to the plateau of the pyramids, while the covering was of costly stone brought down the river from a great distance. On the southern border of Egypt, close to Aswân, stands the 'red mountain' (Tutesherit), composed of a granite sprinkled with black and red, as hard as iron, and shining beautifully when polished. The brilliancy and durability of the syenite—well fitted for buildings that were to last for ever—made the possession of this stone much desired. Quarry marks of those ancient times are still visible; here we meet with the outline of a colossal statue, and there the whole length of the fourth side of an obelisk still waits to be loosened from its bed.

Ten years passed before the workmen had quarried the stone for the Great Pyramid in the mountain of Tûrah, laid the foundation, and closed the dark tomb-chamber in the rock, and twice ten years more before the whole work was completed.

The few contemporary monuments present Khufu in a different light from that in which his character is drawn in the time of the Persian and Greek dominion, when his reputation was at a low ebb. The rock tablets in the Wady-Magharah extol him as the annihilator of his enemies, and represent him as a brave, active ruler. Later tradition says he was barbarous in manners and of a tyrannical nature, and forced the people to do hard labour. He also closed the temples, from an evil motive, fearing that prayer and sacrifices would shorten the time of the people for work.

Three small pyramids facing the east in front of Khufu's gigantic tomb formerly contained the bodies of the king's wife and children.

TATF-RA followed Khufu in the kingdom. His name occurs on the Tablets of Abydos and Saqqarah, but further than this we know nothing of him.

KHAF-RA, the Khefren of the Greeks. His pyramid, ⟍ ⁄, designated by the ancients 'the Great,' stands close to that of Khufu. Although the stones say little of Khaf-Ra, his name is nevertheless well preserved by the wonderful workmanship of his statues.

It is only a few years ago that close to the Sphinx was discovered that building which is still a mystery —small passages, then spacious halls, then again dark side-rooms built with huge, well-cut blocks of hard variegated stone from Aswân, and of shining alabaster fitted to a hair's breadth, each alternate corner stone being clamped into the adjacent wall and perfectly squared, but destitute of any mark or inscription. On the east side the stone-covered space of ground showed in a long hall the shaft of a well, into whose depths a number of statues of Khaf-Ra had been thrown. The greater number of them were destroyed by the violence of the fall. Only one seemed to have survived—the figure of King Khaf-Ra in a sitting posture, of regal appearance, dignified in look and bearing. A sparrow-hawk, hiding itself behind the Pharaoh's head, spreads out its wings in calm repose, as if to protect its royal master. The name and title of the king appear inscribed on the base of the statue. The greenish stone, shining with a high polish, is a hard diorite.

a material seldom chosen for the execution of a monument.

In saying that the discovery of the statues of Khaf-Ra has proved an unparalleled addition to the history of the old empire, and that they must be esteemed the greatest treasure of antiquity, we have not yet nearly exhausted the advantages to be derived from Khaf-Ra's stone image. As that wooden statue of an old Sheikh-el-Belled,[1] which was brought to light out of the tombs at Saqqarah, as the various coloured statues of limestone which came forth from the narrow 'Serdabs'[2] of the tombs as witnesses of ancient life, as every artistic production of those days, in picture, writing, or sculpture, bears the stamp of the highest perfection of art, so the statue of Khaf-Ra also teaches us that in the beginning of history the works of art already redounded to the praise of their authors.

From east to west, almost in the same line with Khaf-Ra's pyramid, lies the colossal Sphinx—the body of a lion united with the face of a man. As if at rest, the lion stretches out his fore paws, between which a narrow path led to the temple which stood at the breast of the monster, while a memorial stone preserves the memory of the gifts made by Tehuti-mes IV. to the god. The lion was of the living rock; but where the hollows in the stone interrupted the rounding of the body, light masonry was introduced to fill in what was wanting in the form.

So far as we learn from an inscription, King Khufu had seen the monster; therefore the statue existed before his time. To the north lay a temple of Isis; a second, dedicated to Osiris, was situated on the southern side; and a third was consecrated to the Sphinx. In

---

[1] See Frontispiece.
[2] Serdab is the Arabic word for the secret chamber in the sepulchral　chapels where the statues of the deceased were placed.

the sacred language the Sphinx is called 'Hu,' a word that only denotes the man-headed lion, while as god the man-lion was called Horemkhu, a word meaning 'Horus on the horizon,' and which the Greek language translated by 'Harmachis.'

Many fragments of antiquity, preserved in the cemetery of Memphis, inform us that Khaf-Ra's wife was named Meri-s-ankh. She appears to have been a devout worshipper of the gods, and in adoring them she obtained honour for herself.

Men-kau-Ra.

After Khaf-Ra had gone to the land where Osiris held the sceptre, King MEN-KAU-RA, the Mycerinus of the Greeks, ascended the throne. His pyramid occupies the south-west corner of the plain of Gîzeh, and is called , Her ('the high one'). When Colonel Howard Vyse found the well-guarded entrance to the chamber of the dead, and entered the room 'of eternity,' he saw, as the last trace of Men-kau-Ra's burial, the wooden cover of the coffin, and the stone sarcophagus, hewn out of a single block of hard stone, and beautifully ornamented outside in the style of a temple. Sent to London as a valuable memorial of antiquity, ship and cargo sank to the bottom of the sea off Gibraltar. The coffin containing the mummy was saved, and is now in the British Museum. The inscription on the cover runs thus: 'O Osiris, king of the north and the south, Men-kau-Ra, living for ever, the heavens have produced thee. Thou wast engendered by Nut;[1] thou art the offspring of Seb.[2] Thy mother Nut spreads herself over thee in her form as a divine mystery. She has granted thee to be a god; thou shalt never more have enemies, O king of the north and south, Men-kau-Ra, living for ever.'

According to Greek testimony, Men-kau-Ra enjoyed

[1] The sky. [2] The earth.

the reputation of being a mild and just man. It also appears certain that he industriously studied the religious writings of his age. The 'Ritual of the Dead,' which was usually buried with every mummy as a guide in the world beyond, mentions this king thus :—

This gate (chapter) was found in the city of Hermopolis, engraved on a block of alabaster and painted in blue colour, under the feet of this god. It was found in the time of King Men-kau-Ra, the deified, by the king's son Hortotef, when he undertook a journey to inspect the temples of Egypt. He brought the stone as a wonderful thing to the king, after he had well understood the contents full of mystery which were on it.

SHEPSES-KA-F, ⟨ 𓀐 𓉐 𓉐 ⟩, is the name of the Pharaoh who succeeded Men-kau-Ra. All doubt on the subject is removed by the inscriptions on a tomb at Saqqarah. The noble for whom it was constructed bore the name of Ptah-Shepses ; he lived at court and was a favourite with the kings. He appears first as an adopted child of Men-kau-Ra, for ' he placed him among the royal children in the royal women's house.' When Men-kau-Ra died Shepses-ka-f placed the young page in his own house and gave him his daughter in marriage. ' He was esteemed by the king above all his servants. He became private secretary for every work that Pharaoh was pleased to execute. He charmed the heart of his master. His Majesty allowed him to embrace his knees and exempted him from the salutation of the ground.' The last words are not without advantage to our knowledge of ancient usages at the court of the Pharaohs. When a servant of high or low degree approached his royal master, custom demanded that he should throw himself repeatedly in the dust and kiss the ground, only favourites being permitted to touch the king's knee. Ptah-Shepses directed the forced labour of the mines, and was also the prophet of the god Sekar

and chief guardian of his sanctuary. The highest
decoration he bore was that of 'chief of the priesthood
of Memphis.' There are but few tombs that give any
further tidings of Shepses-ka-f. We know that he did not
neglect to build himself a pyramid, to which he gave the
name of Qebeh, ⌂, 'the cool.'

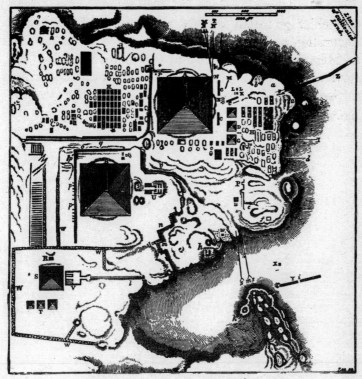

PLAN OF THE PYRAMIDS AND TOMBS OF GIZEH.

A. Entrance to the Great Pyramid.
B. Entrance to the Second Pyramid.
CC. Long pits, by some supposed for mixing the mortar.
D. Pyramid of the daughter of Cheops (Herodotus, ii. 126).
E. Pavement of black stones (basaltic trap), the same as found on the causeways of the pyramids of Saqqarah.
F. Remains of masonry.
G. Round enclosures of crude brick, of Arab date, at N.E. angle of this pyramid.
H. Tombs of individuals, with deep pits.
I. The tomb of numbers.
K. Two inclined passages, meeting underground, apparently once belonging to a small pyramid that stood over them.
L L. The rock is here cut to a level surface.
M. A narrow and shallow trench cut in the rock.
N. A square space cut in the rock, probably to receive and support the corner stone of the casing of the pyramid.
P. Here stood a tomb which has received the title of the Temple of Osiris.
Q. Tomb of trades, to west of tombs H.
R. A pit cased with stone, of modern date.
S. The Third Pyramid.

T. Three small pyramids.
U, V. Ruined buildings, whose original use it is now difficult to determine.
W W W. Fragments of stone, arranged in the manner of a wall.
X. A few palms and sycamores, with a well.
Y. Southern stone causeway.
Z. Northern causeway, repaired by the Caliphs.
a. Tombs cut in the rock.
b. Masonry.
c. Black stones.
d, d. Tombs cut in the rock.
e. The sphinx.
f. Pits, probably unopened.
g. Pits.
h. Stone ruin on a rock.
i. Doorway, or passage, through the causeway.
k. A grotto in the rock.
l. Inclined causeway, part of Y.
m, n. Tombs in the rock.
o. Some hieroglyphics on the rock.
p. Tombs cut in the scarp of the rock.
q. Stone wall.
r. Steps cut in the rock, near the N.W. angle of the Great Pyramid.
s, t. Magnetic south, in 1832 and 1836, corresponding to M N; T N being 'true north.'

CHAPTER III.

DYNASTIES V.–XI.[1]

THE PHARAOHS OF THE FIFTH AND SIXTH DYNASTIES.

USERCHERES heads the list of Pharaohs of the Fifth Dynasty, according to Manetho. He is the same whom the Tablet of Abydos gives as User-ka-f, ⌈ 🔲 ⌉. About his reign we learn little. In the inscriptions on the sepulchral buildings and monuments of his contemporaries he is praised as a Pharaoh at whose tomb a pious priesthood performed divine worship. Although there is no longer any token to indicate the monument of King User-ka-f the name of his pyramid, Ab-asu, 𓏭𓏭, 'the purest place,' has been faithfully preserved. It is otherwise with SAHU-RA, ⌈ 🔲 ⌉, who followed User-ka-f in the kingdom. The cartouche of this king is painted in red on the stone blocks of a pyramid which rose northwards from the village of Abusîr, on the margin of the desert, and was entitled Kha-ba, 🔲, 'rising of souls.' His names are conspicuous also on the smooth cliff in the Wady-Magharah, where he stands sculptured on the rock as the vanquisher of foreign peoples. Beside this an inscription designates him as 'God, who strikes all peoples, and smites all countries with his arm.'

[1] For Table of Kings see p. xx.

Long after Sahu-Ra lay sleeping in his pyramid the pious remembrance of his name continued ; for when the Ptolemies ruled in the Nile valley a sanctuary still stood in Memphis dedicated to his memory, where priests performed their sacred offices for the dead king.

He was succeeded, according to the Tablet of Saqqarah, by a Pharaoh of the name of NEFER-AR-KA-RA, [hieroglyph], doubtless the same that Manetho transcribed Nephercheres. He gave to his pyramid the name Ba, that is 'Soul,' [hieroglyph]. Many fragments of tombs in the cemetery of Memphis have faithfully preserved the memory of this king ; above all the grave of his royal grandson, Urkhuru, who is called 'the royal scribe of the palace, the learned man, the master of writing who serves as a light to all the writing in the house of Pharaoh.' He is also called the 'master of writing for the petitions of the people, he who serves as a light to all the writing which relates to the administration, chief of the provision chambers.' He was also 'general of the forces composed of all the young men.' Another officer of this time, named Pehenuka, performed the duties of secretary of state in faithful service to his master. Of the rulers who followed this king we will mention the thirtieth according to the Tablet of Abydos,

USER-EN-RA, [hieroglyph].

He is the first Pharaoh who adopted a second cartouche with his own private name, An. Following the custom of his predecessors, he built for his sepulchre a pyramid which was called Men-asu, 'the firmest of places,' [hieroglyph]. His name has been found, plainly traced in red, on the middle pyramid of Abusîr, and without doubt he was laid to rest ages ago in its chamber. His name also appears at Wady-Magharah, where a sculptured tablet represents him as conqueror over the ancient people who had their dwelling-places in the Sinaitic valleys. Of the tombs of those court functionaries from whose walls we learn so much of the life-history of this ancient people, the most beautiful that remains is that of Thi. The inscriptions carved in hieroglyphs and filled in with colour give a clear significance to the pictures and enlarge in eloquent language on the worth of the deceased. He served his master as scribe in all his residences, was president of the royal writings, and conducted the king's works, to say nothing of the priestly dignities with which he was invested. It appears strange that in the grave of this noblest of men the name of his father is wanting and no traces of his descent are perceptible. If Thi was a man of low origin, he must certainly have performed something great, to appear worthy of being son-in-law to the king, for Pharaoh gave him his own daughter Nefer-hotep to wife.

The last three sovereigns of this Fifth Dynasty had their places definitely fixed long before the discovery of the Tablet of Abydos.

The first, MEN-KAU-HOR, , built the pyramid called Neter-asu, , which means 'the holiest of places.' A sculptured block, let into a wall of the Apis-tombs (Serapeum), has faithfully preserved for us the portrait of the king in bas-relief, accompanied by his name and titles. It is possible that one of the pyramids of Saqqarah contained the king's tomb. The rocky walls, also, of the Sinaitic mountains, mention this prince several times.

He was followed by TAT-KA-RA, , surnamed

Assa, ⟨ ▭ ⟩.   It is again the Wady-Magharah that gives us information about this king, testifying that new mines were excavated in the mountain when Assa sat on the throne of his fathers.   The name 'beautiful' (nefer), ▮▲, was given to his pyramid, and in ancient days holy men consecrated their services to his memory.

A record worthy of remembrance is preserved in an ancient papyrus written by Assa's son, Ptah-hotep.[1] It is without doubt the oldest manuscript in existence, and contains wise instruction and admonition, praises the practice of virtue and good manners, and points out the path which leads to honour and a happy end.

The king's son must have been very aged when he wrote this book, for he speaks of decrepit old age as one who felt it himself.

'The two eyes,' thus writes the wise man, 'are drawn small, the ears are stopped up, and what was strong becomes continually weak. The mouth becomes silent, it speaks no clear word ; the memory is dulled, it cannot recall past days ; the bones refuse their service. The good has changed to bad.   Even the taste is long since gone. In every way old age makes a man miserable.   The nose is stopped without air.'

After unfolding some of his deepest thoughts in very simple language he adds—

If thou hast become great after thou hast been lowly, and if thou hast amassed riches after poverty, so that thou hast become, because of this, the first in thy city ; and if the people know thee on account of thy wealth, and thou art become a mighty lord, let not thy heart be lifted up because of thy riches, for the author of them is God.   Despise not thy neighbour who is as thou wast, but treat him as thy equal.

·   ·   ·   ·   ·   ·   ·

Let thy countenance shine joyfully as long as thou livest ; did a man ever leave the coffin after having once entered it ?

[1] The Prisse Papyrus, now in the Bibliothèque Nationale, Paris.

The last Pharaoh of the dynasty bore the name of
UNAS, ⌒⌒⌒

We know little more of him than that his sepulchre
was called Nefer-asu, ▌ ▐▐▐ ▲, which means 'the most
beautiful place.'

[The Mastabat-el-Farûn, first explored by Mariette,
was at one time supposed both by the excavator and
Brugsch-Bey himself to be the tomb of this king.
It has now been ascertained by Maspero that Unas
was buried in the pyramid that has since 1881 borne
his name, and which lies to the south-west of the
Step Pyramid. The walls lining the sarcophagus-
chamber are of alabaster and covered with paintings,
the colours of which are still fresh. The fragments of
the king's mummy were found scattered on the floor.]

In accordance with the Tablets of Abydos and Saqqarah, the monuments call the first prince of the Sixth
Dynasty ⌒⌒⌒, TETA. But we also have proof of
his succession in another way. In the grave of
Ptah-Shepses, at Saqqarah, this nobleman's offices and
dignities are enumerated at the usual length. He
was the sacred prophet of the pyramids of Unas, and
of Teta, who was the first king to adopt the title
of Se-Ra, 'Son of the Sun,' ⌒⌒. The pyramid
of this latter was called Tat-asu, ▐▐▐▐▲, 'the most
lasting of places,' surely not without allusion to the
king's own name.

It has been supposed that the name of USER-KA-RA,
which the Tablet of Abydos places after that of Teta,
was the official title of a King ATI, ⌒⌒⌒, who
likewise built a pyramid, called Baiu, ⌒⌒ ▲, ' the pyra-

mid of the souls,' and further that this Ati was the real founder of the Sixth Dynasty, who reigned, perhaps, in Middle Egypt simultaneously with Teta, the last descendant of the ancient kings of Memphis.

One thing is certain, that a nobleman named Una passed immediately from the service of King Ati to that of his successor, MERI-RA, ⟨ ◯ ⁓ 丨丨 ⟩, 'friend of Ra,' whose family name was PEPI, ⟨ ⁝丨丨 ⟩.

The Wady-Magharah, which contains so many memorials of the ancient Memphite Pharaohs, has no less perfectly preserved the memory of Pepi. A great bas-relief, carved in the rock, says that, in the eighteenth year of his reign, a governor named Abton visited the mines to inspect the progress of the work. In the tablet itself the king appears as the conqueror of the foreign people, who in his time dwelt in the valley of caverns. Amongst the ruins which cover the site of the once far-famed city of Tanis, in the Delta, a block of stone was found, covered with the names and titles of Pepi, a proof that the origin of the city extends back to the time of the ancient kingdom. At Denderah also, in the temple of Hathor, the wall of a chamber gives us the information that Pepi enlarged the sanctuary which Khufu had founded before him, while the valleys of Hammamât, the dark rocks near Aswân, and the walls in the quarries of El-Kab, still preserve the memory of the king. When Pepi ruled there was living a nobleman called Una, who began his career at the court of the Pharaohs. By his good services he gained the favour of the king, and when Teta died Pepi became attached to the young man, and placed him in a confidential position in his own house. Among other duties he received orders to quarry a

sarcophagus out of the mountain of Tûrah. Warriors
and sailors accompanied Una to carry on the work.
The monument, which was carved out of one single
block, was conveyed down the river on one of the
king's vessels with its cover and many other hewn
stones destined for the building of the royal pyramid.
Una was next sent in a military capacity against the
Aamu and the Herusha, peoples of the desert east of
Lower Egypt. Everything necessary for the expedition
was prepared, but, as the bands of warriors did not appear sufficiently numerous, levies from a foreign country
subject to the king, and settled on the southern boundary
of the kingdom, were added to the native army; they
were instructed in the proper method of fighting by
captains whom Pharaoh had placed over them. When
the army was at last ready it took the field, destroyed
the land of Herusha, and returned home successful.

After these wars a new contest broke out, and
Pharaoh sent his army against the land of Terehbah (?),
'to the north of the land of the Herusha.' It is difficult
at the present day to recognise this country. Since
ships are mentioned, it does not seem preposterous to
think of Syria, especially of that part of it which lies to
the north of the Arab desert. Pharaoh, as usual, built
himself a pyramid, which was named Men-nefer,
, that is, 'good place' or 'good station' (for
travellers). As a founder of cities, his memory was
immortalised by the city of Pepi, in Middle Egypt.

Amongst the nobles who served him appears a
certain Meri-Ra-ankh, 'president of the public works of
the king,' who is designated on the walls of his tomb
as Governor of Tûrah. He was entrusted with the
direction of the works in the quarries of the Mokattam
mountains. Another at Abydos, the noble Pepi-nekht,
whose grave is in the necropolis, was 'governor of the

city of the pyramids.' By this place is evidently meant
the sanctuary before the king's tomb, in which holy
men offered sacrifices to the deceased Pharaoh, burnt
incense before his images, and performed all other
religious service according to the usual custom.

The Pharaoh Pepi, who, according to Greek accounts,
sat for 100 years on the throne of his fathers, married
a lady not of royal descent, whose father was named
Khua, and her mother Nekebet. After she had received
the honours of an Egyptian queen a royal name was
given to her, and she was called Meri-Ra-ankhnes.
Her tomb, the ruins of which were found in the
necropolis at Abydos, gives us important information
about her descendants. She gave birth to two sons,
Mer-en-Ra and Nefer-ka-Ra. When Pepi died the first-
born took possession of the crown and kingdom. He
figures in the Tablet of Abydos under the name of

, MER-EN-RA.

The long inscription from Una's grave enlightens the
darkness which surrounds this monarch's history. After
the death of Pepi Una rose, under the rule of his
successor, to the dignity of 'Governor of Upper Egypt.'
His government was bounded towards the south by the
town of Elephantiné, and on the north by the nome of
Letopolis, in the Lower Country. He himself acknowledges the rarity of the favour, confessing in his own
words that such a thing had never before happened in
Upper Egypt.

As ancient custom demanded, Mer-en-Ra, when he
had ascended the throne, was at once mindful of the
eternal dwelling which after death should contain his
royal mummy. Una immediately received the command
to prepare everything for the work and to quarry the
hardest stone on the southernmost border of Egypt.

'His Majesty,' so speaks Una himself, 'sent me to the country
of Abhat,[1] to bring back a sarcophagus with its cover; also a small
pyramid and a statue of the king Mer-en-Ra, whose pyramid is
called Kha-nefer,' ☛ ▮ ▲ ('the beautiful rising ').

Scarcely had he executed these orders when he was
commanded to cut blocks of alabaster and bring them
to his lord. The gigantic load was to be sent by water
on great rafts 60 cubits in length and 30 in breadth
($103\frac{1}{2} \times 51\frac{3}{4}$ ft.), which had been previously specially
constructed for this purpose. But the river was found
to have fallen so low that it was impossible to make use
of such large rafts, so the governor was obliged to
build smaller ones in all haste. The wood for this
purpose had to be felled in the neighbouring country,
inhabited by the negroes.   It is thus related by Una :—

His Majesty sent me to cut down four forests in the South, in
order to build three large vessels and four towing vessels out of the
acacia wood in the country of Ua-ua-t. And behold the officials of
Araret, Aam, and Mata caused the wood to be cut down for this
purpose. I executed all this in the space of a year. As soon as
the waters rose, I loaded the rafts with immense pieces of granite
for the pyramid Kha-nefer of the king Mer-en-Ra.

This narrative of the life and actions of a single
man among the contemporaries of the kings Teta, Pepi,
and Mer-en-Ra, exhausts all that we know of their
history. [The mummy of Mer-en-Ra is now in the Gîzeh
Palace.]

After his brother's death NEFER-KA-RA, ⬭o▮ᴜ⬭
followed in the kingdom. His pyramid is called Men-
ankh, ▦ ♀ ᴢ, 'the station of life.' This king is
named in an inscription on the rocks of Wady-Magharah,
in which an officer speaks of him in the second year of
his reign. The tombs also in Middle Egypt frequently

---

[1] Probably near the southern frontier of Egypt.

mention noblemen whom this king had distinguished by honours and offices.

After the death of Nefer-ka-Ra Egyptian history is involved in darkness and confusion, which suggests the probability of a state split up into petty kingdoms, afflicted with civil wars and royal murders, and from among whose princes no deliverer arose who was able with a strong arm to put down the rebels or to guide the monarchy with firmness. The traditional story of Queen NITOCRIS gives us a clue to all this.

, NIT-AQERT or NITOCRIS.

According to Manetho she reigned twelve years, 'the noblest and most beautiful woman of her time, fair in colour (ξανθή), and the builder of the third pyramid.' Herodotus says that the king of Egypt, brother of Nitocris, was killed by conspirators, who however gave the kingdom to her, whereupon she proceeded with subtlety to avenge her brother's death, for she constructed a vast underground building, and, on the pretext of its inauguration, she invited the principal authors of the murder to a feast. During the repast the river was let into the chamber through a hidden channel, so that the whole party of banqueters was drowned. But after she had accomplished this, she plunged into a chamber filled with ashes and killed herself to escape the vengeance of the friends of the deceased. [According to Manetho Nitocris was the builder of the third pyramid, the same which Men-kau-Ra, more than a thousand years before, had prepared for his own resting-place. It has been proved by careful investigations that this pyramid, which contains two sarcophagus chambers, was enlarged in later times; so it is not impossible that Queen Nitocris altered it, left the body of Men-kau-Ra in the lower chamber, and placed her own in the blue basalt sarcophagus contained in the upper one.]

The Tablet of Abydos enumerates the names of twenty sovereigns, who correspond with the unnamed Pharaohs filling up five complete dynasties, according to Manetho. According to the Turin Papyrus the number of Pharaohs immediately preceding the Twelfth Dynasty was six. These, again, were preceded by a series of seventeen or eighteen kings. From Nitocris down to the first of these eighteen kings there was room on the papyrus for the names of about ten kings.

DYNASTIES VII.–XI.[1]

A period of confusion now follows, during which, according to the Tablet of Abydos, twenty kings reigned, of whom we know practically nothing. The first of whom the monuments speak was , NEB-KHER-RA, who was also called , MENTU-HOTEP, like one of his ancestors (his name on the monuments is , NEB-TAUI-RA).

The kings to whom Mentu-hotep belonged were of Theban origin, the feeble ancestors of whose line bore alternately the names of Antef and Mentu-hotep. They had established themselves in Thebes, and their tombs (simple pyramids of brick-work) lay at the foot of the western mountain of the Theban necropolis. Here it was that thirty years ago some Arabs brought to light two very simple coffins of these Pharaohs. They were discovered in that part now called Assassîf, scarcely hidden under heaps of loose stones and sand; one of them contained the mummy of the king, his head

adorned with the regal circlet. The cover of the chest
was richly gilt, and the hieroglyphs on the middle
band bore the cartouche of Antef. In the year 1854,
I had the good fortune to discover the coffin of a
second Antef, distinguished from the first by the title
of 'the Great;' it is now in the Louvre. The remaining traces of this king's tomb were discovered by
Mariette at Drah-abû-'l-Neggah. In the interior of a
brick pyramid was found a simple chamber with a
memorial stone dated in the fiftieth year of the reign
of King Antef 'ao (i.e. 'the Great'), the inscription and
paintings on which have been fully published by Dr.
Birch. The lower part of the king's image is well
preserved. At his feet stand his four favourite dogs.

Of the Mentu-hotep who bore the royal name Neb-
taui-Ra, 'Son of the lord of the country,' a memorial is
preserved on the black rocks of the island of Konosso,
above the First Cataract. A bas-relief chiselled in the
hard stone exhibits him as the conqueror of thirteen
foreign nations, and as the devoted servant of Amsu of
Coptos. This town, situated near Hammamât, was on
the edge of the desert, and was the rendez-vous of
traders to and from the Red Sea, who traced their
names on the rocks, to which they usually added a
pious inscription.

Mentu-hotep also appears immortalised on the cliff
in the valley of rocks, together with his mother Ama.
He had, so the inscription tells, sunk a deep well,
ten cubits in diameter, in the desert, in order to provide water for the refreshment of all pilgrims with
their beasts of burthen, and for all the men who were
commanded by the king to quarry stone in this hot
valley. Another inscription of the second year of his
reign says that a functionary, by name Amenemhat,
received orders to transport the king's sarcophagus

and its cover from the quarry to the eternal resting-place of his lord. The way was long, and the labour of the work heavy, for the enormous mass measured in length eight cubits, while its dimensions in breadth and height were four and two cubits. After offerings had been first made to the gods, 3,000 men moved the gigantic burthen of the stone from its place, and rolled it down the valley to the Nile.

We have less information about the second Mentu-hotep, whose pyramid bore the name of Khu-asu, ﻝ ｜ ⋮ ▵, 'the most shining of places.' A grave-stone found in the cemetery of Abydos commemorates the priest who offered the sacrifices of the dead for the deceased.

This list of sovereigns ends with SANKH-KA-RA, (∘ ⋂ ⼍ ⼫), whom an inscription in the rocky valley of Hammamât commemorates.

The first voyage to Ophir and Punt took place in his reign, under the leadership of a nobleman named Hannu, who gives the following account of his journey :—

I was sent to conduct ships to the land of Punt, to fetch for Pharaoh sweet-smelling spices, which the princes of the red land collect out of fear and dread, such as he inspires in all nations. And I started from the city of Coptos. And his Majesty gave the command that the armed men, who were to accompany me, should be from the south country of the Thebaïd.

. . . .

And I set out thence with an army of 3,000 men, and passed through 'the red hamlet' and through a cultivated country. I had skins and poles prepared to carry the vessels of water, twenty in number. And of people one carried a load daily [*lacuna*], . . . and another placed the load on him. And I had a reservoir of twelve perches dug in a wood, and two reservoirs at a place called Atahet—one of a perch and twenty cubits, and the other of a perch and thirty cubits. And I made another at Ateb, of ten cubits by ten on each side, to contain water of a cubit in depth. Then I arrived at the port Seba (?), and I had ships of burthen built to bring back products of all kinds. And I offered a great sacrifice of oxen, cows, and goats. And when I returned from Seba (?) I had executed the king's command, for I brought him back all kinds of products which I had met with in the ports of the Holy Land. And I came back by the road of Uak and Rohan, and brought with me precious stones for the statues of the temples. But such a thing never happened since there were kings ; nor was the like of it ever done by any blood relations who were sent to these places since the time (of the reign) of the Sun-god Ra. And I acted thus for the king on account of the great favour which he entertained for me.

There seems to be but little doubt that the present coast of Somali, opposite to Arabia, represents the Ophir of the ancient Egyptians. They understood it to be a land of hills and valleys washed by the sea, whence came their choice woods, their balsam and frankincense, their precious metals and costly stones; it was rich also in strange and curious animals and birds. Punt, the ' Holy Land,' possibly represented by the south and west coasts of Arabia Felix, was the original home of the gods. Amen, Horus, and Hathor all came from there, while Bes, who was the most ancient divinity in Punt, is of peculiarly Arab origin.

CHAPTER IV.

DYNASTY XII.[1]

MANETHO states that the princes of the Twelfth Dynasty were of Theban origin, which is more than probable, since the Antefs and Mentu-hoteps have left memorials of themselves in that city. The sanctuary of the great temple of Amen at Karnak, whose ruins are covered with the names of the kings of this house, was gradually enlarged from the time of its foundation to the grandeur of an imperial edifice, whose stone walls reveal to us the history of the Theban kings.

The high distinction of this dynasty does not rest so much on the greatness of the kings as on the wisdom of their government at home and the glory of their victories abroad. Art also was cherished by these rulers, and from the hands of skilful masters arose an immense number of beautiful buildings and pictures. It is from the accession of the Twelfth Dynasty that a more harmonious form of beauty meets the eye of the beholder, alike in architecture and in sculpture.

AMEN-EM-HAT I., ⬚, with the regal name ⬚, SE-HOTEP-AB-RA.

Such is the name of the ruler who greets us on the threshold of this dynasty as the leader of his race.

---

[1] For Table of Kings see p. xxii.

Unless the evidence deceives us, he is a descendant of the prince of the same name who, under Neb-taui Mentu-hotep, received the command to bring enormous stones from the valley of Hammamât, and by so doing earned the praise of the king. His elevation to the throne was no peaceful hereditary succession, but a struggle for the crown. In the instructions which Amen-em-hat I. wrote for his son (Sallier Papyrus II.) he speaks of the trouble which consumed the land from internal wars and conspirators who sought to murder the king. After peace and order were re-established the signal was given for external wars. A memorial stone now in London bears witness that the power of the king extended beyond the limits of the empire. His dominion in the south is confirmed by an inscription engraved on a mass of rock on the road from Korosko, which records his victory over the inhabitants of the land of Ua-ua-t, which country probably co-incided with the auriferous valley of Ollaqi, which extends northwards from Korosko to the sea. The historical information on this stone is also confirmed by contemporary papyri, which tell us of external campaigns and wars carried on against foreign nations, such as the Mazai, the Sati, the Herusha, and other 'rabble' in the South and North, in the East and West. Besides military operations, the service of the gods lay near to the sovereign's heart. He was the founder of the temple of Amen at Thebes, where his own portrait, executed in rose-coloured granite from Aswân, bore witness to his work. Memphis also, the Fayûm, and other places were chosen to be adorned with statues and temples. And even if the last stones of these works were silent, the ancient quarries in the limestone-hill of Mokattam and in the valleys of the much-frequented Wady-Hammamât would tell the tale.

Amen-em-hat followed the ancient custom of the Memphite kings, and built himself, for an 'eternal dwelling,' his own pyramid, with the name of Ka-nefer, 'beautiful and high,' ◢ 𓀀 𓊖 ◣. This Pharaoh also carefully provided, during his lifetime, a stone sarcophagus as the receptacle for his body. The chief of the priests of the god Amsu, Antef, the son of Sebek-nekht, was sent to the mountain of Rohannu in the Wady-Hammamât to cut the stone for the sarcophagus from the wall of rock, and to roll the precious burthen, so immensely great that 'never the like had been provided since the time of the god Ra,' down the valley to the plain of Egypt.

Of the internal condition of the country we may learn something from the 'Story of Sineh.'

From some unknown cause he fled from the court, and endeavoured to escape from the land by the north-eastern frontier. Here he encountered difficulties, first from the keepers of the roads, then from the foreign tribes settled on the frontier. Escaping the vigilance of the watchman on the 'wall,' he reached the desert in safety; and at length gained the little kingdom of Tennu, in the land of Edom, where he was invited to the court of Amen-usha, the king, who gave him his daughter in marriage and the fruitful district of Æa as his residence. Here he lived prosperously for many years, until at last, being seized with an intense desire to see his native land, he obtained permission to return. Pharaoh received him cordially, loaded him with honours, and even had his grave erected for him.

Amen-em-hat reigned the last ten years of his life in common with his son, Usertsen, who was still a boy, and to whom his father addressed the instructions already mentioned.

KHEPER-KA-RA.   USERTSEN I.

Under his rule the land gradually became quiet, and order was completely re-established. Amen-em-hat I. had been obliged to pass through the revolted country with his soldiers, in order to meet and subdue his opponents. It was reserved for his son Usertsen I. to win back men's minds by gaining first of all the favour of the priests, by buildings in honour of the national divinities, works whose ruins exist until the present day.

This king is first mentioned in the inscription on the obelisk of Heliopolis in the immediate neighbourhood of the village of Matarîeh. The Egyptians gave the old town the name of Annu, 'obelisks of the north.' Here there existed from the very earliest known times a temple of the Sun-god Tmu and his wife, to which the Pharaohs were wont to make pilgrimages, in order to fulfil certain sacred rites. The temple and town lay about 6 feet below the present level of the soil, and nearly $11\frac{1}{2}$ feet below that of the high Nile. The long earthen mounds of the circumvallation are now the only visible remains of the city of Heliopolis.

The temple at On already existed in the time of Usertsen, for it is often mentioned in inscriptions of the reigns of his royal ancestors.

The erection of the obelisks proves also that the building was finished as far as the entrance-towers, before which it was the custom to raise these giant needles. But a remarkable document on parchment, now in the Berlin Museum, makes the fact certain, that Usertsen I., at the very beginning of his reign, occupied himself with buildings at the temple of the city of the Sun. This memorial informs us how, in

the third year of his reign, he assembled the first
officials of his court, to hear their opinion and their
counsel as to his intention of raising worthy buildings
to the Sun-god, and gave commands to the proper
court official to watch over the un-interrupted progress
of the work which he was determined upon, and then
began the solemn ceremony of laying the foundation
stone.   The four sides of the great obelisk were deeply
cut with beautiful hieroglyphs in the red granite, which
run thus :—

The Horus of the Sun, | the life for those who are born, | the
king of the upper and lower country, | Kheper-ka-Ra, | the lord of
the double crown, | the life for those who are born, | the son of
the Sun-god Ra, | Usertsen, | the friend of the spirits of On, |
ever living, | the golden Horus, | the life for those who are born, |
the gracious God, | Kheper-ka-Ra, | has executed this work, | at
the beginning of a thirty years' cycle, | he the dispenser of life for
evermore.

Usertsen must have had a special predilection for
this mode of perpetuating his name ; at least, remains
which have been discovered in other parts attest his
inclination for the erection of stone obelisks.   In the
ancient province of the lake of Mœris, near Begig, are
the fragments of a similar memorial, which, according
to the inscription, was executed by the king in honour
of the local gods of the capital.

As his father Amen-em-hat had begun to lay the
foundations of the later temple of Karnak, to the east
of the granite building of the chief sanctuary, so his
son Usertsen enlarged it, as a proof of his veneration
for Amen.   His care was not confined to the dwelling
of the god only, but also to that of his chief servants.
He dedicated to them a separate place, which bore the
name of 'the holy dwelling of the first seers of Amen.'
Though no traces of this ancient building exist, the
fact is proved by an inscription found at Thebes, which

relates to its restoration in the reign of Ramses IX., by Amen-hotep, the first seer of Amen, who restored the great court and the dwelling of the first seers, defraying the cost himself.

As I found the holy dwelling of the first seers of Amen, who of old sat in the house of Amen, the king of the gods, hastening to decay—for what there was of it dated from the time of King Usertsen the First — I caused it to be built anew, in beautiful forms and tasteful work. I restored the thickness of the surrounding wall from behind to the front part. I caused the buildings to be raised, and their columns to be set up of hard stone in tasteful work.

One of the celebrated rock-tombs has preserved some historical memorials of Usertsen I. It is the same tomb which always attracts the attention of the visitor by the new form of the pillar, by the design of the front, and by the peculiar richness of its pictures. Chiselled in the rocks was the sacrificial hall, dedicated to the service of the dead, who belonged to a noble family holding hereditary possession of the neighbouring district.

Here Ameni, the head of the family, relates the incidents of his life as follows :—

In the year 43, under the rule of King Usertsen I.—may he live long, even to all eternity !—which (year) corresponds with the year 25 in the nome of Mah, where the hereditary lord AMEN was governor. In the year 43, on the 14th day of the month Paophi.

Address to those who enjoy life, and to whom death is hateful. Let them recite the prayer of the offerings of the dead.

In favour of the hereditary governor-in-chief of the nome of Mah (some other titles follow), the chief over the holy seers, Amen, who has conquered (i.e. death).

I accompanied my lord when he made an expedition to smite his enemies in the country of the Atu. I went up with him as the son of the most noble lord, who was captain of the warriors and governor of the nome of Mah, as substitute (?) for my father, who was old, and who had received his reward from the king's palace, for he was beloved at court. I entered the country of Cush (the land of the Negroes), ascending the river, and the way brought me to the uttermost boundary of the land. I convoyed the booty of my master, and my praise reached heaven when his Majesty returned home successful. He had smitten his enemies in the miserable country of Cush. I returned home in his retinue, with a joyful countenance. Not one of my warriors was missing.

Again I went up (the river) to convoy the golden treasures to his Majesty King Usertsen—may he live long! I went with the king's eldest son and heir to the throne, Ameni—life, strength, and health be to him! I went up with the number of 400 chosen persons of my warriors. They returned home successful : no one was missing. I brought back the gold. That was the beginning of my distinctions on the part of the kings.

My father praised me. After that I again went up (the river) to convoy the treasures to the town of Coptos, in company with the hereditary lord and chief governor of the town, Usertsen—life, strength, and health be to him! I went up with 400 men, chosen out of the strongest people of the nome of Mah. I arrived happily. My warriors will certify all that I have said.

I was a kind master, of a gentle character, a governor who loved his city. I passed many a year as governor in the nome of Mah. All the works for the palace of the king were placed in my hands. Also the chiefs of . . . of the temples of the nome of Mah gave me thousands of cows with their calves. I received thanks for this on the part of the royal palace, because of the yearly supply of milch cows. I gave up all the produce to the palace, and I kept back nothing for myself out of all the workshops. No child of the poor did I afflict, no widow did I oppress, no landowner did I displace, no herdsman did I drive away, from no 'five-hand master' (small farmer) did I take away his men for (my own) works. No one was unhappy in my time ; no one was hungry in my days, not even in the years of famine, for I had tilled all the fields of the nome of Mah, up to its southern and northern frontiers. Thus I prolonged the life of its inhabitants, and preserved the food which it produced. No hungry man was in it. I distributed equally to the widow as to the married woman. I did not prefer the great to the humble in all that I gave away ; and when the inundations of the Nile were great, then the owner of the seed was master of his property ; nothing of the produce of the field was withdrawn from him by my hand.

The concluding words of this inscription have given rise to the idea that they contain an allusion to the sojourn of Joseph in Egypt and to the seven years of famine

But two reasons especially tell against this supposition. First, there is the difference in the time, which cannot be made to agree with the days of Joseph, and next the indisputable fact that in other inscriptions years of famine are mentioned which thoroughly correspond with the Biblical account. What the inscription of Ameni does really teach, from an historical point of view, is that a military expedition up the river was directed against the black people of the land of Cush, who dwelt from the Egyptian frontier at Syene southwards up to the sources of the Nile. The names of the races of the land of Cush conquered by the first Usertsen, or perhaps rather the names of the countries inhabited by them, are preserved on a memorial stone which was found in the neighbourhood of Wady-Halfah, a little above the Second Cataract. This was, without doubt, the last point to which Usertsen extended his campaign against the above-mentioned inhabitants of the negro-land.

Besides pushing southwards into the gold district of Nubia Usertsen also directed his attention to the caverns and mountains of the Sinaitic peninsula, the mines of which had already been worked under the Memphite kings. New settlers were sent to the lonely valleys of this district to work up 'mafkat'[1] (turquoises) and copper. Some inscriptions of the Egyptian workmen whom the king sent there still bear witness to their presence in the valley of Magharah.

The road from Egypt to Sinai led from the low lands of the Delta by the narrow road along which Sineh was obliged to pass in his flight from Egypt to Edom. Here, also, on the eastern side of the low lands,

---

[1] The green mineral termed 'mafkat' appears to have been of two kinds : the first was marked 'genuine,' and was in all probability the eme- rald ; the second, called 'imitation,' is thought to have been either malachite or smalt.

traces of Usertsen show themselves. In Tanis, 'the great city' of the lower country, surrounded on all sides by races of Semitic origin, the kings of the Twelfth Dynasty raised buildings and sculptures, that so their pillars might do honour even to the gods. The portrait of Usertsen himself has been found on several fragments of this perished world of temples.

Among the numerous nobles who once served the king was Mentu-hotep, whose tombstone, covered with inscriptions, is now at Gîzeh. According to the custom of the time he is introduced as sometimes speaking himself, sometimes as spoken of :—

A man learned in the law, a legislator, one who apportioned the offices, who regulated the works of the nome, who restored order in the whole land, who carried out all the behests of the king, and who as judge gave decisions and restored to the owner his property. As chief architect of the king he promoted the worship of the gods, and instructed the inhabitants of the country according to the best of his knowledge, even as God has commanded to be done. He protected the unfortunate, and freed him who was in want of freedom.

Again :—

Peace was in the utterances of his mouth, and the written learning of the wise Tehuti was on his tongue. Very skilful in artistic work with his own hand, he carried out his designs as they ought to be done. Being the first in the country, the king's heart was full of him : also the great and distinguished men of the court gave him their love.—He knew what was hidden in the heart of every man, and appreciated a man according to his true value.— He compelled the enemies of the king to submit to the court of justice of the thirty. He punished the foreigners, reduced the Herusha to quiet, and made peace with the Negroes.—He was governor in the cities of Ant and the lands of Tesherit. He gave his orders to the land of the South, and imposed the taxes on the North country.

In a word, Mentu-hotep, who was also invested with several priestly dignities, and was Pharaoh's treasurer, appears as the *alter ego* of the king.

When he arrived, the great personages bowed down before him at the outer door of the royal palace.

The panegyric, which occupies twenty-two lines, finishes with a remark relating to certain buildings. Those referred to are the temple of Osiris and the construction of a well at Abydos, both entrusted to him by the special order of the king. He says on this subject :—

I it was who carried out the work for the building of the temple . . . and made the well according to the order of the Majesty of the royal lord.

The well is probably the same about which the Greek geographer Strabo relates that in the Memnonium of Abydos there was a well, to the bottom of which was an arched passage constructed of single stones, admirable for size and workmanship. An overseer of the temple of Abydos, by name Ameni-seneb, who lived in the days of the sovereign just mentioned, says :—

This prince gave me the order, saying thus: 'Thou art commissioned to cleanse the temple of Abydos. Workmen shall be given thee for this purpose, and temple-servants of the district of the holy workplace.' And I cleansed it from bottom to top, and its walls which surrounded the interior. And the writings were filled up with colours, emblems, and other ornamental work ; and thus *what King Usertsen I. had built* was restored.

Long after, under Seti I., the temple, which had suffered much, was re-built.

Among the number of other servants of the king must be named Meri, the son of Menkhtu. From an inscription in the Louvre, dated the ninth year of the reign of Usertsen I., it seems clear that Meri received orders to construct for his royal master 'the sublime place of long duration,' or, in other words, the sepulchre on a grand scale, with columns, gates, and a great front court, all executed in well-hewn limestone from the quarries of Tûrah.

The inscription runs as follows :—

I was an intelligent servant, distinguished in my works, pleasant as a palm-tree. My lord entrusted to me a commission grandly conceived, to erect for him the lofty long-enduring place of his sepulchre. It was to tower up conspicuous on all sides from every place, corresponding to the excellency of the divine one (i.e. the king). Pillars were cut to support the roof ; a canal was dug, to let in the water of the river. The gates and all the *Tekhenen* (?) of the roof were of bright shining stone of Tûrah.

We must here leave King Usertsen I., and turn to his successor, whom the monuments call by the double name of

NUB-KAU-RA   [o ⯈ ⊔ ⊔ ⊔]   AMEN-EM-HAT II.

The second Amen-em-hat trod in the footsteps of his predecessors, extending the southern boundaries of the empire, and defending the inhabitants of the South against the incursions of the negroes, by building well-fortified places on that frontier. The possession of this region was of importance to the Egyptian sovereigns, because its mountains, besides many precious stones, yielded gold.

A stone memorial discovered in Abydos has preserved to us some remarkable notices about the journeys which were undertaken to explore the conquered countries, and to urge on the obtaining of the precious metal. Among these is one in which Se-Hathor, a most distinguished official of the court, relates that he ' opened a mine by the labour of the young men, and forced the old to wash the gold. I brought back the produce. I came as far as the further land (Nubia). The negro inhabitants came to me subdued by the fear with

which the lord of the land inspired them. I entered
the land of He-ha, visited its watering-places, and
opened the harbours.'

The land of He-ha lay above the Second Cataract.
Se-Hathor seems to have been the first who explored
the region. Afterwards, under the third Usertsen, an
immense stone covered with inscriptions was erected at
Semneh, which served as a mark of the Egyptian
boundary for the inhabitants of the country of He-ha.
The same Se-Hathor, who boasts 'that he had been
sent by his Majesty many times on missions of all
kinds,' relates in another passage a service of a peculiar
description :—

I was sent over to the building of (King) Amenu, whose
pyramid is called Kherp—may he live for ever !—to superintend
the execution of the work upon fifteen statues of hard durable stone.
(The restoration of) what had been thrown down in one day was
completed in two months. Never was the like done since the rule
of the sun-god Ra.

King Amenu, whose name and existence we learn
only from this short inscription, appears nowhere else
on the monuments. He must, at all events, have belonged to the rulers immediately before the Twelfth
Dynasty, and in all probability he was one of the ancestors of the Pharaohs of that dynasty.

At Tanis, in Lower Egypt, there are also traces of
the royal power of Amen-em-hat; for there was found,
under the *débris* and ruins of the destroyed temples,
the life-size statue, in black granite, of the wife of this
king, who was called by the name of Nefert, which
means either 'the good' or 'the beautiful.' The royal
lady, with her hair dressed in the ancient fashion, is
seated on a throne, on which her names and titles are
engraved in full. In a memorial tablet at Gîzeh

this queen's name appears again in the following
pedigree :—

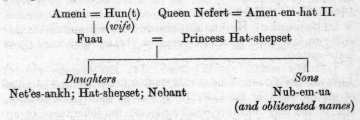

After a reign of twenty-nine years the king associated his son with himself.   He bore the names of

KHA-KHEPER-RA ⎡ o ✦ 🪲 ⎤ USERTSEN II.

His history is found only in an isolated passage
here and there upon the monuments.   We may conclude with certainty from the scattered notices, that
under the rule of this second Usertsen the empire was
at the height of its prosperity.   Some lines which are
engraved on a rock at the town of Aswân, and which
date from the common reign of the two kings, father
and son, bear witness that the sovereign's attention
was constantly directed to the southern borderland
(Nubia).

　　The first kings of the Twelfth Dynasty appear in
their order in the inscription which adorns the lower
border of the hall of sacrifice over Khnum-hotep's rock-
tomb at Beni-Hasan.   In order to give a just representation of the public life of those days, a literal
translation of the inscription is appended :—

　　(1) The hereditary lord and blood relation of the king who loves
his god, the governor (2) of the district of the East, Khnum-hotep, son
of Nehara, who has overcome (death), (3) the son of the daughter of
an hereditary lord, the lady Beket, who has overcome death, (4) the
same has executed this for his memorial.

　　His first virtue consisted in this : that he was a benefactor (5) to
his town, so that he won for his name lasting remembrance for long

long ages, (6) and that he through his good works immortalised it in his tomb (7) of the world below (i.e. the necropolis). He made the name of his people to flourish, (8) who always did good works according to their position. (9) For good men were the inhabitants of his (10) houses. He who distinguished himself among his (11) serfs ; to him stood open every position (12) and all honour (?), as is the custom.

(13) His mouth speaks thus : (14) His Majesty (15–16) AMEN-EM-HAT II. raised me to be (17) hereditary lord and governor of the countries of the East, (18) and to be chief priest of Horus and of the holy lioness Sekhet, and (19) the inheritance of my mother's father in the city of (20) Menat-khufu. He (the king) fixed (21) for me the frontier-pillar in the South ; he set (22) up that of the North corresponding to the quarter of the heavens. (23) He assigned to me the great river in his territory, (24) as had been done to the father (25) of my mother, from the first.

(26) Now an order went forth from the mouth (27) of the king's Majesty (28) SEHOTEP-AB-RA (29) AMEN-EM-HAT (I.). (30) He made him (the father of my mother) hereditary lord and governor (31) of the countries of the East, in the city of Menat-khufu. (32) He fixed the frontier pillar towards the South, and set up (33) the Northern corresponding to the quarter of the heavens. He caused him to distribute the great river (34) over his province. His eastern boundary (35) began from the nome of Tehuti-Horus, and extended to the east country.

(36) It was at that time when his Majesty returned, after he had suppressed (37) the insurrection, manifesting himself like the god Tmu (the evening sun) (38) himself. He restored that which he found (39) destroyed. Taking possession of one town (40) after another, he informed himself of a town and (41) its boundaries up to the next town, placing (42) their boundary pillars (43) according to the quarter of the heavens, taking cognisance of their waters (i.e. the canals, &c., for irrigation) (44) according to the written registers, estimating them by (45) their produce, according to the greatness (46) of his love of justice.

And after this he made him (47) hereditary lord and chief officer of the nome of Mah. (48) He fixed for him the frontier pillars. (49) His southern boundary was towards (50) the nome of Hermopolis, his northern towards the nome of Cynopolis. He distributed for him (51) the great river over his province. (52) His water, his fields, and his groves, and (53) his uncultivated land extended to the districts of the West.

(54) He made his eldest son, Nekht, (55) who has overcome (death), the highly honoured, a governor (or prince : *haq*): (56) his

inheritance was in the city of Menat-khufu, (57) as a sign of great acknowledgment (58) of the royal favour.

A decree (59) went forth from the mouth of his Majesty (60) the king (61) KHEPER-KA-RA USERTSEN (I.)—(62) may his first-born be noble !   (63) My mother entered upon (64) the dignity of an hereditary lady, and (65) as a daughter of a governor (or prince: *haq*) (66) of the nome of Mah, in the city of Ha-Sehotep-ab-Ra (Amenem-hat I.), (67) to become the wife (68) of the hereditary lord and governor (or prince: *haq*) of the cities.   (69) The heart of the king, the lord of Upper Egypt, rejoiced, and enchanted (?) was (70) the lord of Lower Egypt, when he united her to the prefect of the city, (71) Nehara the highly honoured.

(72) King AMEN-EM-HAT (II.) established me (73) as the son of a ruler (*ha*) in the inheritance (74) of the government (or principality, the dignity of a *haq*) of my mother's father, according to the greatness (75) of his love of justice.   The god Tmu (76) he is himself.   And Amen-em-hat II. (77) made me (78) a ruler (*ha*) in his nineteenth year, in (79) the city of Menat-khufu.   There I arranged (80) and established the abundance of necessaries (81) of all sorts of things, and made to flourish (82) the name of my father, and did good for the dwellings (83) of the revered ones (the dead) and their houses, and I caused sculptures (or images, i.e. as memorials of them) to be carried (84) to the holy dwelling, and arranged for them (85) their offerings of pure gifts, (86) and I instituted the officiating priest, and was liberal to him (87) in gifts of land and (88) peasants.   I ordered (89) the funeral offerings for all the feasts (90) of the world below, at the feast of the new year, at the beginning of the year, at the feast of the little year, (91) at the feast of the great year, at the feast of the end of the year, (92) at the great feast of joy (the *panegyry*), at the feast of the great heat (the summer solstice), (93) at the feast of the little heat (the winter solstice), at the feast of the five intercalary days (94) of the year, at the festival of Shetat, at the festival of the sand, (95) at the twelve monthly feasts, at the twelve half-monthly feasts, (96) at the feasts on the plain and on mountain.   And should (97) the priest or any other person (98) cease to do all this, may he perish, and may (99) his son not sit in his seat !

A close examination of the words gives occasion for some very interesting observations, which enable us to form just ideas as to the nature and method of the public administration of the country.   The nobility was in possession of certain rights, either by birth or by alliance with a daughter who was an heiress. These rights became valid through a royal decision; it was requisite that the king should issue his commands with regard to them. Above all, the position of the Haq, or prince-governors of the nomes, was of great importance, and requires to be accurately understood in order to comprehend many events in the course of Egyptian history, which overthrew whole dynasties and interrupted the ordinary course of affairs and of the government of the country.

Another observation which forces itself upon the reader is the mode of fixing the boundaries of nomes at the time of the inundations, which acted as a check upon the inevitable disputes as to boundaries between neighbouring princes of nomes and governors of towns; it facilitated the drawing up of the written registers, which, ' in the name of Pharaoh,' contained an exact survey of the territories thus bounded, according to which the taxes were levied. Another observation of a more scientific nature concerns the festivals of the ancient Egyptian calendar. The learned men on the banks of the Nile occupied themselves in watching the courses of the stars and studying their complete cycles with the regularly recurring seasons. They had already firmly settled ideas of the various lengths thus assigned to the year.

In order the better to judge of this very interesting question, we give the translation of another calendrical inscription engraved in beautifully cut hieroglyphs over the entrance door of the mortuary chapel of Khnum-hotep at Beni-Hasan.

We have arranged in a tabular form the series of the so-called feasts of the dead mentioned therein, in order that they may be easily understood. The days of the months, added here and there, are taken from other

monuments, which thus more clearly determine the
time of the several feasts.

A. *Feasts of the Year :*—
   1. Feast of the New year (vague or civil year).
   2. Feast of the Great Year (Gothic or fixed year).
   3. Feast of the Little Year (lunar year).

B. *Feasts of the Months :*—
   1. Feast of the great heat (at the beginning of Mekhir).
   2. Feast of the little heat (at the beginning of Phame-
      noth).

C. *Feasts of the Days :*—
   1. The feasts on the 1st, 2nd, 4th, 5th, 8th, 15th, 17th,
      29th, and 30th day of each month.
   2. The five intercalary days of the year.

D. *Special feasts :*—
   1. Feast of the rising of Sothis (Sirius).
   2. Feast called Uak (the 17th to 18th of Tehuti).
   3. Feast of Tehuti (the 19th of Tehuti).
   4. Feast of navigation.
   5. Feast of the commencement of the inundation.
   6. Feast of the bark Tebet.
   7. The great feast of joy (Panegyry).
   8. The good feast on the mountain.
   9. The feast called Asha.

A comparison of these feasts with the catalogue of
holidays given in the long inscription just quoted
enables us to perceive that the latter, although on the
whole less complete, nevertheless contains three feasts
more, namely, the feast of the beginning of the year,
another feast at the end of the year, and the feast of
Shetat.

The paintings with which the tomb of Khnum-
hotep is covered are invaluable for teaching of the arts
and trades, as well as of the domestic and public life
of the Egyptians of this time. Among the countless
representations with which the hall of sacrifice is
adorned, attention is due to the scene of the entry of a
strange race into Egypt. A family, belonging to the

people of the Aamu, had left their native land, in the
days of Usertsen II., and migrated to the banks of the
Nile. The immigrants numbered thirty-seven persons,
consisting of men, women, and children, who are represented as coming to Khnum-hotep begging for a gracious
reception and offering him a present of the eye paint
called *mest'em*.

Standing in the place of honour, the prince appears
at the head of the foreign race, the ' haq ' of the land
of Abesha, who approaches respectfully and offers to
Khnum-hotep a magnificent wild goat. Behind their
chieftain appear bearded men, armed with spears, bows,
and clubs, women in the bright-coloured dress of the
Aamu, with their children, and asses laden with the
goods and chattels of the immigrants, whilst a member
of the little band calls forth with the *plectrum* harmonious tones from his antique lyre. The paint in
question was an article much in request, as the
Egyptians used it to blacken their eyebrows, &c.

Khnum-hotep's descendants appear to have received
many honours, his eldest son, Nekht, being made governor
of the Cynopolitan nome, situated to the north of the
nome of Mah, and also of the Southern land, which
apparently embraced several nomes.

KHA-KAU-RA ⟮ ○ ✱ ⊔ ⊔ ⊔ ⟯ USERTSEN III. was a name
of high renown in the most glorious period of the
Egyptian empire, for this king distinguished himself
above all his predecessors by his power and wisdom.
The Egyptians themselves believed that they honoured
the great king Usertsen III. best by regarding him as a
god, to whom they built temples and offered sacrifices.

His martial deeds began by expeditions directed
against the inhabitants of the negro-land of Cush, in hopes
of placing an insurmountable barrier in the way of their

inroads. All his predecessors had extended their campaigns comparatively far southward, but the complete subjection of the people was far from being accomplished. An inscription in the island of Elephantiné names the precise time when 'the king took the field to smite the miserable land of Cush.' In the region beyond the Second Cataract Usertsen built sanctuaries and fortresses commanding both banks of the river; the remains of which still exist in the strongholds of Semneh and Kûmmeh. Two pillars covered with long inscriptions served formerly as boundary-marks between the Egyptian empire and the negro-land called He-ha. They were set up, on the territory of the above-named fortresses, by the order of Usertsen III.

The inscription on the older stone begins thus:—

Here is the southern frontier, which was fixed in the eighth year under the reign of King Usertsen III., the dispenser of life for ever, in order that it may not be permitted to any negro to cross it, with the exception of the ships which are laden with cattle, goats, and asses belonging to the negroes, and except the negroes who come to trade by barter in the land of Aken. To these, on the contrary, every favour shall be allowed. But otherwise it shall not be permitted to any vessel of the negroes to touch at the land of He-ha on its voyage evermore!

The second inscription runs thus:—

Every one of my sons who maintains this boundary, which I have fixed, shall be called my son, who was born of me. My son is like the protector of his father (i.e. Horus), like the preserver of the boundary of his father (i.e. Osiris). But if he abandons it, so that he does not fight upon it, he is not my son, he is not then born of me.

I have caused my own image to be set up on this boundary which I have fixed, not that ye may (only) worship it (the image) upon it (the boundary), but that ye may fight upon it.

Without doubt Aken is the old name of the country of Nubia, called by Pliny Acina; for he mentions it directly after the well-known hill-fortress of Primi

(Qasr Ibrîm), and gives it a distance of 310 Roman miles from Syene. The invasion and final conquest of the region was not effected without cruelty. Memorial tablets of victory of the sixteenth year of Usertsen III. give an idea of the way in which the war was carried on against the negroes. The king marched between the Nile and the Red Sea, made the women captives, seized the people who had gone to their wells, drove away the cattle, and set fire to the standing crops.

More than fifteen centuries after these events had taken place, Tehuti-mes III. erected on the spot, where his great predecessor had raised the fortress of Semneh, a temple which was consecrated to the memory of Usertsen III., as well as to the newly-recognised divinity of the country, Totun, a special form of the ram-headed Khnem of Elephantiné.

Altars were also dedicated to them, and sacrifices instituted, which were to be offered yearly on the great feasts by the priests of the temple of Semneh.

There are a great number of memorials and inscriptions dedicated to the memory of King Usertsen III., which originate from officials who lived in his reign and were employed on the public works.

Ra-n-maat [cartouche] Amen-em-hat III. are the names of the succeeding king, whose remembrance has been preserved for more than twenty centuries by the fame of his works of peace, for he is the founder of the wonderful Lake Mœris and of the Labyrinth.

The prosperity of Egypt depended on the fertility of the soil produced by the regularly recurring inundations of the Nile. If these rise above the height which is necessary to convey sufficient water to the land, they destroy the hopes of the cultivator. If, on the contrary, the rising water stops below the required

height, sterility and famine are the natural consequence of the drought.   In all ages, therefore, the
care of the inhabitants was directed to the state of the
Nile at the time of the inundation, in order that by
dams, sluices, canals, and reservoirs they might divert
the mass of water the moment it reached its due
height.   As in our day the rising of the Nile is tele-
graphed from Khartûm to Cairo, in order that preparations may be made for the approaching inundation, so
in the days of Amen-em-hat and his successors the
southernmost point of the empire (Semneh) served as
the point of observation.   From this place the news
was sent to the lower-lying district.   On the rocks
of Semneh and Kûmmeh the highest point of the inundation was always noted for comparison, and the
mark was accompanied by a corresponding inscription.
Thus we read at one place on the rock :—

Height of the Nile in the year 14, under the reign of his
Majesty King Amen-em-hat III., the ever-living.

From observations made by Lepsius on the spot,
we gather that in the times of the Twelfth Dynasty,
that is, forty-three centuries before our days, the
highest rise was nearly twenty-seven feet above the
greatest height of the inundation in these days ; and
that the average height of the Nile, when Amen-em-hat
III. was king, surpasses that of our times by about
twelve feet.

The attention which this king so evidently devoted
to the rise of the Nile is proved most clearly by his
construction of the enormous basin excavated in the
Fayûm for the reception and storage of the superfluous
water of the inundation.   This lake, which teems with
fish, was protected on all sides by artificial dams, and
communicated with the river by a canal ; while a system
of locks allowed either the influx or the complete shut-

ting off of the waters. The Greeks gave it the name
of Mœris, because, as they report, this was the name of
its constructor, an old king Mœris, which was a corruption of the ancient Egyptian word *meri*, or *meri-uer*,
meaning a ' basin.' Moreover, the Arab-Coptic appellation of the district in which the artificial lake was
situated—now called Fayûm—is easily explained by
the older name P-ium, ' the lake country.'

At last the investigations of Linant-Bey have succeeded in discovering unmistakable traces of Lake
Mœris. He has proved that it lay in the south-eastern
part of the Fayûm, where the depression of the ground
and the ruins of ancient dikes mark its site.

The same king built, in the neighbourhood of the
Lake Mœris, that Labyrinth so famed in antiquity as a
splendid building, as well as the pyramid, his own
monument, not far from this edifice. This wonderful
structure, which is utterly ignored on the Egyptian
monuments, consisted, according to Herodotus (ii. 148),
of three thousand halls and chambers, half of which
were above the ground and half below, with twelve
covered courts, the entrances to which were opposite to
each other. According to Strabo (xvi. 786, 810), the
Labyrinth, like the great kingdom in little, was composed of as many palaces as there were nomes, namely,
twenty-seven.

Fragments of stone, covered with traces of the
names of Amen-em-hat III. and his successor, Queen
Sebek-neferu, near the pyramid of El-Lahûn, are all that
remains of this once celebrated building. The Fayûm,
which, in the times of the above-mentioned king, acquired, through the presence of Lake Mœris, a peculiar importance in a political point of view, has nevertheless not had the fortune to be specially mentioned
in the inscriptions on the monuments. The reason is

simply this, that the province and its inhabitants were
detested as being hostile to Osiris, for in the Fayûm
Sebek and his sacred animal, the crocodile, were held
in high honour, and the pious followers of Osiris recognised in both the mysterious emblem of the god
Set; thus is explained the reason why in the lists of the
nomes the, district of Fayûm was entirely struck out.

There is in the Gîzeh Palace a papyrus representing a plan of the Lake Mœris, together with the
canal connecting it with the Nile. Round the basin
the draughtsman has tried to reproduce a number of
towns and sanctuaries, accompanied by hieroglyphic
explanations, which are of inestimable value for understanding the plan, and for a knowledge of the various
places and their worship. By the help of these notes
we are at once enabled to ascertain the different names
of the lake with all needful clearness. Sometimes it is
called She, i.e. ' basin ' or ' lake ; ' sometimes She-uer,
' the great lake basin,' or, Mi-uer, ' the great lake.'
From the most usual designation, She, the country was
called Ta-She, ' the land of the lake,' of which the
Arab-Coptic word Fayûm is an exact translation.
Another appellation of the lake, including the canal,
is Hunt, ' the water-dam ' or ' weir.' The place at
which the canal leading from the Nile entered the
valley formed by the great mountain basin of the Fayûm
was called Ape-tash, ' the defile of the land of the lake.'
Here was the ' opening (sluice) of the canal,' the La-
Hunt, from which word certainly comes the modern
name of the place, El-Lahûn, which lies near the spot
in question. The same word is beyond all doubt
hidden in the name of the Labyrinth, the Lape-ro-hunt,
that is, ' the temple at the sluice of the canal.' On the
western side of the canal lay the capital of the old
' country of the lake,' in which the kings of the Twelfth

Dynasty founded temples and raised obelisks to the
crocodile-headed Sebek and kindred deities. Situated
in the neighbourhood of the present capital of the
Fayûm, called Medinet-el-Fayûm, the city bore in ancient times the name of Shat (canal?), or Pa-Sebek, i.e.

'the dwelling of Sebek,' ; whence the
Greeks called it by the corresponding name of Crocodilopolis, or 'the city of the crocodile.'

The large stones, which the architects required for
the construction of the Labyrinth, and the other sanctuaries in the district of the Fayûm, came from a great
distance. Rohan and the valley of Hammamât yielded
the most beautiful and durable blocks, as appears with
all certainty from the inscriptions in the quarries there.
Thus, in the second year of the reign of Amen-em-hat
III., an official of the same name was sent there for the
purpose of quarrying stones for the construction of
monuments in Crocodilopolis, among which is mentioned
a statue of the Pharaoh, five cubits in height.

In the dreary mines and quarries of the peninsula
of Sinai traces of the activity of this king's subjects are
visible, and inscriptions dating from the 2nd to the
44th year of his reign bear witness to the long stay
of workmen who were employed in working the mines
of mafkat (emerald) and khemet (copper). The kings
of the Twelfth Dynasty were specially zealous in their
worship of Osiris and the maintenance of his temple at
Abydos. To this new and most convincing testimony
is borne by a monument discovered in 1875 in that
necropolis. It is the tombstone of a certain Sehotep-
ab-Ra, who was buried there, and who during his life,
under the reigns of the kings Usertsen III. and
Amen-em-hat III., was charged with the care of the
temple and the worship of the god 'Osiris in the west'

and of the jackal-headed guardian of the dead, Anpu
He also, it appears, received orders to arrange the
service at the places of the secret mysteries in Abydos,
to regulate the feasts of the gods, to superintend the
priests, and as a skilful artist to build for Osiris the
sacred barque (*bari*) and to cover it with ornamental
painting.

AMEN-EM-HAT IV. and the Queen SEBEK-NEFERU-RA
conclude the Twelfth Dynasty.

The monuments throw no special light on the history
of these two sovereigns.   This princess, his sister, was
an heiress-daughter, like Nit-aqert at the close of the
Sixth and Nefert-ari at the close of the Seventeenth
Dynasty.   After their deaths the inheritance of the
empire passed by marriage to a new family.

Before closing this very remarkable period of
Egyptian history it is necessary to take a backward
glance at the great events which so signally distinguished
the Middle Empire.

Under the rulers of the Twelfth Dynasty the frontiers
of Egypt were extended southwards to the Second
Cataract.   Above this the two fortresses of Semneh and
Kûmmeh formed the frontier, towards the negro-lands
of He-ha and Aken. The peninsula of Sinai was likewise
subject to the Egyptian sceptre.   Officials of the king,
supported by an adequate military force, maintained
the Pharaonic sovereignty in the mountains of the
Mafkat country.

The Egyptians also kept up a very active commerce
with the tribes of Libya on the West, and on the East
with the inhabitants of Palestine and the adjoining
countries.   The immigration into Egypt of people
from these neighbouring territories is proved by paint-

ings and inscriptions in the sepulchral chambers of this
time. The light-coloured Libyans descended into the
Nile valley to entertain the play-loving populace with
dances and warlike games; the dark-coloured inhabitants
of Cush served the great lords of the country as slaves;
and the Asiatics presented themselves at the eastern
frontier to beg for admission in order to carry on trade
on the banks of the Nile. The Egyptian empire appeared
to the world of that time as the centre of civilisation,
and of progress in the provinces of intellectual, artistic,
and commercial activity.

Intellectual life flourished at this period : schools
were established all over the country, and a high tone
of thought prevailed in the temple colleges. The
natural resources of the country were husbanded and
agriculture was thus improved. The land was all
divided up into districts separated by inscribed stones :
and registers were kept at the royal palace giving
statistics as to the area, boundaries, and water supply
of each nome. Temples, pyramids, and rock-hewn tombs
of this period abound; and from the latter we learn
much of contemporary domestic life in the Nile valley.
In the times which comprise the history of the Twelfth
Dynasty the centre of gravity of the Egyptian state was
situated in Middle Egypt. Two cities of that territory—
Crocodilopolis, the city of Sebek, on the shores of Lake
Mœris, and Heracleopolis 'the Great' (Akhnas)—rose
rapidly to an importance the extent of which we can
only judge of by the monuments. Art in its different
branches reached a perfection which we cannot better
describe than in the words of M. de Rougé. 'That long
succession of generations, the date of which we are no
longer able precisely to determine, witnessed various
and changing phases in the development of Egyptian
art. Our museums contain examples sufficient in

number and style to enable us to follow the principal variations. The origin of this art is unknown to us; it begins with the monuments of the Fourth Dynasty, the first to which we can assign a certain rank, in a state decidedly advanced in many respects. Architecture already shows an inconceivable perfection with regard to the working and building up of blocks of great dimensions; the passages in the interior of the Great Pyramid remain a model of exact "joiner's work" which has never been surpassed. We are obliged to guess at the exterior arrangement and ornamentation of the temples of this first period, and to restore them from the basreliefs of the tombs or the decoration of the sarcophagi. This style of architecture was simple, but in the highest degree noble; the straight line and the play of outline in the outer surfaces formed the whole force of the decoration. One specimen of ornament alone gives a certain life to these arrangements; namely, two lotus leaves placed opposite to each other.

'The human form, alike in the statues and the sculptures in relief, is distinguished by somewhat broad and thick-set proportions; it seems that in the course of centuries the race became thinner and more slender under the influence of the soil and climate. In the most ancient monuments, the imitation of nature was aimed at with greater simplicity, and with a truer regard to proportion: in the execution of the single parts, the muscles especially stand out more powerfully, and are strongly indicated. The human figures preserve this character till near the end of the Twelfth Dynasty; from this time forward they become more slender and taller.

'Architecture had already made a great step forward towards ornamentation. We find at this time the first columns which have been preserved in Egypt to

our days; thick, fluted, and with a simple abacus as
capital, they resemble most strikingly the earliest
Doric columns.

'The sculptures in relief, without a trace of per-
spective in the composition, are in the Old Empire often
of incredible delicacy. They were always painted over
with colours. There are examples among them in
which the freedom of the attitudes and the truth of the
movements promise to Egyptian art a great future,
very different from that which was reserved for it in
later centuries. The statues of limestone were often
entirely painted; the figures of˙ granite were only
touched with colour on many parts of the body, such
as the eyes, the hair, or also the drapery. The masterpiece of Egyptian art of the Old Empire is a colossal
leg of black granite, in the Berlin Museum, which
belonged to a [seated] statue of King Usertsen I., and
was discovered in the ruins of the city of Tanis, in
Lower Egypt. This fragment furnishes the most
sufficient proof that the first Egyptian school was on a
more promising track than that of the Second Empire.

'The engraving of the inscriptions on these first
Egyptian monuments leaves nothing to be desired.
It is generally executed in relief up to the Fifth
Dynasty. The characters cut in intaglio of the Twelfth
have never been surpassed. The stone obelisks of
Heliopolis and the Fayûm authorise us to suppose
temples of a grandeur and magnificence in harmony
with these fine remains of the Twelfth Dynasty. We
know, in fact, that one of the wonders of the world,
the Labyrinth of the Fayûm, was constructed by one
of these kings.'

In the histories of art a depreciatory sentence is
constantly pronounced on the artist of those old days,
who, when viewed most favourably, is placed on the

same level with the mechanic. It cannot be too
strongly insisted upon that such a judgment is founded
on complete ignorance of the essence of Egyptian art,
or on a superficial view of it, which is unworthy of
judges of art. The art of Egypt is Art in the truest
sense of the word, as the statues of Ra-hotep and Nefert,
the Sheikh-el-Belled, and Khaf-Ra emphatically prove;
but this art was *Egyptian*, and bound by a chain of
traditions and theories from which the artists—though
they may have rebelled against it—never freed themselves. Attention has sometimes been called to the
fact that history has not transmitted the name of any
Egyptian master. This is not true, for the artist was
the most honoured man in the kingdom. Martisen,
who belonged to a family of artists and lived in the
Eleventh Dynasty, calls himself ' a master among those
who understand art and a sculptor,' who ' was a wise
artist in his art.' He relates his acquirements in the
making of works of sculpture in every attitude, according to the prescribed custom and measure ; and he
mentions, as his particular invention, an etching in
colours (if I have rightly understood the expression),
' which is neither consumed by fire nor washed off by
water ; ' and he adds the further explanation, that ' no
man has arisen who has been able to do this, with the
sole exception of himself and the eldest son of his race '
(Usertsen), ' whom God's will has created ; ' but that
' he has arisen able to do this, and the efforts of his
hand have been admired in masterly works in all sorts
of precious stones, from gold and silver to ivory and
ebony.'

Martisen and his son Usertsen, beyond all doubt,
opened the age when art was at its zenith under the
kings of the Twelfth Dynasty, whose love for it is fully
attested by the monuments of their time.

CHAPTER V.

THE Tablet of Abydos passes at once from the Twelfth to the Eighteenth Dynasty, and places Amen-hotep, the first king, immediately after the princess Sebek-neferu-Ra. The traditions of the ancients concerning this obscure period lead but to confusion and error, and the Turin Papyrus, the only document which could serve as a guide, has such frightful gaps where the list of the Thirteenth Dynasty kings should be, that it is practically useless. Fate has thus done its worst to place the greatest difficulties in the way of the solution of this question. All that scientific research has succeeded in attaining is the well-grounded belief that long after the conclusion of the Twelfth Dynasty native kings ruled with unlimited power in the land until princes of foreign origin, already settled in the eastern lowlands, gradually drove back the old race, so as to establish the right of conquest over the true heirs of the throne.

Before narrating the history of these foreign conquerors it will be advisable to give here the succession of the Egyptian dynasties, the number of their kings, and the time of their total duration, according to the Manethonian sources, and on the authority of the best and most recent researches.

XIIIth dynasty,	of Thebes,	60 kings	453 years.
XIVth	„	of Xoïs,	76 „	484 „
XVth	„	Hyksos,	6 „	260 „
XVIth	„	Hyksos,	? „	251 „
XVIIth	„	of Thebes,	? „	? „

[1] For Table of Kings see p. 87.

Without stopping to examine and establish the numbers—extant and missing—it may be confidently assumed that science can scarcely be mistaken in arranging the preceding lists and periods in the following order:—

Legitimate Kings; of Theban Race.

XIIIth dynasty, 60 kings, 453 years.
XVIIth   „   ? „   ? „

Opposition Kings; of Xoïs.

XIVth dynasty of Xoïs, 76 kings, 484 years.

Foreign Conquerors.

XVth dynasty of Hyksos, 6 kings, 260 years.
XVIth   „   „   ? „   251 „

A glance at the mutilated fragments of the Turin Papyrus will establish the fact that the last five columns were devoted to the kings who belonged to the foregoing dynasties of Manetho. Their total number in the Papyrus may be estimated at about 150 names, and the numbers which have been preserved here and there, as giving the length of reigns of single kings, seldom exceed three or four years. From this it appears probable that the history of Egypt at this period consisted chiefly of revolts and assassinations, in consequence of which the lengths of the kings' reigns were not governed by the ordinary conditions of the duration of human existence. These were the times concerning which Ramses III. remarks in the 'Harris Papyrus,' in the British Museum, that 'the land of Kamit was in the hands of the princes of the cities of the foreigners, of whom the one neighbour killed the other neighbour.'

The kings who immediately followed the Pharaohs of the Twelfth Dynasty were in full possession of Upper and Lower Egypt. For a long time the opinion was prevalent, that the Thirteenth Dynasty marked the exact epoch of the invasion of the foreigners, so that these latter must have already gained a firm footing in Lower Egypt on the east. In opposition to this, however, is the fact that several kings of the Thirteenth Dynasty enjoyed in the Delta perfect leisure and quiet to erect monuments, the remains of which have been preserved to the present time, and whose size and style do not point to their having been hastily constructed. Among these may be mentioned the wonderful stones and statues at Tanis (Zoan), in the neighbourhood of the territory on which, towards the end of the Thirteenth Dynasty, the Hyksos kings pitched their camps. In the extracts from Manetho the names of the kings of the Thirteenth Dynasty are passed over in silence. The Turin Papyrus is, therefore, the only source from which the void can be supplied, and fortunately the extant fragments are just sufficient to establish some of the most important names.

True to ancient custom, nearly all the royal persons are distinguished by means of the official name only. The family names are, however, supplied in the case of no small number of the princes of this dynasty by the contemporary monuments, which bear double cartouches and show that the greater number of these kings bore the name of Sebek-hotep, .

Notwithstanding the Theban origin of this race the seven Sebek-hoteps (servants of Sebek) held in special veneration the crocodile-headed god, to whom the kings of the preceding dynasty had raised monuments in the Fayûm and in the neighbourhood of Lake Mœris. An intimate connection must therefore be supposed between the Twelfth and Thirteenth Dynasties, and it is probable that Sebek-neferu-Ra, the heiress of the Twelfth Dynasty, transmitted the special wor-

ship of that deity to her son—for as such we must re-
cognise Ra-khu-taui, $\boxed{\circ \; \curlywedge \; \rule{1em}{0.4em}}$, 'the protecting son
of the double land,' whom the Turin Papyrus places at
the head of the Thirteenth Dynasty.   The name Sebek-
hotep constantly appears until the commencement of
the Eighteenth Dynasty.

The following Table of the kings who succeeded
Sebek-hotep I. is drawn up from the extant fragment
of the Turin Papyrus.   These Pharaohs belong to the
Thirteenth Dynasty, which, according to Manetho, was
composed of sixty names.   It is possible that he made
a selection from about 140 kings, who, at any rate, are
certified on the authority of the Papyrus.

The Thirteenth Dynasty, according to the Turin Papyrus.

1. Ra-khu-taui (Sebek-hotep I.).
2. Sekhem-ka-Ra.
3. Ra-Amen-em-hat I.
4. Sehotep-ab-Ra I.
5. Aufni.
6. Sankh-ab-Ra.
7. Smen-ka-Ra.
8. Sehotep-ab-Ra II.
9. . . . . . ka-Ra.
10. (one or two names which have been destroyed.)
11. Net'em-ab-Ra.
12. Ra-Sebek-hotep II.
13. Ran-[sen]-eb.
14. Autu-ab-Ra I.
15. Setef . . . . Ra.
16. Ra-Sekhem-khu-taui (Sebek-hotep III.).
17. Ra-user. . . . . .
18. Smenkh-ka-Ra Mermesha.
19. . . . . . ka-Ra.
20. . . . . . user-ser.
21. Ra-Sekhem(suttaui) Sebek-hotep IV.
22. Kha-seshesh-Ra Nefer-hotep, son of a certain Ha-ankhf.
23. Ra-se-Hathor.
24. Kha-nefer-Ra Sebek-hotep V.

25. (Kha-ka-Ra ?).
26. Kha-ankh-Ra (Sebek-hotep VI.).
27. Kha-hotep-Ra (Sebek-hotep VII.) . 4 y. 8 m. 29 d.
28. Uah-ab-Ra Aaah . . . . 10 y. 8 m. 18 d.
29. Mer-nefer-Ra Ai . . . . 13 y. 8 m. 18 d.
30. Mer-hotep-Ra . . . . . 2 y. 2 m. 9 d.
31. Sankh-nefer-Ra Utu . . . . 3 y 2. m. ? d.
32. Mer-sekhem-Ra Anran . . . 3 y. 1 m. ? d.
33. Tat-kher-Ra . . . . . u-Ra . . 5 y. ? m. 8 d.
34. Anemem . . . . . ro.
35–43. (9 or 10 names destroyed.)
44. Mer-kheper-Ra.
45. Mer-ka(Ra).
46–50. (destroyed.)
51. . . . . . mes.
52. Ra . . . . . maat Aba.
53. . . . . . Ra-Uben I.
54–57. (destroyed.)
58. Nahasi-(Ra) . . . . . 0 y. ? m. 3 d.
59. Kha-kheru-Ra . . . . . ? y. ? m. 3 d.
60. Nebef-autu-Ra . . . . . 2 y. 5 m. 15 d.
61. Seheb-Ra . . . . . . 3 y. ? m. ? d.
62. Mer-tefa-Ra . . . . . 3 y. ? m. ? d.
63. Tat-ka-Ra . . . . . 1 y. ? m. ? d.
64. Neb-tefa-Ra . . . . . 1 y. ? m. ? d.
65. Ra-Uben II. . . . . . 0 y. ? m. ? d.
66, 67. (two names destroyed.)
68. . . . . . tefa-Ra.
69. . . . . . Ra-Uben (III.).
70. Autu-ab-Ra II.
71. Her-ab-Ra.
72. Neb-sen-Ra.
73–76. (names destroyed.)
77. Sekheper-en-Ra.
78. Tat-kheru-Ra.
79. Sankh-(ka)-Ra.
80. Nefertum . . . . . Ra.
81. Sekem . . . . . Ra.
82. Ka . . . . . Ra.
83. Nefer-ab-Ra.
84. Ra . . . . .
85. Ra-kha.
86. Nut-ka-Ra.
87. Smen , . , , ,

Unfortunately almost all the names are in such a mutilated condition that they do not admit of transcription, and still less of any proper comparison with those on other monuments.   One peculiarity may be mentioned, which is that they sometimes begin with Sekhem, and sometimes with User.   To the names which manifestly belong to a destroyed part of the foregoing table must be added another, SEBEK-HOTEP VI., KHA-ANKH-RA, ⟨ o ✱ ⚲ ⟩, and who is inserted in his proper place by the help of the Tablet from the Hall of Ancestors.

The most important monuments of the Thirteenth Dynasty in sequence of time are, first, the accompanying Genealogical Table, compiled from a number of inscriptions, and containing family records which will give an idea of the descent of certain kings from persons not of Pharaonic birth, and of their entrance into the royal circle by marriage with the princesses. The Queen Nub-khas, in the fourth generation in the Table on the next page, furnishes a good example.

Among the records of individual sovereigns of this period are two inscriptions at the two extreme limits of the Nubian country—in the one case on the rocky islands at the First Cataract in the neighbourhood of Philæ; in the other at Semneh and Kûmmeh, above the Second Cataract.   At the latter place, SEBEK-HOTEP III., following the example of his predecessors, engraved a record of the highest point to which the inundation of the Nile reached in his day.   It reads simply :—

Height of the Nile in the third year | under the reign of King Sebek-hotep III. | the ever-living.

Ran-seneb, a distinguished courtier and commandant of the fortress of Sekhem-kha-kau-Ra, founded by

GENEALOGICAL TABLE OF A DISTINGUISHED FAMILY, RELATED TO SOME MEMBERS OF THE THIRTEENTH DYNASTY.

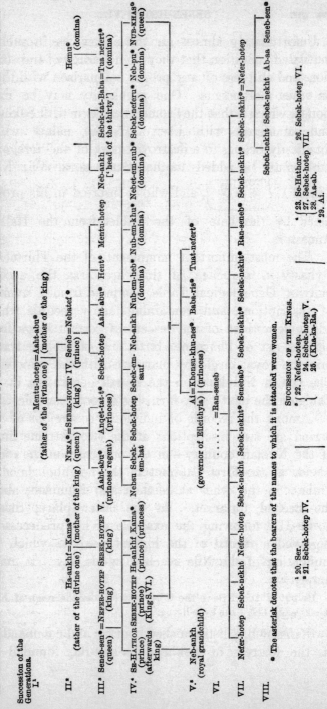

Usertsen III., governed in those days the southern portion of the newly conquered country, and thus possessed the right to place his name by the side of his royal master's.

The eighteenth king, SMENKH-KA-RA, with the family name of Mer-mesha (leader of armies), claims special attention, because Mariette discovered at Tanis two wonderfully perfect colossal statues of this king, on both of which his names were clearly legible. They were originally erected in the great temple of Ptah at Tanis. The Hyksos prince Apepi, as well as Ramses II., about 400 years later, immortalised themselves by cutting their own names on this monument.

SEBEK-HOTEP IV., the son of Mentu-hotep,[1] must have been in possession of the lowlands of the Nile valley, for his statues in granite are found at Tanis, which proves that neither this city nor the country adjacent to it on the east was occupied by enemies. The same fact is made clear from the discovery at Bubastis of a statue of SEBEK-HOTEP V., whose memory was also preserved beyond the boundary of Semneh and Kûmmeh by another statue on the island of Argo. The power of the kings of the Thirteenth Dynasty was therefore neither reduced in the south nor in the north of the empire.

Records of the times of the same kings have been unmistakably preserved in the heart of Egypt itself. Thebes, Abydos, and the rocky valley of Hammamât are rich in proofs of the undiminished power of the empire, and the museums of Europe contain many monuments of this dynasty, notably the memorial-stone at Leyden, which Sebek-hotep VI. dedicated to Hor-Amsu-nekht, the god of Panopolis. The group of kings beginning with Sebek-hotep III. and finishing

[1] See Genealogical Table, p. 90.

with Sebek-hotep VII. are connected with the most
distinguished families of the country, and form a separate series of Thirteenth Dynasty sovereigns. As proof
of this may be cited the much-discussed but little
understood representation in the Hall of Ancestors.
As is well known, this relates to a selection of kings
who received a place in a chamber devoted to them
by Tehuti-mes III. The right side of the hall shows
the portraits and names of the Theban princes of the
Thirteenth Dynasty, but only in a selection the meaning of which is at once evident.

*Table of the Chamber at Karnak compared with the
Papyrus of Turin.*

1. . . . ka.
2. Sut-en-Ra.
3. Sankh-ab-Ra .   .   . No. 6. Sankh-ab-Ra.
4. Ra-Sekhem-khu-taui   .   „ 16. Sebek-hotep III.
5. Ra-Sekhem-tat-taui .   .   „ 21. Sebek-hotep IV.
6. Kha-seshesh-Ra   .   .   „ 22. Nefer-hotep.
7. Kha-nefer-Ra .   .   .   „ 24. Sebek-hotep V.
8. Kha-ka-Ra   .   .   .   „ 25. (destroyed.)
9. Kha-ankh-Ra   (Sebek-   „ 26. (destroyed, Sebek-hotep VI.)
   hotep VI.)
10. Kha-hotep-Ra .   .   .   „ 27. Sebek-hotep VII.

For it appears to contain only the names of those
kings whose importance is confirmed by contemporary
inscriptions, while the rest of the names mentioned
in the Turin Papyrus are passed over in silence.

Among these princes is KA-MERI-RA, (o ⊔ ⌐ II),

known to us from the wall of the rock-hewn tomb
of T'efab the son of Kheti, in the mountain behind
Assiût. T'efab, according to his own account, was
the governor of the south country. Although the
hieroglyphs are much destroyed it seems certain that
the owner of the tomb had been commissioned by his
royal master to execute certain works for the enlarge-

ment and restoration of the temple of Anpu, the tutelary deity of the city just named. There are also indications which lead us to infer warlike events in Upper Egypt. The tombs at Assiût (Lycopolis) all point to a common origin—the times of the Twelfth and Thirteenth Dynasties. The most valuable historically is that of T'efaa-hep, commonly called the 'Stabl Antar,' who was high priest of Anpu and filled a number of other offices at the royal court.

The interior wall, facing the entrance of the sepulchral hall, contains a long and fairly well preserved inscription. After the deceased has set forth his various titles and offices, and has extolled the way in which he fulfilled his duties towards gods and men, he calls upon the future priestly guardian of his grave to care for him (the deceased), as he in his lifetime had cared for the deities in Siût—Lycopolis. He also takes this occasion for fixing the kind and number of the sacrifices, mentioning the feast-days on which they are to be offered, and gives evidence, for the first time in an Egyptian inscription, that the inhabitants of the Nile valley were accustomed to dedicate the first-fruits of their harvest to the deity. The feasts named in this inscription took place at the end and at the beginning of the year. The inscriptions which adorn the walls of the rock-chambers of these tombs, as well as those of El-Kab (the ancient Eileithyiapolis), all point to their belonging to the Thirteenth Dynasty. Quite apart from identity in style and from the presence of the cartouche of

Sebek-hotep IV., (cartouche), which was found in

one of the tombs of this place, whose former tenant

bore the name of Sebek-nekht, (hieroglyph), the proper

names which belonged to the dead certainly point in the most unmistakable way to this period.

[In 1887 Mr. Ll. Griffith made a careful survey of the tombs at Assiût, and discovered in a large scene in the great hall, now unfortunately much obliterated, the owner of the grotto in adoration before the cartouche of Usertsen I., thus fixing the date at the Twelfth Dynasty. Moreover, from the inscriptions in the tombs of Kheti I., T'efaba, and Kheti II., it is clear that the princes of Heracleopolis[1] were extremely hostile to the Theban lords, and that the magnates of Siût sided with the former. For further information see 'Babylonian and Oriental Record,' vol. iii. pp. 121, 164, 174, 244. A splendid translation of the inscription in the tomb of T'efaba was made by Professor Erman in the 'Zeitschrift' for 1882, and another by Maspero was published in 'Trans. of Soc. of Bib. Arch.,' vol. ii. p. 12 et seq.]

SEMITISM IN EGYPT.

In opposition to the kings of the Thirteenth Dynasty of Theban origin there were, according to Manetho, seventy-six Pharaohs who fixed their royal abode in Xoïs. These internal schisms, promoted by the ambitious plans of sovereigns both of Upper and Lower Egypt, give us the key to the long silence of the contemporary monuments, and to the full understanding of the success of an invasion which brought a foreign race into Egypt, who would never have dared to oppose the armed might of the united empire.

The sovereigns of this period had something else to do than to think of constructing monuments to the divinities of the country, and the high functionaries saw their masters change too often to have confidence in the stability of the state, and to occupy themselves with hewing out in the mountain rock those funereal chapels,

[1] The Tenth Dynasty was Heracleopolitan.

witnesses to the glory and riches which permitted men to devote themselves at their leisure to these peaceful labours.—*French Edition.*

Before reviewing the time of this foreign dominion —during which the old native kings sank into the position of simple governors of nomes—it is necessary to examine carefully the countries which were to be the scenes of future events, and to direct particular attention to the tribes by which those regions were peopled. In the lowlands the inhabitants between the branches of the Nile were, for the most part, of pure Egyptian race. Those of the western or Libyan adjacent lands belonged to the light-coloured Tehen, and further westward to the races of the Libu and Tamahu. The wanderings of these restless migratory groups of tribes extended northwards as far as Lake Tritonis, at the bottom of the lesser Syrtis, and eastwards to the Canopic branch of the Nile, called in the cuneiform inscriptions Karbanit. In this direction, near a branch of the Nile which bore its name, lay T'a-an (Zoan), called also Zar, and in the plural Zaru (city of *Zars* or forts). The name Tanis, which was given to it by the Greeks, is to be referred back to the Egyptian word T'a-an. It is everywhere designated in the inscriptions as an essentially *foreign* town, the inhabitants of which are mentioned ' as the peoples in the eastern border-land.'

This eastern border-land is frequently spoken of as Ta-Mazor, that is, ' the fortified land,' in which may easily be recognised the original form of the Hebrew name for Egypt, Mazor or Mizraim.

On the granite memorial stone of Ramses II., discovered in Tanis, there appears a ' commandant of the fortress Zar,' who, besides this office, held also the dignity of ' commander of the foreign peoples,' a reference doubtless to the inhabitants of foreign origin in that part of the Egyptian Delta.

The papyri frequently allude to this city by name, adding also another appellation, Pa-Ramessu, 'the city of Ramses,' identified by M. Naville with Phacûs. Lying east of the Tanite nome was the eighth, or Sethroïte, whose capital bore the name of Pa-Tmu, 'city of Tmu,' the Pithom of the Bible. This town formed the central point of a district, the name of which is of foreign origin, for Thuku, or Succoth, is a Semitic word signifying a 'tent' or 'camp.' This was pasture-land and the property of Pharaoh, and on it the wandering Bedâwi of the eastern deserts pitched their tents in order to procure necessary food for their cattle. Here the Israelites first encamped at the time of the Exodus, moving on the second day to a place called Etham, which was either in the country of Succoth or in its close neighbourhood. It is the place called, in various hieratic papyri, Khetam, the meaning of which, 'a shut-up place, fortress,' completely agrees with the Hebrew Etham.

In this same Sethroïte nome lay, without doubt, the town of Ha-Uar, [hieroglyphs], 'the house of the leg,' the Avaris of Manetho, a town which in Hyksos days became so celebrated. It was on the east of the Pelusiac arm of the Nile and appears to have been connected with the river by a canal. The gradual silting up of the ancient bed of the river has made the situation of the towns on its banks so difficult to determine that there is scarcely a hope of finding again the site of the lost city of Avaris. But that Ha-Uar must in any case be sought in the neighbourhood of a lake is evident from the inscription in the tomb of Aahmes, the navigator, at El-Kab, who relates how he was present when the Egyptian fleet was fighting the foreign enemies on the waters of Pa Zetku, near the town of

Ha-Uar. This name also, in spite of an Egyptian article—*pa*—placed before it, has a Semitic appearance, and is doubtless connected with corresponding roots of that language.

Another place, situated in the Sethroïte nome, bears the purely Semitic name Maktol or Magdol, which is the Hebrew Migdol, 'town,' 'fortress,' out of which the Greeks formed Magdolon. That the ancient Egyptians were well acquainted with the meaning of this word is proved most conclusively by the masculine article prefixed to it, and the sign of a wall (𝍩) placed after it when written in Egyptian characters. This Migdol—of which mention is made in the description of the Exodus from Egypt and in other occasional passages in the Bible—denotes one of the most northern points of inhabited Egypt, and is identical with the heaps of *débris* at Tell-es-Samût, on the eastern side of Lake Menzaleh. The list of defences which were intended to protect the country on the east is not yet closed. Still further to the north-east, on the western border of Lake Sirbonis, was another important frontier stronghold, called Anbu, that is, 'the wall,' 'the rampart.' The Hebrews knew it as Shur, and the Greeks as τὸ Γέρρον, which means 'the fences' or 'enclosures.' Whoever travelled eastwards out of Egypt was obliged to pass 'the walls' before being allowed to enter the 'way of the Philistines' on his further journey. An Egyptian garrison blocked the passage through the fortress, which only opened and closed on the traveller after a previous communication from the royal authorities. Everywhere in this part of the Delta were towns and fortresses, the names of which point to original Semitic colonists.

There was Annu or On (Heliopolis), the original meaning of which seems to have been 'stone' or 'stone

pillars;' then in the neighbourhood of Mendes was a
fortified place called 'the fortress of Azaba' (idol), the
last part of which name does not belong to the Egyptian
but to the Semitic tongue.

Another town on the east side of the Delta bore the
name of Pa-Bailos (Belbeis), the Semitic origin of which
is made clear by its evident relationship with the
Hebrew, Balas (the large sycomore).[1] In its neighbourhood was the lake Shakana, the meaning of which is
only explained by the root *shakan*, 'to settle down, to
dwell, to be neighbour to.' More inland was the town
of Kahani, a name which at once recalls the Hebrew
kohen, 'priests.'

Then, again, the memorial stones, coffins, and
papyri found in the cemeteries all testify to Semites
who were settled in the Nile valley, and who had
obtained the rights of citizenship, as also do they show
the inclination of the people to give their children half
Semitic and half Egyptian names. There were natives
who bore names like the following : Adiroma, Abaro-
karo, Baal-Mohar, Namurod, and many others, without
any appearance of the slightest objection being found
to their foreign character. The commercial interest,
which extended from the Nile to the Euphrates, contributed to introduce into Egypt foreign expressions for
products of the soil, for animals, and for works of industry and art that were not native, as may be shown
by *sus* for 'horse,' *agalota* for 'chariot,' *camal* for
'camel,' and *abir* for a particular kind of bull. The
endeavour to pay court to whatever was Semitic de-
generated in the time of the Nineteenth and Twentieth
Dynasties into a really absurd mania, so much so that the
most educated and best instructed class of the Egyptians,
the priests and scribes, appear to have taken a delight

[1] The sycomore is a kind of fig.

in replacing good old Egyptian words with Semitic terms, like the following: *rosh*, head; *sar*, king; *beit*, house; *bab*, door; *bir*, spring; *birkata*, lake; *ketem*, gold; *shalom*, to greet; *rom*, to be high; *barak*, to bless, and many others. This Semitic immigration spread so widely that it led finally to the formation of a mixed people who have held their ground firmly in the same parts till the present day.

The Egyptians even proceeded to enrich their theology with divinities of new and foreign origin. At the head of all stood the half Egyptian and half Semitic divinity of Set or Sutekh, with the surname of Nub, 'gold,' who was universally considered as the representative and king of the foreign deities in the land of Mazor. In his essence a primitive Egyptian creation, Set gradually became the contemporary representative of all foreign countries, the god of the foreigners. In mentioning the names of Baal and Astarte, so frequently met with in the inscriptions, it is scarcely necessary to point out that both have their origin in Phœnician theology. As at Sidon, so likewise in Memphis, the warlike Astarte had her own temple. Although less frequently mentioned than the preceding Semitic divinities, places were assigned in the Egyptian pantheon to the fierce Reshpu, 'the lord of long times, the king of eternity, the 'lord of strength in the midst of the host of gods;' and to the goddess Kadesh; and to Bes also, the patron of song and music, of pleasure and all social delights. The Phœnician Onka, and the Syrian Anaïtis are also recognised therein under the names of Anka and Anta.

Semitic influence in Egypt may also be seen in the peculiar chronology adopted on the celebrated memorial stone of Tanis erected in the reign of Ramses II.

Contrary to the custom of giving dates according to the day, month, and year of the reigning king, this stone offers the only example as yet discovered of a foreign system of chronology, mention being there made of the year 400 of King Nub, a Hyksos prince.

The monuments also attest the presence of these foreign families on Egyptian soil, as the following letter will show :—

(I will now pass) to something else which will give satisfaction to the heart of my lord ; (namely, to report to him) that we have permitted the races of the Shasu of the land of Aduma (Edom) to pass through the fortress Khetam (Etham) of King Meneptah-Hotephimaat—life, health, and strength be to him !—which is situated in the land of Succoth, near the lakes of the city of Pithom of King Meneptah-Hotephimaat, which is situated in the land of Succoth, to nourish themselves and to feed their cattle on the property of Pharaoh, who is a gracious sun for all nations.

This extremely important document of the time of Meneptah II., the son of Ramses II., refers to those Shasu tribes, or Bedâwi, who inhabited the great desert between Egypt and the land of Canaan, and extended their wanderings as far sometimes as the Euphrates. According to the monuments they belonged to the great race of the Aamu, of which they were in fact the representatives.

As in the neighbourhood of the city of Ramses and the town of Pithom the Semitic population formed the main stock of the inhabitants from remote antiquity ; so the neighbourhood of Pa-Bailos was peopled by strangers who had pitched their tents in sight of the cultivated land where they found pasture for their cattle. They were Bedâwi, who had in all probability migrated from the dreary region near the town of Suez.

Meneptah II., the son and successor of Ramses II., gives at Karnak a graphic account of the dangerous

character of these unbidden guests. When he succeeded to the throne the danger of a sudden invasion
on this side appeared all the more threatening inasmuch that on the west the Libyans suddenly passed
the frontiers of Kamit, and extended their predatory
incursions into the heart of the populous and cultivated western nomes of the Delta. According to the
inscription of victory, Meneptah II. saw himself obliged
to take needful precautions for the safety of the land.
The capitals On and Memphis were, therefore, provided
with the necessary fortifications, as ' the foreigners had
pitched their *ahil* or tents before the town of Pa-Bailos,'
&c.

Before noticing the remaining neighbours of the
Egyptians of the Delta who carried on war or traffic
with the inhabitants of Kamit we must refer to the
administration of affairs and the regulation of trade
with the foreign people (*Pit*). One portion of these
consisted of the industrial population settled in the
towns and villages; another portion served as soldiers
or sailors; others again were employed in the public
works, the mines, and quarries. Over each division of
the foreigners was placed the *Her-pit*, or steward. His
next superior was the commandant of the district, or
Adon (the Semitic form for this title), while, as the
chief authority, the ' *Ab of Pharaoh*,' or royal Vizier,
issued orders in the name of the sovereign. The control over the foreign people lay in the hands of special
bailiffs (*Mazai*), whose duty it was to preserve public
order in the principal cities, and who were under the
orders of an *Ur*, or commander, to whom also the
erection of public buildings was not unfrequently committed.

Among the people of Palestine who held the most
active intercourse with the Egyptians of earlier times

were the Khar, in whom may be recognised the
Phœnicians. They carried on a brisk trade with
Egypt, and seem to have been a people held in esteem
and consideration, slaves from Khar [1] being a much-
desired merchandise, procured by distinguished Egyptians at a high price, either for their own houses or
for the service of the Egyptian deities.

The strong city of Zoan seems to have been a
primeval habitation of the Phœnicians, since Zoan-Tanis
formed an important centre for intercourse with the
rest of Egypt. The name of Zor, as well as Zoan,
is a reminder of the celebrated Zor-Tyre. The importance of these people culminates in the fact that a
Phœnician named Arisu towards the end of the Nineteenth Dynasty was able to make himself master of
the throne of Egypt. The Khar spoke their own
language—Phœnician—which is the only foreign
tongue mentioned on the monuments with a distinct
reference to its importance. Whoever lived in Egypt
spoke Egyptian; whoever stayed in the south had to
speak the language of the Nahasu, or dark-coloured
people; while those who went northwards to the
Asiatic region had to be acquainted with the language
of the Phœnicians, in order to converse at all intel-
ligibly with the inhabitants of the country.

The latest descendants of this old race may be
seen to-day in the same region where their forefathers
settled thousands of years ago, and the traveller still
meets on the shores of Lake Menzaleh, near the old
district of Ramses and Pithom, a race of fishermen
and sailors, whose manners and customs, whose
historical traditions, and whose ideas on religious
matters characterise them as foreigners. They are
the same whom the Arab writers mention sometimes

---

[1] The name Khar denoted both the people and their country.

as Biamites, sometimes as Bashmurites, names whose origin is unknown. The Bashmurite dialect of the Coptic language is a kind of peasants' *patois*, containing a large number of ancient Semitic words.

What, however, forms the most characteristic mark of their foreign descent is their non-Egyptian countenance, as if borrowed from the pictures of the Hyksos, with the broad cheek-bones and defiantly pouting lips.

CHAPTER VI.

THE HYKSOS.

THE name of 'Hyksos,' which comes down from the days of Manetho, deserves very special attention; and the monuments confirm what we know of the lost book of that historian. Quoting him, Josephus says :—

'There was a king called TIMÆUS (Timaius ; *var. lect.* Timaos, Timios). In his reign, I know not for what reason, God was unfavourable, and a people of inglorious origin from the regions of the East suddenly attacked the land, of which they took possession easily and without a struggle. They overthrew those who ruled in it, burnt down the cities, and laid waste the sanctuaries of the gods. They ill-treated all the inhabitants, for they put some to the sword, and carried others into captivity with their wives and children.

'Then they made one of themselves king, whose name was SALATIS (*var. lect.* Saltis, Silitis ; in the list, Saïtes). He fixed his residence at Memphis, collected the taxes from the upper and lower country, and placed garrisons in the most suitable places. But he especially fortified the Eastern frontiers, for he foresaw that the Assyrians, who were then the most powerful people, would endeavour to make an attack on his kingdom.

'When he had found in the Sethroïte nome a city very conveniently situated to the east of the Bubastite arm of the Nile— on account of an old religious legend, it was called Avaris—he extended it, fortified it with very strong walls, and placed in it a garrison of 240,000 heavily-armed troops. Thither he betook himself in summer, partly to watch over the distribution of provisions and the counting out of the pay to his army, and partly to inspire the foreigners with fear by making his army perform military exercises.

He died after he had reigned . . . 19 yrs.

His successor, by name BNON (or Banon,
    Beon), reigned . . . 44 yrs.

After him another, APACHNAN (or Apach-
nas) . . . . 36 yrs. 7 months
After him APHOBIS (or Aphophis, Apophis,
Aphosis) . . . . . . 61 yrs.
And ANNAS (or Janias, Jannas, Anan) . 50 yrs. 1 month
Last of all ASSETH (or Aseth, Ases, Assis) 49 yrs. 2 months

'These six were the first kings. They carried on uninterrupted war, with a view to destroy the land of Egypt, even to extermination.

'The whole people bore the name of HYKSOS, that is, "king shepherds" (commonly called "shepherd kings"). For *hyk* in the holy language signifies a "king," and *sos* in the dialect of the people a "shepherd" or "shepherds." Thus combined they form *Hyksos*. Some think they were Arabs.'

Now the word *sos* corresponds exactly to the old Egyptian *shasu*, hence they have been identified with the *Haq Shasu* (Bedâwi). Their old national name in the course of time obtained, in the popular language, the secondary sense of 'shepherds,' that is, a nomad people, who followed the occupation of rearing cattle, which has at all times formed the sole wealth of the inhabitants of the desert.

If the objection should be raised that the monuments (*as yet* discovered) pass over the name of Hyksos in silence, it must be remembered that by far the greater number of contemporary monuments have completely disappeared from off the Egyptian soil. Meanwhile it may be well to compare the information existing in the few extant inscriptions with the accounts of Greek tradition. Manetho's name *Hyksos* is undoubtedly in complete agreement with the supposed Egyptian word *Haq Shasu*, king of the Arabs, wanderers or shepherds, and it is not therefore necessary to maintain that they invented for themselves and assumed it on account of their office. Rather is it probable that the Egyptians, after the final expulsion of their Semitic tyrants, formed the nickname Haq-Shasu as a contemptuous expression for those princes, who for several centuries had regarded themselves as the legitimate kings of Egypt.

A tradition of the Middle Ages furnishes a contribution to the proofs of the Arab origin of the foreigners, for a legend tells of a certain Sheddad ('a mighty man'), the son of Ad, who conquered Egypt, and extended his victorious campaign as far as the Straits of Gibraltar. He and his descendants, the founders of the Amalekite dynasty, are said to have maintained themselves for more than two hundred years in Lower Egypt, where they made the town of Avaris their royal residence.

According to Julius Africanus (who epitomised the work of Manetho), the Hyksos kings are said to have been Phœnicians, who took possession of Memphis and made Avaris, in the Sethroïte nome, their chief fortress. This tradition is not without a certain appearance of truth. The ancient seats of the Shasu-Arabs and of the Phœnicians extend westwards to the city of Zor-Tanis; consequently the two races must have come into the closest contact. That amidst such a mixture of nations the cultivated Khar would obtain the foremost place scarcely needs a proof, but whether they or the Shasu were the originators of the movement against the native kings is a question which scientific research has hitherto been unable to answer. The inscriptions on the monuments designate that foreign people who once ruled in Egypt by the name of *Men* or *Menti*. On the walls of the temple of Edfû it is stated that 'the inhabitants of the land of *Asher* are called Menti.' By the help of the demotic translation of the trilingual [1] inscription on the great stone of Tanis, known as the 'Decree of Canopus' (Ptolemaic times), we can establish

[1] The inscription is in Hieroglyphs, Demotic, and Greek. The stone is at Gizeh.

that such was the common name of Syria in the popular language of the Egyptians, while the older name of the same country, cited in the hieroglyphic part of the stone, was *Rutennu*, with the addition of 'the East.' In the different languages, therefore, and in the different periods of history, the following names are synonymous : Syria, Rutennu of the East, Asher, and Menti.

It is possible that in the late Egyptian *Asher* the Semitic Asshur, or Assyria, may survive. The old national name Rutennu plays an important part in the history of the Eighteenth Dynasty. It would appear from the catalogue of the towns of western Asia conquered by Tehuti-mes III., whose inhabitants submitted to the Egyptian rule after the battle of Megiddo, that this name must have coincided almost exactly with the country included later within the boundaries of the twelve tribes of Israel. This information is a great help to the right understanding of the movement of the tribes in the eastern Delta. It is certain that, immediately after the expulsion of the Menti, the Egyptian kings of the Eighteenth Dynasty directed their campaigns against the countries inhabited by the Rutennu ; there must have lain, therefore, at the bottom of these constantly repeated invasions the fixed motive of revenge and retribution for losses and injuries received. No doubt the irruption of the foreigners into Egypt proceeded from the Syrians, who, in their progress through the arid desert, found in the Shasu-Arabs welcome allies who knew the country ; and in the Semitic inhabitants settled in the eastern marches of Egypt they welcomed brothers of the same race, with whose help they succeeded in giving a severe blow to the Egyptian kingdom, and in robbing it for centuries of all independent energy.

Historical research concerning the history of the Hyksos may be summed up as follows :—

I. A certain number of non-Egyptian kings of foreign origin, belonging to the nation of the Menti, ruled for a long time in the eastern portion of the Delta.

II. These chose as their capitals the cities of Zoan and Avaris, and provided them with strong fortifications.

III. They adopted not only the manners and customs of the Egyptians, but also their official language and writing, and the order of their court was arranged on Egyptian models.

IV. They were patrons of art, and Egyptian artists erected, after the ancient models, monuments in honour of these usurpers, in whose statues they were obliged to reproduce the Hyksos physiognomy, the peculiar arrangement of the beard and head-dress, as well as other variations of their costume.

V. They honoured Sutekh, the son of Nut, as the supreme god of their newly acquired country, with the surname Nub, 'the golden.' He was the origin of all that is evil and perverse in the visible and invisible world, the opponent of good and the enemy of light. In the cities of Zoan and Avaris, splendid temples were constructed in honour of this god, and other monuments raised, especially Sphinxes, carved out of stone from Syene.

VI. In all probability one of them was the founder of a new era, which most likely began with the first year of his reign. Down to the time of the second Ramses, four hundred years had elapsed of this reckoning, which was acknowledged even by the Egyptians.

VII. The Egyptians were indebted to their contact with them for much useful knowledge. In particular their artistic views were expanded and new forms and shapes, notably that of the winged sphinx, were introduced, the Semitic origin of which is obvious at a glance.

The number of monuments which contain memorials of the time of the Hyksos is very limited; and names of these kings, on their own memorial-stones, as well as those of earlier Egyptian kings of the times before them, have in many cases been carefully chiselled out, so that, in deciphering the faint traces which remain, we have to contend with great difficulties. This gap in the sequence of the monuments may be explained by the fact that when the native rulers were re-established they carefully obliterated every record of the hated usurpers.

The names of the Hyksos kings which cover the more than life-size statue at Tell Mukhdam, the border of the colossal sphinx in the Louvre, the Baghdad lion, and the sacrificial stone at Gîzeh, are erased with such care as to be almost illegible, and science owes merely to an accident the preservation and deciphering with certainty of the names of two of them. These are Aaqenen-Ra, with the family name of Apepi, and Nub, with the official name of Set, 'the powerful.'

The name of the first, which would have been pronounced in the Memphite dialect Aphephi, differs little from that of the king Aphobis, who, according to Manetho, was the fourth of the above-named Hyksos kings.

The names which designate the other are strikingly similar in sound to those which the god 'Set-Nub the powerful' usually bears on the Egyptian monuments.

In the Sallier Papyrus in the British Museum we find the name of the foreign king Apepi in connection with an Egyptian under-king, Seqenen-Ra.

PAGE I. (1) ' It came to pass that the land of Kamit belonged to the enemies. And nobody was lord in the day when that happened. At that time there was indeed a king Seqenen-Ra, but he was only a Haq of the city of the South, but the enemies sat in the town of the Aamu, and (2) Apepi was king (Ur) in the city of Avaris. And the whole world brought him its productions, also the North country did likewise with all the good things of Tamera. And the king Apepi (3) chose the god Set for his divine lord, and he did not serve any of the gods which were worshipped in the whole land. He built him a temple of glorious work, to last for ages [. . . And the king] (4) Apepi [appointed] feasts [and] days to offer [the sacrifices] at every season to the god Sutekh.'

Seqenen-Ra had, according to all appearance, incurred the special displeasure of the tyrant of Avaris, who designed to hurl him from his throne, and sought for a pretext to carry out his intention.

Before this there had evidently been an interchange of letters between them, in which the latter, among other things, required of the former to give up his own gods, and to worship Sutekh alone. Seqenen-Ra had declared himself prepared for all, but had added a proviso to his letter, in which he expressly declared that he was not able to pledge his assent to serve ' any other of the gods that were worshipped in the whole country, but Amen-Ra, the king of the gods, alone.'

This new message to the Haq of the southern city had been drawn up by a council and approved of by King Apepi. The papyrus relates this in these words :—

Many days later, after these events King Apepi sent to the governor of the city in the South country this message (. . .) which his scribes had drawn up for him, and the messenger of King Apepi betook himself to the governor of the city of the South. And (the messenger) was brought before the governor of the city in the South country. He spake thus when he spoke to the messenger of King Apepi : ' Who hath sent thee hither to the city of the South ? How art thou come, in order to spy out ?'

The messenger of Apepi, thus addressed, first answered the governor in these simple words : 'It is King Apepi who sends to thee,' and thereupon he delivered his message, the purport of which was very disquieting and related to the stopping of a canal.

(6) And the governor of the city in the South country was for a long time troubled, so that he could not (7) answer the messenger of King Apepi.

After the foreign messenger had been hospitably entertained, Seqenen-Ra nerved himself to reply. The messenger then returned to Apepi, and Seqenen-Ra called

his great and chief men, likewise the captains and generals who accompanied him, (2) in order [to communicate] to them all the messages which King Apepi had sent to him. But they were silent all of them (*lit.* all with one mouth) through great grief, and wist not what to answer him good or bad.

Although the narrative is frequently interrupted by holes, owing to the splitting of the papyrus, sometimes in the most important passages, that which remains is quite sufficient to make clear the persons, the scenes, and the subject of the historical drama. Apepi is the chief hero ; his residence is at Avaris ; he worships his own divinity, Sutekh ; the Egyptian form of the Semitic Baal-Zapuna, the Baal-Zephon of Holy Scripture. He builds a splendid temple to his god, and he appoints festivals and offerings to him.

At No, the city of the South, that is, at Thebes, there resides a scion of the oppressed Pharaohs, Seqenen-Ra, who is invested with the title of a Haq, or petty king.

Apepi is the all-powerful lord. Among his courtiers are some who bear the title of *Rekhi-khet*, that is, 'temple-scribes.' These give the king bad counsel, for they induce him to send a messenger to the petty king in No, with severe demands.   Seqenen-Ra receives him with the same question which Joseph, his contemporary, put to his own brethren when they went down to Egypt to buy corn, saying to them, 'Whence come ye? Ye are spies, and ye are come here to see where the land lies open' (*nudata castra*).

After the Haq heard the demands of Apepi from the mouth of his messenger he was deeply moved. The great lords and chief men of his court were summoned to a council, and the leaders also of the army; but no one dared to make a proposal for fear of the unfortunate consequences.

Such is an abstract of this remarkable document, the subject of which was, without doubt, *the history of the uprising of the Egyptians against the yoke of the foreigners*.   In order to find the termination of this story it is necessary to go to the ancient city of El-Kab, where towards the east rise rocky hills with long rows of tombs, in which may be seen a painted world of the olden times, peopled with the forms of deceased ancestors.   Among these are contemporaries of the Hyksos kings, whose descendants were among the heroes of the great war of liberation.   In the sepulchral chamber dedicated by his grandson to the hero Aahmes, the son of Abana-Baba, and his whole house, is a wide-branching genealogical tree of the family, which covers the walls of the narrow and much-damaged room.   Aahmes, and his daughter's son, Pahir,[1] form the chief persons of the pedigree.

In a great text on the wall of the sepulchral chamber the hero relates in simple language the history of his life :—

(1) The deceased captain of the sailors, Aahmes, a son of Abana :—

----

[1] See Table opposite.

GENEALOGY OF THE FAMILY OF THE CAPTAIN OF THE SAILORS, *AAHMES.*

DRAWN UP ON THE SPOT FROM THE INSCRIPTIONS IN THE TOMB AT EL-KAB, IN UPPER EGYPT.

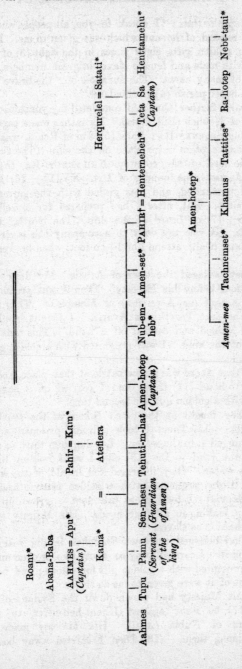

N.B.—The names marked with an asterisk (*) are those of women.

† This is the Pahir who constructed the tomb and set up the inscription.

(2) He speaks thus : 'I speak to you, all people, and I inform you of the reward of honour which was given to me. I was presented with golden gifts eight times in the sight (3) of the whole land, and with male and female slaves in great numbers. I had a possession of many acres. The surname of "the brave" which I gained will never perish (4) in this land.'

He speaks further thus : 'I completed my youthful wandering in the city of Nekheb (Eileithyia). My father was a captain of the deceased king SEQENEN-RA ; Baba (5), son of Roant, was his name. Then I became captain in his place on the ship "The Calf," in the time of the lord of the country, NEB-PEHUTI-RA, the deceased (i.e. King AAHMES, the founder of Dyn. XVIII.) (6) I was still young and unmarried, and was girded with the garment of the band of youths. But, after I had prepared for myself a house, I was taken (7) on board of the ship "The North," because of my strength. It was my duty to accompany the sovereign—life, prosperity, and health attend him !—on foot, when he went forth in his chariot.

'(8) They besieged the town of Avaris. My duty was to be valiant on foot before his Majesty. Then I was promoted (9) to the ship "Ascent (or Accession) in Memphis." They fought by water on the lake Pazetku of Avaris. I fought hand to hand, and (10) I gained and carried off a hand. This was shown to the herald of the king. I was presented with a golden gift for my bravery.

'After that there was a new battle at that place, and I fought again hand to hand (11) there, and I carried off a hand. I was presented with a golden gift the second time.

'And they fought at the place Takem at the south of that city (Avaris). (12) There I took a living prisoner, a grown-up man. I plunged into the water. Leading him thus, so as to keep away from the road to the (13) city, I went, holding him firmly, through the water. They informed the herald of the king about me. Then I was presented with a golden present again. *They* (14) *took Avaris.* I took there prisoners, a grown-up man and three women, making in all four heads. His Majesty gave them into my possession as slaves.

'(15) They besieged the town Sherohan in the year VI. His Majesty took it. I carried away as booty two women and a hand. (16) I was presented with a golden gift for valour ; and besides, the prisoners out of it were given to me as slaves.

'After his Majesty had mown down the Syrians of the land of Asia, (17) he went against Khent-hen-nefer, to smite the mountaineers of Nubia (*Anti*). His Majesty made a great slaughter among them. (18) Then I carried away booty there, two living grown-up men and three hands. I was presented with a golden gift the second time : I also received two female slaves.

'(19) His Majesty went down the river. His heart was joyful because of his brave and victorious deeds. He had taken possession of the South and the North country.

'Then an enemy came from the South country. (20) He approached. His advantage was the number of his people. The gods of the South country were against him (*lit.* his fist). His Majesty found him at the water of Tent-ta-tot. His Majesty carried him away (21) as a living prisoner. All his people brought back booty. I brought away two young people, for I cut them off from the ship of the enemy. There were (22) given me five heads, besides the portion of five hides (*sta*) of arable land in my city. It happened to all the sailors in the same way. Then (23) came that enemy whose name was Teta-an. He had assembled with him a wicked company. His Majesty annihilated him and his men, so that they no longer existed. Then were (24) given to me three people and five hides of arable land in my city.

'I conveyed by water the deceased king SER-KA-RA (AMENHOTEP I.), when he went up to Cush to extend (25) the borders of Egypt. He smote these Nubians (*Anti*) in the midst of his warriors. Being hard pressed, they could not escape. Bewildered, (26) they remained on the ground just as if they had been nothing. Then I stood at the head of our warriors, and I fought as was right. His Majesty admired my valour. I carried off two hands (27) and brought them to his Majesty. We pursued his inhabitants and their herds. I carried off a living prisoner and brought him to his Majesty. I brought his Majesty in two days to Egypt (28) from Khnumt-hert ('the upper spring'). Then I was presented with a golden gift. Then I carried off two female slaves besides those which I had led (29) to his Majesty. And I was raised to the dignity of a "warrior of the king."

'I conveyed the deceased king AA-KHEPER-KA-RA (TEHUTI-MES I.), when he went up by water to Khent-hen-nefer (30) to put down the rebellion among the inhabitants, and to stop the raids from the land side. And I was brave [before] him on the water. Things went badly with the [attack] (31) of the ship on account of its stranding. They raised me to the rank of a captain of the sailors. His Majesty—may life, strength, and health be granted him !—'

(32. Here follows a gap, which, judging by the context, should be filled up to the effect that a new occasion called the king to war against the people of the South.)

'(33) His Majesty was furious against them like a panther, and his Majesty shot his first arrow, which remained sticking in the body of this enemy. He (34) fell down fainting before the asp (on the royal diadem). A [great defeat] took place there in a short time, and their people were carried away as living captives, (35) and his Majesty travelled downwards. All nations were in his power. And this miserable king of the Nubian people (*Anti*) was bound on the fore part of the ship of his Majesty, and he was placed on the ground (36) in the city of Thebes.

'After this his Majesty betook himself to the land of Rutennu, to slake his anger among the inhabitants of the land. His Majesty reached the land of Naharain. (37) His Majesty—life, strength, and wealth to him !—found these enemies. He set the battle in array. His Majesty made a great slaughter among them. (38) Innumerable was the crowd of living prisoners which his Majesty carried away after his victory. And behold, I was at the head of our warriors. His Majesty admired my valour. (39) I carried off a chariot of war and its horses, and those who were upon it, as living prisoners, and brought them to his Majesty. Then was I presented with gold once more.

'(40) Now I have lived many days and have reached a grey old age. My lot will be that of all men upon the earth. [I shall go down to the nether world, and be placed in the] coffin, which I have had made for myself.'

The grievous time of distress and oppression was now past : the reign of tyranny was broken up ; Avaris had fallen, and the fortress of Sherohan had been taken by storm. In the sixth year of the reign of King Aahmes, the founder of the Eighteenth Dynasty of the Pharaohs, Kamit was freed from the long oppression of the foreigners. Seqenen-Ra was the third king of this name ; he also bore in common with his two predecessors the family name of TAA. The inscriptions distinguish them, however, by special surnames, so that TAA II. was known by the addition of Aa, or ' the great,' and TAA III. by the epithet Ken, ' the brave or victorious.' They were buried in Thebes, and therefore must probably have reigned in that city, an opinion which the Abbot Papyrus strengthens.[1]

---

[1] See *Royal Mummies of Deir-el-Bahari*, p. 361.

King Taa III., surnamed 'the brave,' a predecessor of Aahmes, the conqueror of Avaris, built a Nile flotilla for the purpose of one day attacking the town, which lay in the watery lowlands of the Delta.

His successor, named KAMES, ⊔ ⚕ ∫, seems to have reigned but a short time. He was the husband of the much-venerated Queen AAH-HOTEP, ⟋━ ╤▪, whose coffin with the golden ornaments on her body was discovered by some Theban peasants in 1860 in the ancient necropolis of No, buried only a few feet below the surface of the ground.

The cover of the coffin has the shape of a mummy, and is gilt from top to bottom. The uræus decks the brow. The eyelids are gilt. The whites of the eyes are quartz, and the pupils black glass. A rich imitation-necklace covers the breast and shoulders; the uræus and the vulture—the sacred symbols of sovereignty over the Upper and Lower land of Kamit—lie below the necklace. A pair of closed wings seems to protect the rest of the body. Beneath the feet stand the statues of the mourning goddesses Isis and Nephthys. The inscription gives the name of the queen, Aah-hotep, that is, 'delight of the moon.'

When the coffin was opened there were found in it daggers, a golden axe, a chain with three large golden bees, and a breastplate, while a golden chain with a scarabæus attached, a fillet for the brow, armlets, and other objects were on the body. Two little ships in gold and silver, bronze axes, and great anklets lay immediately upon the wood of the coffin. The golden barque and the bronze axes exhibited the cartouche of Kames, but the most valuable of the ornaments bore that of Aahmes with the surname of Nekht, 'the victorious.'

Without doubt Queen Aah-hotep was buried in Thebes, where also was the tomb of her royal husband. She is the real ancestress of the Eighteenth Dynasty, and it was her son Aahmes who afterwards rose up as the avenger of his native country.

It would seem as if the hatred of the Egyptians against the Hyksos kings was by no means so intense as the story handed down by Manetho appears to represent it; for had it been, how is the strange fact to be explained that these same Egyptians could prevail upon themselves to give their children pure Semitic names, borrowed from the language of their hereditary enemies ; or how could they themselves offer their homage to those gods of the strangers?

There was a family actually employed in the temple of Amen whose ancestor called himself Pet-Baal, the ' servant of Baal; ' his wife was Abrakro, and among his descendants we find such names as Atu, Tina, Tetaa, Ama, Tanafi, and Tir.

It is to the Theban kings of the Eighteenth Dynasty that the questionable fame belongs of having destroyed the monuments of the hostile kings, in order to falsify historical truth, and they almost succeeded in extirpating all contemporary memorials of the Hyksos. Aahmes, their conqueror, and after him Amen-hotep III., certainly rebuilt and restored the temples, which 'had fallen into ruins,' though inscriptions in no way attribute this decay to the destructiveness of the Hyksos.

They simply remark that ' the temples had fallen into ruin since the time of their forefathers.' The only allusion to foreigners—and this has nothing to do with any destruction by them—is found on the rock-tablets of the twenty-second year of King Aahmes. It runs thus :—

This stone was drawn by oxen, which were brought here, [and entrusted to the] care [of the] foreign people of the Fenekh.

These Fenekh, , appear clearly to be the most ancient representatives of the Phœnicians on Egyptian soil.

Before concluding this chapter the chronological relations of these historical events, with special reference to the sojourn of the Hyksos, and of the children of Israel, in the land of Egypt, must be mentioned. First there is the memorial stone of the days of Ramses II., found in Tanis, the inscription on which commences, 'In the year 400, on the 4th day of the month Mesori of King Nub.' This tablet, of red granite, engraved with an act of homage, in memory of Seti I., was set up by a high officer of state by the order of Ramses II. After the usual glorification of the king the inscription proceeds as follows :—

His Majesty King Ra-messu II. gave orders to raise a great memorial of granite (of Syene) to the exalted name of his father, animated by the desire to uphold thereby the name of his (royal) father and of his forefathers. May the remembrance of King Ma-men-Ra (Seti Meneptah I.) remain and endure for ever, to-day and every day. In the year 400, the month Mesori, the fourth day of King Apehuti Nub, the friend of the god Horemkhu—may he live for ever and ever ! When there had come (to this city) the hereditary lord and the chief governor of the city, the fan-bearer on the right of the king, the leader of the foreign legions and captain of the foreigners, the constable of the fortress of Khetam (the Etham of Scripture) in Zar, the leader of the Mazai (police), the royal scribe, the chief master of the horse, the high priest of the Ram-god in Mendes, the high priest of the god Sutekh and the praying-priest of the goddess Buto Aptani, the chief of the prophets of all the gods, Seti, the son of the hereditary prince, the commander of the foreign legions, the captain of the foreigners, the constable of Khetam in Zar, the royal scribe and master of the horse, Pa-Ra-messu, the child of the lady and priestess of the sun-god Ra, Thaa,—then spake he thus : ' Hail to thee, Set, son of Nub, thou strong one, in the holy ship,' &c. ; ' grant me a fortunate existence, that I may serve thee, and grant me to remain [in thy house for evermore]'

Since, on the basis of the most recent and best investigations in the province of ancient Egyptian chronology, we reckon the year 1350 B.C. as a mean computation for the reign of the above-named Ramses, the reign of the Hyksos king Nub, and probably its beginning, falls in the year 1750 B.C., that is, 400 years before Ramses II. Although we are completely in the dark as to the place which King Nub occupied in the succession of the kindred princes of his house, yet the number mentioned is important, as an approximate epoch for the stay of the foreign kings in Egypt. According to the statement in the Bible, the Hebrews from the immigration of Jacob into Egypt until the Exodus remained 430 years in that land. Since the Exodus from Egypt took place in the time of Meneptah II., the son of Ramses II.—the Pharaoh of the oppression—the year B.C. 1300 may be an approximate date. If we add to this 430 years, as expressing the total duration of the sojourn of the Hebrews in Egypt, we arrive at the year 1730 B.C. as the approximate date for the immigration of Jacob into Egypt, and for the time of the official career of Joseph at the court of Pharaoh. In other words, the time of Joseph (1730 B.C.) must have fallen in the period of the Hyksos domination, about the reign of the above-mentioned foreign prince Nub (1750 B.C.).

This singular co-incidence of numbers appears to have a higher value than the dates given in the chronological tables of Manetho and the fathers of the Church, and shows the probability of a fixed time for an important section of universal history on the basis of two chronological data which correspond in a way almost marvellous. In fact the supposition that it was under the

Hyksos that Joseph was sold into Egypt, as resulting from the relations thus explained, obtains stronger probability from the writings of Georgius Syncellus, who states that Joseph ruled the land in the reign of Apophis, whose age preceded the commencement of the Eighteenth Dynasty by only a few years. On the basis of an old inscription at El-Kab, the author of which must have been a contemporary of Joseph, it is possible to establish the proof that Joseph and the Hyksos are inseparable from one another.

It must be remembered that in the days of the patriarch a seven years' famine occurred, in consequence of a deficiency in the inundation. Although there is no royal cartouche in the tomb to which the inscription refers, there is internal evidence to show that Baba, its owner, must have lived immediately previous to the Eighteenth Dynasty. Baba, 'the risen again,' speaks thus :—

I loved my father ; I honoured my mother ; my brothers and my sisters loved me. I went out of the door of my house with a benevolent heart ; I stood there with refreshing hand ; splendid were my preparations of what I collected for the festal day. Mild was (my) heart, free from violent anger. The gods bestowed upon me abundant prosperity on earth. The city wished me health and a life full of enjoyment. I punished the evil-doers. The children who stood before me in the town during the days which I fulfilled were—great and small—60 ; just as many beds were provided for them, just as many chairs (?), just as many tables (?). They all consumed 120 ephahs of durra, the milk of 3 cows, 52 goats, and 9 she-asses, a hin of balsam, and 2 jars of oil.

My words may seem a jest to a gainsayer. But I call the god Mentu to witness that what I say is true. I had all this prepared in my house ; in addition I put cream in the store-chamber and beer in the cellar in a more than sufficient number of hin-measures.

I collected corn, as a friend of the harvest god. I was watchful at the time of sowing. AND WHEN A FAMINE AROSE, **LASTING MANY YEARS**, I DISTRIBUTED CORN TO THE CITY EACH YEAR OF FAMINE.

Not the smallest doubt can be raised as to whether the last words of the inscription relate to an historical fact or not. However strongly we may be inclined to recognise a general way of speaking in the narrative of Ameni where 'years of famine' are spoken of, just as strongly does the context of the present statement compel us to refer this record of '*a famine lasting many years*' to an epoch historically defined. Now, since famines succeeding one another are of the very greatest rarity in Egypt, and Baba lived and worked under the native king Seqenen-Ra Taa III. in the ancient city of El-Kab about the same time during which Joseph exercised his office under one of the Hyksos kings, there remains for a satisfactory conclusion but one fair inference: that the '*many years of famine*' in the days of Baba must correspond to the *seven years of famine* under Joseph's Pharaoh, who was one of the Shepherd Kings. The account of the elevation of Joseph under one of them, of his life at the court, of the reception of his father and brothers in Egypt with all their belongings, is in complete accordance with the pre-suppositions connected with the persons, and also with the place and time. Joseph's Pharaoh resided at Zoan (Avaris) with his court in the thorough Egyptian fashion, yet without excluding the Semitic language. He gave orders to proclaim in the Semitic language an *abrek*, that is, ' bow the knee,' [1] a word which is still retained in the hieroglyphic dictionary, and was adopted by the Egyptians to express their feeling of reverence at the sight of an important person or object. He bestowed on Joseph the high dignity of a *Zaphnatpa'neakh*, i.e. ' governor of the district of the living one,' or Sethroïte nome.[2]

---

[1] See paper by M. Le Page Renouf in *Proc. of Soc. Bib. Arch.*, Nov. 1888.

[2] ' The place of life ' was a special designation of the capital of this nome in the sacred language. The whole long word may be analysed into its component parts in the old Egyptian language:—

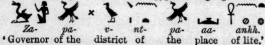

Za-	pa-	v-	nt-	pa-	aa-	ankh.
'Governor	of the	district	of	the	place	of life.'

The name of Joseph's wife, Asenath (Snat), was pure Egyptian, and is seldom met with except in the Old and Middle Empire. His father-in-law, the priest of On, was an Egyptian whose name, Puti-pera, meant the 'gift of the sun.' The chamberlain who bought Joseph from the Midianites bore also the same designation; yet his titles are given in the Semitic language, although the word *sari*, or chamberlain, is found written in Egyptian characters.

The Tale of the Two Brothers in the D'Orbiney Papyrus is of great value for the special relation in which it stands to the history of Joseph. Anpu, a married man, as the papyrus relates—

sent his younger brother, saying to him, ' Hasten and bring us seed corn from the village ;' and the young brother found the wife of his elder brother occupied in braiding her hair, and he said to her, ' Rise up, give me seed corn, that I may return to the field, for thus has my elder brother enjoined me, to return without delay.' The woman said to him, ' Go in, open the chest, that thou mayest take what thine heart desires, otherwise my locks will fall by the way.' And the youth entered into the stable, and took thereout a large vessel, for it was his wish to carry away much seed corn. And he loaded himself with wheat and grains of durra and went out with it. Then she said to him, ' How great is the burthen on thine arm !' He said to her, ' Two measures of durra and three measures of wheat, making together five measures, which rest on my arms.' Thus he spake to her. But she spake to the youth and said, ' How great is thy strength ! Well have I remarked thy vigour every time.' And her heart knew him ! . . . And she stood up and laid hold of him, and she said to him, ' Come, let us enjoy an hour's rest. The most beautiful things shall be thy portion, for I will prepare for thee festal garments.' Then the youth became like to the panther of the south for rage, on account of the evil word which she had spoken to him ; but she was afraid beyond all measure. And he spoke to her and said, 'Thou, O woman, hast been to me like a mother, and thy husband like a father, for he is older than I, so that he might have been my parent. *Why this so great sin, that thou hast spoken to me?* Say it not to me another time, then will I not tell it this time, and no word of it shall come out of my mouth about it, to any man whatsoever.' And he loaded himself with his burthen, and went out into the field.

And he went to his elder brother, and they completed their day's work.

When it was now evening, the elder brother returned home to his dwelling.   And his younger brother followed behind his oxen, which he had laden with all the good things of the field, driving them before him to prepare for them their resting-place in the stable in the village.   And behold, the wife of his elder brother was afraid because of the word which she had spoken, and she took a jar of fat, and she was like one to whom an evildoer had offered violence.   She wished thereby to say to her husband, 'Thy young brother has offered me violence.'   And her husband returned home at evening according to his daily custom, and entered into his house, and found his wife lying stretched out and suffering from injury. She gave him no water for his hands according to her custom. And the lamp was not lighted, so that the house was in darkness. But she lay there and vomited.   And her husband spoke to her thus : 'Who has had to do with thee ?   Lift thyself up ! '   She said to him, ' No one has had to do with me except thy young brother, for when he came to take seed corn for thee he found me sitting alone, and said to me, "Come ! let us make merry an hour and rest !   Let down thy hair ! "   Thus he spake to me, but I did not listen to him (but said), "See ! am I not thy mother, and is not thy elder brother like a father to thee ? "   Thus I spoke to him, but he did not hearken to my speech, and used force with me, that I might not make a report to thee.   Now if thou allowest him to live, I will kill myself.'[1]

The reader will at once perceive that Potiphar's wife and Anpu's wife precisely resemble each other, and Joseph's and Bata's temptations and virtue appear so closely allied that one is almost inclined to suppose a common origin of the two stories.

That Joseph was actually invested with the highest rank at court, next to the king, is evident from the office he filled of an Adon 'over all Egypt.' (Gen. xlv. 9.)   According to the monuments, Adon answers to the Greek ' epistatis,' a president, one set over others. The rank of such a dignitary varied according to his special duties.   We find an Adon of the city of Amen,

[1] The whole story is translated by M. Le Page Renouf in *Records of the Past*, vol. ii. p. 137 *et sea.*

of the seat of justice, of the infantry, of the beer cellars, and so forth.   Quite different from all was the office of Joseph as Adon over the whole land, a title met with only once among the inscriptions.   Before King Hor-em-heb of the Eighteenth Dynasty ascended the throne, he was invested with several very high offices. At last the Pharaoh was so pleased with him that he named him Rohir—procurator of the whole land.   In this capacity, without having any colleague beside him, he was called to be 'great lord in the king's house,' and 'he gave answer to the king and contented him with the utterances of his mouth.'   In such a service Hor-em-heb was 'an *Adon of the whole land* during the course of many years,' and at length rose to the dignity of 'heir to the throne of the whole land,' until finally he placed the royal crown on his own head.

Seventeen hundred years before the birth of Christ is about the epoch when the Middle separates from the New Empire.   The devastated regions of Avaris and Zoan were forgotten and forsaken, and with the new race came the time of requital and vengeance on the descendants of the former conquerors of Egypt, even to the fourth and fifth generations.   The theatre of these great events was removed to Western Asia, where Megiddo, Kadesh, Carchemish, henceforth formed the focus of all warlike movements.

The monuments begin from this point to afford us clear and intelligible history, for they cease not to celebrate in poetry and prose the glory and splendour of their authors.

Neb-peh-tet-Ra. Ser-ka-Ra. Aa-kheper-ka-Ra. Aa-kheper-en-Ra. Vaat-ka-Ra. Men-kheper-Ra.

Aahmes. Amen-hotep I. Tehuti-mes I. Tehuti-mes II. Hatshepsu. Tehuti-mes III.

CHAPTER VII.

DYNASTY XVIII.

Neb-peh-tet-Ra Aahmes I. (Amosis).   1700 B.C. cir.

The dominion of the Hyksos of necessity gave rise to profound internal divisions, alike in the different princely families and in the native population itself. Factions became rampant in various districts, and reached their highest point in the hostile feeling of the inhabitants of Patoris or the South country against the people of Patomit or the North country, who were much mixed with foreign blood. The indolent descendants of the old royal races had made their residences the centres of petty kingdoms ; and just as, in the strong fortress of El-Kab, in Thebes, in Khmun (the Hermopolis of the Greeks), in Khinensu (Heracleopolis), the Upper land kept up its branching dynasties from generation to generation, so the oppressed children of the ancient monarchs in the Lower Egyptian cities of Memphis, Xoïs, Zoan (Tanis), and elsewhere awaited a brilliant future of sole dominion over the re-united divisions of the empire of Horus and of Set.[2]

From this condition of divided power and of mutual jealousy the foreign rulers obtained their advantage and their chief strength, until King Aahmes made himself supreme. Manning his ships with a sufficient number of warriors, he led them down the river

---

[1] For Table of Kings see p. xxii.   [2] See p. 6.

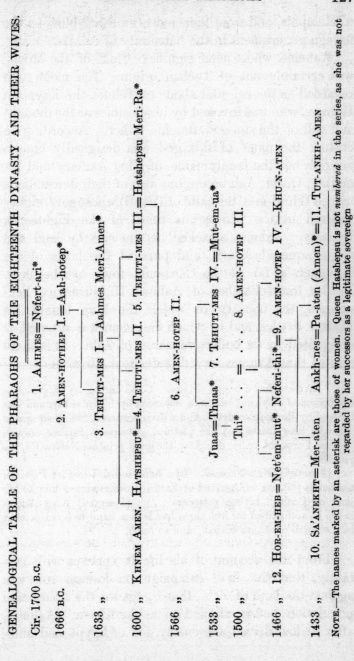

GENEALOGICAL TABLE OF THE PHARAOHS OF THE EIGHTEENTH DYNASTY AND THEIR WIVES.

Cir. 1700 B.C.   1. AAHMES=Nefert-ari*

1666 B.C.   2. AMEN-HOTEP I.=Aah-hotep*

1633 „   3. TEHUTI-MES I.=Aahmes Meri-Amen*

1600 „   KHNEM AMEN. HATSHEPSU*=4. TEHUTI-MES II. 5. TEHUTI-MES III.=Hatshepsu Meri-Ra*

1566 „   6. AMEN-HOTEP II.

1533 „   Juaa=Thuaa* 7. TEHUTI-MES IV.=Mut-em-ua*

1500 „   Thi* . . . . = ... 8. AMEN-HOTEP III.

1466 „   12. HOR-EM-HEB=Net'em-mut* Neferi-thi*=9. AMEN-HOTEP IV.—KHU-N-ATEN

1433 „   10. SA'ANEKHT=Mer-aten   Ankh-nes=Pa-aten (Amen)*=11. TUT-ANKH-AMEN

NOTE.—The names marked by an asterisk are those of women. Queen Hatshepsu is not *numbered* in the series, as she was not regarded by her successors as a legitimate sovereign to Memphis, and from thence dealt a death-blow to the foreign government in the hated city of Avaris.

Aahmes, whose name signifies 'Child of the Moon,' was certainly not of Theban origin. The moon was regarded as the celestial abode of Tehuti, the Egyptian Hermes, who was invoked by his disciples as the thought and will of the sun-god Ra, his father. According to custom the name of this god was designedly chosen not only as the family name of King Aahmes and his mother, Queen Aah-hotep, but also of their descendants named Tehuti-mes (the child of Tehuti), whose sovereignty ushered in the prosperous times of the Eighteenth Dynasty. Aahmes attacked his enemies by land and sea, conquered Avaris, and pursued the hosts of the foreigners as far as the Canaanite town of Sherohan. In the tomb-chamber of Aahmes II., surnamed Pen-nukheb, the country in which the king fought his Eastern battles, and in which Sherohan was situated, is designated by its collective name of Zahi. It is there related that Aahmes served under four kings :—

'I have reached a happy old age. I was during my existence in the favour of the king, and was rewarded by his Majesty, and was beloved by the royal court. And a divine woman, the great queen Maat-ka-Ra (Hatshepsu), the justified, gave me a further reward, because I brought up her daughter, the great princess Neferu-Ra, the justified.'

'[I served] King Aahmes. In a hand-to-hand combat I gained ten hands for him in the land of Zahi. I accompanied him to the land of Cush. Living prisoners . . . . [I served] King Amen-hotep I., and gained for him three hands in a hand-to-hand combat in the north of Aamu Kahak,' and so forth.

From this account of his life it appears with certainty, that the first campaign on foreign soil was against the land of Zahi, that is, against the *Phœnician* population before alluded to as the Kharu. Aahmes, after he had driven the enemy out of Egypt and sufficiently protected the eastern frontier of the low-country by a line of fortresses, attempted to restore peace and order in the kingdom by gradually reducing the petty kings to submission. They remained as under-kings in their several districts, and as such bore royal titles and received Pharaonic homage. Thus, on the monuments, by the side of Aahmes there appear, as legitimate princes and 'kings' sons,' the princes Benipu, Uotmes, Ramses, Aahmes, Sipar, &c., with their double names enclosed in a royal cartouche. It was only in such a manner that he was able to secure himself against insurrection and jealous opposition in the country, and also to lead his warriors from Patoris against the rebellious negroes on the southern frontier of the country.

Taking advantage of the weakness of the empire during the foreign dominion, the inhabitants of the Nubian districts threw off the yoke of the Pharaohs, and even founded independent kingdoms in the valleys near the Cataracts, which the kings of the Twelfth Dynasty had wrung almost step by step from their dusky neighbours. Aahmes, the chief of the sailors, has already related how Aahmes the king came out victorious from this struggle also, in which a king named Tetan offered an obstinate resistance.

Thus not only were the two halves of the empire re-united under the powerful sceptre of Pharaoh, but the South also was for a time again subjected to Egyptian supremacy. At last a time of leisure arrived, which allowed the king to prove his gratitude to the gods by embellishing, rebuilding, or enlarging their temples, which during the long dominion of the foreigners ' had fallen into decay.'

Aahmes, in the twenty-second year of his reign, re-opened the abandoned quarries in the Arab chain of mountains, to obtain limestone for the building of the temples in Memphis, Thebes, and the other principal cities of the kingdom.

The following is a translation of the inscription on two rock-tablets at Tûrah and Massaarah :—

In the year 22 of the reign of King Aahmes, his Majesty gave the order to open the rock-chambers anew, and to cut out thence the best white stone (limestone) of the hill country, (called) An, for the houses of the gods, whose existence is for endless years, for the house of the divine Ptah in Memphis, for Amen, the gracious god in Thebes, . . . and for all other monuments, that his Majesty caused to be executed. The stone was drawn by bullocks, which were brought thither and given over to the foreign people of the Fenekh.

The fact which the inscription relates, about the drawing of the stone by oxen, is represented beneath it in a picture. Six pairs of oxen are drawing a block of stone by the help of a kind of sledge.

But the building of the Egyptian sanctuaries occupied centuries. The immense imperial temple of the god Amen at Thebes, in the neighbourhood of the modern Arab village of Karnak, was begun in the middle of the third millennium before Christ, but down to the thirteenth century the work had only reached a partial completion. It is proved by the inscriptions, even to the very year and day, that the re-building, under the Ptolemies, of the great Temple of the Sun at Edfû occupied the architects, with slight interruption in the progress of the work, for 180 years, 3 months, and 14 days, from the year 237 B.C. to the year 57 B.C. Aahmes, therefore, could not expect to see the completion of the work he had begun ; and, in fact, it was reserved for his late descendants to finish, according to the ancient plan, the buildings he commenced.

The name of Aahmes as a builder has fallen into

oblivion on the walls of the Theban temples, but the rock-tablets of Massaarah have preserved the remembrance of him and of his wife, the great queen

NEFERT-ARI-AAHMES,

that is, ' the beautiful consort of Aahmes.' Not only in the rock-caves of Tûrah and Massaarah, opposite to Memphis, but also on a number of public monuments, in the interior of the sepulchral chambers of the Theban Necropolis, has the name of this queen been preserved, surrounded by laudatory inscriptions. Long after her decease, this great ancestress of the New Empire was venerated as a divine being, and her image was placed beside those of the eternal inhabitants of the Egyptian heaven. In the united assembly of the deified first kings of the New Empire, this divine spouse of Aahmes sits enthroned at

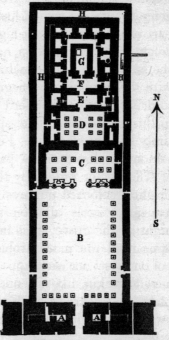

PLAN OF THE TEMPLE OF EDFÛ.
(Built under the Ptolemies B.C. 237-57.)

A A, the plyon, with staircases leading to the top. B, first hall, with peristyle. C, second hall. D, third hall. E, a small chamber, communicating with staircases, one leading to the roof, the other to numerous small passages and chambers. F, another small chamber. G, the sanctuary, in a corner of which is a magnificent monolith of grey granite, the shrine (ναός) of the hawk, which was the emblem of the god Horemkhu.

the head of all the Pharaonic pairs, and before all the kings' children of her race, as the revered founder of the Eighteenth Dynasty. She is ' the daughter, sister, wife, and mother of a king,' besides being the ' wife of the god Amen,' an expression which denoted the chief priestess of the tutelary God of Thebes (but nothing more than that).

On several monuments she is represented with a black skin, and the conclusion has hence been drawn that she was descended from negro stock. In spite of the ingenious surmises which have been put forward, on the part of scholars, to infer high political relations from the colour of her complexion, namely, that this marriage was the seal of a treaty concluded by the Pharaoh Aahmes with the neighbouring negro tribes for a common effort to drive out the Shepherd Kings, it seems to me that, in this supposition, two special points have been entirely left out of sight. First, the dark colour was not seldom employed in the paintings of the kings' tombs at Thebes, in order, by the contrast with the usual brightly coloured pictures of the Pharaohs, to suggest a clearly visible allusion to their abode in the dark night of the grave. This intention of the painter would appear all the more probable in this case as she does not on every occasion appear black, but sometimes with a yellow skin, like all native women. In the second place, the negroes, with an Egyptian queen of their own race, would. have earned a poor return of gratitude from the house of Egypt, if Aahmes, after the victory over his enemies in the North, had immediately turned his arms against the brethren and the people of his own wife, by whose help alone he had been able to obtain the victory over his hereditary enemy.[1] Her son and successor was—

SER-KA-RA, AMEN-HOTEP I.

According to all appearances Amen-hotep was a child at his father's death, so that his mother, Nefert-ari, assumed the reins of government. When he grew up the young Pharaoh turned his attention to the south and led a campaign against the land of Cush, in which

[1] See *Royal Mummies of Deir-el-Bahari*, p. 362.

the brave warrior Aahmes the son of Abana took part in the capacity of captain of the royal ships. His object, which was to extend the boundaries of Egypt, was fully attained, and besides this a rich booty in captive negroes and cattle was brought home.

A second campaign was directed towards the North, where the Libyan people of the Aamu-Kahak had shown themselves hostile to the Egyptians. This people belonged to the great tribe of the 'light-coloured' Thuhen, or, as the Greeks designated them, the Marmaridæ, whose country was known in classic times under the name of Marmarica. At that time they inhabited the northern coast of Africa. In this mention of the Aamu-Kahak are seen the first traces of that enmity which under Meneptah II. assumed an aspect so threatening for the Egyptians. For the rest, 'those from the land of Thuhi' considered themselves as cousins to the Egyptians.

Towards the East Amen-hotep I. remained inactive, and, like his predecessor, contented himself with protecting the frontiers. In the interior of the country the inscriptions prove his erection of the great temple at Thebes, and of sanctuaries for individual gods in the western part of the great Theban plain. After his death divine honours were accorded to him, as to his predecessors.

He had by his consort Aah-hotep a son, who was his successor on the throne, and as such bore the names—

AA-KHEPER-KA-RA TEHUTI-MES I.   1633 B.C. CIR.

His name, written by the Greeks Thotmosis, means 'Tehuti's child.' The victories and wars of this king, who for the first time undertook a campaign in the East as far as the banks of the Euphrates, form the principal events of his history.

The inscription in the tomb of Aahmes, the captain of the ships, first mentions an expedition of Tehuti-mes I. against the country of Khent-hen-nefer, an inclusive term which comprehended all the known countries in Africa situated to the west of the Nile as far as the north coast of Libya, in contradistinction to Cush, now called the Sûdan. On a tract of such an enormous extent there naturally lived an immense number of tribes whose original stock was pure African; they are the black or brown negro races called Nahasu on the monuments.

Among these, lighter-coloured tribes of Semitic or Cushite origin had settled themselves, whom a later monument of the time of the Ptolemies calls by the name of *Senti* (*Sati* ?). According to the situation of these countries, and the habitations of these tribes, we have substituted for the Egyptian appellations of *Ta-Khent* and *Cush* the better known names of 'Nubia' and 'Ethiopia;' and in like manner have translated *Nahasu* by 'Negroes,' and *Annu* by 'Cushites.' For all these nations as well as for the Egyptians, the Nile afforded the one great waterway. In spite of all the efforts of the inhabitants of these remote regions to bid defiance to the Egyptian kings and to destroy their monuments there are still traces enough left to prove their supremacy. Among them the name of Tehuti-mes I. is not wanting; for the rocks in the neighbourhood of the Cataracts of Kerman (the Third Cataract) have preserved the remembrance of his great deeds, and relate how—

'Tehuti-mes I. had taken possession of the throne of Horus, in order to extend the boundaries of the Thebaïd;'—how 'In the territory of the quarter of Thebes called Khefti-neb-s, the inhabitants of the desert (Heru-sha), and the Aamu and all foreign nations were obliged to work;'—how 'The northern people of Khebau-neb are bowed down and the Agabot (Libyans) are quelled;'—how

'Peace is now there, because the inhabitants of the southern lands are driven downward and the northern people are driven upward, and they have all together subjected themselves to the king ; '—how 'The inhabitants of the inner regions hastened to Pharaoh to bow down before his throne ; '—how 'He smote the king of the Annu (the Cushites), and of the Negroes ; '—how 'The Annu of Nubia were hewn in pieces and scattered all over their lands, and how their stench filled the valleys.'

Then the inscription continues :—

The lords of the great king's house have made a frontier garrison for his warriors, so that they may not be surprised by the foreign tribes ; they have gathered together like the young panther against the bull. He remains still ; he is blinded. The king came even to the uttermost limits of his realm ; he reached the extreme boundary by his mighty arm. He sought the battle, but found no one who could have offered him resistance. He opened the valleys, which had remained unknown to his forefathers, and which had never beheld the wearers of the double crown. His southern boundary was at the beginning of this land, the northern boundary at that water where the traveller downwards turns for his upward journey.[1] Never had this been the case under any other king.

The inscription concludes with the words :—

The land in its complete extent lay at the feet of the king.

The office of governor of Cush, to which at first the real sons of the king (called ' King's sons of Cush) laid claim, is mentioned for the first time under the rule of Tehuti-mes I. on the wall of the temple at Semneh, where an official called Nahi, who had won his spurs under Aahmes and Tehuti-mes I., was raised by the latter king to this new dignity.

The richness of Nubia and Ethiopia made them most desirable objects of conquest ; and governors were at once sent to administer the 'land of Cush' and collect the tribute. Cattle and rare animals, panther-skins, ivory, ebony, balsam, sweet-smelling resin, gold, and precious stones, as well as captive negroes, all were

---

[1] Possibly an allusion to the great bend of the river at Gebel Barkal.

brought into Pharaoh's treasuries.   The prisoners were many of them sent to work in the emerald mines at Wady-Magharah, or to the scorching country of Ua-ua-t to dig for gold.   In the neighbourhood of the local temples villages sprang up, whose busy inhabitants were supported by the supplies of Egyptian corn which their own soil denied them.   The natives of the cataract districts were employed as sailors by the king, his generals, and his merchants, nor did the reward of their labour fail them.

When Pharaoh visited the Nubian country in his richly adorned Nile ship, there was no end to the wonder and admiration, the joy and the hurras, for the king and his courtiers bestowed rich gifts on the inhabitants.   For it was well worth while for the kings to leave behind them generous presents, to teach the inhabitants that Pharaoh was the father and benefactor of his subjects.   Then those dusky-coloured men might well sing—

> Hail to thee ! king of Egypt, | Sun of the foreign people !
> Thy name is great | In the land of Cush,
> Where the war-cry resounded through
> The dwellings of the men.
> Great is thy power, | Thou beneficent ruler.
> It puts to shame the peoples.
> The Pharaoh !—life, safety, health to him !—
> He is a shining Sun.

After Tehuti-mes I., in the first years of his reign, had undertaken a campaign against Cush, and had fixed the boundaries of his empire to the South, it seemed to him that the favourable moment had arrived to send troops eastward to attack the hated inhabitants of Asia.   Thus began that great war of 500 years, which was carried on by successive Pharaohs with almost uninterrupted good fortune.

It may be as well to say a little about these

Asiatic people. First of all there were the wandering
Shasu, whose chief territory was the mountainous
country of Edom. Here the Bedâwi of antiquity lived
'like foxes in their holes;' while the kindred tribes
settled at the angle of the sea coast were generally
faithful allies of the Egyptians. Their three chief
places—Rhinocolura, Anaugas, and Jamnia—formed a
sort of Tripolis. After passing the fortress of Sherohan
the road touched the stronghold of Gaza. Along the
edge of the sea lay Phœnicia, of which Askalon, Joppa,
Tyre, Sidon, Berŷtus were the principal places on the
royal road till in the valley of Eleutherus, at the northern
slope of Lebanon, the ancient way took an easterly
direction, and finally opened into the wide plain of
Kadesh on the Orontes, and thence into the heart of the
land of the Amorites. Another much-frequented
though dangerous road led from Gaza in a northerly
direction along the whole length of the Jordan; the
valley of the Leontes and Orontes had to be passed in
order to reach from this side the same city of Kadesh
in the land of the Amorites. Damascus and the towns
of Cœle-Syria were left to the east on the other side of
Anti-Libanus, Carchemish and Kalybon being the last
halting-places on the road in Syria proper, which was
bounded on the east by the broad water-way of the
Euphrates, while on the west the chain of Mount
Amanus and the spurs of the Taurus range set a limit
to the further march of the great army. The whole of
this territory was divided into a number of small kingdoms, the names of which were commonly connected
with a fortified capital, and which were inhabited by
races whose exact designations are as yet unknown.

The Hittites or Kheta held a distinguished place
among them, while the kingdoms of Carchemish, Kadesh,
and Megiddo were looked upon as the most important

points for defence and attack, and as general gathering-places for the allied kings.

The Egyptian inscriptions of this period frequently mention the name of Naharain, or land of two rivers, as a large country in the neighbourhood of the Upper Ruthen.   It is generally understood to be the country of Mesopotamia.   The Arabs at the present day are accustomed to call the fertile country to the west of Damascus, which is watered by many rivers, by the name of Naharain.   Tehuti-mes I. chose as the object of his campaign against the East this land of Naharain. The two contemporaries and namesakes Aahmes, already mentioned, agree completely in their accounts of this expedition, which the king undertook in order ' to wash his heart,' i.e. to satisfy his anger against the inhabitants of the land of Ruthen.   He won the victory, and took numerous prisoners, besides horses and chariots of war.

This campaign was the beginning of a brisk trade between the Nile and the Euphrates, which lasted through many centuries.

Trade and art went hand in hand.   The descriptions of the chariots of war, which blazed with gold and silver, of the armour and weapons, from the most beautiful coats of mail to richly ornamented lances, of the vessels of gold and silver and bronze, of the household furniture down to tent-poles and footstools, and those thousand small objects which appear necessities to civilised men, represent the art and civilisation of that day.   Long before the heroes of the 'Iliad' and ' Odyssey' appear on the battle-field in their ornamental armour, the kings and ' marinas' of the land of Canaan careered in brazen harness in their war-chariots over the plains of Shinar and Mesopotamia and the valleys of Palestine, to measure themselves in battle with the warriors of Egypt.

In the conduct of war also their Asiatic neighbours exercised an influence on the Egyptian military administration. The distribution and arrangement of the troops, and the position of the leaders, were carefully settled, from the common soldier to the highest general. The horse was now introduced into the valley of the Nile under his Semitic name of *sus*, and the war-chariot, with its pair of grey horses, henceforth took a prominent place in the Egyptian order of battle. In the tomb of the brave warrior Aahmes at El-Kab there appears a picture of a pair of horses with a chariot. The driver, *Kazan*, standing behind the chariot, holding the reins, waits for his lord, who 'loves the clever steeds.'

The king returned victorious from his campaign against Naharain. Crowned with glory and laden with booty, he entered Thebes, and, as a lasting monument in remembrance of his expedition, caused a tablet to be set up on which were inscribed his victories. He further showed his thankfulness to Amen by continuing the works begun by his forefathers at Karnak.

The temple, which was at that time small, and surrounded by a wall with rows of chambers built against it, received on the western side an addition of massive buildings and rows of columns; and in front of these two granite obelisks, covered with inscriptions, were to serve as witnesses of the prowess of the king and his piety towards the gods.

It seems that Tehuti-mes I. enjoyed but a comparatively short life and reign. With this agrees the fact that the two Aahmes, as also Nahi, the governor of the southern country, were able to serve their country faithfully under the first four Pharaohs of this dynasty. Tehuti-mes I. left behind him three children, an heiress daughter and favourite of her father, the bold and able Hatshepsu, and two sons, both of whom bore the name of their father, Tehuti-mes. The elder was already able to carry on the government alone, while the other was a very young child, whose future was entrusted to the care of his elder brother and sister.

AA-KHEPER-EN-RA TEHUTI-MES II. 1600 B.C. CIR.

After the death of his father the eldest son, Tehuti-mes II., ascended the vacant throne, not without exciting the jealousy of his energetic sister and wife, Hatshepsu. This favourite child of the late king, superior to her brother both in courage and capacity, risked everything to get the government into her own hands. Whether the means she took to serve her end were legitimate, is now difficult to decide ; but the fact is certain that they met with a hostile reception, for after the death of her elder brother she erased his name from the monuments with the greatest care, a token of the unfriendly feeling that existed between the brother and sister. As an heiress, whom her father had in his lifetime already allowed to take part in the affairs of government, she felt herself strengthened by the influence of her position and her birth, like that by which her mother, Aah-hotep, herself the daughter of a legitimate king of the old race, had held so distinguished a place.

Tehuti-mes II. reigned only a short time in conjunction with his sister. He succeeded, however, in conducting a campaign against the southern people, as well as another against his neighbours, the Shasu, on the eastern frontier, who had attempted an attack upon the Egyptian lowlands.

A rock tablet in the neighbourhood of Aswân informs the wayfarer of the relations of this king with the southern country. It commences with the date of the 8th Paophi in the first year of his reign. On the

left bank of the stream the two-fold names of the royal
brother and sister were especially recorded on buildings
on the site of the modern Medînet Habû (called by the
special name of 'the mountain of Neb-ankh,' that is
'the coffin mountain,' on account of the tombs which
are found there), and on those at the place called Deir-
el-Bahari.   At the site last named, in the north-western
corner of the Theban valley, the white limestone rocks
rise steep and abruptly from the plain.   On the left
hand, where the hill of Gûrnah juts into the plain, not
far from Deir-el-Bahari, the rock is penetrated by
thousands of caves, which lead to the chambers of the
dead.

Here the queen resolved that a magnificent sepulchre should be hewn in the rock, with a temple to the
dead in front of it, in memory of the princes of the
royal house, the like of which should not be found
again in Egypt.   While the steep wall of rock was
pierced with grottoes in the shape of vast halls, which
served as sacrificial chambers to the yet undiscovered
tombs of the families of the race of Tehuti-mes, richly
adorned with variegated representations and corresponding inscriptions of pious import, there rose in
front a gigantic temple in the form of a long, extensive
building approached by broad steps which descended
to the plain.   A sacred avenue (*dromos*), bordered on
each side by sphinxes, led in an easterly direction to the
river.   Such was the splendid erection of Queen Hatshepsu, which called to mind the wonderful buildings
on the banks of the Euphrates that have been so often
described.   In the subterranean chambers which have
not yet been discovered in the interior of the steep
wall of rock, and perhaps connected with the tombs of
the kings which lie behind them in the valley of
Bibân-el-Molûk, were placed the bodies of Tehuti-mes

I. and his wife and sister Queen Aahmes. Here reposed near their parents the princess Kheb-neferu-Ra, who died young, by her side Tehuti-mes II., and his restless, ambitious consort Hatshepsu, and lastly the Pharaoh Tehuti-mes III.

Scarcely had the brother and husband of Hatshepsu closed his eyes when the proud queen laid aside her woman's dress, clothed herself in man's attire, and adorned herself with the crown and insignia of royalty. She assumed the sole government of the country, while her younger brother, Tehuti-mes III., was put aside. Her name was now expanded to

MAAT-KA-RA-KHNEM-AMEN. HATSHEPSU.

The first deed of the new woman-king shows her hatred of her deceased brother and husband, whose memory she sought to obliterate in every conceivable manner. She erased his names from the monuments they had erected together, and replaced them by her own or those of her father. The buildings which had been planned on a great scale were now continued, and before all others the Stage Temple of Deir-el-Bahari was carried to completion by untiring efforts.

The friend and architect of the queen was named Senmut, the son of Rames and of Ha-nefer. After his death the queen raised to him 'as a mark of gratitude' a stone monument, his likeness in black granite, in a sitting posture, and on the right shoulder was this short but significant inscription : *Nen kem em an apu,* 'his ancestors were not found in writing.' In the inscriptions on his monument he abstains from mentioning the woman-king otherwise than as 'he,' for thus the will of the queen commanded.

I lived under the *lord* of the country, the *king* Maat-ka-Ra : may *he* live for ever !

I was a distinguished man, who loved *him*, and who gained for myself the admiration of the *lord* of the country. *He* made me great in the country ; *he* named me as the chief steward of *his* house, and as the governor of the whole country. So I became the first of the first, and the master of the works of all masters of the works.

The buildings of Hatshepsu are some of the most tasteful, most complete, and brilliant creations that the hands of Egyptian artists ever wrought. They belong to the time of the matchless splendour of Egyptian art, whether as regards the manipulation of the stone, or the form and manner of the execution, or the effect of the rich coloured decoration. Even in their ruin they exercise a wonderful charm on the spoilt taste of modern times. Hatshepsu's desire for glory and a certain adventurous turn of mind caused her to look towards the remote shores of the Indian Ocean, and a voyage of discovery must be accomplished to. the land of Punt, the cradle of many marvellous stories told by sea-faring men.

The front walls of the Stage Temple of Deir-el-Bahari are covered with coloured sculptures and inscriptions, of which the representation that has become so famous, of the expedition by sea to the balsam-land of Punt, is conspicuous above all the rest.

Incited thereto by the oracle of Amen, the queen determined to undertake a voyage of discovery to this unknown land. The Egyptians were acquainted from hearsay with the wonders of that distant region on the coasts of the Red Sea and the Indian Ocean, the home of the pine incense so much coveted for the service of the temples, and of many other precious products of the soil. A number of seagoing ships were prepared for the voyage. They were manned by able seamen and warriors, and a profusion of friendly gifts was not forgotten.

A royal ambassador accompanied the expedition, with many noble princes and lords. How long the voyage lasted the inscriptions do not state. When the fleet had reached its destination, a landing was made on the coast of the 'incense terraced-mountain' near Cape Guardafui. Then

Each of the princes of the land of Punt approached, with rich and costly gifts as offerings to the holiness of Hathor, the lady of Punt, of whom the Egyptian queen is the living image.

The inhabitants apparently lived on pile-buildings, in little dome-shaped huts, the entrance to which was effected by a ladder, under the shade of cocoa-nut palms laden with fruit, and splendid incense-trees, on whose boughs strange birds rocked themselves, and at whose feet stately herds of cattle peacefully reposed.

The picture shows the royal ambassador, accompanied by his warriors, as in the act of receiving a number of chains, rings, hatchets, and daggers, the presents of ' the prince of Punt, Parihu,' who, accompanied by his wife Ari . . . , his two sons, and his daughter, greets the royal ambassador with uplifted arms. An ass serves to carry his enormously fat wife. The appended words run thus :—

The princes of the land of Punt have arrived, bowing themselves in greeting, to receive these warriors of the queen. They praise and exalt the King of the Gods, Amen-Ra.

As appears from the continuation of the inscription, they express their natural astonishment that it was possible for foreign men to reach such a distant and unknown country, and they add the prayer, that the queen, the mighty ruler of Egypt, would grant them peace and freedom.

The royal ambassador, ready to take into account the peaceful desires of the princes of Punt, on his side puts forward the condition that the country of Punt should be subjected to the supremacy of the queen of Egypt, as also that some of the products of the country, and particularly incense, should be delivered as a tribute to the royal court.

The ambassador and his suite had in the meantime pitched their camp on the sea-shore. That this was done with the friendly intention of receiving the princes of Punt, whose favourable answer must have been given, and of entertaining them hospitably as the friends of the Egyptian queen, is shown in the clearest manner by the inscription :—

The camp of tents of the royal ambassador and his warriors was pitched in the neighbourhood of the balsam terraced-mountain of the country of Punt, on the shore of the great sea, to receive the princes of this country. There was offered to them bread, mead, wine, meat, dried fruits, and everything else from the country of Tamera (Egypt), just as the royal court had ordered.

The chief representative of the princes of Punt, Parihu, who was mentioned above, accompanied by his wife, did not keep them waiting, for

The prince of Punt came, bringing with him the tribute to the shore of the great sea.

Golden rings, ivory, and a great heap of precious balsams, were laid out before the tents. Inhabitants of Punt bearing loads, and drivers leading laded asses, with herds of cattle behind, showed clearly the willingness of the natives to submit themselves to the Egyptian sovereign. The ambassador 'of the queen received the gifts of the prince of Punt.' Thereupon peace and friendship were concluded, and everything was prepared for the return home.

The treasures of stones and plants and animals, which Punt had cheerfully offered to the Egyptians, were increased by a singular addition, which presents to us the first and oldest attempt, of which we have

any record, to transplant a tree to a foreign soil.
Thirty-one incense trees, packed in tubs, were dragged
to the shore by the natives. Six men toiled under the
burthen of each tree. When all the products of the
land stood ready for embarkation, the difficult work of
packing and loading commenced. The picture shows
us the labours of the sailors and of the natives. The
inscription explains that

the ships were laden to the uttermost with the wonderful
products of the land of Punt, and with the different precious
woods of the divine land, and with heaps of the resin of incense,
with fresh incense-trees, with ebony, (objects) of ivory set in pure
gold from the land of the Aamu, with sweet woods, Khesit-wood,
with Ahem-incense, holy resin, and paint for the eyes, with dog-
headed apes, with long-tailed monkeys and greyhounds, with leopard
skins, and with natives of the country, together with their children.
Never was the like brought to any king (of Egypt) since the world
stands.

Soon the ships were set in motion. Sails and oars
had to help alternately. The incense-trees stood on
deck between chests and sacks: to the great amuse-
ment of the voyagers the apes sprang about here and
there in full freedom among the sails. The inscription
added to the picture informs us that among the people
who travelled with them were even princes of the land
of Punt.

The warriors of the lord of the land betake themselves to the
ship, they return happily home, they take the road to Thebes in
joyfulness of heart. The princes are with them from this country.
What they bring is of a kind, the like of which was never brought
to any other king.

The return of the fleet to Thebes must, of course,
have been celebrated as a great event. Egypt had
quietly become possessed of a newly discovered region
in the East, and with it the wealth of the most precious
productions of this Eldorado. In a solemn court the
queen received the princes of the tribes, who respect

fully prostrated themselves before her who had now become their queen, and in the usual court language in their solemn address designated her as 'the Queen of Tamera, and the Sun who shines like the disk of heaven,' not without at the same time addressing her as 'their queen,' and as 'ruler of Punt.'

They have now become the subjects of her Majesty.

In a long procession the beasts and the other natural products were brought before the queen, and even the heavy incense-trees were dragged past her.

In consequence of the fortunate result of this voyage, which carried the Egyptian name to the coast of Africa and opened new sources of wealth, it was proper and natural to dedicate the treasures which had been brought home to Amen, and to institute grand festivals in his honour.   Pictures and inscriptions leave not the slightest doubt upon this point.

The woman-king appeared in full royal attire, honoured by the most distinguished insignia of her dignity, before the great god, to testify her gratitude, and to prove the same in very deed, by the dedication and presentation of all the treasures which had been brought home from the distant South. The productions of Punt were heaped up in groups, and the incense-trees were planted in Egyptian soil. Giraffes, panthers, hunting-leopards, bulls, panther-skins, gold, copper, ebony, and other woods fit for building purposes, called Aamu-timber, ivory, paint for the eyes, 'kash' (?), and whole mountains of precious incense-resin, were offered to the god, and the number and measure of them inscribed in the temple-books. This last act is shown in a symbolical manner in the picture, where Tehuti, the divine temple-scribe, and Safekh, the Goddess of libraries, write down on the roll of a book the pieces weighed out and counted over by Horus.

The exact and just scales of Tehuti, which the queen had had prepared for her father, the Theban Amen, in order to weigh out silver, gold, blue stone, green stone, and all other precious stones :

so run the words.

On the one scale lie thirty-one rings of precious metal, on the other scale the 'Ten-' (or 'pound-') weights, in the shape of reclining oxen, and the smaller weights in the forms of heads of oxen and bricks. The present occupation of Horus, ' the watcher of the scale,' is designated as

the weighing out of the gold and silver and copper, and the works of the inhabitants of the South, for the Theban God Amen.

In the picture below, the spectator sees two large heaps of incense-resin. Four men are occupied in determining the amount exactly with a hollow measure. An inscription above it says :—

Very active measuring of the fresh incense for the Theban god Amen, from the most wonderful of lands, that of Punt, of the most excellent (incense) of the land of god.

With these transactions there was connected a great feast in honour of Amen. The queen herself was arrayed in a spotted leopard-skin with copper clasps, and her limbs were perfumed like freshly fallen dew. All the inhabitants gave utterance to their joy in song and music. The brother of the queen, Men-kheper-ka-Ra, had the honour of presenting an offering of the best incense to the holy bark of Amen, which was borne in solemn procession on the shoulders of the officiating priests, a long procession of whom, with court officials, warriors, and people, bearing palm-branches, approached the temple of the divine protector of Thebes.

Closely connected with these events was the dedication of the temple to the tutelary deities Amen and

Hathor, in which the king of Punt and his nobles took part.   Hatshepsu's reign was not weakened by external enemies.   In the East the Canaanite kings left Egypt unmolested, and rather showed their friendly feeling by sending the tribute imposed upon them, and in the South the governors delivered to the court the products of their country.   In the meantime Tehuti-mes grew up to manhood, and according to the Egyptian law claimed a share in the throne, which his sister could not withhold from him; and, yielding to force, she placed beside her on the throne, as associate king, the rightful heir to the crown and lineal representative of the royal house.   With deep rancour in his heart Tehu-ti-mes III. assumed the royal dignity.

His first exercise of kingly power bears the date of the year 15, on the 27th day of the month Pakhons.

A rock-tablet at Wady-Magharah exhibits the two sovereigns, Hatshepsu and Tehuti-mes III., united in presenting their offerings to Sopt and Hathor, the protecting deities of the district.   The inscription begins with the date of the year 16.   A year previously a work had been begun which claims attention for two reasons.   On the plinth of one of the obelisks of rose granite, with which the queen adorned the great temple at Karnak, there is an historical statement, the chief contents of which are as follows.   The woman-king— to translate by an approximate phrase the masculine style in which the queen speaks of herself—had cut out the work in question from the wall of rock in the 'red mountain' of Aswân, and had raised it in its place in the inconceivably short space of seven months, namely, from the first day of the month Mekhir of the 15th year of her reign to the last of Mesori of the following 16th year.   If such was the case, the commencement of the first year of her reign must have fallen in the time between the two months; consequently, the reckoning of the regnal year does not begin, according to the system hitherto received, from the first day of that year, in which she ascended the throne as king.

This assumption of the real day of her accession to the throne is fully confirmed by a date from the reign of Tehuti-mes III., who, according to the authority of the monuments, ascended the throne of Egypt on the 4th day of the month Pakhons.

In agreement with this, the great tablet of victories at Karnak announces that the same king, in the 22nd year of his reign, in the month Pharmuthi, left the Egyptian frontier to arrive at Gaza a few days later, in the 23rd year, on the day of his coronation, the 4th of Pakhons.

According to the inscription in the tomb of his contemporary, Amenemheb, the Adon of the warriors, the king died on the last day of the month Phamenoth, in the 54th year of his reign. Tehuti-mes III. accordingly reigned exactly 53 years, 11 months, and 1 day, that is including the years of his sister's reign, whose sole rule appeared to him unjust and illegal. With this length of his reign the Manethonian records of 12 years for the double reign of the two together, and 26 years for his sole reign, in no way agree; a striking example in proof of the corrupt form in which Manetho's numbers have come down to us. The date on the plinth of the obelisk named above can now be perfectly explained. The 15th year ends with the 3rd of Pakhons; and the 4th day of the same month began the 16th year. Thus they laboured at this work for 3 months and 3 days of the 15th year, and 3 months and 27 days of the 16th year: altogether, therefore, for just 7 full months.

Whether Tehuti-mes III., after reaching manhood, drove his sister by force from the throne, or whether she quietly passed out of life, we have not the means of knowing, as the monuments are silent on the point.

CHAPTER VIII.

DYNASTY XVIII.—continued.

MEN-KHEPER-RA TEHUTI-MES III.   1600 B.C. CIR.

(The Alexander the Great of Egyptian History.)

DURING so long a reign as 53 years, 11 months, and 1 day, an energetic king could accomplish much for his country, and that Tehuti-mes did so is proved by innumerable ruined monuments which date from his time. Egypt itself now forms the central point of the world's intercourse, and affords us an insight into the national histories of antiquity. For this king undertook to measure himself in battle with the mightiest empires, and carried his arms to the frontiers of the then known world, bringing home with him the spoils of the conquered people.

We shall be astonished at the countless riches which were laid up in the treasuries of the temples. The same inscriptions on the temple walls which, then in a better state of preservation, the wise men of Thebes read and explained to Germanicus, on his visit to the old city of Amen, still confirm what Tacitus has related. ' There were read to him,' says the Roman historian, ' the tributes imposed on the nations, the weight of silver and gold, the number of weapons and horses, and the offerings to the temples in ivory and sweet scents, also what supplies of corn and utensils each nation paid, which were no less immense than are now imposed by the might of the Parthians or the power of Rome.'

The records of this Pharaoh's wars were carved in hieroglyphs on the walls of the holy of holies at Karnak.   Only isolated portions of the long inscriptions have been preserved; but these are still. important enough to enable us to put together the principal parts of the record of the victories of Tehuti-mes III., and to gain a general idea of his campaigns.

During a period of almost twenty years he carried on more than thirteen campaigns, in the course of which towns had to be stormed, rivers crossed, and many countries traversed under the difficulties of a foreign climate and a hostile population.   Under the rule of Hatshepsu the yearly tributes imposed on the conquered peoples had gradually ceased to be paid, and a deaf ear had persistently been turned to repeated warnings, until at last the foreign kings renounced the Egyptian supremacy under the sceptre of a 'woman-king,' and made a stand against the empire.   A great revolution took place at this time in the Chaldean empire.   The ruling dynasty was attacked by the Arabs from the South and overthrown.   A new era began, the era of the Arab kings in Babylon, who from this time bore rule for many years in Mesopotamia.   All these events, which a short time before the sole reign of Tehuti-mes III. had made a great revolution in the life of the nations from the Euphrates as far as the Western Sea, could not fail to exercise an influence on Egypt.   The tribes of the Upper Ruthen, the Phœnician Kharu, and their southern neighbours in Zahi, declared themselves independent of the yoke of Egypt, and the king of Gaza was the only one who preserved his ancient friendship for the Egyptians.

Ruthen and Zahi formed the main points of attack in the different years of the war.   After victories had been won the king with his army marched out from

the Egyptian frontier in the month of Pharmuthi, probably towards its close, the point of departure being
the fortress on the eastern frontier of Zaru or Zoan-
Tanis.   The following literal translation of the Egyptian
record gives the further course of the campaign :—

FRAGMENT 1.—'(2–5) The king, Men-kheper-Ra (Tehuti-mes III.)
[may he live for ever], has issued the command that there should
be put up [the report of his victories which his father Amen granted
him] in the form of a memorial tablet in the temple which the king
has erected to his father [the Theban god Amen.   Therein is set
forth the list of the towns which he has conquered in his] campaign
according to their names, with the addition of the booty which was
brought away by [the king out of] all [lands], which his father, the
sun-god Ra, had delivered to him.   (6) In the year 22, in the month
Pharmuthi, [on the ? day, the king found himself in] (7) the fortress
of Zaru on his first campaign to [extend] (8) the frontiers of Egypt
by [his] victories.

'(9) Now the duration of the same was $x + 2$ years .   [The
foreign kings had sown] (10) discord.   Each was in the . . . against
. . . (11) The [tribes ?] which lived there (12) in the city of Sherohan, made the beginning with Irza, (13) and found their termination at the extremest limits of the earth, with the exception of those
who had raised themselves up against the king.

' *In the year* 23, *on the 4th day of the month Pakhons, the day of
his accession to the throne,*

'(14) he found himself in the town, which the ruler of Gazatu
(Gaza) had within . . . . (15) *On the 5th of Pakhons*
he left this place full of power [and strength,] (16) in might and
triumph to conquer that miserable enemy, and to extend (17) the
boundaries of Egypt, according to the commands of his father Amen
[who gives him] what he possesses.

'(18) *In the year* 23, *on the 16th of Pakhons* (he went) to Ihem.
[The king] (19) gave the order for a consultation with his warriors
on account of the war, speaking thus :

'"That hostile king (20) of Kadeshu has arrived.   He has
entered into Makitha (Megiddo).   He is [there] (21) at this moment.
He has assembled with him the kings [of all] the tribes [which
dwell] (22) over against the water of Egypt as far as the land of
Naharain [the . . . .], (23) the Kharu (Phœnicians), the Kidu
(Kittim), the . . . . their horses, their warriors [in great num-
bers].   (24) Thus he speaks : I will withstand [the king of Egypt]
(25) at Makitha (Megiddo).   Tell me [which is the way to break
into this city ?]"

'(26) They spake before the king : "How would it be, to force the way along (27) that road which leads to the narrow passes? for there is [intelligence] (28) that the enemy stand there [in ambush, and impassable is] (29) the road for a numerous body. For lo! a horse cannot go behind [another, nor a man behind] (30) a man in like manner. Will not then [the enemies rise up to] (31) fight there, while [the army] stands still? A broad road goes (32) out from Aluna ; it offers them no opportunity for attack, and with respect [to the way on] a broad road (33) it is the only way. Take it into consideration. [Let us go by it, we shall] come [out at] (34) Ta-an-na-ka (Thaanach). Another [way] which you might take into consideration (35) is the road north of Ziftha (Zaphat). We come out upon this to the north of Makitha (Megiddo). (36) Wherever our victorious ruler will go, [we will follow] him on it (the way). (37) Only let him not lead us on the impassable road."

' And lo (38) the spies [arrived, whom the king had sent out] on account of the intentions [of the enemy, and] (39) they spake in the presence of the king.

' Then spake the Majesty of Pharaoh—may he live, and be safe and well !—[thus] : (40) "As truly as the sun-god Ra loves me, I call to witness my father Amen, I the son of the [sun-god Ra] (41) with a pure life, I will enter on the road of A- (42) luna. Let him, whoever among you has the wish, enter on [other] (43) roads, which you have named. But let [those] of you come (44) who will follow me. For thus would speak (45) the enemies, who know not Ra : Does not the king advance on one (46) of the other roads? He wishes to retreat for fear of us." Then they assented, (47) speaking thus before the king : "May thy father Amen of Thebes grant (48) to us protection and safety if we follow thee, the king, into all places wherever thou wilt go : (49) for the servant should be behind [his] lord." [Then the king showed himself] (50) in the sight of his assembled warriors [while he spoke to them thus] : (51) "May Amen give guidance into [good ways] ! " Each one of the warriors took an (52) oath, speaking thus : "I will not advance (53) before the king in order to [protect him against the enemy. I will leave him, the king,] (54) to go himself before his warriors." [Then the king left his horse and went] (55) on foot, and those who went on foot, their horse was behind [them. Thus the king advanced] (56) at the head of his warriors.

' *In the year* 23, *on the* 19*th of Pakhons,* (57) the king's tent was pitched at the city of Aluna. But the king went on (58) forwards. His divine father Amen-Ra [the ruler of Thebes] (59) was before him, and the god Horemkhu [the god of light of Heliopolis]

by [his side] . . . . (60) His father Amen-Ra, the lord of
Thebes, victory for [thine] arm . . . . (61) for the king. The battle
begins on the side [of the enemy] . . . . . (62) In the tumult of
battle, numerous are . . . . . . (63) The southern horn (wing) at the
town of Ta-a-[na-ka] (Taanach) . . . . . . (64) the northern horn
(wing) at the corner south [of the town of Megiddo] (65) the king
was in face of them. (66) They fall to the ground, and the hostile
king . . . . (67) . . . they . . . .'

Then follows, after a gap of three or four lines, the
following large fragment :—

FRAGMENT 3.—'(1) Aa-lu-na. The rear-guard of the brave
warriors of the king [remained] at [the town of] (2) Aluna. The
advanced guard came out into the valley. (3) They filled all
the ground of this valley. Then they spake thus to the king:
(4) " Would the king advance, accompanied by his warriors, to the
battle ? the valley is full of them : (5) we will obey our war-chief in
the [fight] ; (6) we will protect our lord and the rear-guard of his
warriors together with his people. (7) We have (left) the rear of the
warriors behind, [that] they may fight against (8) the country . . .
of the Aam, that we may not act according to our will . . . . .
(9) our warriors." And the king took up a position outside them
(10) there, to protect the rear of his warriors in the battle. Then
they reached the . . . . (11) and the warriors came out on this
road. (12) The sun had rolled downwards, when the king reached
the south of Megiddo on the bank of the brook Quinaa (Kanaah).
There had (further) passed by six hours of the day. Then was
the camp pitched, and the king showed himself in the sight of all
his warriors (speaking thus) : " Keep yourselves ready, look to your
arms, for we shall meet this miserable enemy in battle early to-
morrow morning, because . . . ." (13) assembled at the tent of
Pharaoh ; it was composed of the baggage of the guides, and the
utensils (?) of the servants. When the watch had been set, which
the soldiers kept, they spoke thus : "Firm courage, firm courage !
Watch ! watch ! Watch over his life at the king's tent ! "

'Tidings were brought to the king : "Meru (Egypt) is of good
courage, and the noble races and the warrior people of the South
and the North land alike."

'In the year 23, on the 21st of Pakhons, on the feast of the
new moon, which is the anniversary of the coronation of the king,
in the early morning all the warriors were ordered that they should
open . . . .

'(14) The king went forth on his chariot of copper ; he was
equipped with all the necessary panoply ; he was like Horus the

smiter, the lord of might, and like Mentu, the lord of Thebes. His father Amen made his hands strong. The horn (wing) of the warriors of the king at the southern mountain [was stationed at the brook] of Qina, the northern horn to the north-west of Megiddo, the king in their midst, Amen at his side . . . (15) his limbs. Then the king prevailed over them before his warriors. They (the enemy) wondered at the king, how he became their lord. Then they fled head over heels to Megiddo, with terror on their face, and left behind their horses and their gold and silver chariots, and were drawn up by their clothes as by ropes into that town, for the people had barricaded the town itself on account of [the deeds of the king].

'(16) While they were being drawn up by their clothes from without into this town, oh that the warriors of the king had not yielded to their desire to plunder the goods of the enemy! . . . . Megiddo at the same hour. For the miserable king of Kadesh had gone up together with the miserable king of that town (Megiddo), so that they escaped and went into their town. Then was the king enraged . . . . (17) and his crown gained power over them . . . . Then their horses, their gold and silver chariots, which had been made in the land of the Asebi (Cyprus), were made spoil. They (the enemy) lay kicking in heaps like fishes on the ground. The brave troops of the king counted up their goods. See! they have captured the tent [of the miserable king], in which his son [was]. (18) Then the warriors all at once raised a shout of joy and gave honour to Amen [the lord of Thebes] who had given to his son [the victory]. And the . . . . of the king avouched his power. And they exhibited the spoil, which they had taken, in hands, and in living prisoners, in mares, in chariots, in gold and silver, and [all other things]. Then spake the king : "Thank Amen for the protection which he has afforded [me his beloved son], the (19) sun-god Ra on this day. Concerning all the kings of that people, who have shown themselves as enemies in their inward thoughts, and concerning the fact that the might of Megiddo is the might of a thousand towns, you must make yourselves masters of it " . . . . . . (20) the leaders of the bodyguard [to return] each to his place. And they left that [town and remained] at the rampart which was encompassed with fresh green trees of all kinds of wood in the country. And it was a delight to the king to be within it, as in a fortress, on the east of that town.

'(21) [The king gave the order] to finish building the place and to surround it with thick walls and with thick [battlements], and the king gave it the name of " Men-kheper-Ra, who has taken possession of the plain of the Asiatics ; " and guards were set before the dwelling of the king, and the word was given to them, " Firm courage, firm courage ! Watch, watch ! watch over the life in the king's tent." The king [commanded the hostile inhabitants, that none of them should show himself] (22) outside, behind this wall ; except at the exit in an opposite direction, at the gate of their fortress. All this did the king to this miserable king and to his miserable warriors. It (the record) was set up by day in his name, and in the name . . . . (23) and it was set up on a roll of leather in the temple of Amen on the same day. Then the kings of that land came [together with] their [children ?] to· worship before the king, and to implore breath for their nostrils, because of the strength of his arm, and because of the greatness of his spirit. (24) [And the children of the kings came] before Pharaoh, and presented their gifts of silver, gold, blue stone and green stone, and they brought also wheat and wine in skins, and fruits for the warriors of the king, for every one of the Kiti had taken care to have such provisions for his return home. Then the king graciously pardoned the foreign princes because of . . . . '

There follows a complete list of the spoils, which consist, among other things, of 2,503 captives, cattle, silver, gold, and electrum, ivory and precious stones, cedar-wood and ebony, furniture for tents and houses, costly inlaid work, fine cloth, and armour. The princes of Ruthen and Asshur, the lands of Punt, Cush and Zahi, Ua-ua-t, Cyprus, and the powerful ruler of the Kheta tribes were all forced to pay heavy tribute.[1]

Then the king gave orders to set up the record of the victories which he had gained from the year 23 to the year 32, which coincides with the erection of the memorial table on this temple wall.

Thus has he done. May he live for ever !

The rich tributes and taxes which King Tehuti-mes III. received in what are called the ' halting-places ' on his campaigns, and those which the foreigners, especially the Ethiopians, brought to Egypt in person, were given over to the Theban officials, that they might estimate

[1] For a full account of the spoil carried away, and the tribute imposed upon the conquered peoples, see Birch's translation of the *Statistical* *Tablet of Tehuti-mes III.*, and 'Annals of Thothmes III.,' in *Rec. of Past*, vol. ii. p. 17 *et seq.*

them accurately according to number and weight, and enter them in the account-books of Pharaoh. The tributes of the tribes of the South, of the land of Punt, of the lands of Ruthen and Kefa, occupied the first place in the registers.

If Lepsius's explanation of the Usem-metal as electrum be right, according to a representation in a tomb mentioned below, not less than 36,692 lbs. of it were carried into the treasuries at Thebes under Tehuti-mes III.; that is, a mass of 67 cwts., which, considering the rarity of this precious metal, seems hardly probable. This Usem seems much more likely to have been a mixture of metals, resembling our brass, in which copper formed the principal ingredient.

The tributes of the countries situated directly on the Nile in Upper and Lower Nubia were delivered to the Egyptian governor of the Southern country. In the time of Tehuti-mes III. the 'king's son' Nahi occupied this post, and, according to the inscriptions in the rock-grotto of Ellesîeh,

he filled the king's house with gold, and made joyful the countenance of the king by the products of the lands of the South. The recompense for this is a reward from the lord for Nahi the king's son and the governor of the South.

After his brilliant campaigns on Canaanitish soil, the return of the king to Egypt must have been one grand triumphal procession. The sight of the captive princes, their children, and their subjects, in the train of the young hero; the numberless troops of horses, oxen, goats, and rarer animals—in a word, all the riches of the then known world—could not fail to make a deep impression on the Egyptians, and must have inclined the hearts of all to the young sovereign.

The first thing was to offer homage and thanksgiving to the gods for the victories he had won. The

Theban Amen was first thought of, and his temple-treasury in Apet of the South was filled with princely munificence.   In all quarters of the great city of Thebes new buildings were added to those already existing, and before them were erected great ' gate-towers ' with double wings and obelisks surmounted with copper tops.   The broad surfaces served to receive the records of victory and the catalogue of the foreign nations which had been conquered.   Before returning to Thebes the king took care to found in the northern portion of the land of Ruthen a fortress of unusual strength, which bore the name of Men-kheper-Ra Uaf-shema (i.e. Tehuti-mes III., who has bound the land of the foreigners).   It was situated near the Phœnician cities of Arathu and Zamira, at the foot of Lebanon.

Another inscription, still fairly preserved, gives a full record of the expression of the king's grateful feelings towards Amen.   Directly after his return to Thebes he instituted three feasts of victory in remembrance of his campaigns, in which naturally the national deity had the lion's share of the presents and sacrifices connected with them.   They co-incided with the days of the feasts of Amen, of which, according to the calendar of feasts under Tehuti-mes III., there were eleven.   The calendar just named comprehended in all more than forty feast-days, the list of which is given as follows :—

Eve (called Khet) of the feast of Amen   .   .   . 1 day
Amen's feast-days, which take place every year .   . 11 days
The 4th Pakhons, feast of the accession of Tehuti-mes
III.   .   .   .   . 1 day
Feast of Neheb-hau on the 1st of Tybi   .   .   . 1 day
Feast of the new moon (the 1st) and of the 6th day of
each month   .   .   .   . 24 days

The king dedicated to the god rich presents and sacrificial offerings for all times on the three ' feasts of

victory,' likewise on the great festival ' of the 14th of
Paophi, when the majesty of this glorious god came in
procession, to celebrate the feast of his voyage in the
city of Apet in the southern land of Patoris,' to 'thank
him for the victories over the land of Upper Ruthen.'
By order of the king three cities were assigned to the
domain of this god, to pay yearly to his temple the
taxes laid upon them.

The edifice erected by Tehuti-mes III. to the honour
of the god as a memorial of victory, called the Khu
Mennu, 'splendid building of the hall of pillars,' was
endowed from the booty brought home.   Four obelisks
of immense height were erected, and statues were dedicated to his royal ancestors, while special feasts were
instituted to Horemkhu and Amsu.

The first campaign of the king against the Upper
Ruthen was the most important of all his wars.   Its
history may be seen in a very perfect condition on the
lower story of one of the gate-towers at Karnak, and is
of inestimable importance for a knowledge of ancient
geography and ethnology.[1]

The general superscription, which relates to the
towns of Upper Ruthen, is translated as follows :—

This is the catalogue of the inhabitants of the country of
Upper Ruthen, who were taken prisoners in the hostile town of
Megiddo.   His Majesty took away their children as living prisoners
to the town and fortress of Suhen in Thebes on his victorious
campaign, as his father Amen, who had led him on good paths,
commanded him.

Suhen designated a particular fortified place, situated
on Theban territory and used for the reception of
prisoners.   A second similar catalogue of the same
people, or rather of their towns, is introduced by the
following inscription :—

[1] *Les Listes Géographiques des*   *Palestine, l'Ethiopie, le Pays de*
Pylones de Karnac, comprenant la   *Somâl.* Leipzig, 1875.

These are in their entirety the unknown peoples of the furthest end of Asia, whom his Majesty carried away as living prisoners. [Unknown was their land]; it had never been trodden by the other kings of Egypt, with the exception of his Majesty.

In a third catalogue we find the following words:—

This is the catalogue of the inhabitants of Upper Ruthen, whom his Majesty captured in the hostile town of Megiddo. His Majesty carried away their children as living prisoners to the town of Thebes (*Us*) to fill the house of his father Amen (the Lord) of the town of Thebes on his first victorious campaign, just as his father Amen, who led him in good paths, commanded him.

The value of the catalogue on the pylon at Karnak lies in the indisputable fact, that, more than 300 years before the entrance of the Israelites into the land of Canaan, a great confederacy of tribes of a common race, which the monuments call by the name of Ruthen, existed in Palestine under petty kings, who dwelt in the very same towns and fortresses which, in later times, mostly fell by conquest into the hands of the Jewish immigrants. Among these the king of Kadesh on the Orontes, in the land of the Amorites, played the first part; the kings and their subjects, from the Wady-el-Arish to the land of Naharain, obeyed him as their chief leader. With these were joined the Phœnician Kharu, who dwelt in the country on the sea-coast, called Zahi by the Egyptians, and whose capital was Aradus, as also the Kiti (the Chittim of Holy Scripture), who had taken possession of the island of Cyprus, and in all probability of the sea-coast lying to the north of Phœnicia. The triangle between the three points, Kadesh, Semyra, and Aradus, formed the oft-mentioned theatre of hostile encounters.

The statements on the tablet of victory and in the list of conquered towns are confirmed by another witness.

Amenemheb (an officer who took an active part in the campaign) has described on his tomb his course of life in plain and simple language, according to the style of writing in his day, and he often takes occasion to admire the great deeds of the king, whom he accompanied in the closest attendance on his campaigns.

The following is a literal translation, according to Professor Ebers, of the inscription :—

(1) I served (2) my royal lord on his campaigns in the North and South lands. He wished me to stand by his side. (3) And I fought hand to hand against the people of the (4) land of Negeb (S. Palestine). I carried off three grown-up Aamu as living prisoners.

Then when his Majesty went to the land of Naharain (5) I carried off three grown-up men in hand-to-hand combat. I brought them before his Majesty as living prisoners.

(6) Again I was in a hand-to-hand combat in that campaign against the people of the high plains of Uan (probably the mountainous country on the banks of the Orontes) westward of the land of Khalibu. I made of the (7) Aamu, living prisoners 13 men, 70 live asses, and 13 iron spears inlaid with gold.

(8) Again I fought hand to hand in that campaign against the people of Karikaimesha (Carchemish). I carried away (9) [some inhabitants] as living prisoners. I waded through the water of Naharain (Euphrates), while they were in my hand [without letting them go]. (10) I brought them before my royal lord. Then he rewarded me with a rich reward, namely [. . .].

(11) I admired the brave deeds of King MEN-KHEPER-RA (Tehuti-mes III.), the dispenser of life, against the people of Zor. He had done [. . . (12) against] them. I was a hand-to-hand combatant before the king. I made spoil of a hand. He gave me a golden reward for this, namely [. . .], and (13) two rings of white gold.

And again I admired his valour, while I belonged to his servants. He took (14) Kadesh. I did not remove from the place where he was. I carried off from among the nobles two men as [living prisoners. I brought them] (15) before the royal lord of the land, Tehuti-mes—may he live for ever ! He gave me a golden gift for my valour before all the people, (16) namely, of the purest gold one lion, 2 necklaces, 2 helmets, 2 rings.

And I admired my lord [. . . (17) . . .] in all his appearances, on account of the strength of [his] arm [. . . land . . .]

. . . ha. When it happened another time, (18) I mounted up to the [. . .].

(19) Again I admired his strength against the land of Takhis, which is situated on the shore (?) of Lake Nesru. (20) I fought hand to hand on it before the king. I carried off three men of the Aamu as living prisoners. Then my lord gave me (21) golden rewards of honour : namely, 2 golden collars, 4 rings 2 helmets, a lion, and a slave.

(22) Again [I admired] another extraordinary deed, which the lord of the country performed in the neighbourhood of Ni.[1] He hunted 120 elephants for the sake of their tusks on [his chariot ?] (23) I encountered the greatest among them, which attacked his Majesty. I cut through his trunk. Being still alive [(24) he pursued me]. Then I went into the water, between two rocks. Then my royal lord rewarded me with a golden gift : (25) namely, [. . .], and with three dresses.

Then when the king of Kadesh sent forward a horse (26) with the head of a [. . .], which dashed in among the warriors, then I ran after him (27) on foot, holding my dagger, and ripped up his belly. I cut off its tail and gave (28) it to the king. Praise on the part of the divine one for this. The joy which he bestowed filled my body, and pleasure thrilled through my limbs.

(29) His Majesty caused the bravest of his warriors to go before. The fortress was to be broken into, which the inhabitants of Kadesh had newly erected. I was he (30) who broke into it. I was the leader of all the brave men ; no other did it before me. I went on, I brought back of the nobles (31) two men as living prisoners. My royal lord renewed his thanks to me for this by (32) splendid gifts of every sort. Contentment was with the king.

I achieved these battles while I was a captain. Then [he commanded that] (33) I should be the person to arrange the sails [on his ship. And] I was the first of his suite (34) in the voyage on the river [in honour of Amen] at his splendid festival in Thebes. The inhabitants were full of joy [on that account]. (35) Lo ! the king finished his course of life, after many years, glorified by conquests and by [victory . . . .], (36) and by triumphs, beginning from the 1st year, down to the last day of the month Phamenoth, of the king of Upper and Lower Egypt, (37) MEN-KHEPER-RA TEHUTI-MES, the justified. Then he flew up to heaven, when the disk of the sun went down. The successor of a god joined himself to his parent.

When now the earth became light and the morning (38) broke, the disk of the sun rose, and the heaven grew clear, then was the

---

[1] A town in the land of Naharain often confounded with Nineveh.

king AMEN-HOTEP II. (may he live for ever !) (39) placed in the seat of his father, and he took possession of the throne.   The greatest fulness of strength was his.   For the foreign [inhabitants] (40) of the Red Land (Tesherit) and their chiefs had he subdued.   Appearing like Horus, the son of Isis, he took possession [of Egypt. (41) And the inhabitants of this land] and they who dwell in the land of Kenemti (the Oasis Magna), and all people bowed down before him.   Their gifts were on their backs, (42) [while they] begged [of him] the breath of life.

Then it was that his Majesty looked on me during the festive voyage that he celebrated on the ship, (43) the name of which was 'Kha-em-ua-suten.'   I [conducted the disembarkation] at the splendid festival of joy of the Southern Thebes, in observance of the prescribed order [of the festival].   (44) Then they took me up into the interior of the king's house, and I was made to stand before [the king, and they spake before him], Aa-kheperu-Ra, (45) concerning my merit.   Then I fell down forthwith before his Majesty. And he spake to me thus :

'I know thy worth.   I lay still yet in the cradle as [the child] of the [deceased] lord of the land (46) when thou didst [already] serve my father.   Let an office be granted to thee by my order. Be from this time forth a commander (*Adon*) of the army.   In pursuance of what I have said, watch over the brave troops of the king.'

The commander Mah accomplished all that he had said.

The brave captain had evidently several campaigns in view in his account.   But the first certainly formed the chief part of his own history.   On his return home our hero had the honour of conducting, in his own person, the holy ship of Amen 'on his journey (to Thebes) to his splendid festival,' allusion no doubt to the same festival which Tehuti-mes III. had mentioned in his record of his donations, and which fell on the 14th day of the month Paophi.

An examination of the tablet of victory which relates the campaigns of the king, from the first battle of Megiddo onwards, leads us to the certain conviction, that, from the 23rd to the 40th year of his reign, Tehuti-mes III. undertook fifteen campaigns against the inhabitants of Western Asia.   So far as the fragments

will allow the following is the general summary of
them :—

Year.	Campaign.	
23	I.	Against Ruthen.
24–28	II.–IV.	Against Ruthen.
29	V.	The points of attack were the towns of Tunep and Aradus. The land of Zahi (Phœnicia) was laid waste.
30	VI.	Against Ruthen. The cities of Kadesh, Semyra, and Aradus were laid under contribution.
31	VII.	Against Ruthen as far as Naharain, where two memorial stones were set up at the river. Contributions levied on the towns and lands of Ananruth, Ni, Libanon, Singara, and Kheta. Nubia and Ethiopia deliver their tributes.
32	VIII.	Against Ruthen, for the levying of the war-tax in which the king of Assur is assessed.
34	IX.	Against Ruthen and Zahi. The king of the island of Asebi (Cyprus) appears with his tribute. Nubia and Ethiopia likewise deliver their tributes.
35	X.	Against the land of Zahi.
36	XI.	
37	XII.	
38	XIII.	Zahi brought under tribute; likewise the island of Asebi (Cyprus), and the king of Arrech (Erech ?) Ethiopia and Nubia appear as tributaries.
39	XIV.	Against Ruthen. The Shasu-Arabs and the inhabitants of Zahi laid under contribution.
40	XV.	Against Ruthen.

According to this the hostile towns were summoned
to surrender. If they did so, the inhabitants were
treated as friends, and a moderate war contribution was
imposed ; if not the king proceeded to the attack, put
the inhabitants under tribute, and imposed a heavy
annual tax. Repeated and obstinate rebellion was
punished by the destruction of the towns, the devasta-
tion of the crops and trees, the carrying away of hos-

tages, and increased demands. With regard to the last, it may not appear superfluous to compare the Egyptian accounts of their nature with others transmitted to us by the ancients. According to Professor Movers, they consisted of the following articles, brought from Palestine and Phœnicia : corn, from the land of the Ammonites, the chief supply from Galilee, also from Samaria and Moabitis; Joppa also was rich in it : olive oil, from Judæa and Galilee ; wine, a considerable amount of honey (date-honey and grape-syrup), woollen garments, linen, and fabrics of byssus, the balm of Gilead (gum of the mastich tree), storax (*nekoth*, used as incense) from Phœnicia, Syria, and Palestine, resin (*loth*, the Greek *ledanon*, a third kind of resin), asphalte (*khemar*, much in request for embalming), dates, palm-wine, and date-honey from the date-palm-tree. The Phœnician trade embraced gold, silver, copper, tin, and iron, as well as slaves, who were carried away from Syria and Palestine. The Assyro-Phœnician trade consisted of costly stuffs and magnificent garments, of byssus, coloured embroidery, wool, precious ointments, Aram-wine (the best being from Kalybon and the neighbourhood of Damascus), purple, fine ointments, coral, carbuncles, rubies, and other precious stones. The staple of the trade for these articles was Babylonia. From Arabia were brought gold, precious stones, spices, and sweet-smelling wood.

It seems unlikely that Tehuti-mes III. carried on his campaigns to the South in person. The inscriptions observe an obstinate silence upon this point. The list of names, for the most part of a barbarous sound, which comprehended the lands and peoples of Nubia and Ethiopia, and the catalogue of which in a three-fold repetition was placed like a southern tablet of victory opposite to the northern lists of the nations of

Upper Ruthen, appears rather to be the product of vainglory than of real conquests.

In the two halls situated to the north-west of the Hall of Pillars Mariette-Pasha discovered a succession of wonderful representations, which are clearly copies of similar objects on the Temple at Deir-el-Bahari. I refer to the pictures, so true to nature (that is, in an Egyptian sense), of the new plants and animals acquired during the campaign.

By command of the king, who manifested so strong an inclination for researches in natural history, that four unknown birds gave him greater pleasure than the war contribution of a whole country, an artist was commissioned to depict the new fauna and flora—water-lilies as tall as trees, cactus-like plants, all sorts of trees and shrubs, leaves, flowers, and fruits, melons and pomegranates (the latter are represented in profusion, and seem to have been especially liked by the Egyptians), oxen and calves, among which is a wonderful animal with three horns, herons, sparrow-hawks, geese, and doves. The principal inscription re-marks :—

Here are all sorts of plants and all sorts of flowers from the land of Ta-neter ('Holy Land') — [which] the king [discovered] then, when he went to the land of Ruthen to conquer that land, as his father Amen had commanded him. They are under his feet [from henceforward] until an eternity (of coming) years. The king speaks thus : 'I swear by the Sun, and I call to witness my father Amen, that everything is plain truth ; there is no trace of self-deception in that which has happened to me. What the splendid soil brings forth as its productions, that I have had portrayed (in this picture) in order to offer it to my father Amen, in this great temple of Amen, as a memorial for all times.'

A second shorter inscription is valuable from the date affixed to it, namely :—

In the year 25, under King Tehuti-mes III.—may he live for ever !—these are the plants which the king found in the land of Ruthen.

The first and longer inscription appears to contain an evident misrepresentation of real facts. The historical records of the monuments do not relate one syllable about any expedition of the king to the Holy Land, situated far in the south, at least not before the 25th year of the reign of Tehuti-mes III. ; nor did the way to Ruthen, or Canaan, lie through the Holy Land. The tributes imposed upon the lands of the South were brought every year by the inhabitants to Egypt, without their being compelled to do so by any special campaigns.   There remains as the result only this supposition, that the name of the 'Holy Land' (or more literally the 'Land of God') was applied to the whole of Arabia, so that the king became acquainted with it in his passage through the Arabian territory to Canaan.

The priests of Amen, whose temple and treasuries the king had remembered in the most liberal manner, did not content themselves with perpetuating the victories of this incomparable Pharaoh on the inscribed memorial tablet, for an unknown poet has told in rhythmic words of the glory of the king and the power of Amen.   The monument is now in the Gîzeh Palace.

(1) Come to me (said Amen), rejoice thyself, and admire my glory, | Thou, my son, who honourest me, MEN-KHEPER-RA, ever living. | I shine in the light of the morning sun through thy love. (2) And my heart is enraptured, if thou directest thy noble step to my temple. | My hands sink on (embrace) thy body for the salvation of thy being. Delightful is thy goodness for my holy image. | I stand upright there (3) in my dwelling.

Therefore I will distinguish thee marvellously. I give thee power and victory over all lands. | All people shall feel a terror before thy soul, | And shall fear thee to the utmost ends of the world, to the (4) four pillars of Heaven. | I make thy strength to be great in all bodies, | I make thy war-cry to resound in all the lands of foreign peoples. | Let the kings of the world be all at once in thy grasp.

(5) I stretch out my own hands, | I bind for thee with bands and

gather together for thee | the wandering Nubians by tens of thousands and thousands. | Those who inhabit the North shall be taken prisoners by hundreds of thousands. | (6) I make thy enemies to fall under thy feet. | Smite the hosts of thine enemies. | Thus I commit to thee the earth, in its length and in its breadth. Let the inhabitants of the West and of the East be subject to thee.

(7) Pass through with joyful heart the lands which none have trodden till thy time. | I will be thy leader ; reach them.
Pass through the great ring of water | (8) in the land of Naharain, in full victorious power. | It is my will that the peoples hear thy war-cry, which penetrates into their caverns. | I have taken away from their nostrils the breath of life. | (9) I make thy manly courage to penetrate even to their hearts. | My crown on thy head is a consuming fire : | It goes forth and conquers the false brood of the Kittim. | (10) By its flaming beams the lords among them are turned to ashes. | It cuts off the heads of the Aamu ; they cannot escape. | It strikes to the ground every one who turns his back before its strength.

(11) I make thy victories to go on through all nations. | My royal serpent shines on thy forehead, | And thy enemy is annihilated as far as the horizon. | They come and bear the tribute on their shoulders, | And bow themselves (12) before thy Majesty, | for such is my will. | I make the rebel fall down exhausted near thee, | A burning fire in his heart, and a trembling in his limbs.

(13) I came, and thou smotest the princes of Zahi.
I scatter them under thy feet over all their lands.
I make them behold thy Majesty like the beaming (sun).
Thou shinest in sight of them in my form.

(14) I came, and thou smotest those who dwell in Asia :
Thou madest prisoners the shepherds of Ruthen.
I make them behold thy Majesty in the panoply of thy royal
    dignity,
How thou graspest the weapons on thy war-chariot.

(15) I came, and thou smotest the land of the East :
Thou camest to those who dwell in the Holy Land.
I make them behold thy Majesty like the star Canopus,
Which pours out his light in a fiery glow,
When he disperses the morning dew.

(16) I came, and thou smotest the land of the West :
Kefa (Phœnicia) and Asebi (Cyprus) fear thee.
I make them behold thy Majesty like a young bull.
Full of courage, his horns whetted, he is unapproachable.

(17) I came, and thou smotest the subjects of their lords;
The land of Mathen trembles for fear of thee.
I make them behold thy Majesty like a crocodile,
The terrible one in the water ; he is not to be encountered.

(18) I came, and thou smotest the islanders in the midst of the
great sea : | Thy war-cry is over them.
I make them behold thy Majesty as the avenger,
Who appears (riding) on the back of his victim.

(19) I came, and thou smotest the land of the Thuhen :
The people of the Uthent is under thy power.
I make them behold thy Majesty as a lion with a fierce eye,
Who leaves his den and stalks through their valleys.

(20) I came, and thou smotest the hinder lands :
The circuit of the Great Sea is bound in thy grasp.
I make them behold thy Majesty like the hovering hawk,
Which seizes with his glance whatever pleases him.

(21) I came, and thou smotest the lands in front :
The dwellers upon the sand thou hast fettered alive.
I make them behold thy Majesty like the jackal of the South :
A hidden wanderer, he passes through the land.

(22) I came, and thou smotest the nomad tribes of Nubia,
Even to the land of Shat, which is in thy grasp.
I make them behold thy Majesty like thy pair of brothers,
Whose hands I have united to bless thee.

(23) I make thy two sisters shed on thee health and welfare.
My hands in the height of heaven ward off misfortune :
I protect thee, my beloved son,
The powerful bull, who rose up as king in Thebes,
Whom I have begotten out of [my loins],

(24) TEHUTI-MES, who lives for evermore,
Who has shown all love to my Being.
Thou hast raised my dwelling in long-enduring works,
More numerous and greater than they have ever been.
A great gate [guards against the entrance of the impious].

(25) Thou hast established joyful feasts in favour of Amen.
Greater are thy monuments than those of all former kings.
I gave thee the order to execute them,
And thou hast understood it.
Therefore I place thee on the seat of Horus for never-ending
many years. | Conduct and guide the living generations !

Hymns of praise to the Pharaohs, in the spirit of
this song of victory, were a favourite exercise with the
ancient poets ; our modern languages are powerless to

render the tone which pervades the songs of antiquity. A Homer remains Homer only in his Greek garb.

The foregoing epic by the unknown Theban poet, the similar pæans in honour of the kings Ramses II. and III., the heroic song of the poet Pentaur on the great deeds of Ramses II., during his campaign against the king of Kadesh and his allies, will remain for all times unrivalled specimens of the old Egyptian language in its highest vigour. Only one of these songs, the poem of the priest Pentaur, has as yet undergone an examination worthy of its contents, through the exhaustive researches of the late Viscount E. de Rougé.

The victories of Tehuti-mes III., who during his numerous campaigns brought the countries and cities of Western Asia into his power, to whom were subject Libya and the people of Nubia and Ethiopia, as far as the promontory now called Guardafui, opposite to the south coast of Arabia, had brought to Egypt numberless prisoners of every race, who found their occupation in the public works. It was principally on the great imperial edifices, and among these the temple of Amen, that they were forced to labour, under the superintendence of the overseers (*Rois*), who had to carry out the orders and directions of the king's chief architect. In those days a certain Puam (his name, 'one who has his mouth full of food,' is of Semitic origin) was invested with this high office.

Fate has preserved, on the walls of a sepulchral chamber in the hill of Abd-el-Gûrnah, in the region of the melancholy 'land of the coffin-hill' (Du-neb-ankh), a representation in which the artist has portrayed in lively colours the industry of the prisoners. Far more convincingly than the explanations, written by the side, do these curious drawings themselves enable us to realise the hard work of the unfortunate prisoners.

Some fetch water in jugs from the pond hard by; others knead and cut up the loamy earth; others again, by the help of wooden moulds, make the bricks, or place them in long well-arranged rows to dry, while the more intelligent among them carry out the work of building the walls. The words which are added as a superscription to each occupation inform us that the labourers are 'a captive people which Tehuti-mes III. carried away to build the temple of his father Amen.' They explain that the 'baking of the bricks' is a work 'for the new building of the storehouse of the god Amen of Apet' (the east side of Thebes), and they finally describe, in a detailed manner, the strict super-intendence of the taskmasters over the foreigners in the following words :—

[Here are seen] the captives who were carried away as living prisoners in very great numbers; they work at the building with dexterous fingers; their overseers show themselves in sight; these attend with strictness, obeying the words of the great skilful lord [who prescribes to them] the works, and gives directions to the masters. [They are rewarded] with wine and all kinds of good dishes; they perform their service with a mind full of love for the king; they build for Tehuti-mes III. a Holy of Holies for (the gods). May it be rewarded to him through a number of many endless years! The overseer (*Rois*) speaks thus to the labourers at the building :—' *The stick is in my hand, be not idle.*'

According to the contents of the preceding inscriptions these buildings were connected with the temple of Karnak. The one consisted in the building of a store-house, the other the erection of a Sekhem, or 'most holy place,' which was usually situated in the innermost room of the temples, surrounded on three sides by a row of secluded chambers. In an inscription which covers an entire wall near the most holy place of the Temple of Amen at Apet mention is made of this build-ing, while another wall, much destroyed on the upper

side, gives us information concerning the good deeds of
Tehuti-mes III. for the god Amen at Apet and his
temple there. It relates how the king dedicated to the
temple as a perpetual possession various gifts for the
different yearly feasts. Among these was

a beautiful harp, inlaid with silver and gold, with blue, green,
and other precious stones, that upon it might be sung the praises
of the majesty of the god at all his festivals and under all his
names.

Next is mentioned how Pharaoh had given orders to
construct numerous gates (*sebkhet*), with locks of copper
and dark bronze, to protect the Holy of Holies against
unwarranted intrusion. Statues of the god with the
face of the king were executed by a distinguished
artist, with the added note that

the execution was of such a kind as no one had ever lived to see
in this country since the time of the sun-god Ra.

To this is appended the description of obelisks, in the
erection of which silver, gold, iron, and copper were
not spared, and which now

are reflected in their splendour on the surface of the water, and
fill the land with their light like the stars on the body of the
heavenly goddess Nut.

In like manner the impression produced by the obelisks
of Queen Hatshepsu is described in an inscription on
the base :—

The woman-king Maat-ka Ra, the gold among the kings, has had
(these obelisks) constructed as her memorial for her father, Amen
of Thebes, inasmuch as she erected to him two large obelisks of hard
granite of the South. Their tops are covered with copper from the
best war tributes of all countries. They are seen an endless number
of miles off; it is a flood of shining splendour when the sun rises
between the two.

A statue of the 'successor of Horus,' that is, of the
king, a 'beautiful sacrificial table,' and several altars,
are added to the previous works. 'Many other gifts'

follow, such as a large jar, made of copper, seven cubits high, and 'many kinds of utensils of silver, gold, and iron.'

In his 15th year, on the 27th of Pakhons, the king ordered a completely new establishment of the property of the temple.   Among other things the temple was provided with a number of foreign people from the South and North, among whom were children of the kings of the land of Ruthen (Canaan) and of the southern Khent-hen-nefer.   Gardens and 1,800 acres of arable land in various parts of Upper and Lower Egypt were assigned as permanent property of the temple.   The contributions also in vegetables, wine, birds, beasts, and so forth, were fixed once for all, and the number of the temples of the god ('his favourite abodes') in other districts of the country was carefully designated, and the sacrifices in them were in like manner granted with royal generosity.   In a word :—

The king did more than all his predecessors from the beginning, and proved himself a complete master of sacred knowledge.

The artists in useful works found here their special employment.   Their remarkable works were chiefly gates, the names of which may be read clearly on the spot at the present day.   Of one particular part of the temple it is written :—

The king found it in the form of a brick building, in a very dilapidated condition, being a work of his predecessors.   The king with his own hand performed the solemn laying of the foundation-stone for this monument.

Thus the temple was restored as a new building.

The several 'dwellings of the gods in it (they were called Naos, ναός, by the Greeks) were carved out of monoliths, with new doors of acacia wood.   In these were placed the statues of the gods, as also the statues of his ancestors, the kings of Upper and Lower Egypt.'

After the building had been constructed in a 'position corresponding to the four quarters of heaven,' the great stone gateways were erected.

The first 'had doors of real acacia wood, covered with plates of gold, fastened with black bronze, [copper,] and iron. On these were placed the full name of the king in copper, gold, and black bronze.'

The whole was shut off by a splendid *Bekhen* or winged building (*propylon*) on both sides. Three gates were connected with it; the first bore the name

Gate of Tehuti-mes III.; he glorified the greatness of Amen.

The second was called

Gate of Tehuti-mes III.; lasting is the gratitude of Amen.

The third finally :

'Gate of Tehuti-mes III.; a great spirit is Amen.' 'They were covered with plates of pure copper, and the sacrifices were brought in through them.'

The most important work, both as to position and execution, was the *Khesem*, or *Sekhem* (the Holy of Holies), 'the favourite place of Amen,' built of hard stone of the Red Mountain (at Syene).

Thus the building rose; and then followed the thanksgiving of the priests, which the sequel of the inscription recites in poetic terms :—

'He gives to thee his kingdom. The crowns shall be placed on thy head upon the throne of Horus. The remembrance of thee as king of Egypt shall be lasting. To thee has he given over the united world in peace. All nations bow themselves before thee.'—'We have heard,' say the courtiers, 'of the king's court, bringing welfare. Thou breathest in a pure life. Thy Majesty is set upon the exalted throne. The judgments of the divine one himself are like the words of the sun-god Ra at the beginning of all things.'

The king, flattered by the praise bestowed upon him, insists with pleasure on his services to the god.

This building, which was executed in his temple, shall be a remembrance of my good deeds in his dwelling. I shall remain preserved in the history of the latest times.

The distinguished men of the court did not fail to offer to their new lord the utterance of their admiration in poetic terms, to which the king replied :—

'God Amen is more enraptured with me than with all the kings who have existed in this country since it was founded. I am his son, who loves his Holiness, for that is the same as loving my royal being itself.'—'All nations bow themselves before my spirit. The fear of me is in the heart of the nine foreign nations.'—[God Amen] 'he has poured strength into my hands to extend [the boundaries of Egypt].'

The assumption, that this portion of the inscription relates to the accession of the king as having just taken place, is clearly supported by the fact that the origin of the different throne-names of the king is explained by a sort of paraphrase.

I have already remarked on the reference to the god Tehuti in the name Tehuti-mes. The king testifies this expressly in the words, 'My birth is to be compared to that of the God of Hiser' (a special name of the temple of Tehuti in Hermopolis). Among the new names which were given to him after his accession were *Sam-ta* or *Sam-taui*, 'Uniter of the two worlds.' The reason of this is mentioned by the king himself :—

He (Amen) has united (*sam*) the countries (*taui*) of all the gods in this my name, TEHUTI-MES SAM-TA.

The following paraphrase of the injured inscription may be imagined :—

. . . . in this my (name): LORD OF THE DOUBLE CROWN : AUG-MENTER OF THE EMPIRE LIKE THE SUN IN HEAVEN : He has given me the form of a GOLDEN SPARROW-HAWK ; He has given me HIS MIGHT AND HIS STRENGTH ; I shone gloriously with his CROWNS in this my name, (the third) (38) [GOLDEN SPARROW-HAWK, MIGHTY, STRONG, OF SPLENDID CROWNS . . . .] my crowns. The king's name was written for me alone. He has set up my picture of a sparrow-hawk on the base, he has MADE ME STRONG like a STRONG BULL. He has granted my CORONATION in the interior of THEBES

(39) [(in this my name) (the first) : STRONG BULL CROWNED IN THEBES.]

The king goes on to speak of his sister :—

'What I relate,'—remarks the king,—'is no invention : *she* was astonishing in the sight of men, and a secret for the hearts of the gods who knew it all.   But *she* did not know it, since no one was (for her) except herself.'   He relates further how—'he became comparable to the young Horus (a phrase frequently used by young kings), in the marshy country of Kheb, and how he was obliged to remain in the *town of Buto of the North.*'

There Tehuti-mes III. remained without office or position in the temple of Amen ; for

'It is no fable '—he assures us—'so long as I was a child and a boy, I remained in his temple ; not even as seer of the god did I hold an office.'

A remarkable inscription, the contents of which throw from all sides an unsuspected light on Tehuti-mes and his solitary youth.   He had been banished to the almost inaccessible marsh-country of Buto, in order to remove him from the sight of his subjects, and to destroy all remembrance of him.

The date of the laying of the foundation-stone of a temple is given as follows :—

According to the express order of the king himself, this was set down in writing, concerning the communication orally carried on as to the erection of a memorial-building, on the three sides which bend toward the canal, ... for I (the king) wished to raise a memorial to my father Amen-Ra in Apet, to erect (his) dwelling, which glorifies the horizon, to restore (the temple territory of) Kheft-her-neb-s, the favourite abode of my father from the beginning. I wished to execute this for him, the Theban Amen-Ra, on this territory, of hard stone, and of a gigantic size. But because [the canal was there, which conducts] the water to the shrine of the god Nun, on the arrival of his season, I built him another temple, with a loving heart; and caused him to be brought in thither. What I did for him happened for the first time (i.e. had never been done before). The shrine stands ready in the east of that temple. Then I found that the circuit wall was built of brick, and that the ground was [deeply hollowed out, so that the ground sank in], to give more room for the water to this temple. It had to be cleaned out.

I had the dirt removed and the dams pulled down which were near it. Thus the space was now clear. I caused this site to be built upon, on which the surrounding wall stood, in order to erect on it this memorial-building, desiring to found a splendid temple to [the god Amen of] Apet. It was to be constructed anew. The (official) drawing of (the architect) made the beginning. Never have I placed the like on the monument of any other. I say this in all truth, for *I know every one who knows nothing about me,* and speaks lies. But that which has happened is no feigned invention in place of the truth, nor an intentional deception calculated to bear the appearance of truth. He knows me, whoever agrees with me about this. I gave the order to place cord and pegs in readiness (for laying the foundation-stone) in my presence. The beginning of the day of the new moon was fixed for the festival of the laying of the foundation-stone of this memorial.

In the year 24, on the last day of the month Mekhir, on the festival of the 10th day of Amen's [festival on his splendid feast of the southern Apet ? . . . .] there was a sacrifice offered to the god (at) his great abode. After this I went in, to accompany my father Amen. The god went thither on his feet, to celebrate his beautiful festival. And the Holiness of this god was wonderful to behold. [Then drew near the form] of this god. Pegs and cord were ready. Then his Holiness placed me before him, towards this monument. And I began. Then the Holiness of this god was full of joy at this monument, on account [of my love for him]. Then [the Holiness] of this god went further, and the beautiful feast was celebrated to my lord. Then I came forward, yes I, to complete the business of the laying of the foundation-stone, because . . . . [before] him. He went out, and the work of the first stroke of the hammer for the laying of the foundation-stone was to be performed. Then the Holiness of this divine one wished himself to give the first stroke of the hammer . . . . [to keep out the water] of the inundations of the fields . . . . of the pickaxe. The lines of the fields were drawn . . . . all that he had done. Then was I full of joy, when I saw the great wonder, which my father had done for me . . . . My heart was in a joyful humour at that beautiful procession, to make a beginning of this memorial. There was laid [in the foundation-stone a document] with all the names of the great circle of the gods of Thebes, the gods and the goddesses . . . . And all men rejoiced. After this . . . . of copper was prepared for him.

The memorial-stone just cited was found, Mariette assures us, in a side-room to the north-west of the holy of holies in the temple at Karnak. As the plan of the Sekhem or holy of holies had already been described in the inscription of the 15th year as completely built, there is no alternative but to suppose that Tehuti-mes III., in the 24th year of his reign, built the whole northern wing of the temple, after diverting the canal which was in the way, and removing the temple of the god of the inundation (Nun) connected with it. The improvements made by him in the buildings of the temple, the ruins of which still stand at Karnak, and their union and restoration according to the plans of their original builders—which Mariette has exhibited in all their details to the learned world in his admirable work on Karnak—enable us to recognise at the first glance the lion's share which belongs to the great Tehuti-mes III., among all the royal builders, as founder of several edifices of the temple.

Besides the magnificent temple buildings of Amen Tehuti-mes III. erected the stupendous Hall of Pillars and the chambers and corridors belonging to it on the east, and the series of gigantic gateways with wings on the south. The Hall of Pillars, called Khu-mennu, or 'splendid memorial,' was dedicated not only to the god Amen, but also to the deified rulers, whom Tehuti-mes III. regarded as his legitimate predecessors on the throne, and as the ancestors of his own house. Here, in one of the southern chambers, was found that celebrated wall which is known under the designation of the Table of Kings of Karnak. In this the Pharaoh traces back his pedigree to Sneferu, of the Third Dynasty (of Memphis), and reckons Assa, Pepi, the petty kings of the name of Antef, the famous sovereigns of the Twelfth

Dynasty, and some thirty princes of the Thirteenth, as his illustrious ancestors.

The great wings of the temple have suffered much both from time and man. But the lonely ruins yet enable us to judge of the high perfection of the artistic powers which created such wonderful buildings, and were able by means quite unknown to us to overcome the resistance of the hardest stone. From whatever point of view we look at Karnak, whether it be as an architectural masterpiece or as an example of the artistic history of the nation, we must admit that as a whole its conception is grand, and the execution full of taste and refinement. Among the sculptures which have survived, and are of great historical importance, are the statues of the royal predecessors of Tehuti-mes III.—his grandfather, father, and brother—which stand before one of the southern temple-wings. The first, a ruined colossal torso of reddish siliceous sandstone, represents a Pharaoh seated. An inscription on his girdle designates him as Tehuti-mes I., the father of the king Tehutimes II.

Tehuti-mes II. 'erected this monument as a memorial to his father, and to the Theban Amen-Ra, the heavenly inhabitant of Apet.'

A second inscription contains a new contribution to our knowledge of the destructive anger of Hatshepsu, who mutilated the monument erected by her brother in honour of her own father, until at last Tehuti-mes III. ordered the statue to be re-erected in good condition.

[The lord of the land and] King Tehuti-mes III., the worshipper of the Theban Amen, [restored this monument, which had been mutilated, when he entered] the town Ni (Thebes) of the South country in the year 42, on the 22nd day of the month Tehuti, with the intention that the name of his father Tehuti-mes I. should be preserved.

By the side of her father is the small image of his daughter, the hitherto unknown 'king's daughter and king's wife, the worshipper of her father,' Mut-nefert. A second statue of the same king bears his name on a half-destroyed inscription, which may easily be completed in the following manner :—

This statue was re-erected in good condition in the year [22 of the reign of Tehuti-mes III.]

A similar notice m·v also be read on the statue of Amen-hotep I., the grandfather of Tehuti-mes III. The care shown by this king to honour in every way the memory of his relations presents a strong contrast to Hatshepsu, with whom self-honour and self-glorifi-cation seem to have been the only object. The Hall of Ancestors at Karnak was founded by Tehuti-mes III., in reference to which runs the following inscription :—

Long live King Tehuti-mes III. ! He has built this his monu·ment for his memorial to his father Amen-Ra of Thebes in Apet. To *them* (*sic* in the inscription) this great festive hall was built for the duration of an endless number of years, all new, of splendid clear stone of the mountain of An. It shines brilliantly like the vault of heaven : it is well executed as a work for eternity. The king had given the order that the names of his ancestors should be placed upon it, to make their remembrance bloom afresh, that all their likenesses (?) should be cut out of [. . . .], and that great sacrifices to them should be re-established anew, more than [had been done in the times of earlier kings].

In another hall of the temple at Karnak may be read :—

[Because no one] has provided new stone to cover the building of my father Tehuti-mes I., and because no one has finished the building of my father Tehuti-mes I., and the building of the fore-fathers of the kings of Upper and Lower Egypt, opposite his building, may my name be preserved everlastingly on the building which has been executed for my father Amen to all eternity !

A reproach is here meant against Hatshepsu, because she had so entirely neglected the monuments

of her father and of her ancestors in Apet. The
Stage-Temple of Deir-el-Bahari lay, doubtless, nearer
to her heart than the good old custom of continuing
the buildings at the imperial temple of Apet in honour
of the gods and of her ancestors.

The magnificent building at the foot of the steep
wall of rock which descended by broad steps to the
plain in the direction of the Nile,—the wonderful
structures of many-coloured colonnades and richly
painted wall-surfaces,—must naturally have accorded
better with the mind and taste of a queen who loved
art, than the solemn though stately buildings of the
temple of Amen, the design of which had long been
marked out by an old ground-plan of former kings.

Whatever other architectural works Tehuti-mes III.
caused to be erected on the territory of the 'great
city' (Ni-aa) we must pass over in silence, since only
ruins and fragments prove their existence, and no
important historical records are connected with them.

In conclusion, we will only remark upon the restoration of an older temple, which had fallen into
decay, and which lay in ruins on the land of the
town of Medînet Habû. Tehuti-mes erected an entirely
new temple structure, of hard stone, round the newly
completed Khesem, or 'holy of holies.'

He restored it as a lasting building, when he had found that
it was hastening to decay,

as a text on the spot says of it. Another inscription at
the same place says :—

He erected this memorial-building to his father, the king of the
gods, Amen-Ra, for he caused this great house of the gods to be
constructed on the site of the ruins of the west district. It is the
splendid seat of Amen (built) by Tehuti-mes.

Victorious wars during the long and fortunate
reign of a Pharaoh always enabled him to execute

numerous buildings and works of art, which adorned the temples in the chief cities. For the mass of the captives were employed on buildings, and their painful existence was thus turned to the best account. Under the government of Tehuti-mes III. the land, from its furthest southern boundary to the coast of the Mediterranean, soon had to boast of a whole world of monuments, ruins of which remain to this day.

It is difficult to say how far south the Egyptian boundary extended during this king's reign. The inscriptions commonly designate by the general expression *Ap-ta* or *Up-ta*, that is, 'horn, point of the land,' the furthest southern boundary for the time being; while other inscriptions designate the region on the south frontier as Kali, and as the country of Karu. These names have been supposed to refer to the Galla tribes, but are more probably connected with the old name Koloë, which, according to Ptolemy, was situated in 4° 15' of north latitude.

In these regions all monumental history is naturally silent. The works of Tehuti-mes III. first appear sixteen degrees further north, in the lower Nubian country, from the frontier fortress of Semneh as far as the island of Elephantiné, opposite to the present town of Aswân. The king erected the temple of Semneh in honour of the Nubian-Libyan god Didun, and in memory of his great ancestor Usertsen III. An earlier structure had been erected here; but the dedicatory inscription, dated in the 2nd year, on the 7th Paoni, states emphatically that the ancient work in brick had entirely fallen into decay.

On the opposite side of the river, in the district of Kûmmeh, the king founded another temple, the stones of which were quarried in the mountains of Shaa-t, and dedicated it to the god of the Cataracts, Khnem.

In the neighbourhood of the Second Cataract, on
the western shore of the river, opposite to the large
village of Wady-Halfah, I discovered, in the winter of
1875, the last remains of a temple, on which the
traces of a long dedicatory inscription can be clearly
made out. The temple lay close upon the river, and
steps led up to it. This was the great temple of
Buhan, the Boôn of the Greek writers.

In the rock-tombs of Ellesîeh, not far distant from
the very ancient fortress of Ibrîm Primis, there is
still to be seen a memorial of the king and of Nahi, the
governor of the South. The inscriptions mention 'the
assessments of the peoples of the South, in gold, ebony,
and ivory,' which Nahi was bound to forward to his
royal master.

Wonderfully beautiful to behold must have been
the temple which rose on the island of Elephantiné, a
building of Tehuti-mes III. and his successors down to
the third Amen-hotep, in honour of the god of the
country, Khnem. As recently as the beginning of this
century the draughtsmen of the French expedition
were able to transfer it to paper in its full completeness, but at the present day scarcely more than two or
three stones are left on the old site.[1]

Science has all the more deeply to deplore such a
loss, since even these few last traces of it have proved
of great service. One of the inscribed blocks, a fragment of a once complete catalogue of the yearly feasts
and their days, has given us the important information,
that in the reign of Tehuti-mes III. the rising of the star
Sothis, which took place on July 20, and marked the
beginning of the fixed Egyptian year, happened on the
28th day of the month Epiphi.

This date, in consequence of its connection with the

[1] It was destroyed in 1822 by the Turkish governor of Aswân.

movement of the stars according to fixed laws—independently of every calculation on the basis of the unsettled chronological tables of a later tradition—will serve for all times as the sole foundation for determining the regnal years of Tehuti-mes III.

At the crocodile city of Ombos, where the inhabitants worshipped the god Sebek;—at Latopolis (now Esneh), with a temple to the god Khnem;—at Eileithyia (now El-Kab), where a temple to Nekheb, the goddess of the South, was much frequented;—at Hermonthis, with its temple to the warrior god of light, Mentu, the ancient tutelar lord of Thebes;—the last ruins which have survived the ravages of time point to former temples, which by their inscriptions boast of Tehuti-mes III. as their builder.

The same king erected a sanctuary to Ptah on the north side of the great temple at Karnak, and raised monuments to the glory of Osiris at Abydos. This city was the chief seat of the worship of that divinity, and was one of his burial-places. Pious pilgrims of those days were wont to visit the mysterious place of the tomb of Osiris, and distinguished Egyptians of Patoris longed to be buried in the neighbourhood of the King of the West and of the dead. The kings (as can be proved from the Eleventh Dynasty onwards) strove to show their peculiar veneration of the great god by buildings and presents to his temple. At the general feast of the dead on the 18th and 19th of Tehuti, as well as at the special feasts of Osiris on the 30th of Tybi and the 3rd of Phamenoth, the holy Seshem bark of the god was borne through the field of U-pek, as the sacred soil around the town was called, and was launched on the lake with mystic ceremonies, and the festival of ‘the voyage’ of the god was celebrated in the stillness of night.

This will explain the following inscription. It is the reply of Tehuti-mes III. to the priests who had gone to the king with the petition that he would generously remember the temple and god of Abydos, for, as its words declare—

then the king gave to the keeper of his seal the command to set about the work, and to assemble [workmen in numbers and to deliver] all provision for his servants : and each one of his temple-artists knew the plan and was skilful in his own cunning. No one withdrew himself from that which was given him to do [namely, to build] a monument to his father [Osiris], with the purpose of dedicating it for a long duration, and of restoring in good work the sublime mystery, which no one can see, no one can explain, for no one knows his form ; and to prepare beautiful head-rests, and frames for lying down, of silver, gold, blue stone, black metal, and all kinds of precious stones.

The king now speaks in person :—

I dedicated to him (all sorts of sacred utensils), cymbals, chaplets, incense-burners, dishes, for the sacrifices. Nothing was wanting, nothing was left to wish for. I also filled the holy bark with pure acacia-wood from the ridge of the step-mountain. Its fore part and its hinder part were of pure copper. I dedicated to it a lake, so that the god might make his voyage in it to the festival of the land of U-pek. Also, I gave him . . . . for the goddess (Dud), the mother of the great circle of the gods of Abydos.

These were each named as follows :

  Khnem, the lord of Herur, in Abydos ;
  Khnem, the lord of Elephantiné, in Abydos ;
  Tehuti, the great master of Hermopolis Magna ;
  Hur, of Letopolis ;
  Hur, the avenger of his father ;
  Ap-Maten of the South ;
  Ap-Maten of the North.

The secret place, which contained their splendid forms, and the poles with which to carry them, were of pure copper; they were more beautifully wrought than they had ever been before, more glorious than what is created in heaven, more secret than the place of the abyss, more [invisible] than what is in the ocean. All this I have had executed for my father Osiris, corresponding to the greatness of my love for him, more than for all the other gods, with the intention that my name may endure, and that my remembrance may continue to live in the house of my father Osiris, the prince of the western land, the lord of Abydos, in all times and to eternity.

—[I call upon] you, ye holy fathers of this house, ye priests and singers, ye assistants and artists, as you are there, offer the sacrificial gifts, with the tables for offerings [in your hand, lay] them down on the top of the altar. Preserve my memorial, honour my name, and remember my royal dignity. Strengthen my name in the mouths of your servants, and let my remembrance be ever preserved by your children, because I, the king, am a benefactor to him who is at one with me, and a severe lord against him who remembers my name in word only. What I have done in this land, that is in your knowledge. It does not appear a fable in your sight, and no man can dispute it. I have caused monuments to be raised to the gods, I have embellished their sanctuaries, that they may last to posterity, I have kept up their temples, I have restored again what was fallen down, and have taken care for that which was erected in former times.

I teach the priests what is their duty: I turn away the ignorant man from his ignorance. I have accomplished more than all the other kings before me. The gods are full of delight in my time, and their temples celebrate feasts of joy. I have placed the boundaries of the land of Egypt at the horizon. I gave protection to those who were in trouble, and smote those who did evil against them. I placed Egypt at the head of all nations, because its inhabitants are at one with me in the worship of Amen.

In the time of Tehuti-mes III., and his son Amen-hotep II., Neb-aiu filled the office of high-priest of the temple of Osiris at Abydos. The summary of his life has been handed down to us on stone, which was probably set up by command of the king, in the tomb of the deceased :—

(1) A gracious expression of the gratitude of King TEHUTI-MES III.—may he live for ever !—(2) for the high-priest of Osiris, NEB-AIU. Thus he speaks :—I was charged with various work in (3) the temple of Osiris, of silver, gold, blue stone, green stone, and other precious stones. (4) All this was kept under my key and seal. He (the king) recognised my skill. (5) It was his intention that I should render the most valuable service to my lord, as guardian of the temple of his father. (6) I attained thereby to high honour, and gained therefrom gracious royal reward. Then I was called (7) to his gold-house. My place was in the midst,

among his great court officials.   (8) I had to look great in the grand hall (of the king), and anointed myself with hair oil.   (9) A garland rested on my neck, just as the king does for him whom he will reward.

Again (10) a gracious reward fell to my share from his son, AMEN-HOTEP II.—may he live long!—He committed to me the statue of his father, King (11) Tehuti-mes III.—may he live for ever !—and his (own) statue of indestructible duration, in the temple of Osiris ; moreover, a possession of the temple, consisting of (12) arable land and garden land, each marked out, and remaining according to its position for (the service of) the image of the king, (13) Amen-hotep II., the friend of Osiris of Abydos, the prince of the West.

Four lines further on he concludes with the words :—

(17) Call upon those, who live there (18) on the earth, on the priests and singers, on the assistants and holy fathers of this temple, and on the artists of the sanctuary, even as they are ready : —(19) Let each who approaches this stone read what is upon it. Sing praise and bear love to Osiris, the king of Eternity. (20) Add also the invocation : ' May the north wind be pleasant for the nose of the high-priest of Osiris, NEB-AIU the conqueror by help of Osiris.'

A stone record at Denderah tells us that

King Tehuti-mes III. has caused this building to be erected in memory of his mother, the goddess Hathor, the Lady of An (Denderah), the Eye of the Sun, the heavenly queen of the gods. The ground-plan was found in the city of An, in archaic drawing on a leather roll of the time of the Hor-shesu : it was found in the interior of a brick wall on the south side of the temple in the reign of King Pepi.

In spite of the brevity of these words it appears to be certain that first Pepi, and after him Tehuti-mes, undertook to re-build the ancient temple of the goddess. In the time of the Ptolemies it had again fallen into decay, and those princes re-built it from the very foundations.   Inscriptions which have been found in the tombs at Abusîr and Saqqarah place it beyond doubt that Tehuti-mes III. erected a temple to the god

Ptah of Memphis, and dedicated priests and gifts to his service.

Likewise the old city of On, situated near the present hamlet of Matarîeh, was not forgotten by the king. He beautified and finished the ancient temple of the Sun, and surrounded it with a stone wall in the 47th year of his reign. By a remarkable combination of fortune, the name of the architect who carried out the building of the temple of Tehuti-mes in Heliopolis has been preserved. He was

the hereditary lord and first governor in Memphis, the true author of the order of the feasts (for the temple); the architect in the city of the Sun, the chief superintendent of all offices in Upper and Lower Egypt, the head architect of the king, the chief field-officer of the lord of the land, the steward in the royal palace of Tehuti-mes III., AMEN-EM-ANT;

and he was, we ought to add, the forefather of Amen-em-ant, who was chief architect to Ramses II.

Among the obelisks which King Tehuti-mes III. raised before the great wings of the temple, and which are so frequently mentioned in the inscriptions, the gigantic stone at Constantinople occupies a distinguished place. Inscriptions beautifully carved on the four sides of this huge block of rose-coloured granite contain the king's names and the praise of his deeds. One of these is important from an historical point of view :—

King Tehuti-mes III. passed through the whole extent of the land of Naharain as a victorious conqueror at the head of his army. —He placed his boundary at the horn of the world, and at the hinder (i.e. northern) water-lands of Naharain.

One of the obelisks at Karnak was taken to Rome, and set up in the Lateran square. On it are the two following inscriptions :—

I. 'The king has raised these immense obelisks to Amen in the forecourt of the house of the god on the soil of Apet, as the first beginning of the erection of immense obelisks in Thebes.'

II. 'The king has erected to him these immense obelisks *at the upper (first) door of the temple* of Apet, over against the city of Thebes.'

This boastful but untruthful statement that Tehuti-mes III. was the first who cut obelisks vividly reminds us of the assurance of the Roman, C. Plinius Secundus, that 'Mesphres (Tehuti-mes III.), who reigned in the city of the Sun, first introduced this practice in consequence of a dream.'

That he did, in fact, adorn the city of the Sun with obelisks is proved by the existence of the two commonly known as 'Cleopatra's needles,' one of which is at Alexandria, the other on the Thames Embankment. On one side of the latter is this inscription :—

King Tehuti-mes has caused this monument to be executed in remembrance of his father, the god Horemkhu (i.e. Helios, the Sun). He has had two great obelisks set up to him with a point of gilt copper.

On the other sides the names of the city of On and its Phœnix-temple (Ha-Bennu) are expressly mentioned.

Several inscriptions in the peninsula of Sinai mention Tehuti-mes III. The double representation of the year 16 at Sarbut-el-Hadim refers to the time of the united reign of Queen Hatshepsu and her brother, while another rock-inscription of the year 25 mentions the king as ruling alone. The last is intended to certify the presence of a distinguished Egyptian named Ki, belonging to the court of the king, who betook himself to the valleys of Sinai, in the service of his master, 'at the head of his warriors,' to bring to the king an immense quantity of green stone from the 'land of the gods.'

After a long reign of 53 years and 11 months Tehuti-mes III. passed away, leaving behind him an undying fame as the conqueror and governor of the then known world. His rule extended from the southernmost lands of inner Africa to the limits of the Naharain, all of which brought their treasures to him as annual tribute; hence arose those magnificent temples, statues, and obelisks bearing his name which are to be found throughout the land of Egypt.

CHRONOLOGICAL SUMMARY OF THE REIGN OF TEHUTI-MES III.

Year.	Events.
1	On 4th Pakhons : Accession.
	(NOTE.—*All the ensuing regnal years date from this day of the month.*)
2	On 2nd Payni : Restoration of the temple-fortress at Semneh.
3-4	. . . .
5	On 1st Tehuti : Date of a papyrus at Turin.
6-14	. . . .
15	On 1st Mekhir : Beginning of the erection of Hatshepsu's obelisk.
	On 27th Pakhons : Institution of the sacrifices to Amen.
16	On 30th Mesori : Completion of the obelisk, after seven months' work.
	Inscription at Sarbut-el-Hadim of the time of the joint reign of Tehuti-mes III. and his sister Hatshepsu.
17-21	. . . .
	(Tehuti-mes III. reigning alone.)
22	Restoration of the statues of Amen-hotep I. and Tehuti-mes I.
	On x Pharmuthi : Opening of his First Campaign.
23	On 4th Pakhons : Tehuti-mes III. in Gaza.
	On 21st Pakhons : New Moon.
24	On 30th Mekhir : Laying of the foundation-stone of a temple at Thebes.
25	Inscription at Sarbut-el-Hadim.
	The King's Second Campaign.
26-28	Campaigns III., IV.
29	Campaign V.
30-40	Campaigns VI.–XV.: one in each year.
41	. . . .
42	On 22nd Tehuti : Restoration of the statue of Tehuti-mes I.

Year.	Events.
43–46	. . . .
47	The Temple at Heliopolis enclosed by a wall.
48–50	. . . .
51	On 5th Payni: Dedicatory Inscription at Ellesîeh.
52, 53	. . . .
54	On 30th Phamenoth: Death of Tehuti-mes III., after a reign of 53 years, 11 months, and 1 day.

THE GREAT GATEWAY OF AN EGYPTIAN TEMPLE.

a is the gateway (*pylon*); *b b*, the flanking towers, called the towers of the pylon.

The whole edifice is often called *Pylon, Propylon,* and, in the plural, *Propyla* and *Propylæa,* and by Dr. Brugsch *Thurinthoren,* 'tower-gates.' The simple inversion of Brugsch's term gives us the very suitable name of 'gate-tower,' 'gate-towers,' which is already in familiar use with reference to castle-architecture.

Aa-kheperu-Ra.	Men-kheperu-Ra.	Maat-neb-Ra.	Nefer-kheperu-Ra-ua-en-Ra.	Ser-kheperu-Ra.
Amen-hotep II.	Tehuti-mes IV.	Amen-hotep III.	Amen-hotep IV., or Khu-n-aten.	Hor-em-heb (Horus).

CHAPTER IX.

DYNASTY XVIII.—*continued*.

AMEN-HOTEP II.—TEHUTI-MES IV.—AMEN-HOTEP III.

AA-KHEPERU-RA AMEN-HOTEP II. 1566 B.C. CIR.

IT is a difficult and dangerous position to be the son of a great father, for even the good has always an enemy in the better. Thus it is that Amen-hotep II. shines with diminished lustre, although he also, according to the testimony of the monuments, strove to do useful work for his country and his people.

According to the narrative of the warrior Amen-emheb, the contemporary of Tehuti-mes III. and his son, this last king, before his accession to the throne, on the 1st of Pharmuthi, in the 54th year of the reign of his father, had already distinguished himself in battles, which he had been obliged to undertake against the inhabitants of the 'Red Land,' the mountainous desert valleys between the Nile and the Red Sea, inhabited by the Bedâwi. Amen-hotep, when heir-apparent, had succeeded in overcoming these people, and forcing their chiefs into submission to the king of Egypt; for, as the inscription remarks, 'he possessed the fullest abundance of might.'

After the death of Tehuti-mes III., a spirit of independence seems to have risen up in Asia. Again did those leagues of the towns spring up, which sought by united action to withdraw themselves from subjection to Egypt. A monument, now very much injured, at one of the southern wings of the temple of Amen, in Apet, contains an exact record of the campaign which Amen-hotep II. undertook for the punishment of the rebels in the Upper Ruthen, and it ended victoriously. Seven kings were taken prisoners in the town of Thakhis, and were brought to Egypt.

From what this great historical inscription enables us to learn, in spite of its lacunæ, the war against Asia was this time a war of vengeance in the fullest sense of the word. The several towns were visited in succession, thoroughly pillaged, and the booty registered. All that can be made out as to the names of the towns is confined to the fortresses of Arinath, Ni, and Akerith, and to the mention of the king of Naharain. The campaign, therefore, extended pretty far towards the north. The town of Ni, one of the most important in the land of Naharain, appears to have surrendered to the Egyptians without any serious defence, for

the Asiatics, inhabitants of this town, both men and women, stood above on their walls to glorify the king.

Akerith, on the contrary, proved obstinate, for

it had formed the resolution of driving out the garrison of Pharaoh.

The booty which the king brought back to Egypt cannot have been insignificant. Among the prisoners (of whom the king had taken 18, together with 19 oxen, with his own hand) there were, besides others, 640 merchants, who were carried away, together with their servants. The Nubian temple at Amada, which the king furnished and decorated, has a memorial tablet let into the wall of one of the inner chambers,

which was intended to recall to memory these victories, and to serve as a warning to the inhabitants of
the South.   It also informs us in detail as to the fate of
the kings taken captive in Western Asia.

The actual inscription begins with the date—year 3,
month Epiphi, day 15, and the names of Pharaoh—and
is as follows :—

'At that time' (in the year and on the day of the month
which we have mentioned) 'the king beautified the temple [which
had been executed by] his father, King Tehuti-mes III., in memory
of all his forefathers and the gods.   It was built of stone, as a
lasting work, with a protecting wall of brick around : the doors
were of the best acacia wood, from the ridge of the Table Mountain,
the gates of durable stone, all done with the intention of perpetuating in this temple the great name of his father, the son of the
Sun, Tehuti-mes III.   The king Amen-hotep II. celebrated the
festival of the laying of the foundation-stone in honour of all his
forefathers, dedicating to him (*sic*) a massive gate-tower (propylon)
of hard stone, in front of the protecting wall of this splendid dwelling of the god ; a corridor, with columns of hard stone, as a lasting
work ; many sacrificial vessels, and utensils of silver and iron,
stands, altars, an iron kettle, fire-holders, dishes, and censers (?).
After that, the king had this memorial stone set up and placed in
the temple, at the place where the statue of the king stands, and
engraved upon it in writing the great name of King Amen-hotep II.
in the house of his forefathers and of the gods, after he had returned from the land of Upper Ruthen, where he had conquered all
his opponents, in order to extend the boundaries of Egypt in his
first campaign.
    'The king returned home with his heart full of gratitude
towards his father Amen.   He had with his own hand struck
down seven kings with his battle-axe, who were in the territory of
the land of Thakhis.   They lay there bound on the forepart of the
royal ship, the name of which was "Ship of Amen-hotep II., the
upholder of the land."   Six of these enemies were hung up outside
on the walls of Thebes, their hands likewise.   Then the other enemy
was carried up the river to Nubia, and was hung up on the wall of
the city of Napata, to make evident for all time the victories of the
king among all the peoples of the land of the negroes ; since he had
taken possession of the nations of the South, and had made captive
the nations of the North as far as the ends of the whole extent of
the earth on which the sun rises [and sets] without finding any op-

position, according to the command of his father, the sun-god Ra, the Theban Amen.

'Thus has he done, the king Amen-hotep II.   May he have for his portion a stable, bright, and healthy life, and joy of heart to-day and for ever ! '

The statements of the memorial stone of Amada are confirmed by the inscriptions, bearing the name of Amen-hotep II., which cover one of the southern pro-pylæa of the great temple of Amen at Karnak, and by pictures with explanatory inscriptions in the sepulchral chambers of the king's contemporaries.   In a tomb at Abd-el-Gûrnah, among other pictures, the king appears as a little child, on the lap of his deceased nurse.   The heads and backs of five negroes and of four Asiatics serve him for a footstool.   In another representation he is seated in the attire of a Pharaoh on his throne, the lower part of which is ornamented with the names of the nations and countries which were regarded at that time as subjects of the empire.   The inscriptions name the land of the South, the inhabitants of the Oases, the land of the North, the Arabian Shasu, the Marmaridae (Thuhen), the Nubian nomad tribes, the Asiatic husbandmen, Naharain, Phœnicia, the Cilician coast, and Upper Ruthen—in short, neither more nor less than what Tehuti-mes III. had already conquered.

The building and extension of the temples in Egypt and Nubia were continued by Amen-hotep II. as far as his means allowed.   The temples at Amada and Kûmmeh (opposite to Semneh) bear witness to this. If the newly added works within the precincts of the great temple at Apet may be taken as a measure of the power of the government for the time being, Amen-hotep II. hardly kept up to the usual standard of his predecessors.   The temple erected by him is in no way remarkable either for the beauty of its building, for the

artistic perfection of the sculptures, or for the importance of its inscriptions.

Among this king's contemporaries must be mentioned his son Khamus, and the governor of the
nations of the South, a certain Usati ; as also the high-
priest of the goddess Nekheb at Eileithyiapolis, who,
as such, bore the distinguished title of a 'first king's
son of Nekheb.'

MEN-KHEPERU-RA TEHUTI-MES IV., SURNAMED KHA-KHAU.
B.C. 1533 CIR.

On his memorial tombstone, now in the British
Museum, a certain Amenhotep, servant and soldier of
Tehuti-mes IV., relates that

he accompanied the king on his campaigns against the people of
the South and of the North, travelling with his Majesty from the
river land of Naharain to the Karu.

We have here a proof that Tehuti-mes IV. sought
to uphold the greatness and power of the empire by
conflicts against unruly tribes and subjects. The furthest limits of his campaigns, Naharain in the North,
Karu in the South, allow us to form an idea of the
unusual activity of the king.   Unfortunately no document, giving us information on the details of these
campaigns, has survived the ravages of time.   A fragment in the temple of Amen at Apet mentions 'the
first campaign of the king against the land of Kheta.'
A rock inscription on the little island of Konosso, in
the midst of the boiling floods of the First Cataract of
the Nile, bearing as an introduction the date of the
year 7, the month Athyr, day 8, relates how the
Libyan deities had given the nomad tribes of the Annu
and all lands into the power of the king.   Another
inscription, in the temple at Amada, gives the same
sort of general information about victories of the king

over the land of Cush and the nomad tribes, and
contains, as its only other statement of importance, the
assurance that they had been so completely beaten
'that they were no longer (for the time) to be found.'

Tehuti-mes IV. attributed his elevation to the throne
to the active protection and aid of the god Horemkhu,
if the account of the interference of the divine hand
is not merely a cloak for the intrigues of the king to
reach his high aim.

The account referred to is contained in the inscription on the memorial stone, fourteen feet high, which is
placed directly before the breast of the Sphinx of Gîzeh.

At the time when Tehuti-mes IV. ascended the
throne, the space before the pyramids was an already
abandoned burial-ground, the king of which, Osiris-
Sekar, was invoked in prayer by the pilgrims to this
spot, in his temple, close to the figure of the Sphinx.
At the foot of the hill on which the pyramids are
raised ran the ancient 'sacred road,' which, turning in
an easterly direction, led to the western boundary of
the Heliopolitan nome over the hill of Babylon, in the
neighbourhood of the present Old Cairo, opposite
to Gîzeh.   The whole long road was accounted an
enchanted region, and the Egyptians may have whis-
pered many ghost-stories of apparitions and strange ad-
ventures which happened in this neighbourhood.   Behind the Sphinx and the pyramids began the valley of
the desert, 'the land of gazelles,' in which huntsmen
were wont to follow their sport, not without resting a
short time under the shadow of the Sphinx.   The Sphinx
himself represented the image of the god Hor-em-khu,
that is 'Horus on the horizon' (the Harmachis of
the Greeks), who was also called by the names
of Kheper, Ra, and Tmu.   Hor-em-khu seems to
have represented the Sun in his mid-day strength. <small>Hor-
em-khu.</small>

The inscription on the Sphinx runs thus :—

Once upon a time he practised a spear-throwing for his pleasure on the territory of the Memphite nome, in its southern and northern extent, where he slung brazen bolts at the target, and hunted lions in the valley of the gazelles. He rode in his two-horsed chariot, and his horses were swifter than the wind. With him were two of his attendants. No man knew them.

Then was the hour in which he granted rest to his servants. He took advantage of it to present to Horemkhu, near the (temple of) Sekar in the city of the dead, and to the goddess Rannu, an offering of the seeds of the flowers on the heights [and to pray to the great mother Isis, the lady of] the north wall and the lady of the south wall, and to Sekhet of Xoïs, and to Set. For a great enchantment rests on this place from the beginning of time, as far as the districts of the lords of Babylon, the sacred road of the gods to the western horizon of On-Heliopolis, because the form of the Sphinx is a likeness of Kheper-Ra, the very great god who abides at this place, the greatest of all spirits, the most venerable being who rests upon it. To him the inhabitants of Memphis and of all towns in his district raise their hands to pray before his countenance, and to offer him rich sacrifices.

On one of these days it happened, when the king's son Tehutimes had arrived on his journey about the time of mid-day, and had stretched himself to rest in the shade of this great god, that sleep overtook him.

He dreamt in his slumber at the moment when the sun was at the zenith, and it seemed to him as though this great god spoke to him with his own mouth, just as a father speaks to his son, addressing him thus :—

'Behold me, look at me, thou, my son Tehuti-mes. I am thy father Horemkhu, Kheper, Ra, Tmu. The kingdom shall be given to thee . . . . and thou shalt wear the white crown and the red crown on the throne of the earth-god Seb, the youngest (among the gods). The world shall be thine in its length and in its breadth, as far as the light of the eye of the lord of the universe shines. Plenty and riches shall be thine ; the best from the interior of the land, and rich tributes from all nations ; long years shall be granted thee as thy term of life. My countenance is gracious towards thee, and my heart clings to thee ; [I will give thee] the best of all things.

'The sand of the district in which I have my existence has covered me up. Promise me that thou wilt do what I wish in my heart ; then shall I know whether thou art my son, my helper. Go forward : let me be united to thee. I am . . . .'

After this [Tehuti-mes awoke, and he repeated all these speeches,] and he understood (the meaning) of the words of the god and laid them up in his heart, speaking thus with himself : 'I see how the dwellers in the temple of the city honour this god with sacrificial gifts [without thinking of freeing from sand the work of King] Khaf-Ra, the statue which was made to Tmu-Horemkhu.' . . . . . .

Although the following lines of the inscription are destroyed, it is not difficult to guess the conclusion of the narrative.

When Tehuti-mes IV. came to the throne, he thought it incumbent on him to keep the promise made to Horemkhu; he cleared away the sand and set free the gigantic body of the Sphinx. After this had been done, in the very first days of his reign, the memorial stone dated the nineteenth of Athyr was erected on the spot. Tehuti-mes IV. certainly took some precautions to keep off the sand from the Sphinx, the total length of which is 190 feet. It lay there exposed, with its face turned towards the east, hiding a temple between its out-stretched paws, the end wall of which formed the great memorial stone of the king. Thus it was still seen by visitors in Greek times, to judge from the inscriptions found on the spot ('Corpus Inscript. Græc.,' No. 4699 et seq.) As nowadays the Bedâwi of the neighbouring village of Kafr guide the 'Franks' to the pyramid-field of Gîzeh, so here in times past the inhabitants of the village of Busiris (city of Osiris) undertook the business of guides to what were even then marvels of antiquity.

Tehuti-mes IV. was succeeded by his son, the cele-brated king

MAAT-NEB-RA AMEN-HOTEP III., B.C. 1500 CIR.,

whose mother's name was Mut-em-ua, which means 'mother in the boat.' We are led to the conclusion that he was a worthy successor of the great Tehuti-mes from the number and beauty of the monuments he has

left behind him. Among the scarabæi which were
used as amulets against evil magic, and as memorials
of great kings of the country, there are not a few which
bear the name of this Pharaoh on the under side.
Among these are some of considerable size, covered
with inscriptions, which state the extent of the empire
under Amen-hotep III. On the north the river-land of
Naharain, as on the south the land of the negroes,
formed its boundaries; so that its ancient extent was
preserved. Amen-hotep III. appears to have been an
ardent sportsman, and to have been trained in the
school of his father; at least the memorials often inform
us how he speared with his own hand 210 lions on his
hunting expeditions in the land of Naharain.

Tehuti-mes III., in repeated campaigns, had con-
fronted the Canaanitish nations to the north of his
great empire: Amen-hotep III. chose as his battle-fields
the hot countries of Ethiopia, and there gained laurels
such as scarcely any other king of Egyptian history
could boast. A rock inscription of the fifth year of his
reign, on the old road which led from Syene to the
island of Philæ, affords trustworthy evidence that
Amen-hotep III. directed his first campaign against the
inhabitants of the southern regions. More than thirty-
three centuries have passed over this tablet, and have
destroyed or half effaced some of the letters of the
inscription; but this much at any rate we may learn
from it: that

'in the 5th year the king returned home. He had triumphed
in this year on his first campaign over the miserable land of Cush.
He placed his boundary wherever it pleased him.' And then—

'The king ordered that the remembrance of his victories should
be preserved on this memorial stone. No other king has done the
like, except him, the brave Pharaoh, who trusts in his strength,
namely, Amen-hotep III.'

Under the inscription there are written in the well-known turreted cartouches the names of six vanquished nations of the South, among them the land of Cush.

The campaigns of the king were continued up the Nile, above the great cataracts, their aim being the subjugation and plunder of hostile tribes. A tablet at Semneh gives some details which are not without importance for our knowledge of the land of Nubia in those days. 'The king was in the land of Abeha, which begins at the frontier garrison of Beki, and which ends at the frontier garrison of Tari, a length of 52 miles.' The land of Abeha, the oft-mentioned Behan (the Greek Boôn, the modern Semneh), lay to the south and north of the ancient fortress of Semneh, for Beki was evidently to the north. Here follows the complete catalogue of captured negroes :—

Catalogue of the prisoners whom the king captured in the land of Abeha :—

Living negroes	.	.	.	.	150 heads
Boys	.	.	.	.	110 ,,
Negresses	.	.	.	.	250 ,,
Old negroes	.	.	.	.	55 ,,
Their children	.	.	.	.	175 ,,
		Total of living heads	.		740
	Number of hands (cut off)	.	.		312

The total number, together with the living heads, 1,052

In these campaigns the kings remained true to the old custom of cutting off the hands of the slain foes, and bringing them home as tokens of victory. In no other way could the number of slain enemies be more manifestly proved to the Egyptians who stayed peaceably at home.

Amen-hotep III. must have penetrated far into the Sûdan, since the catalogue of his victories over the conquered negro races mentions names the majority of which are not found again; and in the temple of Soleb also, high up in Nubia, new names appear both of people and countries. It may be presumed that the wars against the gold country of Cush opened new sources of wealth to the empire of the Pharaohs, for the 'king's sons of Cush' executed their office as governors of the countries of the South, and collected the tributes which were regularly levied every year. There flourished in the reign of this sovereign the following governors: Merimes, Hi, Amenhotep, and Tehutimes. Their names are found on different rocks in the island of Biggeh, in the midst of the First Cataract—a remembrance of their visits to the temple of Osiris on the island of Philæ.

The Amenhotep mentioned above occupied a distinguished place not only at the court, but also in the favour of Pharaoh. He was one of the wise men of his time, a prudent and experienced vassal whom the king honoured with a richly decorated statue, now in the Gîzeh Palace. He was the son of Hapu, and of the lady A-tu, and recounts his life in the following words:—

King Amen-hotep III., the eldest son of the god Horemkhu, rewarded me and appointed me as royal under-chief-secretary. I was introduced to the knowledge of the holy book, and beheld the glories of the god Tehuti. I was enlightened concerning all their mysteries, and all parts of them were laid before me. I was made master of the art of speaking, in all its bearings.

And a second time my lord the king Amen-hotep III. rewarded me, and delivered over to me all the people, and the names of them were placed under my inspection as the royal upper-chief-secretary of the young men. I arranged the families of my lord, and reckoned the number of the tributes by hundreds of thousands. I gave satisfaction to the people in their place of taxing, to the old man, as to the son who loves him.

I laid the taxes on the houses according to their number. I separated the warriors and their houses. I increased the subjects by the best of the prisoners whom the king had made on the theatre of war. I gave due weight to all their privileges. . . . . .

I placed warriors at the openings of the roads (of the country), to keep back the inhabitants of foreign lands in their place, for they were settled round about the two sides of (Egypt), and opened wide their eyes to make inroads upon the districts of the Nemausha (inhabitants of the desert).

I acted thus at the lake of the Sethroïtic mouth of the Nile. The same was closed by my war captains, chosen for the crews of the king's ships. I was their leader, and they were obedient to my orders.

I was a Ro-hir (lieutenant—an *epitropos* of Greek times) at the head of the bravest warriors, to smite the nations of Nubia and Asia. The thoughts of my lord were continually my care. I penetrated what his mouth concealed, and comprehended his thoughts towards all natives and all foreigners who were about him. It was I also who brought the prisoners from the victories of the king. I was their overseer. I did according to that which he spoke, and took my measures according to that which he prescribed to me. I found that this proved best for the later time.

And for the third time, my lord, the son, Amen-hotep III., the prince of Thebes, rewarded me. He is the Sun-god himself— may there be accorded to him numerous returns of the thirty years' feast without end !—My lord promoted me to be chief architect. I immortalised the name of the king, and no one has done the like of me in my works, reckoning from earlier times. For him was created the mountain of sandstone ; he is indeed the heir of the god Tmu. I acted according to what seemed best in my estimation, in causing to be made *two portrait-statues of noble hard stone* in this his great building. It is like heaven. No king who has possessed the land has done the like, since the time of the reign of the Sun-god Ra. Thus I executed these works of art, his statues— (they were astonishing for their breadth, lofty in their perpendicular height : their completed form made the gate-tower look small ; 40 cubits was their measure)—in the splendid sandstone mountain, on its two sides, that of Ra and that of Tmu (that is, the east and west sides).

I caused eight ships to be built ; they (the statues) were carried down (the river) and placed in his lofty building. They will last as long as the heaven (above them).

I declare to you who shall come hither after us, that of the people who were assembled for the building every one was under me. They were full of ardour ; their heart was moved with joy ; they raised a shout and praised the gracious god. Their landing in Thebes was a joyful event. The monuments were raised in their future place.

These statues of the king, nearly sixty-nine feet high, mentioned in the inscription are the two celebrated statues of Memnon. The measure assigned to them agrees with modern measurements, and so does the description of their size, which must indeed have made the gate-tower behind them look small. Amen-hotep III. was, like his grandfather Tehuti-mes III., a zealous worshipper of the gods, especially of Amen, and erected temples in honour of the divinities in all parts of the land. In the very first years of his reign, new quarries were opened in the limestone hills of Mokattam, opposite to Memphis. In the neighbourhood of the village of Tûrah new rock-chambers were opened in the king's first and second year, and two inscriptions were set up to transmit the fact to posterity.

The king gave orders to open new chambers, in order to quarry the beautiful white stone of An, for the building of a lasting temple, after the king had learnt that the rock-chambers, which are situated in Ro-fu, had long since threatened to fall in.

These were made anew by the king.

The buildings at Karnak were not only carried on, but a new temple also was erected. Before the west front of the temple specially dedicated to Amen, so far as it had then been completed, Amen-hotep III. raised an immense gate-tower (propylon), erected a new temple to the same divinity on the north, and built another on the south to the divine mother Mut, near the holy temple-lake of Asher. He then united all the temples at Karnak with his new temple of Amen at Luqsor by an avenue (dromos) of sphinxes.

According to the inscriptions on the stone lintels at Luqsor, this building, close to the river, was erected in honour of Amen after the victorious campaigns against the negroes of Cush, when 'the king had mounted his horse to reach the extremest boundaries of the negroes, and had scattered the people of Cush, and laid waste their country.' Pharaoh himself 'gave instructions and directions, for he understood how to direct and guide the architects.'

'He had executed great monuments in Apet of the South, wonderful works never seen before, and he had increased and extended Apet of the South.'

On the further bank of the river, in a northeasterly direction from the temple of Tehuti-mes III. at Medînet Habû, a new temple to Amen was raised by the king's command. Its site is indicated from a great distance by the gigantic sitting statues of the king.

Although little more than the foundation walls of the temple itself are left, yet a memorial tablet, which now lies thrown down on its back, bears witness to the size and importance of the original building. The inscription which adorns its surface is in the form of a dialogue between the king and the god. Amen-hotep III. speaks thus :—

Come then, Amen-Ra, lord of Thebes in Apet, behold thy abode, which is prepared for thee on the great place of Us (Thebes). Its splendour rests on the western part (of the city). Thou passest through the heaven to unite thyself with it (the abode, i.e. the temple). And thou risest on the horizon (in the east) ; then is it enlightened by the golden beams of thy countenance. Its front turns towards the east, &c.

Thy glory dwells in it. I have not let it want for excellent works of durable beautiful white stone. I have filled it with monuments in my [name], from the mountain of admirable stone. Those who behold them in their place are full of great joy on account of their size.

And likewise I built a court on the rocky soil, of alabaster, rose granite, and black stone. Also I made a double gate-tower, labouring to dedicate the most beautiful thing to my divine father. Statues of the gods are to be seen everywhere. They are carved in all their [parts ?]. A great statue was made, of gold and all kinds of beautiful precious stones. I gave directions to execute what pleased thee well, to unite thee with its beautiful dwelling-places,

and so on until the god interrupts him with the assurance :—

I hear what thou sayest. I have beheld thy memorial, I thy father who have created thy glory, &c.

Excellent is that which thou hast prepared for me ; never has the like been done for me.

The temple, now in ruins, was carried out according to the plan of the chief architect Amenhotep, the same who boasts of having designed the two gigantic statues of the king in front of it. They represent Amenhotep III. sitting, with his wife Thi and his mother Mut-em-ua standing at his feet. They are at a distance of twenty-two feet from one another. The northern one is that which the Greeks and Romans celebrated in poetry and prose by the name of the *Vocal Statue of Memnon*. Its legs are covered with the inscriptions of Greek, Roman, Phœnician, and Egyptian travellers, written to assure the reader that they had really visited the place, or that they had heard the musical tones of Memnon at the rising of the sun.

In the year 27 B.C., in consequence of an earth-quake, part of the statue was thrown to the ground, and from that time until the reign of Septimius Severus, who restored the figure, the tourists of antiquity scribbled their names upon it, accompanied by remarks pertinent or impertinent. Alexander von Humboldt affirmed that split or cracked rocks, or stone walls, after cooling during the night, emit at sunrise, as soon as the stone becomes warmed, a prolonged ringing (or tinkling) note. The sudden change of temperature creates quick currents of air, which press through the crevices of the rock, and produce that peculiar melancholy singing tone.

The historical legend of the Memnon is thus seen to be a very modern story, of which the old Egyptians knew nothing.

In its place the narrative of Pausanias appears as the correct one, according to which the statue belonged to a man of the country, by name Phamenoph—that is, Amenhotep (Paus. i. 42). It was no easy task that the architect set himself to perform when he conceived the idea of raising colossal statues in his master's honour, for it was not only necessary to hew out the stone from the quarries and work it, but also it had to be conveyed down the Nile to its proper position. He was obliged to build eight ships, in order to carry the burthen of these gigantic statues. Even in our highly cultivated age, with all its inventions and machines, the shipment and erection of the statues of Memnon remain an insoluble riddle. Verily Amenhotep must have been a clever and ingenious man.

He came of an ancient and noble stock. His father, Hapu, surnamed Amenhotep, was a son of Khamus, a contemporary of the Tehuti-mes III. who belonged to the priestly family, of which we have spoken previously (p. 198), the eldest sons of which bore the title of honour of 'king's sons.' His wisdom and his sayings were remembered even in the times of the Ptolemies.

Amenhotep the wise, with the surname of Hui, had himself founded a temple behind the sanctuary of his king, Amen-hotep III., not far from the road to the tombs of the king's daughters and the royal ladies. The district bore the appellation of Kak, and hence the newly founded temple was called Ha-Kak, 'the temple of Kak.' A remarkable memorial stone records ;—

(1) The year 11, on the 6th day of the month Khoiakh, in the reign of King Amen-hotep III.

On this day the king was in the temple of Kak (2) of the hereditary lord and royal secretary, Amenhotep. There were brought before him the governor of the town, Amenhotep, the treasurer, Meriptah, and the royal secretary of the garrison. These words were spoken to them in the presence (3) of the king: Good luck to you! You have understood the orders which have been given for the administration of the temple of Kak of the hereditary lord Amenhotep, called Hui, son of Hapu, whose virtues are well known; (4) that his temple of Kak should remain secure to his sons and daughters for all time, from son to son, from heir to heir, and that they should never take away the same, because it (the temple) is founded by Amen-Ra, the king of the gods in his time on the earth. (5) Being king in eternity, it is he who protects the dead. Those chiefs of the garrison and secretaries of the garrison who come after me, who shall find that the temple of Kak is hastening to destruction, together with (6) the man-servants and maid-servants who are on the flower-knob of my staff, and that people are taken from them; they shall give up the whole place to Pharaoh, together with the whole administration. His body will be satisfied. If he, however, (7) [allows] them to be taken away, so that he does not fulfil their intention, he shall incur the judgment of the Theban god Amen, who will not allow that such should enjoy their dignities as royal secretaries of the garrison, which they have received through him (?); (8) but he will deliver them over to the fire of Sutekh in the day of his wrath, and his serpent-diadem will spit out flames of fire on their head, annihilating their limbs; it will consume their bodies. They shall become like the hellish snake Apophis on the morning of the new year; they shall be overwhelmed in the great flood. (9) He will hide their corpses, and they shall not receive the reward of righteousness; they shall not partake of the feasts of the blessed; the water from the spring of the river shall not refresh them; it shall not come to pass that their posterity should sit in their place. Their wives shall be brought to shame, (10) and their eyes shall see it; the great shall not enter their house, so long as they live on earth. They shall not enter nor be brought into the house of Pharaoh. They shall not hear the words of the king in the hour of joyfulness. (11) They shall be cut down . . . . . . in the day of battle, and they shall be called a serpent brood. Their bodies shall languish away. They shall starve, wanting bread, and their bodies shall languish and die. The governor, the treasurer, the guardian of the temple, the steward

of the corn, (12) the high-priests, the holy fathers, and the priests
of Amen, to whom these words shall be read over, which are
composed with regard to the temple of Kak of the hereditary lord
and royal secretary Amenhotep, son of Hapu, if they should not be
protectors (13) of his temple of Kak ; may these words smite
them, them the first of all.   But if they prove themselves protectors of the temple of Kak, including also the man-servants and
maid-servants that are on the flower-knob of my staff, all the best
prosperity will attend them.   Amen-Ra, the king of the gods, will
reward them with a happy life.   Your end [the beginning and part
of line 14 is missing] king of your land (15) like his end.   Your
claims to honour upon honour shall be doubled.   You shall receive
son after son, heir after heir, who shall be sent on employments,
whom the king of [your] land will reward ; your [. . . . .].   Your
bodies (16) shall rest in the under-world of Amenti, after a course
of life of 110 years.   The sacrificial gifts shall be multiplied to you,
(and so forth) . . . . . .

(17) With regard to the captains of the town watchmen, who
belong to the nome, and (with regard) to the governor of the
West country, namely, the quarter of the town called Kheft-her-
neb-s, who do not join my staff for that day, including my festival
on every month, these words shall smite them, and they shall do
penance for it (18) with their bodies.   But if they obey all the
words which are contained in this order, by following (my) will,
they shall not be deserted, they shall remain good and righteous,
(19) they shall be buried in the graves of the dead full of years and
old age.   In explanation : with regard to the governor of the West
country, he enters into the number of my own servants from this
day forth.

The temple, whose maintenance was assured by
royal command, fell into decay, and was not restored
till under the Ptolemies.   It was dedicated to Amen
and Hathor as the tutelar deities ; and the wise
Amenhotep, surnamed Hui, the son of Hapu, received
in the bas-reliefs his place of honour among the
deities of the place.   What the wise god of learning,
Im-hotep, the son of Ptah, was for Memphis, Amen-
hotep was henceforth for the Thebans down to the
latest times, and Deir-el-Medîneh (as the Arabs of our
day call the spot) was a place of pilgrimage for the
mourning visitors to the Theban Necropolis.

The temple on the island of Elephantiné, which Amen-hotep III. finished and adorned, has been mentioned;[1] also the temple at Soleb, in which the king dedicated 'to his own image on earth' a place of worship and prayer.   A special shrine called 'The temple-garrison of Kha-m-maat,' with a propylon and krio-sphinxes[2] before it, and surrounded by walls and battlements, was founded by the king, far to the south, at the foot of Mount Barkal; and there are traces of the architectural activity of Amen-hotep at El-Kab and in Nubia.   The king also lavished gifts in a royal manner upon the temples, the priests, and his court officials and subjects.   Amen especially had no cause to complain of the niggard hand of his beloved son.   The following is a record of his gifts to the temple at Karnak alone.   No less than 4,820 lbs. of blue stone, 3,623 lbs. of khenti, innumerable masses of gold, silver, and copper, and even a great number of wild lions, appear as his gifts to the temple, not to mention the increased sacrifices and alms.

The thirtieth year of his reign, the festive completion of the first thirty years' jubilee, seems to have been especially propitious for the country.   In the sepulchral chamber of the noble hereditary lord Khamhat may be seen

Pharaoh, on his exalted throne, receiving the catalogues of tributes from the South and North.

Then follows

the reading over of the catalogues of the tributes of the thirtieth year before the king, according to the taxing of the full Nile on the festival of the thirtieth year.   The king [receives the tributes] from the overseers of the houses of Pharaoh, together with the [taxes of the hostile nations], from the South and from the North, and from this miserable land of Cush to the region of the river-land Naharain.

[1] See p. 165.   [2] Ram-headed sphinxes.

The people greet and congratulate the king, some lying prostrate, others bowing before him and stretching out their hands to him in the attitude of worship, and to the faithful subjects, who have punctually paid their taxes in the holy thirtieth year, the customary necklaces (answering to our 'orders') are handed by the courtiers.

Much more might still be related concerning Amenhotep III. and his contemporaries, for the monuments of his time are eloquent, and divulge much.   Here is one statement imprinted with a dark pencil on the two sides of an old potsherd :—

Let a report be made of all thefts which the workpeople of Nekhuemmut have committed. They smuggled themselves into the house ; they stole the . . . and spilt the oil ; they opened the cornchest which contained spelt, and stole the lead at the mouth of the fountain. They went into the bake-house (?) and stole the provision of stale bread, and spilt the lamp-oil,—*on the 13th day of the month Epiphi, on the coronation-day of King Amen-hotep.*

As if such a theft had not been enough, the back of the potsherd continues, in the same strain :—

They went into the store-room and stole three long loaves ; eight ornaments . . . . . . they drew (or rather, they sucked) the beer from the skin which lay on the water, while I was in the house of my father. Will my lord cause that [justice be done] me ?

And all this happened on the coronation-day of Pharaoh, the date of which would otherwise, without this little potsherd, have remained probably for ever unknown to us.

Amen-hotep III. must have reigned more than thirty-five years. The two rock-inscriptions at Sarbut-el-Hadim, in the peninsula of Sinai, bear witness to the fact that in the month Mekhir of the thirty-sixth year of his reign a courtier fulfilled a commission of the king, in connection with the ob-

taining of the ' green stone' called mafkat, while an
inscription in the sandstone quarries of Silsilis dates
from the 1st of Pakhons of the previous year, 35.

A peculiar fate seems to have presided over the
king's nuptial relations; he did not seek his queen
among the fair princesses of his house, but, following
a strong inclination of his heart, chose for his wife
Thi, the daughter of Jua and Thua, who were not
even of Egyptian origin, though their nationality is
unknown.

Amen-hotep III. left behind him several children,
some of whose names are preserved by the monuments.   We give the following, as determined by
Lepsius: his sons Amen-hotep and Tehuti-mes, and
his daughters Isis, Hent-mi-heb, and Set-Amen.   The
last-named was the wife of one of the following
kings.

[In 1888 a number of cuneiform tablets were
found at Tell-el-Amarna in the tomb of a 'royal
scribe' of Amen-hotep III. and IV.   From these we
learn the history of Queen Thi.   It appears that she
was the daughter of Tushratta, king of Mitanni
(possibly Mesopotamia); that Amen-hotep III., when on
a hunting expedition in that country, met the princess,
fell in love with her, and in due course made her
his queen.   Thi went away to her new home accompanied by 317 of her principal ladies.   Doubtless it
was from his Semitic mother that Khu-n-aten learnt
the worship of the sun's disk.]

CHAPTER X.

DYNASTY XVIII.—continued.

THE HERETIC KINGS.

WHEN his royal father died, the throne was ascended by

NEFER-KHEPERU-RA-UA-EN-RA, AMEN-HOTEP IV.,

1466 B.C. CIR.,

' the long-lived prince of Thebes,' or, according to the new name he afterwards adopted, KHU-N-ATEN.

The descent of this king, as the son of Thi, from a house which was not Egyptian, precluded him, according to the existing prescriptions regarding the succession, from any lawful claim to the throne. His deceased father had, by his mis-alliance, passed over the hereditary princesses of the royal race; and the son of the unfortunate marriage had to pay the penalty of his father's fault. In the eyes of the priestly corporation of the imperial temple at Thebes, who jealously watched over the letter of the law regarding the succession to the throne, the young king was an unlawful ruler, whose buildings in honour of the great Amen of Thebes could not mollify the excited feelings of the holy fathers and their dependents. To increase existing difficulties, a circumstance was added, which was alone sufficient to cause the excommunication of the new ruler. This was the aversion of Amen-hotep IV. to the worship of

Amen, and of his fellow-gods, as it had been faithfully handed down to the heirs of the throne from
age to age, by law and teaching and education. In the
house of his mother Thi, the daughter of the foreigner,
beloved by his father, and hated by the priests,
the young prince had willingly received the teaching
about the one God of Light; and what the mouth
of his mother had earnestly impressed upon his
childish mind in tender youth became a firm faith
when he arrived at man's estate.

The king was so little prepared to renounce the
new 'doctrine,' that he designated himself within the
royal cartouche itself as 'a high-priest of Horemkhu'
and 'a friend of the sun's disk,' Mi-aten. Such a
heresy appeared at once a thing unheard of; and
open hate soon took the place of the aversion which
had existed from the first. It was also the great misfortune of the king that his personal appearance was
most unprepossessing. Angry blood was thus roused
on both sides; and, to give public expression to his
hatred against the priests of Amen, the king issued
the command to obliterate the names of Amen and
of his wife Mut from the monuments of his royal
ancestors.

The disaffection of the priests and the people had
now reached its highest point, and open rebellion broke
out against the heretic king, who now assumed the new
name of Khu-n-aten, that is, 'splendour of the sun's
disk.'

Under the conviction that he could no longer remain
in the city of Amen, the king determined to found a
new capital at a place in Middle Egypt, which at this
day bears the name of Tell-el-Amarna.

Artists, overseers, and workmen were called together,
and erected, according to the plans of the king, a

splendid temple of hard stone, in honour of the Sun-God Aten, composed of many buildings, with open courts, in which fire-altars were set up.   The plan of the great building was new, with little of the Egyptian character, and arranged in a peculiar manner.   The dwelling also of the king and of the queen Nefer-it Thi, and the abodes for her children—seven young princesses, Mi-aten, Mak-aten, Ankh-nes-aten, Neferu-aten, Ta-shera, Neferu-Ra, Sotep-en-Ra, and Bek-aten—and for his sister-in-law, Net'em-mut, were executed in great splendour near the temple of the Sun, and suitable buildings were added to those already mentioned, for the use of the court and its servants.

The city was richly adorned with monuments, traces of which, in spite of their later wholesale destruction, are clearly enough preserved in the heaps of *débris*. The most important works of art were made of granite, which the king obtained from the quarries of Syene. The office of architect there was held by an Egyptian named Bek, a son of 'Men, and of the lady Ri-n-an.' Men, a son of Hor-amu, had already served in his office under Amen-hotep III., as 'overseer of the givers of life in the red mountain,' and as 'overseer of the sculptors from life for the grand monuments of the king.'

The works of Bek (the third in this generation of artists) for the new city of the Sun are most clearly proved by the following inscription on a rock near Aswân, in which Bek bears the title of

an overseer of the works at the red mountain, an artist and teacher of the king himself, an overseer of the sculptors from life at the grand monuments of the king for the temple of the sun's disk in the city of Khu-aten.

The tombstone of the artist Bek was put up for sale some years ago in the open market-place at Cairo.   It

is half a mètre, or about 19·7 inches high. Inside a
niche are seen two little standing images of a man and
a woman. The inscription runs :—

(On the right hand)—' A royal sacrifice to Horemkhu, the Sun's
disk, who enlightens the land ; that he may vouchsafe to accept the
customary offerings of the dead on the altar of the living sun's disk,
in favour of the overseer of the sculptors from life, and of his wife,
the lady Ta-her.'

(On the left)—' A royal offering to the living Sun's disk, which
enlightens the world by its benefactions, in order that it may
vouchsafe a complete good life, united with the reward of honour,
joy of heart, and a beautiful old age, in favour of the artist of the
king, the sculptor of the lord of the land, the follower of the divine
benefactor, Bek.'

'The inhaling of the holy incense, the receiving of the unction in
favour of the artist of the king, the overseer of the sculptors, Bek :
The inhaling of the fragrance of the incense in favour of the overseer of the works of the lord of the land, Bek :

' That *thy soul may appear, that thy body may live, that thy foot
may march out to all places,* in favour of the artist of the king, and
overseer of the sculptors, Bek :

' That " *he may grant me to drink wine and milk,*" and that " *the
king may receive the sacrifice of the dead,*" in favour of the lady
Ta-her.'

The phrases marked by italics are the beginnings
of very ancient prayers for the dead, which were frequently used in the offerings for the dead, and were
also quoted as titles at the commencement of similar
inscriptions.

The genealogical tree of this family of artists comes
out as follows :—

Hor-amu
|
Men=Ri-n-an* (under Amen-hotep III.)
|
Bek=Taher* (under Amen-hotep IV.)

Another master, who did not hold such a high office
as Bek, has not been passed over, as a promoter of his

* As in previous genealogies, the names of women are distinguished by *.

art, in the decorations of the tombs at Tell-el-Amarna. He there exhibits himself in the very act of giving the last strokes of the chisel to a statue of the princess Bek-en-aten, which is just finished. This person is 'the overseer of the sculptors of the queen Thi, by name Putha.' Under his supervision two artists are carving, the one a head, the other an arm, from life. And, in fact, if we are to believe the representations we have mentioned in the tombs behind Tell-el-Amarna, the temple of the Sun was almost overladen with the pictures of the king, his wife, and his daughters.

Near the quarry of Aswân, which furnished the artist with rose and black granite, lay the cliffs of Silsilis, on each side of the river, from which the hard brown sandstone was obtained for the works of architecture and sculpture, under the rule of Khu-n-aten.

The building of the new city was now finished. In the midst, not far from the Nile, on the eastern side of the river, stood the great temple of the Sun. In the background towards the east rises a steep mountain, while on the north and south of the city, like an encompassing wall, stand two ranges of hills, reaching almost to the Nile, and leaving only narrow outlets towards the east, to the right and left of the eastern chain of mountains.

The dignity of Chief Prophet in the temple of the Sun-god was bestowed upon a faithful servant of the king, named Meri-Ra, which means 'dear to the Sun.' He bore the title of honour of 'chief seer of the disk of the Sun in the temple of the Sun of the city of Khu-aten.' In the presence of the king he was solemnly invested with his high dignity. Pharaoh spoke to him on this occasion the following words :—

Here am I present to promote thee to be chief seer of the disk of the Sun, in the temple of the Sun of the city of Khu-aten. Be

thou such, according to thy wish, for thou wast my servant, who
wast obedient to the (new) teaching.   Besides thee, none has done
this.   My heart is full of contentment because of this ; therefore I
give thee this office, saying, Eat of the nourishment of Pharaoh thy
lord in the temple of the Sun.

The king then called his treasurer before him, and
spoke to him thus :—

Thou treasurer of the chamber of silver and gold !   Reward the
chief seer of the disk of the Sun in the city of Khu-aten.   Place a
golden necklace round his neck, and join it behind ; place gold at
at his feet ; for he was obedient to the (new) teaching of Pharaoh
in everything that has been spoken in relation to these beautiful
places, which Pharaoh caused to be erected in the chamber of the
obelisk in the temple of the Sun, of the disk of the Sun in the city
of Khu-aten.   The altar of the disk of the Sun is filled with all
good things, with much corn and spelt.

As the chief official who was set over the king's
house, there lived at the court of Pharaoh a certain
Aahmes, who also had the superintendence of the
store-houses of the temple.   Next to Meri-Ra, he was
one of the most zealous adherents of the new teaching.
His prayer to the Sun, which is preserved to us among
the sepulchral inscriptions at Tell-el-Amarna, confirms
this :—

Beautiful is thy setting, thou Sun's disk of life, thou lord of
lords, and king of the worlds.   When thou unitest thyself with
the heaven at thy setting, mortals rejoice before thy countenance,
and give honour to him who has created them, and pray before
him who has formed them, before the glance of thy son, who loves
thee, the king Khu-n-aten.   The whole land of Egypt and all
peoples repeat all thy names at thy rising, to magnify thy rising in
like manner as thy setting.   Thou, O God, who art in truth the
living one, standest before the two eyes.   Thou art he who
createst what never was, who formest everything that is in the
universe.   We also have come into being through the word of thy
mouth.

Give me favour before the king every day ; let there not be
wanting to me a good burial after attaining old age in the territory of Khu-n-aten, when I shall have finished my course of life
peaceably.

I am a servant of the divine benefactor (the king); I accompany him to all places where he loves to stay. I am a companion at his feet. For he raised me to greatness when I was yet a child, till [the day of my] honours in good fortune. The servant of the prince rejoices, and is in a festive disposition every day.

The queen was deeply penetrated with the new faith, which appeared to contemporaries in the light of an open heresy. In an old hymn still extant she thus addresses the rising sun :—

Thou disk of the Sun, thou living god! there is none other beside thee! Thou givest health to the eye through thy beams, Creator of all beings. Thou goest up on the eastern horizon of heaven, to dispense life to all which thou hast created ; to man, four-footed beasts, birds, and all manner of creeping things on the earth, where they live. Thus they behold thee, and they go to sleep when thou settest.

Grant to thy son, who loves thee, life in truth, to the lord of the land, Khu-n-aten, that he may live united with thee in eternity.

As for her, his wife, the queen Nefer-it-Thi—may she live for evermore and eternally by his side, well pleasing to thee : she admires what thou hast created day by day.

He (the king) rejoices at the sight of thy benefits. Grant him a long existence as king of the land.

The mother also of the king, the widow of Amenhotep III., honoured the city and the temple of the Sun by a visit. She arrived at Khu-aten with a great retinue. The king, in company with his wife, himself conducted her into the new temple. The inscription explains the picture that remains to us of this scene in the following terms :—'Introduction of the queen-mother Thi to behold her sun-shadow.'

According to the still extant wall-pictures in the sepulchral chambers of the hills behind the town, Khu-n-aten enjoyed a very happy family life. Surrounded by his daughters and wife, who often, from a high balcony, threw down all kinds of presents to the crowd which stood below, the mother holding on her lap the little Ankh-nes-aten, he reached a state of the highest enjoyment, and found in the love of his family, and the devout adoration of his god, indemnification for the loss of the attachment of the 'holy fathers' and of a great part of the people. His mother Thi also shared this domestic happiness. Her suite used to accompany her, and especially her steward and treasurer, the controller of the women's apartment, Hia.

King Khu-n-aten gave a remarkable expression to his love for his relations in three identical rock-sculptures with inscriptions, which remain on the steep cliff near the city of Khu-aten, but are barely within reach of the eye. The king and queen are seen in the upper compartment, raising their hands in an attitude of prayer to the god of light, whose disk hovers over their heads, each ray terminating in a hand dispensing life. Two daughters, Meri-aten and Mak-aten, accompany their royal parents. The date of the 6th year, in the month Pharmuthi, the 13th day, gives to the whole a fixed historical epoch.

Underneath are the following words—omitting the long titles of honour of the king or the queen :—

On this day was the king in Khu-aten, in a tent of byssus. And the king—life, prosperity, and health to him !—changed Khu-aten, which was its name, into Pa-aten-haru (that is, 'the city of the delight of the Sun's disk'). And the king appeared riding in the golden court-chariot, like the disk of the Sun, when it rises and sheds over the land its pleasant gifts, and he took the road that ends in Khu-aten, from the first time when the king had discovered it, to found it (the city) as a memorial to the disk of the Sun, according as the sun-god king, who dispenses life eternally and for ever, had signified to him to found a memorial within it.

A proper and complete sacrifice was offered on that day in the [temple of the sun] at Khu-aten, to the Sun's disk of the living god, who received the thanks of the love of the royal counterpart, the Pharaoh Khu-n-aten. Thereupon the king went up the river, and went up in his chariot before his father, the sun-god king, towards the mountain to the south-east of the city of Khu-aten.

The beams of the Sun's disk shone over him in a pure life, so as to make his body young every day.

Thereupon King Khu-n-aten swore an oath by his father thus : 'Sweet love fills my heart for the queen, for her young children. Grant a great age to the Queen Nefer-it-Thi in long years ; may she keep the hand of Pharaoh ! Grant a great age to the royal daughter Meri-aten, and to the royal daughter Mak-aten, and to their children ; may they keep the hand of the queen, their mother, eternally and for ever !

'What I swear is a true avowal of that which my heart says to me. Never is there falsehood in what I say.'

With regard to the southern memorial tablet, [of the] four [memorial tablets] on the east of the city of Khu-aten, let this be the memorial tablet which I will have set up in the place which I have chosen for it in the south, for ever and eternally.

This memorial tablet shall be set up in the south-west, towards the middle, on the mountain of Khu-aten, in the midst of it.

With regard to the memorial tablet in the middle, on the mountain to the east of the city of Khu-aten, let this be the memorial tablet for Khu-aten. This I will have set up in its place [which I have appointed for it in sight of] the city of Khu-aten, at the place which I have appointed for it in the east, for ever and eternally.

This memorial tablet in the middle, on the mountain to the east of the city of Khu-aten, let it be in the midst of it.

With regard to the memorial tablet to the north-east of Khu-aten, I will have it set up in its place. Let that be the memorial tablet on the north of Khu-aten. Let this be the place which I have appointed for it.

[In such wise shall the memorial tablets be set up, according to their directions] towards Khu-aten. From the memorial tablet in the south to the memorial tablet in the north [the distance amounts to] 1,000 [. . . . . .]

The following lines are so much destroyed, that little more can be made out of them beyond the fact, that the king also set up a similar memorial tablet to the west of Khu-aten, on the opposite bank of the river.

There is some difficulty about the conclusion, for a postscript, added not quite two years afterwards, relates as follows with respect to the tablets :—

This memorial tablet, which was placed in the middle, had fallen down. I will have it set up afresh, and placed again at the

place at which it was [before] : this I swear. In the 8th year, in
the month Tybi, on the 9th day, the king was in Khu-aten, and
Pharaoh mounted his court-chariot of polished copper, to behold
the memorial tablets of the Sun's disk, which are on the hills in
the territory to the south-east of Khu-aten.

Two of them stand in a valley, covered with blocks
of stone and *débris*, in a south-easterly direction from
Tell-el-Amarna, towards Haggi Qandil, high up on the
wall of rock, at a height of 9 mètres (nearly 30 feet).
The third rock-tablet, on the other hand, is on the
opposite side of the river. At Gebel Tûneh, on the
smooth face of the Libyan mountain, the same picture
and the same inscription as at the above-named places
present themselves to the eye of the traveller.

According to them, the king visited the solitary
mountain district again in his eighth year, to con-
vince himself that his orders had been obeyed. The
memorial tablets had, soon after their erection, 'tumbled down,' that is, had been destroyed purposely by
disaffected Egyptians, so that the king found himself
obliged to order their re-erection.

The sepulchral chambers of Tell-el-Amarna, which
received the deceased generations of the strange court
of the heretical king, show us repeatedly in their
pictures the king taking a journey in his chariot in
the bright sunshine, accompanied by his daughters,
who likewise, according to the fashion of the times,
used two-horsed and two-wheeled chariots.

In the twelfth year of his reign, on the 18th day of
the month Mekhir, Khu-n-aten celebrated his victories
over the Syrians and Cushites. He could hardly have
taken a personal part in these campaigns, but his appearance at the festival of victory was none the less brilliant.
In full Pharaonic attire, adorned with the insignia of
his rank, he appears on his lion-throne, carried on the
shoulders of his warriors. At his side run servants,

who with their long fans wave the cool air upon their
heated lord.

We know nothing more precise either as to the
direction or the duration of the campaigns in the North
and South thus announced in general terms. Only
the pictures and inscriptions of the king on the propyla
of the Temple of Amen at Soleb lead us to suppose
that the warriors of Khu-n-aten must have gone thus
far on their campaign against the South. There is also
a remarkable monument in the Egyptian collection at
Leyden, on which Hor-em-heb (who was afterwards
king), in his character as the first official of his then
reigning lord, causes the prisoners of all nations to
be brought before his lord by the servants of the king.
Stupid negroes, sly Syrians, and small-featured Marmaridæ (whose women lead horses by the bridles as
presents), form the chief members of the motley,
cringing, submissive assemblage of foreigners before
the king's throne.

The king, as we have seen, died without male issue.
Of his daughters, the eldest had married a certain
Saa-nekht; the third, Ankh-nes-pa-aten, or, as she was
obliged to call herself later in honour of Amen, Ankh-
nes-Amen, was married to the noble lord Tut-ankh-
Amen; while the sister of the queen Neferit-Thi, whose
name was Net'em-mut, became the spouse of the later
king, Hor-em-heb.

The husbands of all these princesses became kings.
Among the first was Tut-ankh-Amen, whose viceroys
in the south were the same Hi and Amenhotep who
had already held that office under Amen-hotep III.
It is only under King Ai that we find a new governor,
of the same name, Ai, whose son Amenape afterwards,
under Seti I., takes the place of his father.

The succession of the kings, to whose combined

reigns there was allotted a very short time, scarcely the length of a single generation, is as follows :—Saa-nekht, Tut-ankh-Amen, Ai, Hor-em-heb.

SAA-NEKHT,

the husband of the princess Mer-aten, disappeared quickly from the stage of history.   His successor,

TUT-ANKH-AMEN,

'the living image of Amen,' the royal husband of the third daughter of Khu-n-aten, Ankh-nes-Amen, has, on the contrary, had his memory preserved by one of the most remarkable representations in a sepulchral chamber at Gûrnah.

This shows us the king on his throne, holding a public court, in presence of his two governors of the South, Hi and Amenhotep.   The richly laden ships, which contain the tributes and presents of the negro peoples, have arrived at Thebes.   A negro queen herself has not felt ashamed to appear in person on this conspicuous scene.   She is introduced on a chariot drawn by oxen, surrounded by her servants, who lay the rich gifts and presents of their dusky mistress at the feet of Pharaoh, to his great delight and that of all his court.

As if to enhance their joy, the princes of the land of Ruthen appear at the same time from the distant north, in rich variegated dresses, with their black hair elegantly curled, to offer to the king the costly and beautiful works of their country.

The inscription runs thus :—

Arrival of the tributes for the lord of the land, which the miserable Ruthen offer under the leadership of the (Egyptian) royal ambassador to all countries, the king's son of Cush, and governor of the South, Amenhotep.

Above the princes of Ruthen are the significant words :—

These kings of the land of Upper Ruthen knew nothing of Egypt since the time of the divine one. They beg for peace from the king, speaking thus : 'Grant us freedom out of thy land. Indescribable are thy victories, and no enemy appears in thy time. All lands rest in peace.'

Above the costly gifts of the princes (among them horses), brought by red-bearded servants, of a light colour and an almost dwarf-like build, is the following explanatory inscription :—

This is the best selection of all sorts of vessels of their land, in silver, gold, blue-stone, green-stone, and all kinds of jewels.

Of the tributes and presents of the negroes, on the other hand, it is said :—

This is the arrival of the splendid Ethiopian tributes, the best selection of the productions of the lands of the South, and their landing in Thebes under the conduct of the king's son of Cush, Hi.

The Northern presents, valuable in themselves from their materials, gain a still higher interest from the artistic character of their treatment. Under the guidance of the Phœnicians, who, besides their commerce, had so remarkable a genius for handicrafts and for art, there had sprung up, along the eastern coast of the ' inner sea,' a cultured school, which not only had the skill to make what was necessary, but also to create beauty. In the course of trade the artistic productions of Phœnicia found an entrance and a sale in all parts of the then known world, especially among the enlightened people of Egypt. The exhibition of Phœnician works before the eyes of the astonished Pharaoh remains therefore for all times a precious contribution to the history of the oldest Phœnician school of art. Judgment may be passed on the condition of culture and of handicraft

in the lands of the negroes in the fifteenth century
B.C., from the coloured representations in these sepulchral chambers.   A certain artistic spirit manifests
itself in the construction and execution of the exterior
forms of the objects.   Passing over the golden vessels
set with precious stones, the manifold utensils of
domestic life, the chariots, ships, weapons, and all the
articles which the queen brings to Thebes, exhibit an
unmistakable development of artistic power, which
must without doubt be ascribed on the one hand to
Egyptian influence, and on the other to the natural
talent of these so-called savage tribes, and to their
imitative instinct.

Tut-ankh-Amen, whose very name serves as a
proof that he had thrown aside the new teaching of
his royal father-in-law about the one living Sun's
disk, reigned in Thebes with the consent of the priests
of Amen.   By a brilliant external pomp, he seems to
have obtained the power and commanded the respect
which were denied him on account of his birth and
marriage.   Yet in spite of this he remained an ille-
gitimate ruler, to whom, in the eyes of the priests
of Amen, the full Pharaonic blood was wanting.
Neither did his reign last long.

The throne became vacant; the female line of
King Khu-n-aten, the heretic, had left no descendants;
and so, by stratagem or force, the empire was seized
by Khu-n-aten's former master of the horse,

'THE HOLY FATHER' AI.

The king's foster-mother, Thi, was married to one
of the lords of the court, a 'holy father' of the
highest grade, by name Ai.   This connection with
the king's own nurse led, as a natural consequence,
to Ai's mounting continually up the ladder of dignities,

until he at last held the highest offices. He was named 'fan-bearer on the right hand of the king, and superintendent of the whole stud of Pharaoh.' He seems to have occupied himself with the science of law, and was also promoted to be 'the royal scribe of justice.' The king bestowed many presents on the ennobled pair. 'The high nurse, the nourishing mother of the divinĕ one, the dresser of the king,' must, of course, have stood in peculiar favour. The riches of her house increased visibly.

Ai, however, appears to have been an excellent king for the country, and at the same time to have returned to the ancient ways prescribed for the kings by the priests of Amen, for he calls himself 'a prince of Thebes,' and shows no remembrance of the new teaching of his deceased king. He sacrifices to Amen and his associated gods according to the old traditional custom, and he honours the god, that is, the priests of the god, in a marked manner.

The holy fathers appear clearly to have been supported by their former colleague on the throne, for they allowed him to prepare for himself a tomb in the Bibân-el-Molûk, near Thebes, where it and his sarcophagus are still to be seen. Ai, 'conqueror of the Asiatics,' and 'distinguished for power,' must in fact have carried on wars in the North, and have won great successes for Egypt. His acknowledged supremacy in the South is vouched for by the presence of his 'king's son of Cush and governor, Pauer,' whose memory has been faithfully preserved beside that of the king, in the Nubian rock-grottoes of Shetaui. He is the father of that governor in the South, Amenemape, who, under King Seti I., exercised the same office in Nubia. This family connection, which is of great importance as bearing on the succession of the generations, gives ground for the supposition that the following kings, Hor-em-heb, Ramses I., and his son Seti I., were contemporaries, and consequently each possessed the throne for a comparatively short period.   This supposition is strengthened by the probability that the sister-in-law of King Khu-n-aten, Net'em-mut, was no other than the princess who was afterwards the wife of King Hor-em-heb.

SER-KHEPERU-RA MER-AMEN HOR-EM-HEB;
THE KING HORUS OF MANETHO.

Who was to be king ?   That was the great question after the funeral of the master of the horse.   There was in Middle Egypt a man whom, in all probability, Amen-hotep III. had known and honoured with his confidence.   His right to the throne of Pharaoh had but a slight foundation; it rested only on his marriage with the sister of Queen Neferit-Thi, the high lady Net'em-mut, who has been already mentioned.   But another helper stood by: this was the god Horus, under whose protection the future heir to the throne lived in quiet retirement at the town of Ha-suten, 'the house of the king.'

This place stood on the right side of the river, and formed the capital of the eighteenth nome of Upper Egypt.   The monuments give it a second name, Ha-Bennu, 'the Phœnix city;' it is the Hipponon of the Greek travellers in Egypt, the Alabastrônpolis (alabaster-city) of the geographer Ptolemy.   It stood probably in the neighbourhood of the city of Khu-aten, behind which lie rich alabaster quarries, if it be not Khu-aten itself.

The future heir to the throne bore the name of Hor-em-heb.   As to how he obtained his royal dignity, we will allow his own monument in Turin, which is at least 33 centuries old, and needs no elucidation, to speak for itself.

While he was yet carried as a suckling in arms, both old and young touched the ground before him.

His tutelar god, Horus of Ha-Suten, had chosen him for great things.

He knew the day of his good fortune, to grant to him his kingdom, for this god made his son great in the sight of mortals, and he willed to prolong his career till the arrival of the day on which he should receive his office (as king).

Hor-em-heb was presented to the then living Pharaoh.

And he enraptured the heart of the king, who was contented because of his qualities, and rejoiced on account of his choice. And he named him as Ro-hir (guardian) of the country, until he should attain to the title of a son as crown-prince of this land, as it is and remains, he alone without a rival.

Hor-em-heb fulfilled the duties of his calling as councillor to the king to his entire satisfaction.

'For (he contented the) inhabitants of Egypt by the judgments of his mouth. And he was called to the royal court, so that he was far from anxiety. He opened his mouth and gave answer to the king, and consoled him by the utterances of his mouth. So that he was the sole benefactor, like none [other beside him].' In such a way did he show himself, 'who took pleasure in justice alone, which he carried in his heart,' standing in the same grade with the gods Tehuti and Ptah. 'In all his deeds and ways he followed their path, and they were his shield and his protection on earth to all eternity.'

After this he was also named Adon of the land.

'When he had now been raised to be Adon during the space of many years,' in consequence of his fortunate administration, every kind of distinction was showered upon him. 'The distinguished men at the court bowed themselves before him outside the door of the palace. And when the kings of the nine foreign nations of the South and of the North came before him, they stretched out their hands at his approach, and praised his soul, as if he had been God. Then all was done that was appointed to be done, under the orders which he [gave].' Thus 'his authority was greater than that of the king in the sight of mortals, and all wished him prosperity and health.   He punished the guilty (?), and bestowed prosperity on men.'

' After this the eldest son of Horus was raised from the dignity of a guardian to be the crown-prince of the land, as it is established. Then had this glorious god, Horus of Alabastrônpolis, the desire in his heart to place his son upon his throne for evermore.   And [this glorious god] Amen gave command that they should conduct the god Horus, with a joyful mind, to Thebes, the eternal city, and his son on his breast, to Apet ; to bring him in with festivity before Amen, to deliver to him his royal office, and to establish it for the term of his life.   Then [they arrived full of joy] during his splendid festival in Apet of the South country ; and they beheld this god Horus, the lord of Alabastrônpolis, in company with his son, in the coronation procession, that he might bestow upon him his office and his throne.   Then was Amen-Ra moved with joy. And he beheld [the king's daughter . . . and wished to unite her] to him. And behold! he brought her to this prince, the crown-prince Hor-em-heb.   And he went into the palace, and he placed him before himself on the exalted place (of the throne) of his glorious distinguished daughter.   (And she) bowed herself, and embraced his pleasing form, and placed herself before him.   And all the divinities of the chamber of fire were full of ecstasy at his coronation : Nekheb, Buto, Nit, Isis, Nephthys, Horus, Set, the whole circle of the gods on the exalted place, [raised their] song of praise to the height of heaven, and there was joy because of the grace of Amen.   After this there was an interval of rest.   Then went Amen, with his son before him, to the hall of kings, to set his royal helmet on his head, and to lengthen his term of life, as it should in fact be. (Then the gods cried out), "We are assembled ; we will to invest him with his kingdom ; we will to bestow upon him the royal attire of the sun-god Ra ; we will to praise Amen in him. Thou hast brought him to us, to protect us.   Give him the thirty years' festivals of the sun-god Ra, and the days of Horus as king. Let him be one, who does that which is pleasing to thy heart in Apet, just as in On (Heliopolis), and in Memphis : let it be he who glorifies these places."   And the great name of this divine one was settled, and his title recorded, corresponding to the Holiness of the sun-god, as follows :—

'" 1. As HORUS, the powerful bull, always at hand with counsel ;

2. As LORD OF THE DOUBLE CROWN, great from his wonderful works in Apet :

3. As GOLDEN HORUS, who rests himself on justice, the up holder of the land :

4. As KING SER-KHEPERU-RA, who is elected by the sun-god :

5. As the SON OF RA, Mer-Amen Hor-em-heb.

May he live for ever ! "

'Then came forth from the palace the Majesty of this glorious god Amen, the king of the gods, with his son before him, and he embraced his pleasing form, which was crowned with the royal helmet, in order to deliver to him the golden protecting image of the sun's disk.   The nine foreign nations were under his feet, the heaven was in a most festive disposition, the land was filled with ecstasy, and as for the divinities of Egypt, their souls were full of pleasant feelings.   Then the inhabitants, in high delight, raised towards heaven the song of praise ; great and small lifted up their voices, and the whole land was moved with joy.

'After this festival in Apet of the Southern country was finished, then Amen, the king of the gods, went in peace to Thebes, and the king went down the river on board his ship, like an image of Horemkhu.   Thus had he taken possession of this land, as was the custom since the time of the sun-god Ra.   He renewed the dwellings of the gods, from the shallows of the marsh-land of Nathu as far as Nubia.   He had all their images sculptured, each as it had been before, more than . . . And the sun-god Ra rejoiced, when he beheld [that renewed which] had been destroyed in former times.

'He set them up in their temple, and he had a hundred images made, one of each of them, of like form, and of all kinds of costly stones.   He visited the cities of the gods, which lay as heaps of rubbish in this land, and he had them restored, just as they had been from the beginning of all things.   He took care for their daily festival of sacrifice, and for all the vessels of their temples, formed out of gold and silver.   He provided them (the temples) with holy persons and singers, and with the best body-guards ; and he presented to them arable land and cattle, and supplied them with all kinds of provisions which they required, to sing thus each new morning to the sun-god Ra : " Thou hast made the kingdom great for us in thy son, who is the consolation of thy soul, King Hor-em-heb.   Grant him the continuance of the thirty years' feasts, give him the victory over all countries, as to Horus, the son of Isis, towards whom in like manner thy heart yearned in On, in the company of thy circle of gods."'

It is noticeable that the late king Ai is passed over in silence.   The passage is also obscure, in which mention is made of 'the daughter'—in all probability his heiress-daughter—who had taken refuge in the temple of Amen. Thus it was possibly Net'em-mut, afterwards the king's wife, whose dependence on the godhead of Amen the priests wished to reward by a marriage with Hor-em-heb.

After the newly-elected king had ascended the vacant throne with a grand ceremonial at Thebes, where, as the inscription informs us, he was crowned, his first work was the enlargement and beautifying of this temple. To this end a gigantic obelisk at Karnak, raised by Khu-n-aten, was destroyed, and the blocks of stone were broken up and used for the building of the fourth gate-tower of the great temple of Amen in Apet.

A second gate-tower was added, both being connected by walls with a large court; and in front of the outermost gate an avenue of sphinxes was set up in honour of Amen, in the name of Hor-em-heb.

Thus speaks Amen-Ra, the king of the gods : Splendid is the monument which thou hast erected for me, O Horus, thou wise king ; my heart rejoices in thy love. I am enchanted with the sight of thy memorial. Therefore we grant thee a life as long as the sun, and the years of Horus as king of the land.

The entrances to this gate were also adorned with statues of the king. The eastern side walls also were sculptured with representations of the princes of Punt, who appear before the king, to whom they present a number of heavy sacks filled with gold, saying :—

Hail to thee, king of Egypt, sun of the nine foreign nations ! By thy name ! we did not know Egypt. Our fathers never trod it. Present us with freedom out of thy hand. We will be thy subjects.

Hor-em-heb undertook a victorious expedition against the Sûdan, as may be seen at Silsilis. The bas-reliefs are best described by Champollion.

'The Pharaoh is represented standing, as, with his battle-axe on his shoulder, he receives from Amen-Ra the emblem of divine life, and power to subdue the

North and to conquer the South. Beneath lie
Ethiopians, some prostrate on the ground, others
stretching forth their hands in prayer to an Egyptian
leader, who, according to the inscription, upbraids
them with having shut their hearts to wisdom, and with
refusing to hear when it was said to them, " Behold the
lion who has fallen upon the land of Cush." '

The king is carried on a throne by his generals,
accompanied by the fan-bearers. Servants clear the
road by which the procession is to pass ; behind him
appear warriors, who lead with them hostile generals as
prisoners ; other armed men, with shields on their
shoulders, put themselves in motion, with the trumpeters
at their head. A troop of Egyptian officers, priests,
and other officials, receive the king, and do homage to
him.

The hieroglyphs run as follows :—

The divine benefactor returns home after he has subdued the
princes of all countries. His bow is in his hand, as if he were the
(god of war Mentu) the lord of Thebes. The powerful glorious
king leads the princes of the miserable land of Cush with him. The
king comes back from Ethiopia with the booty which he has taken
by force, as his father Amen had commanded him.

In the tomb of an official (at Gûrnah) is a vivid
representation of the arrival of the booty from the
Sûdan. The inscription above it says, in short and
pithy terms :—

Reception of the silver, gold, ivory, and ebony into the treasure-
house.

But Hor-em-heb was not only mindful of Amen ;
Ptah also received his full share. An inscription
found in Thebes says :—

In the first year, in the month Khoiakh, on the 22nd day, of
King Hor-em-heb, the day of the feast of the Memphite Ptah in
Thebes, on his festival, [the sacrifices] were appointed [for this god
according to the command of the king].

That Hor-em-heb knew how to reward his followers, is testified by the grave of his faithful servant, the priest Neferhotep, in the necropolis of Thebes :—

In the third year, under the reign of the king of Egypt, Hor-em-heb, his Majesty showed himself comparable to the sun-god Ra, in his own sepulchre, for the purpose of making an offering of bread to his father Amen.   As he came out from the Golden Chamber, cries of joy sounded through the whole region, and the shout rose up heavenward.   Then was the holy father of Amen, Neferhotep, summoned to receive the king's thousandfold gracious rewards in all manner of presents, consisting of silver and gold, stuffs, fine oils, bread and drinks, flesh and condiments.   According to the command of my (or his) lord Amen, the rewards were presented to me (or him) in the most exalted presence by the chief singer of Amen, Hotep-ab.

Neferhotep speaks thus : ' One rich (in —) makes acknowledgment by presents.   So is the god, the king of the gods, who acknowledges him that acknowledges Him, and rewards him that works for Him, and protects him that serves Him.'

What further can be known of Hor-em-heb is only from the ruins of contemporaneous monuments, amongst which is a very remarkable fragment in the British collection which runs thus :—

In the 7th year of King Hor-em-heb, that was the day of the conveying of the people of Ai my father to the abodes of the dead. The burgomaster of the city (that is, Thebes), Tehutimes, had assigned the burial-places, which are situated at the necropolis which belongs to the territory of Pharaoh ; and he granted the tomb of Amen to Ai my father for appropriation.   It was, namely, Qu-an . . . . my mother, his daughter by birth, and he left behind no male child.   All his burial-places would therefore have remained deserted afterwards.

In the 21st year, on the first day of the month Paoni, they stood before Amenhotep, (and I) spake to him : ' Grant, I pray thee, to each one the burial-places of their fathers ! '   Then he gave me the burial-places of Ai by a writing, and so I came into their full possession.

However insignificant this formless piece of limestone may be, still it is valuable on account of its historical testimony, that Hor-em-heb lived to see the twenty-first year of his reign.

GENEALOGICAL TABLE OF THE RAMESSIDES.

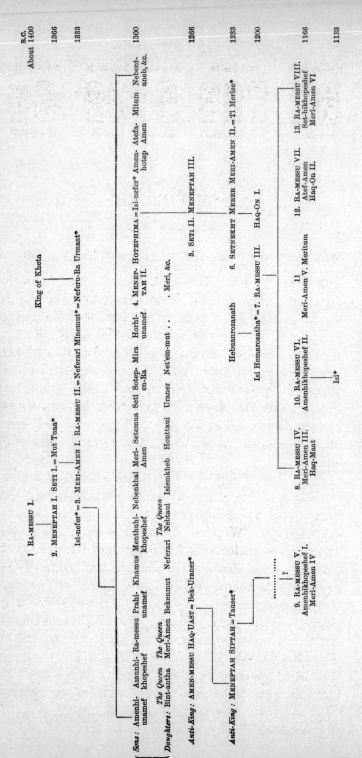

Note.—(1) The Nos. show the succession of the kings. (2) The Names with * are those of women.

Men-pehtet-Ra.	Maat-men-Ra.	Ra-user-maat-Sotep-en-Ra.	Hotep-her-maat.
Ramses I.	Meneptah I., Seti I.	Ramses II., Meri-Amen.	Meneptah II.

CHAPTER XI.

DYNASTY XIX.[1]

Men-pehtet-Ra. Ra-messu. (Ramses I.) b.c. 1400 cir

The death of King Hor-em-heb closed the Eighteenth
Dynasty. The heretic king Khu-n-aten had by his
teaching about Amen somewhat diminished his prestige
in the eyes of the orthodox priests and people, and had
created a schism in the internal life of the nation, for the
new teaching, with its Semitic origin, had gained many
adherents among the Egyptians. How peace was
brought about it is now difficult to say, but Hor-em-heb
certainly appeared as a mediator between the adherents
of Amen and the persecuted followers of the god of the
Solar Disk.

While the kingdom was being disturbed by this
burning question a nation on the north-east had been
growing up, which now began to endanger the Egyptian
supremacy in Western Asia. Already during these
annual wars, undertaken by Tehuti-mes III. against the
Syrian peoples, the Kheta, under the leadership of their
own kings, had shown themselves to be a dominant race.
Contemporary inscriptions designate them as ' the great
people,' or ' the great country,' less with respect to the
space they occupied, than from their just reputation for
those brave and chivalrous qualities which they were
acknowledged even by their enemies to possess. We
believe we are falling into no error if we recognise in

[1] For Table of Kings see p. xxiii.

these people the Hittites of the Bible. When Tehuti-mes III. fought with them and conquered their towns, they were an important people in the north of Syria. At the commencement of the Nineteenth Dynasty their power extended over the whole of the surrounding nations. These predecessors of the Assyrian Empire held the first place in the league of the cities and kings of Western Asia. The Egyptian inscriptions do not hesitate to refer to their sovereigns in a conspicuous manner, and to speak of their gods with reverence. When Ramses I. ascended the throne Sa-pa-li-li, Saplel, or Saprer, ruled as their king, and was followed by his son and heir Mauro-sar. At his death he left two sons, of whom the elder was Mauthanar, who appears as a contemporary of Seti I. and an enemy of Egypt, while the younger Kheta-sar was the friend, ally, and father-in-law of Ramses II. At the head of their divinities stood Sutekh—the Kheta counterpart of Amen—and his wife the steed-driving queen of heaven, Astartha-Anatha.

Among the towns of the Kheta, Tunep (Daphnæ) and Khilibu (Haleb) are two points certainly fixed by their definite position, and both had temples of the great Baal-Sutekh. On the other hand, the name of the country of Qazauatana points with certainty to the region of Gozan (Gauzanitis) to the east of the Euphrates, between the towns of Circesium in the south and Thapsacus in the north. The situation of the countries of the Kheta—Zaranda, Pirqa or Pilqa (Peleg, Paliga?), Khissap, Sarsu, Sarpina, Zaiath-khirra (hinder Zaiath)—must be determined by future enquiries. Perhaps we may find an answer to these questions in the Assyrian inscriptions.

If it is allowable to form a judgment on the origin of this cultivated and powerful people from its outward appearance, it seems to be very doubtful whether we should reckon it among the Canaanites. Beardless, armed in a different manner, fighting three men in each chariot of war, arranged in their order of battle according to a well-considered plan previously laid down, the Kheta present a striking contrast to their Canaanite allies. In the representations of the wars of Ramses II. against Kheta-sar, the foreign king appears surrounded by his generals and servants, who are mentioned by name, down to the 'letter-writer Khirpa-sar.' His warriors were divided into foot-soldiers and fighters in chariots, and consisted partly of Kheta, partly of foreign mercenaries. Their hosts were led to battle by *Kazans*, or 'commanders of the fighters in the chariots,' by 'generals,' and *Herpits*, or 'captains of the foreigners.'

In the battle of Kadesh 8,000 *Tuhir* (chosen ones) stood in the foremost rank, under the command of Kamaiz; while 9,000 others followed their king. In the same battle, the noblemen Thargannas and Pais led the chariots; Thaadar commanded the mercenaries; Nebisuanna was at the head of the foreign warriors from Annas; and another chief appears as the general of the mercenaries from Nagebus. Sapzar and Mazarima are spoken of as brothers of the king; whether real brothers, or only allies, is not clear. Among other names of Kheta origin, the following are mentioned: Garbitus, Thargathazas, Tadar or Tadal, Zauazas, Samarius, and that of the 'ambassador' Tarthisebu. It is evident at once that these names do not bear a pure Semitic stamp. The endings in *s, r,* and *u,* prevail. In the proper name Thargatha-zas, in which the ending *zas* plays the same part as in the proper name Zaua-zas, Thargatha seems to answer to the goddess called by the Greeks and Romans Atargates or Atargatis, Derketo and Dercetis, who possessed very celebrated temples in

Askalon and Astaroth-Karnaim, as well as in the Syrian
town of Hierapolis (Mabog).

The peculiarities of the language are for the most
part found in that hitherto unexplained series of names
of towns which form the second division of the northern
peoples in the lists of the victories of Tehuti-mes III.
at Karnak. These lists are of the greatest value as
a memorial of times and people who have long since
vanished :—

120. Pirkheta	164. Tariza
121. Ai	166. Anriz
122. Amau	167. Aares
124. Thuka	168. Khazrezaa
125. Thel-manna	169. Arnir
126. Legaba	170. Khathaai
127. Tunipa (Daphne)	173. Thenuzuru
132. Ni	184. Anauban
134. Ar	185. Khatuma
135. Zizal	186. Magnas
136. Zakal	187. Thepkanna
139. Arzakana	188. Thuthana (Susan ?)
140. Kharkakhi (or Kharkaka)	189. Nireb
141. Bursu	190. Theleb (Thalaba)
142. Lerti	191. Atugaren
145. Unai	196. Nishapa (Nisibis)
146. Aunfer	197. Ta-zeker
147. Ithakhab	198. Abatha
148. Uniuqa	199. Ziras
150. Sakti	200. Authir
151. Aubillina	201. Natub
152. Zanruisu (Zarruisu)	202. Zetharseth
153. Suka	203. Aithua
154. Pazalu	204. Sukaua
155. Sathekhbeg	205. Tuaub
156. Amarseki	206. Abir[na]th
157. Khalros	207. Shainarkai
158. Nenuranaantha	208. Aurma
159. Shauirantha	212. Kainab
160. Mairrekhnas	213. Ares
161. Zagerel	214. Anautasenu
163. Kanretu	215. Azana

216. Zetharsetha
217. Tulbentha
218. Mauthi
221. Atur
222. Kartha-meruth
223. A-sitha
224. Taniros
226. Athebena
227. Ashameth
228. Athakar
229. Tazet
230. Athrun
231. Thukamros
232. Abetha
235. Anzakeb
236. Ares
237. Artha
247. Farua
252. Sur
253. Papaa
254. Nuzana
255. Zamauka
259. Suki-beki
263. A-thini
264. Karshaua
265. Retama
271. Zazker
272. Maurmar
279. Khaitu
280. Pederi (Pethor)
281. Athrithan

282. Mashaua
283. A-anreka
284. Nepiriuriu (Nipur)
285. Nathkina
286. Athetama
287. Abellenu
288. Airanel
289. Airanel (sic)
290. Annaui
292. Thalekh
293. Aurna
296. Papabi
306. Aiber
307. Kel-maitha (Khilmod)
308. Amak
309. Kazel
310. Aumai
311. Khalbu (Haleb)
312. Piauanel (Pnuel)
315. Aukam
316. Puroth
318. Aripenekha
320. Puqiu
322. Thinnur
323. Zarnas
333. Iurima
338. Thethup
343. Shusaron
347. Thamaqur
348. Retep (?) (Re-ap ?)
349. Maurika

Although we possess no information from the monuments about the family ties which united the king, who was the head and founder of the Nineteenth Dynasty, with his predecessor Hor-em-heb, there must have been a close connection between them. Whether Ramses I. was the son, son-in-law, or brother of Hor-em-heb, is as yet undecided, but his reign was neither remarkable nor of long duration. His fame consists chiefly in being the father of one very celebrated man and the grandfather of another. His recognition by the priests of Amen as the legitimate king is authenticated by the representation of his coronation on the entrance gate of the temple at Karnak.

A memorial stone at Wady-Halfah, dated in the second year of his reign, the 20th Mekhir, informs us that King Ramses I. founded there a storehouse for the temple of his divine father, Amen - Amsu, and filled it with captive men-servants and maid-servants from the conquered countries.

Ramses I. was laid in his own tomb-chamber in the valley of the kings' sepulchres, and was succeeded by his son, to whom the monuments give the name of MAAT-MEN-RA. MENE-PTAH I. SETI I. (SE-THOS.) 1366 B.C. CIR.

The great national temple at Thebes records the honours of Seti I., for the king executed works to the glorious god Amen the splendour of which is

PLAN OF GREAT TEMPLE AT KARNAK.

A. First Propylon. B. Open Area, with corridors, and a single column erect. C. Second Propylon. D. Great Hall. E. Third Propylon. F. Fourth Propylon. G. Hall with Osirid figures. H. Granite Sanctuary and adjoining chambers. I. Open Court. K. Columnar Edifice of Tehuti-mes III. L. Temple of Ramses III.

a. Sculptures of Seti I. b. Sculptures of Shishak. c. Sculptures of Ramses II. d. Small Obelisks. e. Large Obelisks. f. Pillars of Usertsen I. g. Hall of Ancestors.

only surpassed by their extraordinary size. We refer to

the building of that wonderful ' Great Hall' in the temple at Karnak, where 134 columns of astonishing height and circumference still attract the admiration of the present age.

The wars of Seti arose from the constant advances of the neighbouring peoples upon the Delta. The long duration of peace, as well perhaps as the weak reign of Ramses I., had caused them, and especially the Shasu, to take the bold resolve of pressing forward over the eastern frontier, 'to find sustenance for their cattle on the possessions of Pharaoh.' Six battle paintings, ranged in a series on the outer wall of the north side of the Great Hall of Pillars in the temple at Karnak, describe the principal events of this campaign. War broke out in the East in the very first year of Seti's reign, ' from the fortress of Khetam (Etham), in the land of Zaru (Tanitic nome), as far as Kanaan,' which proves that they had pressed westward into Egyptian territory to make good their claims derived from the Hyksos. The king assembled his army and himself rode in his war-chariot against the invading Bedâwi; the road the Egyptians took is clearly indicated by the pictures and inscriptions.

The campaign was begun from the fortress of Khetam, which was situated on both sides of an arm of the Nile, which swarmed with crocodiles, and whose banks were covered with reeds. The king took thence the direction of the ' way of the Philistines,' and first reached the fortified but otherwise unknown place, Taa-pa-mau, Leontopolis, ' the house of lions,' near a small fountain of sweet water enclosed by a wall. His march was next directed to the Egyptian fortress of Migdol, close to the springs in the country of Hazina or Hazian (the Kasion or Mount Casius of the ancients), and along the road to the 'north' fortress Uti (Buto), also near a spring. Here stood the often-mentioned temple on Mount Casius, in which an Amen was worshipped, who was the Baal Zapuna of the Egyptian inscriptions, the Baal Zephon of Holy Scripture The army passed along the sea-shore to Ostracine, where there was a tower, designated Pa-Nekhtu, or ' the conqueror's tower' of King Seti. At this point the boundary of Egypt proper ended, and the land of the Philistines began. The next halting-place was a fortified spot, newly built by Seti, at the water of Absaqab. Two other fortresses lay on either side of the road. The larger one was called ' the town, which the king had built at the spring of . . . tha.' It is also called ' a strong place' in a second passage, and its water is designated as that of Ribatha, without doubt the Rehoboth of the Bible, to the south-west of Beersheba, in Negeb or the south country of Palestine. The smaller fortress stood near Takhnum-net'em, ' the sweet spring.' It is called A-Nekhtu, ' the fortress of victory.' Passing by a new fortress (the name is unfortunately destroyed), the end of the road was reached, and at the same time the eastern boundary of the land of Shasu, marked by the hill-fortress of ' Kanaan of the Land of Zahi,' near which a stream seems to have fallen into a lake. The fortress was stormed, and the king took possession of the land of the Shasu to its extremest boundary, thus becoming lord of the whole of the Edomitish Negeb. Their first victory is thus celebrated :—

In the first year of King Seti there took place by the strong arm of Pharaoh the annihilation of the hostile Shasu, from the fortress of Khetam of the land of Zaru, as far as Kanaan. The king was against them like a fierce lion. They were turned into a heap of corpses in their hill-country. They lay in their blood. Not one escaped to tell of his strength to the distant nations.

The Shasu next attempted to make head against the Egyptians, but were completely routed in the territory

of the Phœnicians. These latter were speedily punished
for going to the help of the Shasu, for 'Pharaoh annihilated the kings of the land of the Phœnicians in the
battle of Inu-aamu (Jamnia). The Egyptians next
turned against the Rutennu of Canaan. The kings of
the several cities were successively overcome in many
battles, in which a son of Seti fought by the side of his
father. Pharaoh evidently took special delight in this
combat, for he says that

his joy is to undertake the battle, and his delight is to dash into
it. His heart is only satisfied at the sight of the stream of blood
when he strikes off the heads of his enemies. A moment of the
struggle of men is dearer to him than a day of pleasure. He slays
them with one stroke, and spares none among them. And whoever
of them is left remaining finds himself in his grasp, and is carried
off to Egypt alive as a prisoner.

In his victorious campaign throughout the whole
land of Canaan, through which he was borne by his
pair of horses named 'big with victory,' the great
fortress of Kadesh, which had already played such an
important part under Tehuti-mes III., was reached.
The inscription thus designates the campaign:—

This is the going up of Pharaoh, to conquer the land of Kadesh
in the territory of the Amorites.

The arrival of the army was unexpected. The
herdsmen were pasturing their cattle under the trees
which surrounded the city, when Pharaoh appeared.
Each sought to save himself; the herds fled with their
keepers; the warriors of Kadesh, as they sallied out,
were pierced by the arrows of Seti, and fell from their
chariots. The defenders in the fortress fared no better.
They also gave way before the violent assault of the
Egyptian army, and fortress and people fell into the
hands of Pharaoh.

From Kadesh onwards, the land of the Kheta lay

open before the hosts of Pharaoh. Mauthanar, the
king, had broken the treaties which had been made between his predecessor and the Egyptians, and had given
notice to Pharaoh of the termination of their alliance.
Seti, as the avenger of broken treaties, made no delay
in falling upon the Kheta, and success crowned his
enterprise. Although the well-ordered hosts of the
Kheta, on foot, on horseback, and in chariots, offered a
determined resistance to the Egyptians, yet for all this
they were unsuccessful. An inscription describes thus
the Egyptian victory :—

> He is a jackal which rushes prowling through this land, a grim
> lion that frequents the most hidden paths of all regions, a powerful
> bull with a pair of sharpened horns. . . . He has struck down the
> Asiatics, he has thrown to the ground the Kheta ; he has slain
> their princes.
>
> .   .   .   .   .   .
>
> The king was victorious, great was his strength. His war-cry
> was like that of the son of Nut (that is, Baal-Sutekh). He returns
> home in triumph ; he has annihilated the peoples, he has struck
> to the ground the land of Kheta, he has made an end of his ad-
> versaries. The enmity of all peoples is turned into friendship.
> The terror of the king has penetrated them, his boldness has opened
> their hearts. The kings of the countries find themselves bound
> before him.

After the battle peace was concluded, and the king,
taking with him an immense number of prisoners, prepared to return home. He went by the royal highway
through Kadesh, but made a diversion into the country
of Mount Lebanon. The inhabitants, Canaanites of the
purest race, received the king in the most reverential
manner, lifting up their hands to hail the conqueror
An inscription says :—

> The priests and elders of the land of Limanon, they speak thus,
> while they pray before the lord of the land to exalt his renown :
> 'Thou appearest like thy father, the Sun-god ; men live in thy
> glance.'

The king, it appears, had made known certain wishes, for an Egyptian scribe assures him, ' All shall be accomplished as thou hast said.' They related to the felling of cedars in the wooded mountain region of Lebanon for the building of a new Nile ship, to be used in the service of Amen and for the fabrication of those tall masts which adorned the front of the temple gate-towers. In the lively representation still preserved the Canaanites are seen employed in felling the highest and straightest trees. With this the deeds of Seti, in the East, had reached their conclusion.

He had smitten the wandering peoples (An), and struck to the ground the agricultural peoples (Menti), and had placed his boundaries at the beginning of the world, and at the utmost borders of the river-land of Naharain . . . which the great sea encircles.

His return took the form of a specially festive triumphal procession. Laden with booty from the land of Ruthen, with silver and gold, with blue, green, red, and other precious stones, accompanied by numerous captives from lands, which he had again subjected to the supremacy of Egypt, Seti reached his home by the same road which had led him from Egypt into the foreign countries. At the frontier, near Khetam, the priests and great men of the land waited to meet him with gifts of flowers.

The priests, the great ones, and the most distinguished men of South and North Egypt have arrived to praise the divine benefactor on his return from the land of Ruthen, accompanied by an immensely rich booty, such as never had happened since the time of the Sun-god Ra. They speak thus in praise of the king and in glorification of his fame :

' Thou hast returned home from the foreign countries which thou hast overcome. Thou hast triumphed over thy enemies which are subjected to thee. May the duration of thy life as king be as long as the sun in heaven ! Thou hast quenched thy wrath upon the nine foreign nations. The Sun-god himself has established thy boundaries. His hand protected thee, when thy battle-axe was raised above the heads of all peoples, whose kings fell under thy sword.'

Then comes a list of the conquered nations, of which the following are those generally mentioned on the monuments :—

1. Kheta, the land of the Kheta.
2. Naharain, the river-land (Mesopotamia).
3. Upper Ruthen, Canaan.
4. Lower Ruthen, Northern Syria.
5. Singar, the city and the land of Singara, the Sinear of Holy Scripture.
6. Unu, an unknown island or coast land.
7. Kadesh, in the land of the Amorites.
8. Pa-Bekh ⎫
9. Kadnaf ⎬ both names require to be more accurately defined.
10. Asebi, the island of Cyprus.
11. Mannus, the city and land of Mallos.
12. Aguptha, the land of Cappadocia.
13. Balnu, Balaneæ, to the north of Aradus.

To these may be added the Canaanitish cities mentioned on the temple of Abydos :—

Zithagael.
Zor or Tyre.
Inuam or Jamnia.
Pa-Hir (Hil), Galilee ? or Hali in the tribe of Ashur.
Bitha-antha or Beth-anoth (in what was afterwards Judah).
Qartha-anbu or Kiriath-eneb (in Judah).

That the wars of the king did not take place only in the first year of his reign is evident from several inscriptions; as, for example, the record in the temple of Redesîeh, built in the ninth year of Seti's reign, which cites the following names of the people who had been conquered :—1. Sangar, i.e. Singara; 2. Kadeshu; 3. Makita, i.e. Megiddo; 4. Ha . . . . . .; 5. the Shasu-Arabs of Edom; 6. Asal or Asar, a name which we can hardly venture to identify with Assur.

Seti carried his wars to the west, and in particular against the Libyan tribes, who now appear for the first time on the Egyptian monuments.   The double plume on the crown of the head and the side locks of hair mark in the most striking manner these races, which the inscriptions designate by the name of Thuhi, Thuhen, or Tuheni, i.e. 'the light or fair people.'[1]   To this campaign Seti took his son and heir Ramses.   In the battle itself the king appears in a chariot, whose pair of horses bore the name ' Victorious is Amen.'   An inscription says :—

He (the king) utterly destroyed them, when he stood on the field of battle.   They could not hold their bows, and remained hidden in their caves like foxes, through fear of the king.

Of course after these extensive campaigns, Amen and his temple in Apet would be remembered, as is proved by the following record :—

The king presents the booty to his father Amen, on his return from the miserable land of Ruthen, consisting of silver, gold, blue, green, red, and other precious stones, and of the kings of the peoples, whom he holds bound in his hand, to fill therewith the storehouse of his father Amen, on account of the victory which he has granted to the king.

The kings of the peoples which had not known Egypt are brought by Pharaoh in consequence of his victory over the miserable land of Ruthen.   They speak thus to glorify his Majesty and to praise his great deeds :—

' Hail to thee ! mighty is thy name, glorious thy renown.   The people may well rejoice which is subjected to thy will ; but he appears in fetters who oversteps thy boundaries.   By thy name ! We did not know Egypt ; our fathers had not entered it.   Grant us freedom out of thy hand ! '

The prisoners are presented by the divine benefactor to his father Amen, from the hostile kings of the nations which had not known Egypt—their gifts rest on their shoulders,—to fill therewith all the storehouses, as men-servants and maid-servants, in

[1] See p. 133.

consequence of the victories which the god has given the king over all lands !

The great kings of the miserable land of Ruthen are brought by the king in consequence of his victory over the people of the Kheta, to fill with them the storehouse of his noble father, Amen-Ra, the lord of Thebes, because he has given him the victory over the southern world and the subjection of the northern world.

The kings of the nations speak thus, to praise Pharaoh and to exalt his glory :—

'Hail to thee ! king of Kamit, sun of the nine peoples, exalted be thou like the gods !'

From the above inscription it is clear that Seti I. must have proved his entire devotion to the Theban priests, or, to speak in the official tone of the Egyptians, to the Theban Amen. His buildings, wonderfully beautiful creations of the unknown masters of his time, bespeak the efforts of the Pharaoh to express his gratitude for the distinguished position which the priests had allowed him. His rich presents complete the proof of his regard for the temple at Apet. A special reason for this lay in the peculiar position of Seti with regard to the great question of the hereditary right to the throne.

The monuments name as the wife of the king, or rather as mother of his great son and successor Ramses II., the queen Tui, whose name at once reminds us of the family of Khu-n-aten. In genealogical succession, she was a granddaughter of that heretical king, whom the Theban priests had so bitterly excommunicated, although he belonged to the legitimate race of kings. But however hateful this connection might be to the priests, yet it was in accordance with the law of the hereditary succession. The remembrance of her grand-mother's origin must have been all the more distasteful to the priests, as King Seti and his race worshipped the foreign gods in the most obtrusive manner, and at the head of them all the Canaanitish Baal-Sutekh or Set, after whose name his father, Ramses I., had called him Seti—the 'follower of Set.' Thus he had to avoid an open breach, and though as a conqueror Seti had done his part for Egypt, he was bound to try to win over the priests as a benefactor and a generous king. Yet he seems to have had but little success, since at an early period he conferred the highest dignity of the empire on his infant heir, Ra-messu, and made him associated king. In the great historical inscription at Abydos Ramses II. relates that

the lord of all himself nurtured me, and brought me up. I was a little boy before I attained the lordship ; then he gave over to me the land. I was yet in my mother's womb, when the great ones saluted me full of veneration. I was solemnly inducted as the eldest son into the dignity of heir of the throne on the chair of the earth-god Seb. And I gave my orders as chief of the body-guard and of the chariot-fighters. Then my father presented me publicly to the people : I was a boy on his lap, and he spake thus : 'I will have him crowned as king, for I desire to behold his grandeur while I am still alive.' [Then came forward] the officials of the court to place the double crown on my head (and my father spake), 'Place the regal circlet on his brow.' Thus he spake of me while he still remained on earth, 'May he restore order to the land ; may he set up again [what has fallen into decay]. May he care for the inhabitants.' Thus spake he [with good intention] in his very great love for me. Still he left me in the house of the women and of the royal concubines, after the manner of the damsels of the palace. He chose me [women] from among the [maidens], who wore a harness of leather.

In another inscription of the times of Ramses II., the early reign of the king is mentioned in the following words :—

Thou wast a lord (Adon) of this land, and thou actedst wisely, when thou wast still in the egg. In thy childhood what thou saidst took place for the welfare of the land. When thou wast a boy, with the youth's locks of hair, no monument saw the light without thy command ; no business was done without thy knowledge. Thou wast raised to be a governor (Rohir) of this land

when thou wast a youth and countedst ten full years. All buildings proceeded from thy hands, and the laying of their foundation-
stones was performed.

When Ramses II. ascended the throne, he may have
been about twelve years old, or a little more. From
this epoch we should count the years of his reign up to
its sixty-seventh year, so that he was an old man of
eighty when he died.

After Seti had assured the birthright of his race, in
the manner we have described, by the elevation of his
eldest son to the throne, it must have been easy for him
to meet the reproach that he was not of royal descent.
While he actually ruled the land as king, Ramses, his
son, as legitimate sovereign, gave authority to all the
acts of his father.

It seems to have been under their double reign that
those wars took place which were waged against the
nations to the south of Egypt. When Seti, in the list of
conquered peoples on the wall of Karnak, mentions the
countries of Cush and Punt, with all the great and
small races of the southern lands of Africa, as the
subjects of his crown, we must not forget that the
ancient usage was followed of exhibiting to the Egyptians with more or less detail the whole catalogue of
those peoples, transcribed from the temple books of the
'subjects of Egypt.' Several records of this time bear
witness to campaigns beyond the frontier town of Syene.
Egyptian viceroys known as 'king's sons of Cush' acted
as governors in the place of Pharaoh in the South, and
took care that the tributes imposed were regularly paid.
As such are mentioned, in the joint reign of Seti I. and
Ramses II., Ani and Amenape a son of Pauer.

The reign of Seti belongs to that period in the history of the country during which Egyptian art enjoyed
the peculiar favour of the king, and answered to his

patronage in the most worthy manner by the creation
of real master-pieces. The Hall of Columns at Karnak,
in so far as it was carried out during the king's life, and
the temple of Osiris at Abydos are works of the highest
order, the splendour of which consists, above all else,
in the beauty of the sculpture, even to the hieroglyphic
characters. The celebrated tomb also of Seti is one of
the most remarkable achievements of Theban art. It
is the one called after the name of its discoverer,
'Belzoni's tomb,' and to this day forms the chief point
of attraction to visitors to the Valley of the Tombs of
the Kings at Thebes. It contains an abundance of
pictures and inscriptions, which are chiefly mythological, but which also involve a special significance in
relation to astronomy, as do the very instructive roof-
pictures of the so-called Golden Chamber. Unique in
its kind is the mythological substance of a long text,
found in a side chamber of the same tomb, and which
(as M. Naville has proved) has for its subject a description of the destruction of the corrupt human race.

As Seti had erected one of the most splendid works
to the god Amen on the right bank of the Theban
metropolis, so also at his command there rose on the
western bank of the river that wonderful temple, which
he dedicated to the memory of his deceased father
Ra-messu I. I mean the 'Memnonium' of Seti at Old
Gûrnah. In many places on this monument, which
belonged to the West country and consequently to
the realm of Osiris, the king avoids giving himself
the name of Seti. He calls himself generally Usiri, or
Usiri Seti. The sanctuary bore the designation of 'the
splendid temple-building of King Meneptah Seti, in the
city of Amen, on the western side of Thebes;' frequently
also with the addition 'in sight of Apet.' The temple
was dedicated to his deceased father, to the gods of

the dead, Osiris and Hathor, besides Amen and his company. The death of Seti took place while the temple was in course of building. We are told by the inscription which Ramses II. put up :—

King Ramses II. executed this work, as his monument to his father Amen-Ra, the king of the gods, the lord of heaven, the ruler of Thebes ; and he finished the house of his father King Meneptah (Seti). For he died, and entered the realm of heaven, and he united himself with the sun-god in heaven, when this his house was being built. The gates showed a vacant space, and all the walls of stone and brick were yet to be raised ; all the work in it of writing or painting was unfinished.

Seti dedicated a special document to the memory of his royal ancestors in the temple of Abydos, namely, the celebrated Tablet of the Kings, called that of Abydos, containing the names of seventy-six kings, up to the founder of the empire, Mena.

In Memphis and Heliopolis, Seti I. raised temples, or added new parts to temples already existing, which are likewise designated as 'splendid buildings.' Although their last remains have disappeared, without leaving a trace, their former existence is most surely proved by the testimony of inscriptions. In the same way we know that at the foot of the mountain behind the old town of El-Kab he erected a temple to the goddess Nekheb and another in the form of a rock-grotto to Hathor in her lioness form.

Among the sculptors of the time the name of a certain Hi has been preserved ; and among the painters Amen-uah-su is expressly celebrated as the 'first painter.' Both worked by the king's order in the decoration of the tomb which was destined for Pauer, the reigning governor of Thebes, the son of the chief priest of Amen, Neb-neteru, surnamed Thera, and of the oldest among the sacred priestesses of the god Mer-Amen-Ra, and also for her brother Tathao.

The abundant tributes and taxes which under Tehuti-mes III. were yearly contributed by the conquered nations and his own subjects, seem, from the reign of Seti, to have flowed in less vigorously, while the wants of the kings were the same, and the erection of costly buildings required a great expenditure. New sources must needs therefore be opened for the requisite means. So the king began to devote special care to the regular working of the gold-mines in Egypt and Nubia, and to the formation of wells in the midst of the parched mountain regions, from which the gold was to be won. One of these was the desert on the eastern side of the Nile, opposite to Edfû, which at this day bears the name of Redesîeh, and contains the remains of an old rock-temple. It marks the site of one of the resting-places on the road which led straight through the desert from the town of Coptos, on the Nile, to the harbour of Berenice, on the Red Sea. The inscriptions on the temple date from the time of Seti I. They not only establish the existence of gold ore in the interior of the mountain, but also the position of a well (*hydreuma*, as the Greeks called it), made by royal command, and relate how, in the ninth year of Seti, in the month Epiphi, on the 20th day, that king undertook a journey to see the gold mines which existed there. After he had gone many miles he halted to consider the information he had received, that the want of water made the road almost impassable, and that travellers died of thirst in the hot season of the year. At a suitable place a well was bored, and a small rock-temple built there ' to the name of King Seti.' Thereupon everything was done to carry on the gold-washing with success. The people who followed this laborious occupation were placed under the supervision of a *her-pit*, or ' overseer of the foreign peoples,' and measures were taken to ensure the keeping up of the temple and the worship of its deities, Osiris, Isis, and Horus, besides the three chief divinities of the country, Amen and Horemkhu of Thebes, and Ptah of Memphis. The inhabitants were highly pleased with this work, for

King Seti did this for his memorial for his father Amen-Ra and his company of gods, namely, he built anew for them a house of God, in the interior of which the divinities dwell in full contentment. He had the well bored for them. Such a thing was never done before by any king, except him, the king. Thus did King Seti do a good work, the beneficent dispenser of water, who prolongs life to his people ; he is for every one a father and a mother. They speak from mouth to mouth, 'Amen grant him (a long existence), increase to him an everlasting duration. Ye gods of the well ! assure to him your length of life, since he has made for us the road to travel upon, and has opened what lay shut up before our face. Now can we travel up with ease, and reach the goal and remain living. The difficult road lies open there before us, and the way has become good. Now the gold can be carried up, as the king and lord has seen. All the living generations, and those which shall be hereafter, will pray for an eternal remembrance for him. May he celebrate the thirty years' jubilee-feasts like Tmu ; may he flourish like Horus of Apollinopolis; because he has founded a memorial in the lands of the gods, because he has bored for water in the mountains.'

In the execution of the work Ani, the ' King's son of Cush,' as well as commander-in-chief of the Mazai, was present as the directing architect. This fact is attested by rock-inscriptions, accompanied by pictorial representations, as, for example, that of the warlike foreign goddess Antha, who rides on horseback wielding a battle-axe and shield, like Bellona.

Whether, after all, the mines yielded rich produce, and the gold-washers delivered to the ' reckoner of silver and gold of the land of the country of Upper and Lower Egypt, Hi-shera,' the results of their laborious employment in satisfactory quantity, we do not know, for upon this point the monuments are silent.

As Seti's reign runs parallel with that of his son Ramses, we will suppose, with the ancients, that his soul suddenly flew away like a bird to the Egyptian heaven, to enjoy a better existence in the barque of the sun.

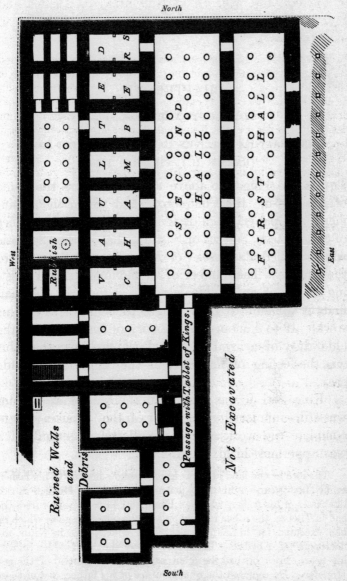

TEMPLE OF SETI I. AND RAMSES II. AT ABYDOS.

CHAPTER XII.

DYNASTY XIX.—continued.

User-maat-Ra sotep-en-Ra Ra-messu meri-Amen (Ramses II.) cir. b.c. 1333.

This is the king who above all others bears the name of A-nekht-u, 'the Conqueror,' and whom the monuments and papyri often designate by his popular names of Ses, Sestesu, Setesu, or Sestura, that is, the 'Sethosis who is called Ramesses' of Manetho, the Sesostris of the Greeks. The number of his monuments still existing in Egypt and Nubia is so great that the historian finds it difficult to know where to begin or to end his work. If to honour the memory of his father be the chief duty of a loyal son—and we shall see that this was the feeling of Ramses II.—the beginning is made easy.

King Seti I. was dead, and the temple at Abydos was still unfinished. The first care of Ramses was to complete the work and to record the intention which was uppermost in his mind.

The lord of the land arose as king, to show honour to his father, in his first year, on his first journey to Thebes. He had caused likenesses of his father, who was King Seti I., to be sculptured, the one in Thebes, the other in Memphis at the entrance gate, which he had executed for himself, besides those which were in Nifur, the necropolis of Abydos. Thus he fulfilled the wish which moved his heart, since he had been on earth, on the ground of the god Unnefer. He renewed the remembrance of his father, and of those who rest in the under world, in that he made his name to live, and

caused his portraits to be made, and fixed the revenues set apart
for his venerated person, and filled his house and richly decked out
his altars.   The walls were rebuilt, which had become old in his
favourite house ; the halls in his temple were rebuilt, its walls were
covered, its gates were raised up ; whatever had fallen into decay in
the burial-place of his father in the necropolis was restored, and
[the works of art which] had been carried away were brought back
into the interior.

.   .   .   .

The king (now) returned from the capital of the land of the South.
[As soon as] the sun [had risen], the journey was commenced.   As
the ships of the king sailed on, they threw their brightness on the
river.   The order was given for the journey down the stream to the
stronghold of the city of Ra-messu, the Conqueror.

Then the king, in order to behold his father, made the rowers
enter the canal of Nifur, with the intention of offering a sacrifice to
the beneficent god Unnefer with his choicest libations, and of praying to [the divinity] of his brother Anhur, the son of Ra in . . . as
which he abides there.

There he found the halls of the dead of the former kings, and
their graves, which are in Abydos, hastening to the beginning of
desolation.   Their burial-places had become dilapidated from the
foundations.   [The stones were torn away] out of the ground, their
walls lay scattered about on the road, no brick held to another, the
hall ' of the second birth' lay in ruins, nothing had been built up
[for the father by his son], who should have been busied in preserv-
ing it according to his expectations, since its possessor had flown up
to heaven.   Not one son had renewed the memorial of his father,
who rested in the grave.

There was the temple of Seti.   The front and back elevations
were in process of building when he entered the realm of heaven.
Unfinished was his monument ; the columns were not raised on
their bases, his statues lay upon the earth ; they were not sculptured
according to the corresponding measure of ' the golden chamber.'
His revenues failed.   The servants of the temple without distinction
had taken what was brought in from the fields, the boundary marks
of which were not staked out on the land.

The king speaks to the chamberlain at his side : 'Speak, that
there may be assembled the princes, the favourites of the king, the
commanders of the body-guards, as they are (i.e. all of them), the
architects, according to their number, and the superintendents of
the house of the rolls of the books.'

When they had come before the king, their noses touched the
ground, and their feet lay on the ground for joy ; they fell down to

the ground, and with their hands they prayed to the king. They praised this divine benefactor, while they exalted his grace in his presence.

. . . . . .

The king speaks to them after an interval : 'I have called you because of a determination regarding that which I am about to do. I have beheld the houses of the necropolis, the graves of Abydos. The buildings of them require labour from the times of their possessors down to the present day. When the son arose in the place of his father, he did not renew the memorial of his parent. In my mind I have pondered with myself the splendid occasion for good works for coming times (?). The most beautiful thing to behold, the best thing to hear, is a child with a thankful breast, whose heart beats for his father. Wherefore my heart urges me to do what is good for Meneptah. I will cause them to talk for ever and eternally of his son, who has awakened his name to life. My father Osiris will reward me for this with a long existence, like his son Horus. Let me do what he did ; let me be excellent, just as he was excellent, for my parent, I, who am a scion of the sun-god Ra.

. . . . . .

'[I gave orders for the buildings], I myself laid their foundation-stone to build [the work. I had an image] made of him who begat me, my father, of gold, quite new.

'In the first year of my reign as king I had given orders to provide his temple with stores. I secured to him his fields, [and fixed their boundaries,] and appointed him revenues for his worship, [and arranged the sacrifices of oxen and geese and bread] and wine and incense and other things. I planted for him groves to grow up for him. Thus was his house under my protection ; I took upon myself all his buildings from the time that [I was crowned as king]. And thus I was a child [whose heart was full of thanks towards] his father who had exalted me.

'I will renew the memorial. I will not neglect his tomb as children are accustomed to do, who do not remember their father. [Men shall speak of me] as of a son who did good, and shall estimate the strength of my father in me his child. I will complete it because I am lord of the land. I will take care of it because it is fitting and right.

'I clothe the walls in the temple of my parent. I will commission the man of my choice to hasten the buildings for him, to build up again what was sunken of its walls, [and to raise up] his temple wings on the [front side,] to clothe his house, to erect his pillars, and to place the blocks on the places of the foundation-stone.

Beautifully shall the most splendid double memorial be made at
once.   Let it be inscribed with my name, and with the name of my
father.   As the son is, so was the father [who begat him].'

The king's friends speak in answer to the divine benefactor :

'[That which thou hast determined,] O king, do it.   Remember
that which was sunk in forgetfulness, renew the monuments in
the necropolis, and all the plans which were behindhand, execute
them as is right and fitting.—Thou art now king of Upper Egypt
and Lower Egypt.   Do good even as thou willest.   Let thy heart
be satisfied in doing what is right.   For that which is done for the
honour of the gods, that will be accepted and [rewarded by the
immortals] when thou hereafter shalt rise to heaven.   When thy
grace raises himself to the orb of light, then shall the eyes see thy
glorious virtues in the sight of gods and men.   Thus do thou.   Renew memorial after memorial to the gods.   Therefore shall thy father
Ra command that thy name shall resound in all lands, beginning
in the south with Khent-hen-nefer, northwards from the shores
of the sea as far as the nations of Ruthen.   The foreign fortresses
and towns of the king and the cities, well guarded and occupied
with their inhabitants, and [the dwellers in all places, they speak
of thee,] that thou art as a god for every one.   They awake to
offer incense to thee.   Thus according to the will of thy father Tmu,
the black land (Egypt) and·the red land (Tesherit) praise thee,
O king.'

.   .   .   .

When [this speech] from the lips of the princes before their lord
[was ended,] then the king commanded, and gave commission to the
architects, and separated the people of the masons and of the stone-
cutters with the help of the graver, and the draughtsmen, and all
kinds of artists, to build the most holy place for his father, and to
raise up what had fallen into decay in the necropolis, and in the
temple of his father, who sojourns among the deceased ones.

Then [he began] to have the statues of his father carved, from
the first year.   The revenues were doubled for his worship, his
temple was enriched according to the number of its wants.   He
appointed its register of fields and peasants and herds.   He named
its priests according to their service, and the prophet, to raise in his
hands [the incense-vessel], and he appointed the temple servants
for the performance of the works for him.   His barns were many,
full of wheat [and his storehouses in all plenty].   His domain was
immense in the South and in the North, and was placed under the
administration of the superintendent of his temple.   In such wise
did King Ramses II. for his father, King Seti, under the protection
of Unnefer.

He repeated what he had done for his honour in Thebes, in On, and in Memphis, where his statues rested in their places, and in all the places of the granaries.

These are the words of King Ramses II., [to sing] what he did for his father, the Osiris-king Seti. He speaks thus :

'Awake, raise thy face to heaven, behold the sun, my father Meneptah, thou who art like God. Here am I, who make thy name to live. I am thy guardian, and my care is directed to thy temple and to thy altars, which are raised up again. Thou restest in the deep like Osiris, while I rule like Ra among men (and possess) the great throne of Tmu, like Horus, the son of Isis, the guardian of his father. Beautiful is that which I have done for thee.—

'Thou enterest on a second existence. I caused thee to be fashioned, I built thy house which thou didst love, in which thy image stands, in the necropolis of Abydos for ever. I set apart revenues for thee for thy worship daily, to be just towards thee. If anything is in my power, which seems to be wanting to thee, I do it for thee. Thy heart shall be satisfied, that the best shall be done for thy name. I appoint for thee the priests of the vessel of holy water, provided with everything for sprinkling the water on the ground, besides meat and drink. I myself, I myself am come here to behold thy temple near that of Unnefer, the eternal king. I urged on the building of it, I clothed [the walls], I did that which thou didst wish, that it may be done for thy whole house. I established thy name therein to all eternity. May it be done in truth, may it succeed according to my intention. I dedicated to thee the lands of the South for the service of thy temple, and the lands of the North, they bring to thee their gifts before thy beautiful countenance. I gathered together the people of thy service one and all, assigning them to the prophet of thy temple. All thy property shall remain in one great whole, to keep up thy temple for all time. I made presents to thy silver chamber; it is rich in treasures which are well pleasing to the heart, and I apportioned to thee the tributes at the same time. I dedicated to thee ships with their freight on the great sea, which should bring to thee [the wonderful productions] of the holy land. The merchants carry on their commerce with their wares, and their productions of gold and silver and bronze. I fixed for thee the number of the fields according to the proportion of the claims [of thy temple]. Great is their number according to their valuation in acres. I provided thee with land-surveyors and husbandmen, to deliver the corn for thy revenues. I dedicated to thee barks with their crews, and labourers for the felling of wood, for the purpose of building what is wanting in ships for thy house. I gave thee herds of all kinds of cattle to increase thy revenues, according to what is right. I fixed for thee the tribute of birds in the marshes for thy necessary sustenance. I [caused to be delivered to thee] living geese, to keep up the breed of the birds. I gave to thee fishermen on the river and on all the lakes, to feed the workmen who load the sea-going ships. I have provided thy temple with all kinds of guilds of my handi[craftsmen]. Thy temple servants have been made up to their full number from the best people, and the peasants pay their taxes in woven stuffs for thy drapery. Thy men-servants and maid-servants work in the fields in all the town districts. Each man thus performs his service, to fill thy house.

'Thou hast entered into the realm of heaven. Thou accompaniest the sun-god Ra. Thou art united with the stars and the moon. Thou restest in the deep, like those who dwell in it with Unnefer, the eternal. Thy hands move the god Tmu in heaven and on earth, like the wandering stars and the fixed stars. Thou remainest in the forepart of the bark of millions. When the sun rises in the tabernacle of heaven, thine eyes behold his splendour. When Tmu (the evening sun) goes to rest on the earth, thou art in his train. Thou enterest the secret house before his lord. Thy foot wanders in the deep. Thou remainest in the company of the gods of the under world.

'But I obtain by my prayers the breath (of life) at thy awaking, thou glorious one! and I praise thy numerous names day by day, I who love my father.—I let myself be guided by thy virtue. So long as I stay on earth, I will offer a sacrifice to thee. My hand shall bring the libations for thy name to thy [remembrance] in all thy abodes.

'Come, speak to Ra [that he may grant long years] of life to his son, and to Unnefer, with a heart full of love, that he may grant length of time upon length of time, united to the thirty-years' feasts of jubilee, to King Ramses. Well will it be for thee that I should be king for a long time, for thou wilt be honoured by a good son, who remembers his father. I will be a [protector and] guardian for thy temple day by day, to have regard to the wants of thy worship in every way. If I should hear of any injury which threatens to invade it, I will give the order immediately to remove it in every way. Thou shalt be treated as if thou wert still alive. So long as I shall reign, my attention shall be directed continually to thy temple. My heart beats for thee; I will be thy guardian for the honour of thy name. If thou also remainest in the deep, the best, the very best shall be thy portion as long as I live, I, King Ramses.'

The spirit of the deceased king then appears from the under world to answer the vows of Ramses. To him, the son, be all good fortune, glory, health, and joy, and whatever else a man could wish, but above all what Ramses most coveted, a very long term of life, to be measured by the thirty years' feast of jubilee. What gives this inscription its special value in relation to history may be stated in a few words. It is that Seti I. was apparently buried first of all in Abydos, where the soil, impregnated with salt, is favourable to the preservation of the dead; and the position of his temple, dedicated to Osiris, quite agrees with this. His body was probably removed afterwards to Thebes.

In the course of his long reign Ramses II. completed the temple begun by his father at Abydos. He must have been advanced in years when it was finished, since not less than sixty sons and fifty-nine daughters greeted in their effigies the entrance of the pilgrims at the principal gate.

In proportion as the works executed under Seti I. present splendid examples of Egyptian architecture and sculpture, just so poor and inferior are the buildings executed by Ramses II. The feeling also of gratitude towards his parent seems to have gradually faded away, as years increased upon him, to such a degree that he did not even deem it wrong to chisel out the names and memorials of his father in many places of the temple walls, and to substitute his own.

In the fifth year of this king's reign a great war broke out between Egypt and the Kheta, in which Kadesh was the rallying-point. Besides the prince of the Kheta, there were as his allies the kings and peoples of Arathu (Aradus), Khilibu (Haleb), of the river-land of Naharain, of Qazauadana (Gauzanitis—Goshen), of Malunna, of Pidasa (Pidasis), of Leka (the Ligyes), of the Dardani, or Dandani (Dardanians in Kurdistan), of the Masu (the inhabitants of Mount Masius), of Kerkesh (the Girgesites?) or Keshkesh, of Qirqimosh (Carchemish), of Akerith, of Anau-gas (Jenysus), of Mushanath, all ' peoples from the extremest end of the sea to the land of the Kheta.'

It was a slaughter of peoples, in the fullest sense of the word, that was prepared at Kadesh, out of which Ramses came but as a doubtful conqueror, and had to thank his own personal bravery for his life and preservation, since 'he was all alone and no other was with him.'

This heroic feat was the theme of the celebrated epic poem of Pentaur the scribe, of which we not only possess a papyrus copy but its words cover the whole surface of walls in the temples at Abydos, Luqsor, Karnak, the Ramesseum, and Abû Simbel. An unknown painter has chiselled in deep work on the wall of the temple at Karnak a vivid representation of the battle of Kadesh—the storming of the fortress, the overthrow of the enemy, and the details of the camp life of the Egyptians. The tent of Pharaoh is seen in the middle of the camp, and near it the movable shrine of the divinities of Egypt. Above the picture is the inscription, ' This is the first legion of Amen, who bestows victory on Ramses II.; Pharaoh is with it. It is occupied in pitching its camp.' Not far off sits the king, enthroned, receiving the reports of his generals, while the soldiers are dragging forward two foreigners about whom the inscription says, ' This is the arrival of the spies of Pharaoh; they bring two spies of the people of the Kheta before Pharaoh. They are beating them to make them declare where the king of the Kheta is.' The war-chariots and legions of Amen, Ptah, Phrah, and Sutekh are seen passing in good order before the king.

Mercenary troops are not wanting, for the Colchian Shardana, whose fine linen was well known to antiquity under the name of Sardonian, appear among the Egyptian allies. They are distinguished by their helmets with horns and a ball-shaped crest, by their long swords and the round shields on their left arm, while their right hand grasps a spear.

The Kheta and their allies are also vividly represented. The Canaanites are distinguished in the most striking manner from the allies, of races unknown to us, who are attired with turban-like coverings for the head, or with high caps such as are still worn at the present day by the Persians. Short swords, lances, bows and arrows, form the weapons of the Egyptian enemies. Among the *Tuhir*, ' chosen ones,' who follow in the train of the Kheta king are the *Qelau*, or ' slingers,' who formed his body-guard.

Wonderfully rich is the great battle-picture which represents the fight of the chariots before Kadesh on the banks of the Orontes. While the gigantic form of Ramses, in the very midst of the mass of hostile chariots, performs deeds of the highest prowess, to the astonishment of the Egyptians and of their enemies, his brave son, Prahiunamef, as the chief commander of the chariots, heads the attack on the chariots of the enemy. Several of his brothers, the children of Ramses, take part in the battle. The chariots of the Kheta and their warriors are thrown into the river; and among them the king of Khilibu, whom his soldiers have just dragged out of the water, and are endeavouring to restore to animation. They hold him head downwards by the legs. The inscription by the side runs thus :—

This is the king of Khilibu. His warriors are raising him up after Pharaoh has thrown him into the water.

The beginning of the battle is described in a short inscription annexed to the picture :—

When the king had halted, he sat down to the north-west of the town of Kadesh.   He had come up with the hostile hosts of Kheta, being quite alone, no other was with him.   There were thousands and hundreds of chariots round about him on all sides.   He dashed them down in heaps of dead bodies before his horses. He killed all the kings of all the peoples who were allies of the (king) of Kheta, together with his princes and elders, his warriors and his horses.   He threw them one upon another, head over heels, into the water of the Orontes.   There the king of Kheta turned round, and raised up his hands to implore the divine benefactor.

The battle, or rather butchery, seems to have been as little agreeable to the people of the Kheta as to their lords, for

the hostile Kheta speak, praising the divine benefactor thus : 'Give us freedom (literally, breath) from thy hand, O good king ! Let us lie at thy feet ; the fear of thee has opened the land of Kheta.   We are like the foals of mares, which tremble in terror at the sight of the grim lion.'

In the customary manner, as already described, the inscriptions sing the praise of their king :—

The brave and bold conqueror of the nations, of the highest valour in the field of battle, firm on horseback, and glorious on his chariot, whom none can escape when he seizes his bow and arrows.

A less poetical and ornate description of the great battle of Kadesh is preserved in a record repeated several times on the temple walls.   It runs as follows :—

(1) In the 5th year, in the month Epiphi, on the 9th day, in the reign of King Ramses II., the Pharaoh was (2) in the land of Zahi, on his second campaign.   Good watch was kept over the king in the camp of Pharaoh on the heights to the south of (3) the city of Kadesh.   Pharaoh came forth as soon as the sun rose, and put on the (war) array of his father Mentu.   And the sovereign went further (4) upwards, and came to the south of the town of Shabatun.   There came to meet him two Shasu, in order to speak to (5) Pharaoh thus :—

'We are brothers, who belong to the chiefs of the tribes of the
Shasu, which are (6) in the dominion of the king of Kheta. They
commanded us to go to Pharaoh, to speak thus : We wish to be
servants (7) to the house of Pharaoh, so that we may separate ourselves from the king of Kheta. But now (8) the king of Kheta
stays in the land of Khilibu, to the north of Tunep, for he fears
Pharaoh, intending forwards (9) to advance.'

Thus spake the two Shasu. But the words which they had
spoken to the king were vain lies ; (10) for the king of Kheta had
sent them to spy out where Pharaoh was, so that the (11) soldiers of
Pharaoh should not prepare an ambush in the rear, in order to fight
with the king of Kheta. For the king of Kheta had (12) come
with all the kings of all peoples, with horses and riders, which he
brought with him in great numbers, and stood there ready (13) in
an ambush behind the town of Kadesh, the wicked. And the king
did not discover the meaning of their words.

And Pharaoh went further downwards, and came to the region
to the north-west of Kadesh, where he stayed to rest on (14) a
golden couch of repose. There came in the spies, who belonged to
the servants of the king, and brought with them two spies of the
king of (15) Kheta. When they had been brought forward, Pharaoh spake to them : 'Who are ye?' They said, 'We belong to
(16) the king of Kheta, who sent us to see where Pharaoh is.'
Then spake to them (17) Pharaoh : 'He, where stays he, the king
of Kheta? For I have heard say that he is in the land of Khilibu?'
They said : 'Behold (18) the king of Kheta stays there, and much
people with him, whom he has brought with him (19) in great
numbers from all countries which are situated in the territory of
the land of Kheta, of the land of Naharain (20) and of all the Kiti.
They are provided with riders and horses, who bring with them (21)
the implements of war, and they are more than the sand of the sea.
Behold, they stay there in ambush to fight behind the town of
Kadesh, (22) the wicked.'

Then Pharaoh called the princes before him, that they might
hear (23) all the words which the two spies of the land of Kheta,
who were present, had spoken. The king spake to them : 'Behold
the wisdom (24) of the governor and of the princes of the lands
of the house of Pharaoh in this matter ! They stood there speaking daily thus to Pharaoh—(25) "The king of Kheta is in the
land of Khilibu; he has fled before Pharaoh since he heard say that
he would come to him according to the words of Pharaoh daily."
(26) Now behold what I have had to hear in this hour from the
two spies. The king of Kheta is come up with much people,
who are with him with horses and riders (27) as many as the

sand.   They stand there behind the town of Kadesh, the wicked. Thus has it happened that the governor and the princes knew nothing, to whom (28) the countries of the house of Pharaoh are entrusted.   (29) It was their duty to have said, They are come up.'

Then the princes who were before Pharaoh spake thus : ' The fault (30) is great which the governor and the princes of the house of Pharaoh have committed, that they did not make enquiries (31) where the king of Kheta stayed at each time, (32) that they might have given notice daily to Pharaoh.'

Then (33) was the commission given to a captain to urge on in haste the army of the king, which entered into the country (34) to the south of Shabatun, to direct them to the spot where (35) Pharaoh was.   For Pharaoh had relied on the words of the princes, while in the meantime the king of Kheta came up with much people that were with him, with riders (36) and horses.   So exceeding great was the number of the people that was with him. They had passed over the ditch, which is to the south of the town of Kadesh, and they fell upon the army of Pharaoh, which entered in without having any information.   And (37) the army and the horses of Pharaoh gave way before them on the road upwards to the place where the king was.   Then the hostile hosts of the king of Kheta surrounded the (38) followers of Pharaoh, who were by his side.

When Pharaoh beheld this, he became wroth against them, and he was like his father Mentu.   He put on his war array (39) and took his arms, and appeared like the god Baal in his time.   And he mounted his horse, and hurried forth in a quick course.   (40) He was all alone.   He rushed into the midst of the hostile hosts of the king of Kheta and the much people that were with him.   (41) And Pharaoh, like the god Sutekh, the glorious, cast them down and slew them.   ' And I the king flung them down head over heels, one after the other, into the water of the Arantha. I (42) subdued all the people, and yet I was alone, for my warriors and my charioteers had left me in the lurch.   None of them stood (by me).   Then the king of Kheta raised his hands to pray before me.'

(43–44) 'I swear it as truly as the Sun-god loves me, as truly as my father, the god Tmu, blesses me, that all the deeds which I the king have related, these I truly performed before my army, and before my charioteers.'

About two years after the events described above, Pentaur, the poet, finished his heroic song.   Throughout

the poem the peculiar cast of Egyptian thought is
clearly visible ; subjoined is a translation of it :—

THE HEROIC POEM OF PENTAUR.

Beginning of the victory of King Ramses Meri-Amen—may he
live for ever !—which he obtained over the people of the Kheta, of
Naharain, of Malunna, of Pidasa, of the Dardani, over the people
of Masa, of Karkisha, of Qasuatan, of Qarqamish, of Kati, of
Anaugas, over the people of Akerith and Mushanath.

The youthful king with the bold hand has not his equal. His
arms are powerful, his heart is firm, his strength is like that of the
god of war, Mentu, in the midst [of the fight. He leads] his warriors to unknown peoples. He seizes his weapons, and is a wall [of
iron for his warriors], their shield in the day of battle. He seizes
his bow, and no one is equal to him. Mightier than a hundred
thousand united together goes he forwards . . . .
. . . . . . His courage is firm like that of a bull which seizes [the
. . . . . . He has smitten] all peoples who had united themselves
together. No man knows the thousands of men who fell down, nor
the hundreds of thousands that sank before his glance. Terrible is
he when his war-cry resounds ; bolder than the whole world ; [dread-
ful] as the grim lion in the valley of the gazelles. His command
[will be performed. No opponent dares] to speak against him
Wise is his counsel. Complete are his decisions, when he wears the
royal crown Atef and declares his will, a protector of his people
[against unrighteousness]. His heart is like a mountain of iron
Such is King Ramses Meri-Amen.

After the king had armed his people and his chariots, and in
like manner the Shardonians, which were once his prisoners . . . .
. . . then was the order given them for the battle. The king took
his way downwards, and his people and his chariots accompanied
him, and followed the best road on their march.

In the fifth year, on the ninth day of the month Payni, the fortress of Khetam (Etham) of the land of Zar opened to the king
. . . . . As if he had been the god of war, Mentu himself, the
whole world trembled [at his approach], and terror seized all enemies
who came near to bow themselves before the king. And his warriors passed by the path of the desert, and went on along the roads
of the north.

Many days after this the king was in the city of Ramses Meri-
Amen [which is situated in Zahi]. After the king had marched
upwards, he reached . . . . . and arrived as far as Kadesh. Then
the king passed by in their sight like his father Mentu, the lord

of Thebes. He marched through the valley of the river Arunatha,
(with him) the first legion of Amen, who secures victory to the
king Ramses Meri-Amen. And when the king approached the
city, behold there was the miserable king of the hostile Kheta
(already) arrived. He had assembled with him all the peoples
from the uttermost ends of the sea to the people of the Kheta.
They had arrived in great numbers : the people of Naharain, the
people of Arathu, of the Dardani, the Masu, the Pidasa, the Malunna, the Karkish (or Kashkish), the Leka, Qazuadana, Kirkamish,
Akarith, Kati, the whole people of Anaugas every one of them,
Mushanath, and Kadesh. He had left no people on his road
without bringing them with him. Their number was endless ;
nothing like it had ever been before. They covered mountains and
valleys like grasshoppers for their number. He had not left silver
nor gold with his people ; he had taken away all their goods and
possessions, to give it to the people who accompanied him to the
war.

     Now had the miserable king of the hostile Kheta and the many
peoples which were with him hidden themselves in an ambush
to the north-west of the city of Kadesh, while Pharaoh was alone,
no other was with him. The legion of Amen advanced behind
him. The legion of Phra went into the ditch on the territory
which lies to the west of the town of Shabatuna, divided by a long
interval from the legion of Ptah, in the midst, [in the direction]
towards the town of Arnama. The legion of Sutekh marched on by
their roads. And the king called together all the chief men of his
warriors. Behold, they were at the lake of the land of the
Amorites. At the same time the miserable king of Kheta was in
the midst of his warriors, which were with him. But his hand
was not so bold as to venture on battle with Pharaoh. Therefore
he drew away the horsemen and the chariots, which were numerous
as the sand. And they stood three men in each war-chariot, and
there were assembled in one spot the best heroes of the army of
Kheta, well appointed with all weapons for the fight. They did not
dare to advance. They stood in ambush to the north-west of the
town of Kadesh. Then they went out from Kadesh, on the side of
the south, and threw themselves into the midst of the legion of
Phra-Horemkhu, which gave way, and was not prepared for the
fight. There Pharaoh's warriors and chariots gave way before them.
And Pharaoh had placed himself to the north of the town of Kadesh,
on the west side of the river Arunatha. Then they came to tell
the king. Then the king arose, like his father Mentu ; he
grasped his weapons and put on his armour, just like Baal in his
time. And the noble pair of horses which carried Pharaoh, and

whose name was 'Victory in Thebes,' they were from the court of King Ramses Meri-Amen. When the king had quickened his course, he rushed into the midst of the hostile hosts of Kheta, all alone, no other was with him. When Pharaoh had done this, he looked behind him and found himself surrounded by 2,500 pairs of horses, and his retreat was beset by the bravest heroes of the king of the miserable Kheta, and by all the numerous peoples which were with him, of Arathu, of Masu, of Pidasa, of Keshkesh, of Malunna, of Qazauadana, of Khilibu, of Akerith, of Kadesh, and of Leka. And there were three men in each chariot, and they were all gathered together.

And not one of my princes, not one of my captains of the chariots, not one of my chief men, not one of my knights was there. My warriors and my chariots had abandoned me, not one of them was there to take part in the battle.

Thereupon speaks Pharaoh : 'Where art thou, my father Amen ? If this means that the father has forgotten his son, behold have I done anything without thy knowledge, or have I not gone and followed the judgments of thy mouth ? Never were the precepts of thy mouth transgressed, nor have I broken thy commands in any respect. The noble lord and ruler of Egypt, should he bow himself before the foreign peoples in his way ? Whatever may be the intention of these herdsmen, Amen should stand higher than the miserable one who knows nothing of God. Shall it have been for nothing that I have dedicated to thee many and noble monuments, that I have filled thy temples with my prisoners of war, that I have built to thee temples to last many thousands of years, that I have given to thee all my substance as household furniture, that the whole united land has been ordered to pay tribute to thee, that I have dedicated to thee sacrifices of ten thousands of oxen, and of all good and sweet-smelling woods ? Never did I withhold my hand from doing that which thy wish required. I have built for thee propylæa and wonderful works of stone, I have raised to thee masts for all times, I have conveyed obelisks for thee from the island of Elephantiné. It was I who had brought for thee the everlasting stone, who caused the ships to go for thee on the sea, to bring thee the productions of foreign nations. Where has it been told that such a thing was done at any other time ? Let him be put to shame who rejects thy commands, but good be to him who acknowledges thee, O Amen ! I have acted for thee with a willing heart ; therefore I call on thee. Behold now, Amen, I am in the midst of many unknown peoples in great numbers. All have united themselves, and I am all alone ; no other is with me ; my warriors and my charioteers have deserted me. I called to them, and not one of them heard my voice. But I find that Amen is better to me than millions of warriors, than hundreds of thousands of horses, than tens of thousands of brothers and sons, even if they were all united together in one place. The works of a multitude of men are nothing ; Amen is better than they. What has happened to me here is according to the command of thy mouth, O Amen, and I will not transgress thy command. Behold I call upon thee at the uttermost ends of the world.'

And my voice found an echo in Hermonthis, and Amen heard it and came at my cry. He reached out his hand to me, and I shouted for joy. He called out to me from behind : 'I have hastened to thee, Ramses Meri-Amen. I am with thee. I am he, thy father, the sun-god Ra. My hand is with thee. Yes ! I am worth more than hundreds of thousands united in one place. I am the lord of victory, the friend of valour ; I have found in thee a right spirit, and my heart rejoices thereat.'

All this came to pass. I was changed, being made like the god Mentu. I hurled the dart with my right hand, I fought with my left hand. I was like Baal in his time before their sight. I had found 2,500 pairs of horses ; I was in the midst of them ; but they were dashed in pieces before my horses. Not one of them raised his hand to fight ; their courage was sunken in their breasts, their limbs gave way, they could not hurl the dart, nor had they the courage to thrust with the spear. I made them fall into the waters just as the crocodiles fall in. They tumbled down on their faces one after another. I killed them at my pleasure, so that not one looked back behind him, nor did another turn round. Each one fell, he raised himself not up again.

There stood still the miserable king of Kheta in the midst of his warriors and his chariots, to behold the fight of the king. He was all alone ; not one of his warriors, not one of his chariots was with him. There he turned round for fright before the king. Thereupon he sent the princes in great numbers, each of them with his chariot, well equipped with all kinds of offensive weapons : the king of Arathu and him of Masa, the king of Malunna and him of Leka, the king of the Dardani and him of Keshkesh, the king of Qarqamash and him of Khilibu. There were all together the brothers of the king of Kheta united in one place, to the number of 2,500 pairs of horses. They forthwith rushed right on, their countenance directed to the flame of fire (i.e. my face).

I rushed down upon them. Like Mentu was I. I let them taste my hand in the space of a moment. I dashed them down, and killed them where they stood. Then cried out one of them to his neighbour, saying, ' This is no man. Ah ! woe to us ! He who is in our midst is Sutekh, the glorious; Baal is in all his limbs. Let us hasten and flee before him. Let us save our lives; let us try our breath.' As soon as any one attacked him, his hand fell down and every limb of his body. They could not aim either the bow or the spear. They only looked at him as he came on in his headlong career from afar. The king was behind them like a griffin.

(Thus speaks the king) :—

I struck them down; they did not escape me. I lifted up my voice to my warriors and to my charioteers, and spake to them. 'Halt! stand! take courage, my warriors, my charioteers! Look upon my victory. I am alone, but Amen is my helper, and his hand is with me.'

When Menna, my charioteer, beheld with his eyes how many pairs of horses surrounded me, his courage left him, and his heart was afraid. Evident terror and great fright took possession of his whole body. Immediately he spake to me : 'My gracious lord, thou brave king, thou guardian of the Egyptians in the day of battle, protect us. We stand alone in the midst of enemies. Stop, to save the breath of life for us! Give us deliverance, protect us, O King Ramses Meri-Amen.'

Then spake the king to his charioteer : 'Halt! stand! take courage, my charioteer. I will dash myself down among them as the sparrow-hawk dashes down. I will slay them, I will cut them in pieces, I will dash them to the ground in the dust. Why, then, is such a thought in thy heart? These are unclean ones for Amen, wretches who do not acknowledge the god.'

And the king hurried onwards. He charged down upon the hostile hosts of Kheta. For the sixth time, when he charged upon them, (says the king) 'There was I like to Baal behind them in his time, when he has strength. I killed them; none escaped me.'

And the king cried to his warriors, and to his chariot-fighters, and likewise to his princes, who had taken no part in the fight, 'Miserable is your courage, my chariot-fighters. Of no profit is it to have you for friends. If there had been only one of you who had shown himself a good (warrior?) for my country! If I had not stood firm as your royal lord, you had been conquered. I exalt you daily to be princes. I place the son in the inheritance of his father, warding off all injury from the land of the Egyptians, and you forsake me! Such servants are worthless. I made you rich, I was your protecting lord, and each of you who complained supplicating to me, I gave him protection in his affairs every day. No Pharaoh has done for his people what I have done for you. I allowed you to remain in your villages and in your towns. Neither the captain nor his chariot-horses did any work. I pointed out to them the road from their city, that they might find it in like manner at the day and at the hour at which the battle comes on. Now behold ! A bad service altogether has been performed for me. None of you stood by, ready to stretch out his hand to me when I fought. By the name of my father Amen ! Oh that I may be for Egypt like my father, the sun-god Ra ! Not a single one of you would watch, to attend to what concerns his duty in the land of Egypt. For such ought to be the good kind of men, who have been entrusted with work for the memorial-places in Thebes, the city of Amen. This is a great fault which my warriors and chariot-fighters have committed, greater than it is possible to describe. Now behold, I have achieved the victory. No warrior and no chariot-fighter was with me. The whole world from afar beholds the strength of my arm. I was all alone. No other was with me. No prince was by my side, of the captains of the chariots, no captain of the soldiers, nor any horseman. The foreign peoples were eye-witnesses of this. They publish my name to the furthest and most unknown regions. All the combatants whom my hand left surviving, they stood there, turning themselves to wonder at what I did ; and though millions of them had been there they would not have kept their feet, but would have run away. For every one who shot an arrow aimed at me, his own weapon failed, which should have reached me.'

When now my warriors and my charioteers saw that I was named like Mentu of the victorious arm, and that Amen my father was with me, and the special favour he had done for me, and that the foreigners all lay like hay before my horses, then they came forward one after another out of the camp at the time of evening, and found all the people which had come against them, the best combatants of the people of Kheta, and of the sons and brothers of their king, stretched out and weltering in their blood. And when it was light on the (next morning) in the plain of the land of Kadesh, one could hardly find a place for his foot on account of their multitude.

Then came my warriors forward to praise highly my name, full of astonishment at what I had done. My princes came forward to honour my courage, and my chariot-fighters also to praise my strength.

'How wast thou, great champion of firm courage, the saviour of thy warriors and of thy chariot-fighters ! Thou son of Amen, who came forth out of the hands of the god, thou hast annihilated the people of Kheta by thy powerful arm. Thou art a good champion, a lord of victory ; no other king fights as thou dost for his warriors in the day of battle. Thou, O bold one, art the first in the fight. The whole world united in one place does not trouble thee. Thou art the greatest conqueror at the head of thy warriors in the sight of the whole world. No one dares to contend with thee. Thou art he who protects the Egyptians, who chastises the foreigners. Thou hast broken the neck of Kheta for everlasting times.'

Thereupon the king answered his warriors and his chariot-fighters, and likewise his princes : 'My warriors, my charioteers, who have not taken part in the fight, a man does not succeed in obtaining honour in his city unless he comes and exhibits his prowess before his lord, the king. Good will be his name, if he is brave in the battle. By deeds, by deeds, will such a one obtain the applause [of the land]. Have I not given what is good to each of you, that ye have left me, so that I was alone in the midst of hostile hosts ? Forsaken by you, my life was in peril, and you breathed tranquilly, and I was alone. Could you not have said in your hearts that I was a rampart of iron to you ? Will any one obey him who leaves me in the lurch when I am alone without any follower ? when nobody comes, of the princes, of the knights, and of the chief men of the army, to reach me out his hand ? I was alone thus fighting, and I have withstood millions of foreigners, I all alone.

' "Victory in Thebes," and "Mut is satisfied," my pair of horses, it was they who found me, to strengthen my hand, when I was all alone in the midst of the raging multitude of hostile hosts. I will myself henceforth have their fodder given to them for their nourishment in my presence, when I shall dwell in the palace, because I have found them in the midst of hostile hosts, together with the captain of the horsemen, Menna, my charioteer, out of the band of the trusted servants in the palace, who stay near me. Here are the eye-witnesses of the battle. Behold, these did I find.'

The king returned in victory and strength ; he had smitten hundreds of thousands all together in one place with his arm.

When the earth was (again) light, he arranged the hosts of warriors for the fight, and he stood there prepared for the battle, like a bull which has whetted his horns. He appeared to them a likeness of the god Mentu, who has armed himself for the battle. Likewise his brave warriors, who dashed into the fight, just as the hawk swoops down upon the kids.

The diadem of the royal snake adorned my head. It spat fire and glowing flame in the face of my enemies. I appeared like the sun-god at his rising in the early morning. My shining beams were a consuming fire for the limbs of the wicked. They cried out to one another. Take care, do not fall ! For the powerful snake of royalty, which accompanies him, has placed itself on his horse. It helps him. Every one who comes in his way and falls down, there comes forth fire and flame to consume his body.'

And they remained afar off, and threw themselves down on the earth, to entreat the king in the sight [of his army]. And the king had power over them and slew them without their being able to escape. As bodies tumbled before his horses, so they lay there stretched out all together in their blood.

Then the king of the hostile people of Kheta sent a messenger to pray piteously to the great name of the king, speaking thus : 'Thou art Ra-Horemkhu. Thou art Sutekh the glorious, the son of Nut, Baal in his time. Thy terror is upon the land of Kheta, for thou hast broken the neck of Kheta for ever and ever.'

Thereupon he allowed his messenger to enter. He bore a writing in his hand with the address, ' To the great double name of the king ' (and thus it ran) :

' May this suffice for the satisfaction of the heart of the holiness of the royal house, the Sun-Horus, the mighty Bull, who loves justice, the great lord, the protector of his people, the brave with his arm, the rampart of his life-guards in the day of battle, the king Ramses Meri-Amen.

' The servant speaks, he makes known to Pharaoh, my gracious lord, the beautiful son of Ra-Horemkhu, as follows :

' Since thou art the son of Amen, from whose body thou art sprung, so has he granted to thee all the peoples together.

' The people of Egypt and the people of Kheta ought to be brothers together as thy servants. Let them be at thy feet. The sun-god Ra has granted thee the best [inhabitants of the earth]. Do us no injury, glorious spirit, whose anger weighs upon the people of Kheta.

' Would it be good if thou shouldst wish to kill thy servants, whom thou hast brought under thy power ? Thy look is terrible, and thou art not mildly disposed. Calm thyself. Yesterday thou camest and hast slain hundreds of thousands. Thou comest to-day, and—none will be left remaining [to serve thee].

' Do not carry out thy purpose, thou mighty king. Better is peace than war. Give us freedom.'

Then the king turned back in a gentle humour, like his father Mentu in his time, and Pharaoh assembled all the leaders of the army and of the chariot-fighters and of the life-guards. And when they were all assembled together in one place, they were permitted to hear the contents of the message which the great king of Kheta had sent to him. [When they had heard] these words, which the messenger of the king of Kheta had brought as his embassy to Pharaoh, then they answered and spake thus to the king :

'Excellent, excellent is that! Let thy anger pass away, O great lord our king! He who does not accept peace must offer it. Who would content thee in the day of thy wrath?'

Then the king gave order to listen to the words of him (the king of Kheta), and he let his hands rest, in order to return to the south. Then the king went in peace to the land of Egypt with his princes, with his army, and his charioteers, in serene humour, in the sight of his [people]. All countries feared the power of the king, as of the lord of both the worlds. It had [protected] his own warriors. All peoples came at his name, and their kings fell down to pray before his beautiful countenance. The king reached the city of Ramses Meri-Amen, the great worshipper of Ra-Horemkhu, and rested in his palace in the most serene humour, just like the sun on his throne. And Amen came to greet him, speaking thus to him: 'Be thou blessed, thou our son, whom we love, Ramses Meri-Amen!, May they (the gods) secure to him without end many thirty-years' feasts of jubilee for ever on the chair of his father Tmu, and may all lands be under his feet!'

The battles of Ramses II. in Syria must have taken place previous to the battle of Kadesh; for the three rock-tablets near Beyrût, which were as well known to the Greek travellers in the fifth century B.C. as they are in our own day, testify to his presence at this very place in the second year and first campaign, and in the fifth year and second campaign of his reign. After peace had been made with the Kheta their frontiers were spared, although several cities could not prevail upon themselves to acknowledge the Egyptian supremacy. In one of these—'Tunep, in the land of Naharain'—the opposition of the populace assumed such a serious aspect that Ramses was obliged to go in person against the town. The memorial inscription records that

[there arose a new?] war, which was against a city of Kheta, in which the two statues of Pharaoh were set up. The king had reduced them [under his power. Then the king assembled] his warriors and his chariots, and gave orders to his warriors and his chariots [to attack] the hostile Kheta, who were in the neighbourhood of the city of Tunep, in the land of Naharain. And the king put on his armour [and mounted his chariot]. He stood there in the battle against the town of the hostile Kheta at the head of his warriors, and of his [chariots. His] armour was upon him. And the king came again to take his armour, and to put it on. [And he utterly smote] the hostile Kheta, who were in the neighbourhood of the city of Tunep in the land of Naharain. After that he no more put on his armour.

In the eighth year we again find the king in the land of Canaan, where the inhabitants had so angered Pharaoh that he went against them, captured their fortresses, and carried away their king and elders and all men capable of bearing arms to Egypt. The representation of this victory is on the northern gate-tower on the west side of Karnak. Against every fortress is written, 'This is the city which the king took in the eighth year,' to which the particular designation of the place was added. In what has been preserved we can make out the names: Shalama (that is, the town of peace), the place Salem, or Saleim, to the south of Scythopolis; Maroma, that is, Merom; Ain-Anamim, that is, Anim or Engannim; 'Dapur in the land of the Amorites,' the well-known fortress on Mount Tabor; 'the town Kalopu, on the mountain of Beitha-Antha,' that is, the Beth-anath of Scripture, in the land of Cabul.

That Ramses was the ruler ' of the foreign peoples of Singara and Kheta' is proved by the list of conquered places on his monuments at Thebes. They correspond entirely with those taken by Tehuti-mes III. The wars against the cities of Canaan called into play all the military activity of Ramses II., and his storming of Askalon appeared to the Egyptians so great an exploit as to merit a detailed representation on the temple at Karnak. Askalon was in a fertile district on the coast of the Mediterranean, and although strongly fortified belonged sometimes to the Syrians and sometimes to the Egyptians. The king in his war-chariot personally

directed the attack, which resulted in a capture by
storm. Pharaoh's soldiers are seen scaling the city
walls and beating in the barricaded doors with axes,
while men and women are trying to appease the victors.
The king of Askalon submits, saying, 'He rejoices, who
acts according to thy will, but woe to him who transgresses thy boundaries. We will make known thy
glory to all the nations who know not Egypt.'

This seems to have been the only instance in which
Askalon broke faith with the Pharaohs.

As a consequence of the wars in Western Asia a
great number of prisoners were brought into the Nile
valley. On the temple at Luqsor there is a scene with
this superscription: 'Catalogue of the princes of the
people of the Kheta whom Pharaoh has brought back
as living prisoners to fill the house of his father Amen,
and of the people of the Dardani, of Pidasa, and others.'
As leaders of the band of prisoners there appear the
king's sons Amen-her-khopesh-f, Khamuas, Meri-Amen,
and Seti, who had all taken part in the campaign, and
distinguished themselves at the storming of Tabor.
Although Ramses II. is always represented as fighting
on land, it is evident that his campaigns were also
carried on by water, and that his sailors measured
themselves in sea-fights with the most powerful maritime
nations, for the dominion of the sea. A short but
valuable notice on the rock-tablet on the outside of the
temple at Abû Simbel places this fact beyond doubt.
The growing troubles in Canaan, the pushing forward
of whole races in Western Asia, owing to the immigration of warlike tribes of foreign origin, seemed to have
caused anxiety to the kings of Kheta as well as to
Pharaoh. The then lord of Kheta, Kheta-sar, was the
first to make to his Egyptian friend the proposal,
written on a tablet of silver, for an offensive and de-

fensive alliance. Ramses II. was prudent enough not to refuse it, and a treaty was made, which laid the foundation of the intimate friendship, so often mentioned by the chroniclers of the time, between the two great empires of Asia and Africa.

It was couched in the following terms :—

OFFENSIVE AND DEFENSIVE ALLIANCE BETWEEN KHETA AND KAMIT.

In the year 21, in the month Tybi, on the 21st day of the month, in the reign of King Ra-messu Meri-Amen, the dispenser of life eternally and for ever, the worshipper of the divinities Amen-Ra (of Thebes), Horemkhu (of Heliopolis), Ptah (of Memphis), Mut, the lady of the Asher-lake (near Karnak), and Khonsu, the peace-loving, there took place a public sitting on the throne of Horus among the living, resembling his father Horemkhu in eternity, in eternity, evermore.

On that day the king was in the city of Ramses, presenting his peace-offerings to his father Amen-Ra, and to the gods Horemkhu-Tmu, the lord of Heliopolis, and to Amen of Ra-messu Meri-Amen, to Ptah of Ra-messu Meri-Amen, and to Sutekh, the strong, the son of the goddess of heaven Nut, that they might grant to him many thirty years' jubilee feasts, and innumerable happy years, and the subjection of all peoples under his feet for ever.

Then came forward the ambassador of the king, and the Adon [of his house, by name . . . . . , and presented the ambassadors] of the great king of Kheta, Kheta-sar, who were sent to Pharaoh to propose friendship with the king Ra-messu Meri-Amen, the dispenser of life eternally and for ever, just as his father the Sun-god [dispenses it] each day.

This is the copy of the contents of the silver tablet, which the great king of Kheta, Kheta-sar, had caused to be made, and which was presented to the Pharaoh by the hand of his ambassador Tar-thi-sebu and his ambassador Ra-mes, to propose friendship with the king Ra-messu Meri-Amen, the bull among the princes, who places his boundary-marks where it pleases him in all lands.

The treaty which had been proposed by the great king of Kheta, Kheta-sar, the powerful, the son of Maro-sar, the great king of Kheta, the powerful, the son of the son of Sapa-li-li, the great king of Kheta, the powerful, on the silver tablet, to Ra-messu Meri-Amen, the great prince of Egypt, the powerful, the son of Meneptah Seti, the great prince of Egypt, the powerful, the son's son of Ra-messu I., the great king of Egypt, the powerful,—this was a good treaty for friendship and concord, which assured peace [and established concord] for a longer period than was previously the case, since a long time. For it was the agreement of the great prince of Egypt in common with the great king of Kheta, that the god should not allow enmity to exist between them, on the basis of a treaty.

To wit, in the times of Mau-than-ar, the great king of Kheta, my brother, he was at war with [Meneptah Seti] the great prince of Egypt.

But now, from this very day forward, Kheta-sar, the great king of Kheta, shall look upon this treaty, so that the agreement may remain, which the god Ra has made, which the god Sutekh has made, for the people of Egypt and for the people of Kheta, that there should be no enmity between them for evermore.

And these are the contents :—

Kheta-sar, the great king of Kheta, is in covenant with Ra-messu Meri-Amen, the great prince of Egypt, from this very day forward, that there may subsist a good friendship and a good understanding between them for evermore.

He shall be my ally ; he shall be my friend.

I will be his ally ; I will be his friend : for ever.

To wit, in the time of Mau-than-ar, the great king of Kheta, his brother, after his murder, Kheta-sar placed himself on the throne of his father as the great king of Kheta. I strove for friendship with Ra-messu Meri-Amen, the great prince of Egypt, and it is [my wish] that the friendship and the concord may be better than the friendship and the concord which before existed, and which was broken.

I declare : I, the great king of Kheta, will hold together with Ra-messu Meri-Amen, the great prince of Egypt, in good friendship and in good concord. The sons of the sons of the great king of Kheta will hold together and be friends with the sons of the sons of Ra-messu Meri-Amen, the great prince of Egypt.

In virtue of our treaty for concord, and in virtue of our agreement [for friendship, let the people] of Egypt [be bound in friendship] with the people of Kheta. Let a like friendship and a like concord subsist in such measure for ever.

Never let enmity rise between them. Never let the great king of Kheta invade the land of Egypt, if anything shall have been plundered from it (the land of Kheta). Never let Ra-messu Meri-Amen, the great prince of Egypt, overstep the boundary of the land [of Kheta, if anything shall have been plundered] from it (the land of Egypt).

The just treaty, which existed in the times of Sapa-li-li, the great king of Kheta, likewise the just treaty which existed in the times of Mau-than-ar, the great king of Kheta, my brother, that will I keep.

Ra-messu Meri-Amen, the great prince of Egypt, declares that he will keep it. [We have come to an understanding about it] with one another at the same time from this day forward, and we will fulfil it, and will act in a righteous manner.

If another shall come as an enemy to the lands of Ra-messu Meri-Amen, the great prince of Egypt, then let him send an embassy to the great king of Kheta to this effect : ' Come ! and make me stronger than he.' Then shall the great king of Kheta [assemble his warriors], and the king of Kheta [shall come] and smite his enemies. But if it should not be the wish of the great king of Kheta to march out in person, then he shall send his warriors and his chariots, that they may smite his enemies. Otherwise [he would incur] the wrath of Ra-messu Meri-Amen [the great prince of Egypt. And if Ra-messu Meri-Amen, the great prince of Egypt, should banish for a crime] subjects from his country, and they should commit another crime against him, then shall he (the king of Kheta) come forward to kill them. The great king of Kheta shall act in common with [the great prince of Egypt].

[If another should come as an enemy to the lands of the great king of Kheta, then shall he send an embassy to the great prince of Egypt with the request that] he would come in great power to kill his enemies ; and if it be the intention of Ra-messu Meri-Amen, the great prince of Egypt, (himself) to come, he shall [smite the enemies of the great king of Kheta. If it is not the intention of the great prince of Egypt to march out in person, then he shall send his warriors and his two-] horse-chariots, while he sends back the answer to the people of Kheta.

If any subjects of the great king of Kheta have offended him, then Ra-messu Meri-Amen [the great prince of Egypt, shall not receive them in his land, but shall advance to kill them] . . . . . . the oath, with the wish to say : I will go . . . until . . . Ra-messu Meri-Amen, the great prince of Egypt, living for ever . . . . their . . . that he may be given for them (?) to the lord, and that Ra-messu Meri-Amen, the great prince of Egypt, may speak according to his agreement evermore. . . . . .

[If servants shall flee away] out of the territories of Ra-messu Meri-Amen, the great prince of Egypt, to betake themselves to the great king of Kheta, the great king of Kheta shall not receive them, but the great king of Kheta shall give them up to Ra-messu Meri-Amen, the great prince of Egypt, [that they may receive their punishment.

If servants of Ra-messu Meri-Amen, the great prince of Egypt, leave his country,] and betake themselves to the land of Kheta, to make themselves servants of another, they shall not remain in the land of Kheta, [they shall be given up] to Ra-messu Meri-Amen, the great prince of Egypt.

If on the other hand there should flee away [servants of the great king of Kheta, in order to betake themselves to] Ra-messu Meri-Amen, the great prince of Egypt, [in order to stay in Egypt,] then those who have come from the land of Kheta in order to betake themselves to Ra-messu Meri-Amen, the great prince of Egypt, shall not be [received by] Ra-messu Meri-Amen, the great prince of Egypt, [but] the great prince of Egypt, Ra-messu Meri-Amen, [shall deliver them up to the great king of Kheta].

[And if there shall leave the land of Kheta persons] of skilful mind, so that they come to the land of Egypt to make themselves servants of another, then Ra-messu Meri-Amen will not allow them to settle, he will deliver them up to the great king of Kheta.

When this [treaty] shall be known [by the inhabitants of the land of Egypt and of the land of Kheta, then shall they not offend against it, for all that stands written on] the silver tablet, these are words which will have been approved by the company of the gods among the male gods and among the female gods, among those namely of the land of Kheta, and by the company of the gods among the male gods and among the female gods, among those namely of the land of Egypt. They are witnesses for me [to the validity] of these words, [which they have allowed.

This is the catalogue of the gods of the land of Kheta :

      Sutekh, of the city] of Tunep (Daphne),
      Sutekh, of the land of Kheta,
      Sutekh, of the city of Arnema,
      Sutekh, of the city of Zaranda,
      Sutekh, of the city of Pilqa,
      Sutekh, of the city of Khissap,
      Sutekh, of the city of Sarsu,
      Sutekh, of the city of Khilbu (Haleb),
      Sutekh, of the city of . . . . .
      . . . .
      Sutekh, of the city of Sarpina,
      Astartha, of the land of Kheta,
      The god of the land of Zaiath-khirri,
      The god of the land of Ka . . . .
      The god of the land of Kher . . . .
      The goddess of the city of Akh . . . .
      [The goddess of the city of]   . . and of the land of A . . ua,

The goddess of the land of Zaina,
The god of the land of . . . nath . . . er.

[I have invoked these male and these] female [gods of the land of Kheta, these are the gods] of the land, [as witnesses to] my oath. [With them have been associated the male and the female gods] of the mountains, and of the rivers of the land of Kheta, the gods of the land of Qazauadana (Gauzanitis), Amen, Phra, Sutekh, and the male and the female gods of the land of Egypt, of the earth, of the sea, of the winds, and of the storms.

With regard to the commandment which the silver tablet contains for the people of Kheta and for the people of Egypt, he who shall not observe it shall be given over [to the vengeance] of the company of the gods of Kheta, and shall be given over [to the vengeance] of the company of the gods of Egypt, [he] and his house and his servants.

But he who shall observe these commandments, which the silver tablet contains, whether he be of the people of Kheta or [of the people of the Egyptians], because be has not neglected them, the company of the gods of the land of Kheta and the company of the gods of the land of Egypt shall secure his reward and preserve life [for him] and his servants and those who are with him, and who are with his servants.

If there flee away of the inhabitants [one from the land of Egypt], or two or three, and they betake themselves to the great king of Kheta, [the great king of Kheta shall not] allow them [to remain, but he shall] deliver them up, and send them back to Ra-messu Meri-Amen, the great prince of Egypt.

Now with respect to the [inhabitant of the land of Egypt], who is delivered up to Ra-messu Meri-Amen, the great prince of Egypt, his fault shall not be avenged upon him, his [house] shall not be taken away, nor his [wife] nor his [children]. There shall not be [put to death his mother, neither shall he be punished in his eyes, nor on his mouth, nor on the soles of his feet], so that thus no crime shall be brought forward against him.

In the same way shall it be done, if inhabitants of the land of Kheta take to flight, be it one alone, or two, or three, to betake themselves to Ra-messu Meri-Amen, the great prince of Egypt. Ra-messu Meri-Amen, the great prince of Egypt, shall cause them to be seized, and they shall be delivered up to the great king of Kheta.

[With regard to] him who [is delivered up, his crime shall not be brought forward against him]. His [house] shall not be taken away, nor his wives, nor his children, nor his people ; his mother shall not be put to death, he shall not be punished in his eyes, nor

on his mouth, nor on the soles of his feet, nor shall any accusation
be brought forward against him.

That which is in the middle of this silver tablet and on its front
side is a likeness of the god Sutekh . . . . surrounded by an
inscription to this effect : 'This is the [picture] of the god Sutekh,
the king of heaven and [earth].' At the time (?) of the treaty,
which Kheta-sar, the great king of Kheta, made. . . . .

This treaty seems to have been received with great
rejoicings, judging from the letters of that period still
in existence. According to a memorial tablet which
was set up solemnly in the temple at Abû Simbel, and
the long inscription on which begins with the date of
the year 34 of the reign of Ra-messu, the Egyptian king
married the daughter of the king of Kheta. The prince
of Kheta, clad in the dress of his country, himself conducted the bride to his son-in-law. After the marriage
had taken place, the young wife, as queen, received the
name of Ur-maat Neferu-Ra.

The temple at Derr records the presence of Ramses II.
in that country also. There may be seen represented a
razzia of the king against the negroes. In like manner
at Beit-el-Walli are vivid pictures of the Pharaoh's
victories over the land of Cush, the Thuhen, and the
Phœnicians. Evidently he has just returned home and
is holding a court in the temple :—

The deeds of victory are inscribed a hundred thousand times
on the glorious Persea. As the chastiser of the foreigners, who
has placed his boundary-marks according to his pleasure in the
land of the Rutennu, he is in truth the son of Ra, and his very
likeness.

The hereditary prince Amen-her-unam-f appears
before the king, and presents to him a train of captive
negroes, and tributes of leopards' skins, lions, giraffes,
antelopes, gazelles, and of gold rings, ivory, fruits,
and other productions of the south. The king's son of
Cush, Amen-em-ape, a son of Pauer, then stands before

his master to be decorated with a gold necklace as a
reward for honest and successful service. For a campaign had just been brought to a close, which had
subjected the revolted negro tribes anew to the sceptre
of Egypt. In its principal battle, Ramses appeared in
his chariot. His son named above, and his pious
brother Khamuas, accompanied him.

Here is another court of the king in the South. At
his feet lies his faithful attendant, the lion Smam-
kheftu-f, 'the tearer to pieces of his enemies,' and there
his son, who, accompanied by Egyptian warriors, brings
to the Pharaoh some captive Khar-Phœnicians, without
doubt for the purpose of being employed as workmen
on the buildings which Ramses was erecting there.

Prisoners of the Canaanite and Libyan tribes were
also employed on the erection of buildings. His own
words declare of his victories, 'that henceforth sand is
in their dwellings, instead of the fruits of the earth.'
Accompanied by one of his sons, he took their chief
city, the 'miserable king' of which declares to Sesostris,
'No other is to be compared to Baal as thou art. Thou,
O king, art his true son for ever.'

Ramses seems to have subjugated only small tribes
of Ethiopia and Libya in his campaigns into the interior
of the country. Their names are mentioned incidentally
on several monuments : thus the memorial stone of Abû
Simbel cites the Auntom, Hebuu, Tenfu, Temuu, and
Hetau, whom the Memphite god Totunen delivers as
subjects into the hands of his son Ramses. The monuments mention as 'king's sons of Cush' the Egyptian
lords Pauer ; Amen-em-ape, son of Pauer ; Setuan (who
was also entrusted with the administration of the gold-
mines), Amen-em-heb, Nekhtu, and Massui. In order
to increase his revenues, Ramses turned his attention to
the gold districts, and especially to the Nubian mines of

Akita, the modern Wady-Ollaqi. But water was wanting in the sterile valleys, and men and beasts died on the roads. From an old Egyptian map at Turin the situation of the mountain tracks, the roads, the places where the gold was found, the wells, and all the other appurtenances and buildings can be determined. Here, according to the inscriptions, are ' the mountains out of which the gold was extracted ; they are marked with a red colour ; ' there ' the roads which have been abandoned, leading to the sea : ' here ' the houses of . . . . of the gold-washing,' the ' well,' and the 'memorial-stone of King Meneptah I. Seti I. : ' there, ' the temple of Amen in the holy mountain.' Nothing is forgotten which could seem calculated to give the spectator an idea of the state of the region, even to the stones and the scattered trees along the roads. Seti I. had first worked the gold-mines, but without any remarkable success. He made the well named in the inscriptions, and erected near it the memorial-stone of which the inscription on the map speaks. The shaft of the well had a depth of more than 63 yards, but the water soon became exhausted, and the mine was abandoned. The following inscription covers a stone which was found at the village of Kûban, opposite to Dakkeh, on the eastern bank of the Nubian territory. Here stood in ancient times a fortified place, destined as a bulwark against the irruptions of the Nubian tribes. Inscribed stones in the neighbourhood mention Tehuti-mes III., Hor-em-heb, and Ramses II. This place seems at the same time to have been the point of departure for communication with the gold-mines :—

(1) In the year 3, in the month Tybi, on the fourth day, in the reign of King Ra-messu Meri-Amen, the dispenser of life eternally and for ever, the friend of the Theban Amen-Ra of Apet.

(2) A court was held on the throne of Hor (that is, of the king), among the living. Like his father, the everlasting Sun-god,

the divine benefactor, the lord of the south land, the radiant Hut-Hor, a beautiful golden sparrow hawk, he has spread out his wings over Egypt, giving shade to the inhabitants in the protecting wall of the strong and victorious. When he goes forth thence diffusing terror, it is to (3) display his power for enlarging his boundaries. The glittering brilliancy of colour has been granted to his body by the victories of Mentu. He is the lord of the two crowns of Horus and of Set. A shout of joy resounded in heaven on the day of his birth. The gods (spake) thus : 'We have begotten him ;' (4) the goddesses thus : 'He is born of us to govern the kingdom of Ra ;' Amen thus : 'I am he who formed him, to put truth in its place.' The land was set in order, the heaven quieted, the company of the gods satisfied, through his piety. He is a mighty bull for the miserable land of Cush, who pushes back (5) the conspirators from the land of the negroes. His hoof crushes the Annu (the Cushites) and his horn gores them. He has made himself master of the land of Nubia, and his terror, it has reached the land of Karu. His name resounds in (6) all lands, because of the victories which his hands have achieved. The gold appears on the mountains at his name, as at the name of his father Horus, the lord of Baka, the well-beloved in the land of the south, as at the name of Horus in the land of Maama, the lord of Buhan (Boôn). (7) Thus is King Ra-messu Meri-Amén, the dispenser of life eternally and for ever, like his father the everlasting Sun-god.

Then was the king in the city of Memphis to worship his fathers, the gods, and the lords of South and North Egypt, that they might grant him power and victory and a long duration of life of infinitely many (8) years. On one of these days it came to pass, that the king sat there on his great throne of gold, attired with the royal diadem, and with the ornament of the double plume, to consult about the countries from which the gold is obtained, and to consider the method and way of boring (9) wells on the roads, which are accursed for want of water, since he had heard that there was much gold existing in the land of Akita, but that the approach to it was accursed on account of the utter want of water. There were taken some (10) gold-washers to the place where it was ; but those who had gone thither had died of thirst on the road, together with the asses which were with them. They could not find what was required (11) for them to drink on their upward journey, unless it happened that the rain fell from heaven. So could no gold be obtained in this country, on account of the want of water.

Then spake the king to his nobleman, who stood beside him : 'Let the princes be called who are present. (12) I will take counsel with them about this land, as to what measures should be taken.'

As soon as they had been brought before the divine benefactor, they lifted up their hands to praise his name with speeches in his honour, and to pray before his beautiful countenance. And the king described to them the condition of this land, in order to take (13) their advice upon it, with the view of boring wells on the road. And they spake before the king : ' Thou art like the sun. Everything succeeds with thee. What thy heart desires, that comes to pass. When thou conceivest a wish in the night, it is accomplished as soon as the earth becomes light (again). We have hastened to thee to do what there is to do, for (14) great is the number of thy astonishing works, since thou hast appeared as king in the country. We heard nothing, we saw nothing, and yet what is there, it was done just as it is. All the sayings of thy mouth are like the words of Horemkhu. Thy tongue is a balance ; thy lips are a standard measure (15) according to the just scales of the god Tehuti. Where is that hidden which thou didst not know ? Where is the wise man who might be like thee ? There is no place found, which thou hast not seen ; there is no land which thou hast not trodden. Everything excellent found an entrance into thy ears since (16) thou wast an Adon of this land. Thou didst act with wisdom when thou didst still sit in the egg. In thy time of childhood that happened which thou saidst, for the welfare of the land. When thou grewest up to boyhood with the lock of hair of youth, no memorial saw the light without thy command. (17) No business was carried out without thy knowledge. Thou wast raised to be an overseer (Rohir) of this land, when thou wast a youth and didst count ten full years. All buildings went forward under thy hand, and the laying of their foundation stones was carried out. When thou spakest to the water : Come upon the mountain, then appeared the rain (18) immediately at thy command. Thou art like the Sun-god. As the body of the Creator, so is that which he begets. Truly thou art the living likeness of Ra, the heir of thy father Tmu of Heliopolis. Taste is on thy tongue, feeling is in thy heart. The place of thy tongue is the shrine of truth. The divinity sits on thy lips, and all thy words will be performed for ever. (19) What thy understanding has done is like the works of Ptah, the fashioner of the works of art. Thou art ever he whose intentions are all carried out, whose words are all fulfilled, thou our great lord and ruler ! As regards the land of Akita, may a decision be made according to the counsel taken concerning it.'

Then spake the king's son of the miserable land of Cush, (20) saying thus before the king : '(The land) is in this state. It is accursed for want of water since the time of Ra. People die of thirst in it. All former kings wished to bore wells in it, but they were not successful. (21) King Seti I. also did the same. He had a well bored 120 cubits deep in his time, but they abandoned it, for no water made its appearance. If then now thou thyself wouldest speak to thy father, the Nile-god Hapu, (22) the father of the gods : " Let the water come up on the mountain," he will do all that thou sayest, yea, indeed, all which thou hast designed will be accomplished before us, and not only according to hearsay, because thy fathers the gods love thee more than all kings (23) which have been since the time of Ra.'

Says the king to the princes : 'If all is true that ye have spoken, and water has not been opened in that country since the time of the god, as ye have said, then I will bore a well there, to afford water perpetually, yea! that the well (24) may be under the command of the father Amen-Ra, the Theban god, and of Horus, the lords of the land of Nubia, that their heart may be fixed in love. I will therefore appoint that it be called after [their name.' And the princes] (25) praised their lord and worshipped him, and fell prostrate before him (the king), and raised shouts of joy (26) to the heights of heaven.

Then spake the king to a royal scribe [who was near him : 'Prepare thyself and betake thyself to the] (27) road to the land of Akita. Let the second day of the month be the day on [which] thou shalt [carry out thy mission.' The scribe did] (28) just as he was bidden. Behold, he assembled the people [which were skilful in boring, that they should work and form a well, which should furnish water to those who travelled] (29) the road to the land of Akita. Never was the like done since the earlier kings. [And of the water which streamed out brooks were formed, and] (30) fishermen from the islands in the neighbourhood of the lagoons of Natho enjoyed themselves, for they built [small boats and made use of the . . . . . .] (31) as a rudder with the wind.

Then there came the bearer of a letter from the king's son of the miserable land of Cush [about the well, to say to the king : 'All has in fact been done] (32) that thy Majesty has spoken with his own mouth. There has appeared water out of it 12 cubits deep. There were 4 cubits in it . . . . ? . . . . the depth . . . . (33) . . . . . . they . . . . out as was the intention of the work. The god has inclined his heart favourably through thy love. Never has such a thing happened [since the time of the god Ra].'

(34) [And the inhabitants of] Akita made joyful music on great drums (?) Those who had diseased eyes [washed themselves with the water and were healed. They all sang : (35) 'Hail] to the king ! The water which is in the depth was obedient to him. He hath opened the water on the [mountain.' And they offered thanks] (36)

to him through the king's son, because of his mission. That was
more pleasant to [the heart of the king than all else. Thus then
were] (37) his plans well carried out. Beautiful was the acknowledgment which [the inhabitants of the district] uttered. A road
was made from] (38) this well to the well of Ramses Meri-Amen,
the conqueror [in the land . . . .].

So early as the Eleventh Dynasty we find traces of
borings for water in the waste valleys of Hammamât.
Twelve hundred years before the accession of Ramses
II., Sankh-ka-Ra, one of his ancestors, had made four
wells on the old road from Coptos to Kosseir, the
remains of which can still be seen.

CHAPTER XIII.

RAMSES II. (*continued*)—SETNEKHT.

THE name of Ramses II. has come down to us as that of a great builder as well as a valiant soldier. His first important architectural work was at the temple of Abydos, although it is incidentally recorded that he had raised two temple gates at Thebes and Memphis to the memory of his father. Of the buildings erected by Ramses II. at Memphis we have an account written on a stone near the Second Cataract, dated the 35th year and 13th day of Tybi, where, in a conversation between the king and Ptah, information is given as to the relations between the king and the Kheta. The god says :—

I have given thee strength and might and the power of thy arm in all countries. Thou hast wounded the hearts of all peoples, which are placed under thy feet. When thou comest forth on each new day, the great kings of all nations lead to thee a captive people, to do homage to thee with their children. They are given into the power of thy strong arm, to do with them whatsoever pleases thee, O King Ramses II. I have placed in all hearts reverence for thee. The love of all peoples is turned towards thee. Thy manly courage is spread abroad over all the plains, and the fear of thee goes through the mountains. The kings tremble at the thought of thee, and thou art regarded as their established head. They come to thee with a prayer to entreat thy friendship. Thou allowest to live whom thou willest : thou killest whom it pleases thee. The throne of all peoples is with thee.

Some lines further on is the passage which is of importance for us :—

The people of Kheta are subjects of thy palace. I have placed it in their hearts to serve thee, while they humbly approach thy person with their productions and the booty in prisoners of their king. All their property is brought to thee. His eldest daughter stands forward at their head, to soften the heart of King Ramses II. —a great inconceivable wonder. She herself knew not the impression which her beauty made on thy heart. Thy name is great and glorious for ever. Thou art the most complete example of strength and power. He is inconceivably great, who orders and does not obey. Since the times of the traditions of the gods, which are hidden in the house of the rolls of writing, from the times of the sun-god Ra down to thee, history had nothing to report about the Kheta people, but that they had one heart and one soul with Egypt.

To which the Pharaoh replies :—

Thou hast committed to me what thou hast created. I do and I will do again all good for thee, so long as I shall be sole king, just as thou hast been. I have cared for the land, in order to create for thee a new Egypt, just as it existed in the old time. I have set up images of the gods, according to thy likeness, yea, according to their colour and form, which hold possession of Egypt according to their desire. They have been formed by the hand of the artist in the temples. Thy sanctuary in the town of Memphis was enlarged. It was beautified by long-enduring works, and by well executed works in stone, which are adorned with gold and jewels. I have caused a court to be opened for thee on the north, with a splendid double-winged tower in front. Its gates are like the heavenly orb of light. The people offer their prayers there. I have built for thee a splendid sanctuary in the interior of the walled enclosure. Each god's image is in the unapproachable shrine, and remains in its exalted place. I have provided them with priests and prophets of the land of Egypt, with arable land and herds of cattle. The account of the property of the temple in all things amounts to millions. All thy great thirty years' feasts of jubilee are celebrated. Thus has everything which thou hast commanded me been carried out in rich abundance according to thy wish. There are oxen and calves without end ; all their sacrificial meat is provided, to the number of hundreds of thousands ; the smell of their fat reaches to heaven ; the heavenly ones receive it. I cause the whole world to admire the completeness of the monuments which I have dedicated to thee. I brand with a hot iron the foreign peoples of the whole earth with thy name. They belong to thy person for evermore. Thou hast in truth created them.

According to this Ramses II. had erected the whole northern court of the temple of Ptah at Memphis, together with the propyla belonging to it ; and had built a temple within the surrounding wall, remains of which have lately been discovered near the Arab village of Quassarìeh. He had erected images of the gods, and had provided the necessary means for the service of the great Architect. There is no dearth of statues of Ramses II. and the members of his family. The most celebrated and most often visited is the great torso of Ramses, the property of the English nation, which lay in a trench among the ruins of the temple of Ptah (Mitraheny) until 1887, when Major Bagnold, R.E. (with subscriptions collected by Sir F. Stephenson), succeeded in raising it. The statue had become encrusted with the mud left by succeeding Nile deposits, and during the inundation it was almost covered with water. Besides this, the smaller statues of the king, and of his wife and daughters, have been torn away from the grove of palm-trees at the same place. The king also raised in Memphis temples and buildings to the memory of his father. The chief master of the house of Pharaoh and the leader of the Mazai (policemen), Hi, was also administrator of a Ramses-temple in Pa-neb-am, and of the sun-temple of Ra-messu Meri-Amen in the southern part of Memphis. For the building of this last 'the people—the red-skins'—were doomed to the laborious task of dragging heavy blocks of stone from Tûrah—across the river—to Memphis. These people were likewise employed in building the great propylon—called Meriu-ma—of the temple of Ptah, and for which a certain Amen-em-an was architect and chief of the policemen.

The family of Amen-em-an plays an important part in the monumental history of this period: he was probably the immediate oppressor placed by Ramses II. over the Israelites. The accompanying Genealogical Tree has been compiled on the authority of a family group preserved in the collection of antiquities at Naples.

Like Abydos and Memphis, Thebes was also the object of the especial care of Ramses II. New temples were erected on both sides of the river, or those which already existed were enlarged. In the great sanctuary at Apet (Karnak), the king first completed the hall of Seti I., by the erection of the fifty-four columns which were wanting on the south side, and of a stone wall to surround the whole temple on the east as far as the wall of the Hall of Columns just mentioned. In Luqsor the temple of Amen, founded but not finished by Amen-hotep III., was completed, the two splendid propylæa were placed before it, and two beautiful obelisks were erected beside the colossal granite statues of the king. On the western side, the temple of the dead built by Seti I. at Old Gûrnah was finished, and on the south-western side of it a special temple of victory, called the 'Ramesseum,' was dedicated to the God Amen. Here stood also the largest statues of the king, which, according to tradition, Cambyses threw down when he visited Thebes. In Nubia Ramses founded Pa-Ra, near Derr; Pa-Amen, near Wady-Serbûa; and Pa-Ptah, near Gerf Hûssein. Above all he excavated that magnificent rock-temple at Abû Simbel the façade of which surpasses everything which imagination can picture. There in Nubia, in a solitary wall of rock, far removed from human habitations, a temple was hewn out and dedicated to the great gods of the land— to Amen of Thebes, Ptah of Memphis, Horemkhu of

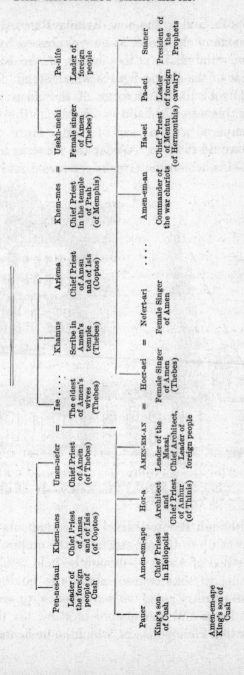

GENEALOGY OF AMEN-EM-AN, THE ARCHITECT OF THE CITY OF RAMSES.

Heliopolis, and to the new divinity Ramses Meri-Amen.
The name of the place, as now expressed by the Arabs,
is Abû Simbel, i.e. 'the father of the ear of corn.'
Neither of the sitting figures which stand out from the
wall of rock like giant forms of the olden time carries
any emblem in his hand which can in the least degree
be compared with an ear of corn.   More correct, perhaps, would it be to consider the name as a corruption
of Pa-Mas, which the Greeks converted into Psampolis.

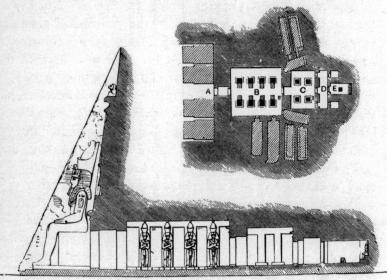

PLAN AND SECTION OF THE GREAT TEMPLE AT ABÛ SIMBEL.

A, Entrance.   B, Great Hall, supported by eight Osirid columns.   C, Second hall, supported
by four square columns, with religious subjects on the walls.   D, Third hall, with similar subjects.   E, Sanctuary, with an altar in the middle, and at the end four seated figures of Ptah,
Amen, Horus, and Ramses himself.

Although Ramses raised his monuments in Thebes,
and went up to the old capital of the empire to celebrate
the festival of Amen ;—though he held public courts in
Memphis, to take counsel about the gold-fields in the
Nubian country ; and visited Abydos, to see the tombs
of the kings and the temple built by his father ;—not
to mention Heliopolis, in which he dedicated a temple

and obelisks to the sun-god;—yet neither these nor other cities formed his permanent abode. On the eastern frontier of Egypt, in the low-lands of the Delta, in Zoan-Tanis, was the royal residence of this Pharaoh. Connected with the sea by its situation on the then broad and navigable Tanitic arm of the Nile, and commanding also the entrance of the great road, covered by 'Khetams,' or fortresses, which led to Palestine either through Pelusium or through Migdol, Zoan-Tanis was, in the proper sense of the word, *the key of Egypt*. Impressed with the importance of the position of this 'great city,' Ra-messu transferred his court there, strengthened its fortifications, and founded a new temple-city, dedicated to Amen, Ptah, and Horemkhu, with whom as a fourth he associated the foreign Baal-Sutekh. With the newly-established divinities the king united himself both in effigy and in name, and there appeared in due course an Amen of Ra-messu, a Ptah, a Horemkhu, and a Sutekh. The new temple-city had a super-abundance of statues and obelisks, memorial stones, and other works, the most remarkable of all being the memorial tablet inscribed with the date of the year 400, of King Nub. From several records found among the ruins of Tanis much information of an historical and mythological character is derived incidentally, for the knowledge of which we are indebted to M. Chabas in his 'Mélanges Égyptologiques.' Zoan—or Pa-Ra-messu—became henceforward the special capital of the empire. The following 'Letter of Panbesa' (Pap. Anas. iii.) describes the new city. The writer says:—

So I arrived in the city of Ramses Meri-Amen, and I have found it excellent, for nothing can compare with it on the Theban land and soil. [Here is the seat] of the court. It is pleasant to live in. Its fields are full of good things, and life passes in constant plenty and abundance. Its canals are rich in fish, its lakes swarm with birds, its meadows are green with vegetables, there is no end of the

lentils ; melons with a taste like honey grow in the irrigated fields.
Its barns are full of wheat and durra, and reach as high as heaven.
Onions and sesame are in the enclosures, and the apple-tree
blooms (?) The vine, the almond-tree, and the fig-tree grow in the
gardens. Sweet is their wine for the inhabitants of Kamit. They
mix it with honey. The red fish is in the lotus-canal, the Borian-
fish in the ponds, many kinds of Bori-fish, besides carp and pike,
in the canal of Pa-Harotha ; fat fish and Khipti-pennu fish are in
the pools of the inundation, the Hauaz-fish in the full mouth of the
Nile, near the 'city of the conqueror' (Tanis). The city-canal
Pshenhor produces salt, the lake-region of Pahir natron. Their sea-
ships enter the harbour ; plenty and abundance is perpetual in it.
He rejoices who has settled there. My information is no jest.
The common people, as well as the higher classes, say, 'Come hither !
let us celebrate to him his heavenly and his earthly feasts.' The
inhabitants of the reedy lake (Thufi) arrived with lilies, those of
Pshenhor with papyrus flowers. Fruits from the nurseries, flowers
from the gardens, birds from the ponds, were dedicated to him.
Those who dwell near the sea came with fish, and the inhabitants
of their lakes honoured him. The youths of the 'Conqueror's city'
were perpetually clad in festive attire. Fine oil was on their
heads of fresh curled hair. They stood at their doors, their hands
laden with branches and flowers from Pa-Hathor, and with garlands
from Pahir, on the day of the entry of King Ra-messu Meri-Amen,
the god of war Mentu upon earth, in the early morning of the
monthly feast of Kihith (that is, on the 1st of Khoiak). All people
were assembled, neighbour with neighbour, to bring forward their
complaints.

Delicious was the wine for the inhabitants of the 'Conqueror's
city.' Their cider was like . . . . , their sherbets were like
almonds mixed with honey. There was beer from Kati (Galilee)
in the harbour, wine in the gardens, fine oil at the lake Sagabi,
garlands in the apple-orchards. The sweet song of women resounded to the tunes of Memphis. So they sat there with joyful
heart, or walked about without ceasing. King Ra-messu Meri-Amen,
he was the god they celebrated.

In spite of the unexplained names of the fishes and
plants the scribe could hardly have given a clearer or
livelier account of the impression made upon him by
the new city of Ramses in its festal attire on the day of
Pharaoh's entry. It is the very same place which is
spoken of in the Old Testament as one of the two places

in which the king caused *arei miskenoth*, i.e. 'treasure cities' or temple cities, to be built for him.

The new Pharaoh ' who knew not Joseph,' and who adorned the cities of Ramses and Pithom with temples and treasuries, can be no other than Ramses II.   He is undoubtedly the Pharaoh of the oppression and the father of that un-named princess who found Moses in the little papyrus barque among the flags of the river.

While the fact that this Pharaoh was the founder of Ramses is so unquestionably demonstrated by the Egyptian records, the inscriptions do not mention the Israelites by name. It must, therefore, be supposed that they were included in the general term of ' foreigners.' From this time, and in the future history of the empire, Zoan-Tanis is of great importance ; here, on the wide plains, the hosts of warriors and chariots were mustered, to be exercised in the manœuvres of battle, and in the harbours on the river the sea-going ships and their crews came to land.   From this place Tehuti-mes III. had started in his war against Western Asia ; it was to Tanis that Ramses II. had directed his return from Thebes ; here he had received the embassy of peace from the king of Kheta ; and from hence Moses led the Hebrews out of the land of bondage to the land of promise.

The numbers of foreign prisoners, who, in the campaigns of the Egyptians, were transplanted to the Nile valley, must under Ramses Sesostris have reached an unprecedented height. If we add to these the descendants of the foreigners brought to Egypt after former wars, a total number is reached, which certainly amounted to a third, and probably still more, of all the families of Egypt. So far as the contemporary information will allow us to judge, it was the custom to place the northern groups in the south, and the southern people in the north, in order by this prudent measure to prevent any dangerous combination of neighbours related by blood.

The foreigners were employed in various services, according to their capacities. Those most active, and most experienced in war, were formed into foreign legions, the commanders of which, for the most part Egyptians, bore the name of *Her-pit* ('captain of the foreigners'). Others, experienced in sea life, were enrolled in the Egyptian fleet. Others again were assigned places in the royal palace, or the temples, or in the households of distinguished personages, while no less a number were employed on the buildings, in the quarries, or in the mines. The king's name was branded upon them, to prevent their flight, and to facilitate their re-capture. On the whole, they were treated with mildness, for their captivity was not regarded as slavery in our sense of the word.

The influx of Semitic hostages and prisoners from Asia exercised a continually increasing influence on religion, manners, and language. The Egyptian language was enriched with foreign expressions, often indeed from mere whim, but more often for good reasons, in order properly to designate unknown objects by their native names. The letters and documents of the time of the Ramessides are full of Semitic words thus introduced. The learned court-scribes, especially, seem to have felt a sentimental craving for the use of foreign words, in order to give themselves in the eyes of the public an air of learned culture. The Egyptian expressions for designating a 'hero' were supplanted by the words *Mohar*, or Ariel, borrowed from the Semitic; the Egyptian Nefer, 'a young man,' was changed for the Semitic name *Na'ara-na*; the army was in the same

way called *Zeba*, and many other incongruous expressions were adopted.

The young Egyptian world, satiated with the traditions of the past thousands of years which had now
vanished away, found a pleasure in the fresh and lively
vigour of the Semitic spirit, to which a different and
more attractive view of the universe gave a forward
impulse. Subjoined is the literal translation of a letter
from a master to his former pupil, who having become
a 'royal scribe' entertained the belief that while por-
traying his hero in an artificial and confused composition he had achieved a masterpiece. The answer of
the priestly teacher is as biting as it is scrupulously
respectful. The words borrowed from the Semitic are
given in the French expressions answering to them :—

Thy piece of writing has too much *glane*. It is a cargo of
high-flown phrases, the meaning of which may be the reward of
those who seek for it ; a cargo which thou hast laden at thy
pleasure. I describe a *champion*, so sayest thou repeatedly ; we on
the other hand say, Is there truth in thy portraiture ?

Set out ! examine thy yoke, the horses gallop like foxes ;
their eye is reddened ; they are like the hurricane when it bursts
forth. Put on the armour ; seize the bow ! We will admire the
deeds of thy hand.

I will portray for thee the likeness of a *champion* ; I will
let thee know what he does. Thou hast not gone to the land of
Kheta, neither hast thou beheld the land of Aupa. The appearance
of Khatuma (Adama ?) thou knowest not. Likewise the land of
Igad'ai, what is it like ? The Zor of Sesostris and the city of
Khilibu (Haleb) is on none of its sides. How is its ford ? Thou
hast not taken thy road to Kadesh and Tubikhi, neither hast thou
gone to the Shasu with numerous foreign soldiers, neither hast thou
trodden the way to the Magar (Migron), where the heaven is
darkened in the daytime. It is planted with maple-trees, oaks,
and acacias, which reach up to heaven ; full of beasts, bears, and
lions ; and surrounded by Shasu in all directions. Thou hast not
gone up to the mountain of Shaua (Shawah), neither hast thou
trodden it ; there thy hands hold fast to the [rim] of thy chariot ;
a jerk has shaken thy horses in drawing it. I pray thee, let us go

to the city of (Ha- ?) Birotha. Thou must hasten to its ascent, after thou hast passed over its ford, in front of it.

Do thou explain the relish for the *champion*! Thy chariot lies there [before] thee ; thy [strength] has fallen lame ; thou treadest the backward path at eventide. All thy limbs are ground small. Thy [bones] are broken to pieces. Sweet is the [sleep]. Thou awakest. There has been a time for the thief in this unfortunate night. Thou wast alone, in the belief that the brother would not come to the brother. Some grooms entered into the stable ; the horse kicks out, the thief goes back in the night ; thy clothes are stolen. Thy groom wakes up in the night, he sees what has happened to him, he takes what is left, he goes to the evil-doers, he mixes himself up with the tribes of the Shasu. He acts as if he were an Aamu. The enemies come, they [feel about] for the robber. He is discovered, and is immovable from terror. Thou wakest, thou findest no trace of them, for they have carried off thy property

Become (again) a *champion*, who is fully accoutred. Let thy ear be full of that which I will relate to thee besides.

The town 'Hidden,' such is the meaning of its name Kapuna, what is its state ? Its goddess (we will speak of) at another time. Thou hast not visited it. Be good enough to look out for Birotha (Berſtus), Ziduna (Sidon), and Zareptha (Sarepta). Where are the fords of the land of Nazana ? The land of Authu (Avathus), what is its state ? They speak of another city in the sea, Zor (Tyrus), the lake is her name. The drinking water is brought to her in boats. She is richer in fishes than in sand. I tell thee of something else. Dangerous is it to enter into Zar'au-na (Zareah, in Heb. 'wasps'). Thou wilt say, it is burning with a very painful sting ! *Champion!* come ! Go forwards on the way to the K'aikana. Where is the road of 'Aksapu (Achsib) ? Towards no city. Pray look at the mountain of User. How is its crest ? Where is the mountain of Ikama ? Who can surmount it ? *Champion!* whither must you take a journey to the city of Huzor (Hazor) ? How is its ford ? Let me (choose) the road to Hamatha (Hamath), Dagana (Beth-Dagon), and Dagal-ael (Migdal-El ?) Here is the place where all *champions* meet. Be good enough to spy out its road, cast a look on I'ana (Ijon). When one goes to Adamin (Adumin), to what is one opposite ? Do not draw back, but instruct us ! Guide us ! that we may know, thou leader !

I will name to thee other cities besides these. Thou hast not gone to the land of Thakhis, to Kafir-Marlena, Thamnah (Thimnah), Kadesh (Kedes), Dapur (Tabor), Azai, Hairnemma (Horonaim), nor hast thou beheld Qairtha-Anbu (Kiriath-eneb) near Bitha Thupail

(Tophel), nor dost thou know Adulma (Adullam), Zidiputha (Jotapata), nor dost thou know any better the name of Khaanroaz, in the land of Aupa, the bull on its frontiers. Here is the place, where all the mighty warriors are seen. Be good enough to look and see how Sina is situated, and tell me about Rehobu. Describe Bitha-Sheal (Bethshean), and Tharqa-ael. The ford of Jirduna (Jordan), how is it crossed? Teach me to know the passage in order to enter into the city of Makitha (Megiddo), which lies in front of it. Verily thou art a *champion*, well skilled in the work of the strong hand. Pray, is there found a *champion* like thee, to place at the head of the army, or a *seigneur*, who can beat thee in shooting?

Drive along the edge of the precipice, on the slippery height, over a depth of 2,000 cubits, full of rocks and boulders. Thou takest thy way back in a zigzag, thou bearest thy bow, thou takest the iron in thy left hand. Thou lettest the old men see, if their eyes are good, how, worn out with fatigue, thou supportest thyself with thy hand. *Il est perdu, le chameau, le champion. Eh bien!* Make to thyself a name among the *champions* and the knights of the land of Egypt. Let thy name be like that of Qazailoni, the lord of Asel, because he discovered lions in the interior of the balsam-forest of Baka, at the narrow passes, which are rendered dangerous by the Shasu, who lie in ambush among the trees. They measured 14 cubits by 5 cubits. Their noses reached to the soles of their feet.

Of a grim appearance, without softness, they ceased not for caresses. Thou art alone, no stronger one is with thee, no *armée* is behind thee, thou findest no *lion de dieu* (ariel), who prepares the way for thee, and gives thee counsel on the road before thee. Thou knowest not the road. The hair of thy head stands on end; it bristles up. Thy soul is given into thy hands. Thy path is full of rocks and boulders, there is no way out near, it is overgrown with thorns and thistles, with creepers and wolf's-foot. Abysses are on one side of thee, the mountain and the wall of rock on the other. Thou drivest in against it. The chariot, on which thou art, jumps. Thou art troubled to hold up thy horses. If it falls into the abyss, the pole drags thee down too. Thy *ceintures* are pulled away. They fall down. Thou shacklest the horse, because the pole is broken on the path of the narrow pass. Not knowing how to bind it up, thou understandest not how it is to be repaired. The *essieu* is left on the spot, as the load is too heavy for the horses. Thy courage has evaporated. Thou beginnest to run. The heaven is cloudless. Thou art thirsty; the enemy is behind thee; a trembling seizes thee; a twig of thorny acacia worries thee ; thou thrustest it aside ; the horse is scratched, till at length thou findest rest.

Explain thou (to me) thy relish for the *champion* !

Thou comest into Jopu (Joppa). Thou findest the date-tree in full bloom in its time. Thou openest wide the hole of thy mouth, in order to eat. Thou findest that the maid who keeps the garden is fair. She does whatever thou wantest of her. She yields to thee the skin of her bosom. Thou art recognised, thou art brought to trial, and owest thy preservation to the *champion*. Thy girdle of the finest stuff, thou payest it as the price for a bad rag. Thou sleepest every evening with a rug of fur over thee. Thou sleepest a deep sleep, for thou art weary. A thief takes thy bow and thy sword from thy side ; thy quiver and thy armour are cut to pieces in the darkness ; thy pair of horses run away. The groom takes his course over a slippery path, which rises before him. He breaks thy chariot in pieces ; he follows thy foot-tracks. [He finds] thy equipments, which had fallen on the ground, and had sunk into the sand ; it becomes again (i.e. leaving only) an empty place.

Prayer does not avail thee ; even when thy mouth says, 'Give food in addition to water, that I may reach my goal in safety :' they are deaf, and will not hear. They say not 'yes' to thy words. The iron-workers enter into the smithy ; they rummage in the workshops of the carpenters ; the handicraftsmen and saddlers are at hand ; they do whatever thou requirest. They put together thy chariot ; they put aside the parts of it that are made useless ; thy spokes are *faconnés* quite new ; thy wheels are put on, they put the *courroies* on the axles, and on the hinder part ; they splice thy yoke, they put on the box of thy chariot ; the [workmen] in iron forge the . . . . ; they put the ring that is wanting on thy whip, they replace the *lanières* upon it.

Thou goest quickly onward to fight on the battle-field, to do the works of a strong hand and of firm courage.

Before I wrote I sought me out a *champion*, who knows his power (*lit.* hand), and leads the *jeunesse*, a chief in the *armée*, [who goes forward] even to the end of the world.

Answer me not, 'That is good, this is bad ;' repeat not to me your opinion. Come, I will tell thee all which lies before thee, at the end of thy journey.

I begin for thee with the city of Sesostris. Thou hast not set foot in it by force. Thou hast not eaten the fish in the brook. . . . . Thou hast not washed thyself in it. With thy permission I will remind thee of Hazina ; where are its fortifications ? Come, I pray thee, to Uti, the strong fortress of Sesostris User-maat-Ra,

to Sabaq-Ael and Ab-saqabu. I will inform thee of the position of 'Aini, the customs of which thou knowest not. Nakhai
and Rehoburotha thou hast not seen, since thou wast born,
O *champion*! Rapih (Raphia) is widely extended. What is
its wall like? It extends for a mile in the direction of Qazatha
(Gaza).

Answer quickly. That which I have said is my idea of a
champion in reply to thee. I let the people keep away from thy
name, I wish them a *seigneur*. If thou art angry at the words
which I have addressed to thee, yet I know how to estimate thy
heart in every way. A father chastises, but he knows the right
measure a hundred thousand times. I know thee. To put on
armour is really beyond thy ability. No man whose hand and
courage is warlike makes himself famous in my esteem. I am open
and clear, like the spring-water of the god Mentu. It matters
very little what flows over thy tongue, for thy compositions are very
confused. Thou comest to me in a covering of misrepresentations,
with a cargo of blunders. Thou tearest the words to tatters, just
as it comes into thy mind. Thou dost not take pains to find out
their force for thyself. If thou rushest wildly forward, thou wilt
not succeed. What comparison is there between one who does not
know the goal that he wishes to reach, and one who reaches it?
Now, what is he like? I have not gone back, but I have reached
(my goal). Soften thy heart, let thy heart be cheerful; may the
way to eat cause thee no trouble!

I have struck out for thee the end of thy composition, and I
return to thee thy descriptions. What thy words contain, that is
altogether on my tongue, it has remained on my lips. It is a confused medley, when one hears it; an uneducated person could not
understand it. It is like a man from the lowlands speaking with a
man from Elephantiné. But since thou art the scribe of Pharaoh,
thou resemblest the water for the land, that it may become fertile.
Take my meaning kindly, and do not say, 'Thou hast made my
name to stink before all other men.' Understand me as having
wished to impart to thee the true position of a *champion*, in doing
which I have visited for thee every foreign people, and placed before
thee in a general view the countries, and (every) city according to
its special character. Acquaint us kindly, that thou so understandest it. If thou findest that the remarks upon thy work are
apposite, thou wilt be for us like the famous Uah.

Ramses II. reigned sixty-seven years, of which probably more than half must be assigned to his joint reign
with his father. His thirty-years' jubilee was the

occasion for great festivities throughout the whole country, which are frequently mentioned in the inscriptions at Silsilis, El-Kab, Biggeh, Sehêl, and even upon several scarabæi. The prince and high priest of Ptah of Memphis, Khamuas, travelled through the principal cities of the land, in order to make the necessary preparations for celebrating duly this great feast of joy. The return of this jubilee seems to have been calculated according to a fixed cycle of years, perhaps when the lunar and solar years co-incided at short intervals of three or four years, in the same manner as the festivals. In the 30th year Khamuas celebrated the feast under his own superintendence, in Biggeh and in Silsilis, where at that time Khai was governor of the district, while at El-Kab the governor Ta conducted the festivities. The recurrence of the succeeding jubilees took place—the second in the 34th year, the third in the 37th year, and the fourth in the 40th year, of the reign of Ramses II.

From the outer wall of the temple at Abydos we learn that Ramses II. had 119 children—60 sons and 59 daughters—which gives ground for supposing a great number of concubines, besides his lawful wives Isi-nefer, the mother of Khamuas, Nefer-ari, Meri-mut, and the daughter of the Kheta king. Among his sons Khamuas held a fond place in his father's heart. He was high priest of Ptah of Memphis, and in that character did his best to restore the worship of Apis, the living type of Ptah-Sekari. His buildings in Memphis and in the so-called Serapeum, the burial-place of the sacred bulls, are celebrated in the inscriptions as splendid works. From all that the monuments relate of Khamuas he seems to have been a learned and pious prince who devoted himself specially to the service of the deity and estranged himself more from state affairs than was altogether pleasing to his royal father.

The elder sons, including Khamuas, died during the long reign of their father : the fourteenth, named Meneptah, was his successor. He had already taken part in the affairs of the government during his father's lifetime, and in this capacity he appears on the monuments by the side of Ramses II.

Of the daughters of the king the monuments name Bint-antha ('daughter of Anaïtis),' Meri-Amen, and Nebtaui. A much younger sister, named Meri, deserves to be mentioned, since her name reminds us of the princess Merris, the daughter of Maat-neferu-Ra, the Kheta princess, who, according to Jewish tradition, found Moses when she went to bathe.

The list of contemporaries of Ramses II. is considerable. Among them a distinguished place was held by that Beken-Khonsu upon whose statue in Munich is the following inscription :—

(1) The hereditary lord and first prophet of Amen, Beken-Khonsu, speaks thus : I was truthful and virtuous towards my lord. I undertook with pleasure that which my god taught me. I walked in his ways. I performed acts of piety within his temple. I was a great architect in the town of Amen, my heart being filled with good works for my lord.

O ye men, all of you altogether, of reflecting mind, (2) ye who remain now upon the earth, and ye who will come after me for thousands and later thousands of years, according to your age and frailty, whose heart is possessed by the knowledge of virtue, I give you to know what services I performed on earth, in that office which was my lot from my birth.

I was for four years a very little child. For twelve years (3) I was a boy. I was the superintendent of the office for the sustenance of the king Meneptah Seti. I was a priest of Amen for four years. I was a holy father of Amen for twelve years. I was third prophet of Amen for sixteen years. I was second prophet of Amen for twelve years. He (the king) rewarded me, and distinguished me because of my deserts. He named me as first prophet of Amen for six years. I was (4) a good father for my temple-servants, in that I afforded sustenance to their families, and stretched out my hand to the fallen, and gave food to the poor, and did my best for my temple. I was the great architect of the Theban palace for his (Seti's) son, who sprang from his loins, the king Ramses II. He himself raised a memorial to his father Amen, (5) when he was placed upon the throne as king.

The skilled in art, and the first prophet of Amen, Beken-Khonsu, speaks thus : I performed the best I could for the temple of Amen as architect of my lord. I erected for him the wing-tower ' of Ra-messu II., the friend of Amen, who listens to those who pray to him,' (thus is he named) at the first gate of the temple of Amen. I placed obelisks at the same made of granite. Their height reaches to the vault of heaven. A propylon is (6) before the same in sight of the city of Thebes, and ponds and gardens, with flourishing trees. I made two great double doors of gold. Their height reaches to heaven. I caused to be made double pairs of great masts. I set them up in the splendid court in sight of his temple. I had great barks built on the river for Amen, Mut, and Khonsu.

Although the day of the death of Beken-Khonsu is not given in the inscription, yet it is clear that he must have departed this life while priest of Amen, after having completed sixty-six years. We can therefore divide his whole life of sixty-six years into the following sections :—

			Years.
Beken-Khonsu was a little child	.	4 years .	1–4
A boy, and at last official of the palace	. . . . .	12 „ .	5–16
Priest of Amen	. . . .	4 „ .	17–20
Holy father of Amen	. . .	12 „ .	21–32
Third prophet of Amen	. . .	16 „ .	33–48
Second prophet of Amen	. . .	12 „ .	49–60
First prophet of Amen	. . .	6 „ .	61–66

The body of Ramses II. was laid in his sepulchral chamber in the rocky valley of Bibân-el-Molûk. The son of Seti I., so full of gratitude to his father, had not left one descendant to beautify his tomb and commemorate his name. At his death he might truly have re-iterated what he had said of himself in his combat with the Kheta--'I was alone ; no other was with me.'

PTAH-MERI-EN-SE-PTAH.   MENEPTAH II.

A careful examination of the monuments shows
that Meneptah II. does not rank with those Pharaohs
who have transmitted their remembrance to posterity
by grand buildings and the construction of new temples,
or by the enlargement of such as already existed. A
glance at the plan of the temple at Karnak is alone
sufficient to prove that Meneptah did as good as nothing
for the great temple of the empire at Apet. With the
exception of small works hardly worthy of being mentioned, the new Pharaoh contented himself with the
cheap glory of utilising, or rather misusing, the monu
ments of his predecessors as far back as the Twelfth
Dynasty, not excepting the works of the Hyksos, for in
the cartouches of former kings, where he had chiselled
out their names, he unscrupulously inserted his own.
Short, unimportant, badly executed inscriptions, for the
most part of the first years of his reign, commemorate
merely his existence, the one exception being an
important record which he caused to be placed on the
inner side-wall at Karnak, to call to the remembrance
of the Thebans his great friendship for the gods. It
also announces the irruption of the Libyans and their
allies into Egypt and their repulse :—

(1) Catalogue of the peoples which were smitten by the king :
[. . . .]-i the A-qa-ua-sha, the Tu-li-sha, the Li-ku, the Shar-dana,
the Sha-ka-li-sha, peoples of the North, which came hither out of
all countries.

(2) [In the year V., in the month . . . . , in the reign of the
lord of the diadem] to whom his father Amen has given power, the
king of Upper and Lower Egypt, Meneptah Hotephima, the dispenser of life, the divine benefactor, was [in the town of Memphis,
to thank the god Ptah] (3) [for] his [benefits]. For all gods protect him, all peoples were in fear of his glance. The king Meneptah
(4) [received at that time a message, that the king of the Libyans
had fallen upon the towns of the country] and plundered them,

and turned them into heaps of rubbish ; that the cowards had submitted to his will ; that he had overstepped the boundaries of his
country, that he had gained the upper hand.

(5) [Then the king caused the towns to be fortified, and measures
to be taken] in all directions for the protection of the breath of life.
He gave it back to the inhabitants who were without it, sitting still
in (their) hiding-places. Powerful was his might to (6) [attain his
end. He had entrenchments drawn] to protect the city of On, the
city of the sun-god Tmu, and to protect the great fortress of Tanen
(i.e. Memphis), and to extend [the works for the protection of other
cities] in great numbers.

(7) [For the foreign peoples had long since made inroads also
from the East, and had pitched] their tents before the town of Pa-
Bailos (Byblus, Bilbeïs) ; they found themselves (already) on the
canal Shakana, to the north of the canal Ao (of Heliopolis), (8) [so
that the adjoining land] was not cultivated, but was left as pasture
for the cattle on account of the foreigners.[1] It lay waste there from
the times of our forefathers. All the kings of Upper Egypt sat in
their entrenchments (9) [and were occupied in building themselves
memorials], and the kings of Lower Egypt found themselves in the
midst of their city, surrounded with earthworks, cut off from
everything by warriors, for they had no mercenaries to oppose to
them.

Thus had it been (10) [until the day when King Meneptah]
ascended the throne of Horus. He was crowned to preserve life
to mortals. He was brought in as king to protect men. There
was the strength in him to do this, because he was the likeness of
the [beautiful] faced (11) [god (Ptah). And the king sent messengers to the land of Ma ?]-bair. The choicest of his mercenaries
were equipped ; his chariots were assembled from all directions ;
and his spies [betook them to the road to keep him informed. Thus
had he] prepared [everything] for his equipment in (12) [a short
time. And thus was he armed for the approaching struggle. For
he is a hero] : he takes no count of hundreds of thousands (of
enemies) on the day of the turmoil of battle. His life-guards
marched forward ; there came on the most powerful warriors ; and
beautiful was the sight at the entrance of the mercenaries for all
the inhabitants [of Egypt].

(13) [And they came to announce to the king : 'In . . . .]
month of the summer has it happened, that the miserable king of
the hostile land of Libu, Mar-ajui, a son of Did, has made an
irruption into the land of the Thuhennu (the Marmaridæ) with his
foreign mercenaries, (14) [the catalogue of whom is as follows :

[1] See p. 98.

the Sh]ar-dana, the Sha-ka-li-sha, the A-qa-ua-sha, the Li-ku, the
Tu-ri-sha : since he has sought out the best of all combatants, and
of all the quick runners of his country.　He has also brought with
him his wife and his children ; (15) [besides there are come with
him the princes] and the captains of the host.　He has reached the
boundaries of the west land at the fields of the town of Pa-Ar-
shop (Prosopis).'

Then his Majesty was enraged against them like a lion, (16)
[and he assembled the princes and leaders of his host and spake
thus :] 'Listen to the sayings of your lord.　I give you [to know]
that I, the king, am your shepherd.　My care is to enquire (17)
[what tends to the good of the land.　He is for you a father who
preserves the life of his children.　Should they be anxious like the
birds ?　You do not know the goodness of his intentions.'　No
answer (was made to this) on the part of (18) [the princes.　And
the king continued : 'It is not my intention to await the enemy,
so that the land] should be wasted and abandoned at the advance
of the foreigners to plunder its borders.　The enemies (19) overstep
them daily.　Each takes [what he pleases, and it is their intention]
to plunder the frontier cities.　They have already advanced into the
fields of Egypt from the boundary of the river onwards.　They
have gained a firm footing, and spend days and months therein.
[They have] settled themselves (20) [near the towns.　Others of
them] have reached the mountains of the Oasis, and the lands in
sight of the nome of Taahu.　It was a privilege ever since the kings
of Upper Egypt, on the ground of the historical records of other
times.　But no one (21) knows [that they ever came in large num-
bers] like vermin.　Let no more be granted to them than their belly
requires.　If they love death and hate life, if their temper is
haughty to do (22) [what they wish, then let them apply to] their
king, let them remain on (their) ground and soil, and go to the
battle, so as always to fill their bodies.　They have come to Egypt
to seek sustenance for their mouth.　They [direct] their mind (23)
[to this, to fill] their belly [with] my property, just like the fishermen.　Their king is like a dog, a bragging fellow.　His courage is
naught.　Having arrived, he sits there planning (24) [a treaty to
carry out with him] the people of the Piti-shu, whom I allowed to
take away wheat in ships, to preserve the life of this people of
Kheta, because I, the king, am he whom the gods have chosen.
All plenty, (25) [all sustenance, lies] in my hand, the king, Meneptah,
the dispenser of life.　In my name are laid [the supporting columns]
of my [buildings].　I act as king of the country.　[All] happens
(26) [in my name in the land of Egypt].　What is spoken in Thebes
pleases Amen.　He has turned himself away from the people of

the Mashauasha (Maxyes), and (he) looks [no more] on the people of the Tamahu, they are (27) [lost.'

Thus spake the king to] the leaders of the host, who stood before him, that they should destroy the people of the Libu. They went forth, and the hand of God was with them. Amen was at their [side] as a shield. The news reached the [people] of Egypt, (28) [namely, that the king in his own person would take part] in the campaign on the fourteenth day. Then his Majesty beheld in a dream as if the statue of Ptah, which is placed at the [gate of the temple,] stepped down to Pharaoh. It was like a giant. (29) [And it was] as if it spoke to him: 'Remain altogether behind,' and, handing to him the battle sword, 'Mayest thou cast off the lazy disposition that is in thee.' And Pharaoh spoke to it: 'Behold! (30) [thy word shall be accomplished].'

And my warriors and the chariots in sufficient number had prepared an ambush before them in the high land of the country of the nome of Prosopis.

Then the miserable king of (31) [the hostile Libu caused his warriors and his mercenaries to advance] in the night of the first of Epiphi, when the earth became light enough for the encounter. When the miserable king of the hostile Libu had arrived, about the time of the 3rd of Epiphi, he had brought (32) [with him all his hosts. But] they held back. When the warriors of his Majesty had charged forward, together with the chariots, then was Amen-Ra with them, and the god Nub reached out to them his hand. Each (33) [man fought bravely. A great defeat was inflicted on them, and they lay there in] their blood. No man was left remaining of them, for the foreign mercenaries of his Majesty had spent six hours in annihilating them. The sword gave (34) [no mercy, so that] the land was [full of corpses].

While they thus fought, the miserable king of the Libu stood there full of fear, his courage deserted him; then fled (35) [he in quick flight, and left] his sandals, his bow, his quiver, in his haste behind him; and [all other things] which he had with him. He, in whose body there was no timidity, and whose form was animated by a great manly courage, (36) [he fled like a woman. Then the mercenaries of his Majesty took what he had left] of his property, his money which he had gathered in, his silver, his gold, his vessels of iron, the ornaments of his wife, his chairs, his bows, his weapons, and all other things which he had brought (37) [with him. All was allotted to the] palace of the king, whither it was brought together with the prisoners. When in the meantime the miserable king of the Libu had hurried forth in his flight, then there [followed] him a number (38) [of the people of his nation, since they had escaped] destruction by the sword. Then did the cavalry who sat upon their horses spring forward to pursue them. [The enemy] (39) fled in haste, [and great destruction was inflicted on them]. No [man] had seen the like in the historical records of the kings of Lower Egypt, at the time when this land of Egypt was in their [power], when the enemy maintained their ground firmly, at the time when the kings of Upper Egypt (40) [would afford no assistance]. But [all] this was done by the gods from love to their son who loves them, to preserve the land of Egypt for its ruler, and to protect the temples of the land of Tamera, in order to exalt (41) [the glory of the king to the latest generations.

Then the governor] of the frontier garrisons of the west land sent a report to the royal court to the following effect : 'The enemy Mauri has arrived in flight ; his body trembled ; he escaped far away only by favour of the night. (42) [His flight, however, does no harm, for] want [will be his fate]. He has fallen. All the gods are for Egypt. The promises which he had made are become vain, and all his words have rolled back on his own head. His fate is not known, whether he is dead, (43) [or whether he is living. Thou, O king !] leave him his life. If he is alive, he will not raise himself up any more. He has fallen down, and his people have become hostile (to him). Thou wilt be the man who will undertake it, by giving orders to kill (44) [the rebels among the inhabitants] in the land of the Tamahu, and [of the Libu]. Let them set up another in his place, one of his brothers, who took part in the battle. He will be obliged to acknowledge him, since he is himself despised by the princes as a (45) [monster without an equal.'

Then the king gave the order that there should return home] the leaders of the foreign mercenaries, the life-guards, the chariots of war, and all the warriors of the army whose service was ended. . . . Then the whole land rejoiced to the height of heaven ; the towns and villages sang the wonderful deeds that had been done ; the (48) river resounded with the joyful shouts of the dwellers on its banks, and they] carried the booty under the window of the palace in order that his Majesty might behold their conquests.

Such was the great battle of Prosopis, which took place in the 5th year of the reign of Meneptah. With the Libyans, who were held in contempt by the Egyptians as uncircumcised, were joined mercenary troops of the Caucaso-Colchian race, who in these times had migrated into their country, and rendered military service, partly in Egypt and partly in Libya. In the times of Ramses III. they appeared again with the following allies :—

1. Qai-qasha : the Caucasians.
2. A-qa-ua-sha : the Achæans of the Caucasus.
3. Shar-dana : the Sardones, Chartani.
4. Sha-ka-li-sha : the people of Zagylis.
5. Tu-ri-sha : the Taurians.
6. Zakar, Zakkari : the Zyges, Zygritæ.
7. Li-ku : the Ligyes.
8. Uashash : the Ossetes.

To identify these *circumcised* tribes, as some have done, with the Achæans, Sardinians, Siculi, Etruscans, Teucrians, Lycians, and Oscans, of classical antiquity, is to introduce a serious error into the primitive history of the classic nations. After her deliverance from such dangerous enemies as the Libyans and their allies, Egypt, freed from a pressing incubus, rejoiced. The chief share in this joy must have belonged to the inhabitants of the Delta, whose cities and villages touched on the borders of the enemies, especially the Colchians and Carians.

In what was afterwards called the Mareotic nome, the Danau were settled in the district named by the geographer Ptolemy Teneia, or Taineia. Their next neighbours were the Purosatha, the Prosoditæ of the same writer ; while along the coast, as far as the great Catabathmus, the last remnant of the Sha-ka-li-sha still remained at the time of the Romans in the village of Zagylis ; and the descendants of the Shardana and the Zakkar were perpetuated in the small tribes of the Chartani and the Zygritæ. The whole coast beyond, as far as Cyrene, appears to have been a gathering-ground of warlike adventurers of the Colchio-Cretan tribes, up to the Dardani, whose name is again reflected in the

Greek designation of the town Dardanis. The officials
and priests at the court of Meneptah were not backward
in extolling their Pharaoh. The fragments of the
writings of some of these officers display a poetical
enthusiasm in lauding the king, whom they commonly
introduce under his throne-name of Ba-n-Ra, 'soul of
Ra.' The relations which Meneptah maintained with
the Kheta towards the East were, in consequence of the
old treaty, of the most friendly nature. His contribution of corn to them gives a full confirmation of this
idea. The fortresses and wells which Tehuti-mes III.
and Ramses II. had established in Canaan, and provided
with Egyptian garrisons, still existed. With them, as
with the inhabitants of Gaza, a constant intercourse
was regularly maintained, and messengers went to and
fro as bearers of the king's orders from the court to the
East. These officials belonged mostly to the Canaanite
peoples, as their names prove.

The nomad tribes of the Edomite Shasu—who
under Seti I. still regarded the eastern region of the
Delta as far as Zoan as their own possession—until they
were driven out by that Pharaoh—bestirred themselves
anew under Meneptah II., but in a manner alike peaceful and loyal. As faithful subjects, they asked for a
passage through the border fortress of Khetam, in the
land of Thuku (Succoth), in order to find sustenance for
themselves and their herds in the rich pasture-lands of
the lake district about the city of Pa-Tmu (Pithom).

On this subject an Egyptian official makes the
following report (Pap. Anastasi, vi.):—

Another matter for the satisfaction of my master's heart. We
have carried into effect the passage of the tribes of the Shasu from
the land of Aduma (Edom), through the fortress (Khetam) of
Meneptah-Hotephima, which is situated in Thuku (Succoth), to
the lakes of the city Pa-Tmu, of Meneptah-Hotephima, which are
situated in the land of Thuku, in order to feed themselves and to

feed their herds on the possessions of Pharaoh, who is there a beneficent sun for all peoples. In the year 8 . . . . Set, I caused them to be conducted, according to the list of the . . . . for the . . . . of the other names of the days, on which the fortress (Khetam) of Meneptah-Hotephima is opened for their passage.

As Ramses II. must be regarded as the Pharaoh under whom Moses first saw the light, so the chronological relations—having regard to the great age of the two contemporaries, Ramses II. and Moses—demand that Meneptah II. should in all probability be acknowledged as the PHARAOH OF THE EXODUS. He also had his royal seat in the city of Ramses, and seems to have strengthened its fortifications. PER-AO—'great house,' 'high gate'—is, according to the monuments, the designation of the king of the land of Egypt for the time being. This does not of itself furnish a decisive argument; but then, besides, the incidental statement of the Psalmist, that Moses wrought his wonders *in the field of Zoan* (Psalm lxxviii. 43), carries us back again to those sovereigns, Ramses II. and Meneptah, who were fond of holding their court in Zoan-Ramses.

Some scholars have recently sought to recognise in the Hebrews the so-called Aper, Apura, or Aperiu, the Erythræan people in the east of the nome of Heliopolis, in what is known as the 'red country' or the 'red mountain;' and hence they have drawn conclusions which rest on a weak foundation. According to the inscriptions, the name of this people appears in connection with the breeding of horses and the art of horsemanship. In an historical narrative of the time of Tehuti-mes III. the Apura are named as horsemen or knights (*senen*), who mount their horses at the king's command. In another document, of the time of Ramses III., long after the Exodus of the Jews from Egypt, 2,083 Aperiu are introduced, as settlers in

Heliopolis, with the words, 'Knights, sons of the kings and noble lords (Marina) of the Aper, settled people, who dwell in this place.' Under Ramses IV. we again meet with 'Aper, 800 in number,' as inhabitants of foreign origin in the district of Ani or Aini, on the western shore of the Red Sea, in the neighbourhood of the modern Suez.

These and similar data completely exclude all thought of the Hebrews.

Pre-supposing, then, that Meneptah is to be regarded as the Pharaoh of the Exodus, this king must have had to endure serious disturbances of all kinds during his reign:—in the West the Libyans, in the East the Hebrews, and in the South a spirit of rebellion, which declared itself by the insurrection of a rival king of the family of the great Ramses II. The events which form the close of his rule are passed over by the monuments with perfect silence.

In looking over names of the most eminent contemporaries of this king there were Mas, his viceroy in Ethiopia, the 'king's son of Cush,' the same who held the like high office under Ramses II., and whose memory is perpetuated in a rock-inscription at Aswân; and also the influential high-priest of Amen, Roi, who held the command of the legion of Amen and administered his treasury, and was chief architect to Pharaoh.

The more troublous the times, the less thought was there of expeditions, and the greater was the attention paid to the pursuit of knowledge. The following temple-scribes are among the brilliant stars: Qa-ga-bu, Horus, Anna, Mer-em-apet, Bek-en-Ptah, Hor-a, Amen-masu, Su-an-ro, Ser-Ptah. If we add to these the name of Pentaur, the author of the epic of Ramses the Great, and also that of Amen-em-hant, the director of the Theban library, as well as those of Amen-em-ape and

Panbesa, we have completed the cycle of literary names
in those times from Ramses II. downwards.

Meneptah II. was succeeded by his son,

User-kheperu-Ra.   Seti II.   cir. b.c. 1266.

Already during his father's lifetime Seti II. enjoyed
a special distinction, inasmuch as he is frequently
designated crown prince of the empire. We possess
records of the first two years only of his rule, which at
that time extended over the whole of Egypt.

The Ramses-city of Zoan-Tanis remained, as before,
the special residence of the court. As in the preceding
times, special attention was devoted to the fortresses
eastward of Tanis, which covered the entrance from
Syria. Here was the old royal road, which offered
fugitives the only opportunity of escaping from the
king's power, though not without danger. That such
attempts were often made, is proved by the following
report of a scribe, who had gone out upon the road in
order to overtake two fugitive servants of the court:—

I set out (he says) from the hall of the royal palace on the 9th
day of the month Epiphi, in the evening, after the two servants. I
arrived at the fortress of Thuku on the 10th of Epiphi. I was informed that the men had resolved to take their way towards the
south. On the 12th I reached Khetam (Etham). There I was
informed that grooms, who had come from the neighbourhood [of
the 'sedge-city,' had reported] that the fugitives had already passed
the rampart (i.e. the Shur of the Bible, Gerrhon of the Greeks) to
the north of the Migdol of King Seti Meneptah.

Notwithstanding the apparent shortness of his
reign, Seti II. found the time and means to erect a
special sanctuary to his father Amen in the great temple
of the empire at Apet. This is the small temple, consisting of three chambers, to the north-west of the great
front court; an insignificant building, which merely
attests the official acknowledgment of the king on the

part of the priestly guild of Thebes. Roi, the high-priest of the god Amen, was friendly to the king, as was also his son and successor in office, Roma. Both were declared adherents of the king, whose affection for the pious fathers of Amen shows itself also in other forms in the extant papyri. It was for him, while he was still crown prince, that a temple-scribe composed that wonderful tale of ' The Two Brothers,' the translation of which we owe to M. Le Page Renouf.[1]

The sepulchre of this king, in the rocky valley of Bibân-el-Molûk, is really princelike and magnificent. In it also we have a new proof of the priestly recognition of his sovereignty over the land of Egypt.

After his death the sovereignty passed in regular succession to his son,

USER-KHA-RA-SOTEP-EN-RA. SET-NEKHT. CIR. B.C. 1233.

All that we are able to say of him can be condensed into a few words; he was the father of a great king, and he lived in times full of disturbance and trouble. As his father had, in all probability, been opposed by a rival king, Amen-messu, so had the son of the latter, Meneptah Siptah, become a dangerous successor against Setnekht. Siptah, the husband of that Queen Ta-user whose grave obtained a distinguished position in the valley of the kings at Thebes, seems to have been favoured by a number of adherents in the city of Amen, and to have owed his elevation to the throne to the help of an Egyptian noble, named Bi. This latter held the office of confidential servant of the king; he declares on his own behalf that ' he put away falsehood and gave honour to the truth, inasmuch as he set the king upon his father's throne—he, the great keeper of the seal for all the land, Ra-messu-kha-em-neteru-Bi.'

[1] Part of this tale is given on p. 123 *et seq.*

Among the remaining adherents of the anti-king, no insignificant part was played by his governor of the southern lands, Seti, whose memory has been perpetuated by an inscription at Abû Simbel. In that representation, this official exhibits himself as a zealous worshipper of the Theban Amen, and there is appended an inscription of four lines, giving the following explanation :—

(1) Worship offered to Amen, that he may grant life, prosperity, and health, to the person of the king's envoy into all lands, the companion (2) of the lord of the land, of the friend of Horus (i.e. the king) in his house, the first commander of the war-chariots of his Majesty, (3) who understood his purpose, when the king came, to exalt (him) the king's son of Cush, (4) Seti, upon his throne (or, the throne of his father ?) in the first year of the lord of the land, Ra-messu Siptah.

On the summit of a group of rocks on the island of Sehêl, near Philæ, there remains the following inscription of the same Seti, annexed to the name of his king :—

In the year 3, Pakhons, day 21. Honour to thy name, O king ! May it attest the acknowledgments of the person of the commander of the chariots, and the king's sons of Cush, and the governor of the southern lands, Seti !

On the last visit I paid to Thebes to the grave of ' the great queen and lady of the land, the princess of Upper and Lower Egypt, Ta-user,' the names of her husband Siptah were still to be seen at its entrance, while in the interior, on the piece which has been laid on to cover the names of the queen, the cartouche of Setnekht meets the eye in a re-engraving. Setnekht took possession of his wife's sepulchre, without in a single case replacing the feminine signs in the inscriptions by the corresponding masculine forms. His rival having been driven out, Setnekht could deal with the tomb at his pleasure.

Nor was it only against native claimants of the

throne that this prince had to wage war; foreigners also contributed to turn Egypt upside down.   A certain Khar, or Phœnician, had seized the throne, maintained himself on it for some time, driven the Egyptians into banishment, and grievously oppressed those left in the land.   This is that Arisu of whom the great Harris Papyrus speaks thus :—

Thus says King Ra-messu III., the son of Setnekht, the great god, to the princes and leaders of the land, to the warriors and to the chariot soldiers, to the Shardana, and the numerous foreign mercenaries, and to all the living inhabitants of the land of Tamera :—

Hearken ! I make you to know my glorious deeds, which I have performed as king of men.

The people of Egypt lived in banishment abroad.   Of those who lived in the interior of the land, none had any to care for him.   So passed away long years, until other times came.   The land of Egypt belonged to princes from foreign parts.   They slew one another, whether noble or mean.

Other times came on afterwards, during years of scarcity.   Arisu, a Phœnician, had raised himself among them to be a prince, and he compelled all the people to pay him tribute.   Whatever any had gathered together, that his companions robbed them of.   Thus did they.   The gods were treated like the men.   They went without the appointed sin-offerings in the temples.

Then did the gods turn this state of things to prosperity.   They restored to the land its even balance, such as its condition properly required.   And they established their son, who had come forth from their body, as king of the whole land on their exalted throne.   This was King Setnekht Meri-Amen.

He was like the person of Set when he is indignant.   He took care for the whole land.   If rebels showed themselves, he slew the wicked who made a disturbance in the land of Tamera.

He purified the exalted royal throne of Egypt, and so he was the ruler of the inhabitants on the throne of the sun-god Tmu, while he raised up their faces.   Such as showed themselves refusing to acknowledge any one as a brother, were walled up.

He restored order to the temples, granting the sacred revenues for the due offerings to the gods, as their statutes prescribe.

He raised me up as heir to the throne on the seat of the earth-god Seb, to be the great governor of the Egyptian dominions in care for the whole people, who have found themselves united together again.

And he went to his rest out of his orbit of light, like the company of the celestials. The (funeral) rites of Osiris were accomplished for him. He was borne (to his grave) in his royal boat over the river, and was laid in his everlasting house on the west side of Thebes.

And my father Amen, the lord of the gods, and Ra, and Ptah with the beautiful face, caused me to be crowned as lord of the land on the throne of my parent.

I received the dignities of my father amidst shouts of joy. The people were content and delighted because of the peace. They rejoiced in my countenance as king of the land, for I was like Horus, who was king over the land on the throne of Osiris. Thus was I crowned with the Atef-crown, together with the Uræus-serpents; I put on the ornament of the double plumes, like the god Tanen [1]; thus I reposed myself on the throne-seat of Horemkhu; thus was I clothed with the robes of state, like Tmu.

[1] Tanen was the personification of the earth, and is also another form of the nightly sun. He was the local god of the district bordering on Lake Mœris.

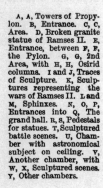

A, A, Towers of Propylon. B, Entrance. C, C, Area. D, Broken granite statue of Ramses II. E, Entrance, between F, F, the Pylon. G, G, 2nd Area, with H, H, Osirid columns. I and J, Traces of Sculpture. K, Sculptures representing the wars of Ramses II. L and M, Sphinxes. N, O, P, Entrances into Q, The grand hall. R, S, Pedestals for statues. T, Sculptured battle scenes. U, Chamber with astronomical subject on ceiling. V, Another chamber, with W, X, Sculptured scenes. Y, Other chambers.

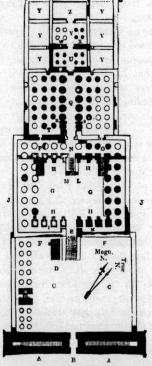

PLAN OF THE RAMESSEUM

GENEALOGICAL TABLE OF THE ROYAL FAMILIES OF THE DYNASTIES XX. TO XXVI.

CHAPTER XIV.

DYNASTY XX.[1]

Ra-messu Haq-On.   cir. b.c. 1200.
(Ramses III.)

As this king's official name was User-maat-Ra, he is only distinguished from Ramses II. by the title Haq-On, 'Prince of Heliopolis.' Among the people he bore the appellation of RA-MESSU-PA-NETER, that is, 'Ramses the god,' from which the Greeks formed the well-known name of Rhampsinitus.

The miserable state of Egypt before his accession could not be better described than in his own words, cited in the last chapter. The same Harris Papyrus gives a comprehensive outline of the eventful life of Ramses III., the following being the chief events:—The king's first care after his accession was the restoration and demarcation of the several castes, which he arranged in their descending degrees, as follows: The Ab en Perao, 'counsellors of Pharaoh,' an office which Joseph held in the Egyptian court; the 'great princes,' governors and representatives of the king in the several nomes; 'the infantry and chariot-soldiers;' the mercenaries of the tribes of the Shardana and the Kahak; and the lowest classes of the officers and servants.

He was next occupied with wars against foreign nations, who had invaded the borders of Egypt. The Danau were pursued to the Cilician coast, and there

[1] For Table of Kings see p. xxiv.

defeated; so in Cyprus were the Zekkaru (Zygritæ), and the Perusatha (Prosoditæ); while the Colchio-Caucasian Shardana (Sardones), and the Uashasha (Ossetes), on the other hand, were exterminated in their settlements west of the Delta, and transplanted to Egypt in great masses, with their families. They were compelled to settle in a Ramesseum, and to pay every year, according to the ·custom of the country, a tribute of woven stuffs and corn to the temples of Egypt.

On the East the king achieved a like success against the Sahir, a branch of the Shasu; he plundered their tents, seized their possessions and cattle, and carried off the people as prisoners to Egypt. A war was next kindled by the Libyans and Maxyes, who, as before under Meneptah II., made an inroad into the Delta, and occupied the whole country along the left bank of the Canopic branch of the Nile, from Memphis as far as Carbana (Canopus). Near the latter place, along the seashore, lay the district of Gautut, the cities of which they had held for many years. They and their allies were defeated by the Pharaoh, and among the latter the king mentions by name the Asbita (Asbytæ), the Kaikasha (Caucasians), the Shai-ap (who cannot be more closely defined), the Hasa (Ausees), the Bakana (Bakaloi). The king of the Libu, his family and people, together with their herds, were transported as captives to Egypt, where some were placed in the fortified 'Ramessea,' and others branded with hot iron 'in the name of the king' as sailors. A magnificent gift was made of their herds to the temple of Amen at Thebes.

For the protection of the frontier towards Suez, the king built a great wall in the country of the Aperiu, and surrounded it with strong defences whose walls had a height of $52\frac{1}{2}$ feet. In the harbour of Suez

Ramses III. built a fleet of large and small ships on purpose to make voyages on the Red Sea to the coasts of Punt and 'the Holy Land,' and to bring back the costly productions of those distant regions, especially incense.

Connected with these objects was the establishing of commercial relations with those coasts, and a caravan trade by land was started on the road from Kosseir to Coptos on the Nile. In a word, Ramses III. opened direct intercourse by land and sea with the shores of the Indian Ocean, which in later times was renewed by the Ptolemies. Not less important was the despatch of a mission by land to the copper-mines of Akita; and the metal, shining like gold, and in the form of bricks, was brought home from the smelting-houses in those parts.

The king also turned his attention anew to the treasures of the peninsula of Sinai, which from the times of Sneferu had appeared to the Egyptians so desirable. Laden with rich presents for the temple of Hathor, protectress of the Mafkat peninsula, distinguished officials went thither to bring back the much-prized greenish-blue copper-stone

Throughout Egypt Ramses planted trees and shrubs to give the inhabitants rest under their cool shade. Rhampsinitus concludes by extolling the peaceful condition of the whole country, in which the weakest woman could travel unmolested on all the roads. The Shardana and the Kahak remained quietly in their cities, and Cush and the Phœnicians then had ceased to annoy Egypt with their attacks. Finally, in the 32nd year of his reign the king recommends his son Ramses IV., whom he had made joint king with himself, to the recognition and obedience of his subjects.

It is quite possible to fill in this general outline

of Ramses III.'s reign with more definite facts supplied by the Ramesseum, which was turned from a
treasure-house into a complete temple of victory. To-
day pictures and words alone replace the treasures
which were once stored there and dedicated by
Rhampsinitus to Amen-Ra. Gold in grains up to the
weight of 1,000 lbs. from the mines of Amamu, in the
land of Cush, of Edfû, of Ombos, and of Coptos; bars
of silver; whole pyramids of blue and green stones,
besides the much-prized bluestone of Tafrer and the
real greenstone of Roshatha; copper ore; lead;
precious sorts of incense from Punt and from the
Holy Land; moreover gold and silver statues, images
of animals, vases, chests, and other ornaments, down
to the seal-rings with the name of the king upon them;
—all these and many other things did the Pharaoh
dedicate to the god in this address :—

I dedicate this to thee as a memorial for thy temple, consisting of clear raw copper, and raw gold, and [of all works of art],
which have come forth from the workshops of the sculptor. The
productions of the land of Ruthen shall be brought to thee as
gifts, to fill the treasury of thy temple with the best things of all
lands.

Again :—

Thou hast received gold and silver like sand on the [sea] shore.
What thou hast created in the river and in the mountain, that I
dedicate to thee by heaps upon the earth. Let it be an adornment
for thy Majesty for ever. I offer to thee blue and green precious
stones, and all kinds of jewels in chests of bright copper. I have
made for thee numberless talismans out of all kinds of valuable
precious stones.

Ramses III. must have enjoyed enormous wealth,
which he lavished on the temples of Amen, Ptah, and
Ra of Heliopolis.

When he came to the throne things looked bad for
Egypt.

The hostile Asiatics and Tuhennu robbers (the Libyan Marmaridæ) showed themselves only to injure the state of Egypt. The land lay open before them in weakness since the time of the earlier kings. They did evil to gods as well as to men. No one had so strong an arm as to oppose them, on account of their hostile intentions.

In the 5th year of his reign the enemies prepared a fresh attack from the West.

The people of the Tamahu assembled together in one place. The tribes of the Maxyes prepared themselves for a raid out of their own country. The leaders of their warriors had confidence in their plans.

As in former times the Libyans were the prime movers of hostilities, so now their kings Zamar and Zautmar appear as instigators and leaders in battle.

The defeat of the enemy was tremendous. Three years after this event a warlike movement broke out in the north, caused by the migration of the Carian and Colchian tribes, but they were at last utterly routed in a naval engagement at Migdol, at the mouth of the Pelusiac branch of the Nile. The inscriptions of the temple of victory thus relate the story :—

A quivering (not of fear) seized the people in their limbs : they (the invaders) came up leaping from their coasts and islands, and spread themselves all at once over the lands. No people stood before their arms, beginning with the people of Kheta, of Kadi (Galilee), and Carchemish, Aradus, and Alus. They wasted these countries, and pitched a camp at one place in the land of the Amorites. They plundered the inhabitants and the territory as if they had been nothing. And they came on (against Egypt), but there was held in readiness a fiery furnace before their countenance on the side of Egypt. Their home was in the land of the Purosatha, the Zakkar, the Shakalsha, the Daanau, and the Uashuash. These nations had leagued together ; they laid their hand on the double land of Egypt, to encircle the land. Their heart was full of confidence, they were full of plans. This happened, since such was the will of this god, the lord of the gods (Amen of Thebes). An ambush was prepared to take them in the snare like birds. He (Amen) gave me strength, and granted success to my plans. My arm was strong as iron when I broke

forth. I had guarded well my boundary up to Zahi (Philistia).
There stood in ambush over against them the chief leaders, the
governors, the noble *marinas*,[1] and the chief people of the warriors.
[A defence] was built on the water, like a strong wall, of ships of
war, of merchantmen, of boats and skiffs. They were manned from
the forepart to the hindpart with the bravest warriors, who bore
their arms, and with the best life-guards of the land of Egypt. They
were like roaring lions on the mountain. The knights were of the
swiftest in the race, and the most distinguished horsemen of a
skilful hand. Their horses quivered in all their limbs, ready to
trample the nations under their hoofs. I was like the war-god
Mentu, the strong. I held my ground before them. They beheld
the battle of my hands. I, King Ra-messu III., I went far forward
in the van, conscious of my might, strong of arm, protecting my
soldiers in the day of battle. They who had reached the boundary
of my country never more reaped harvest. Their soul and their spirit
passed away for ever. They who had assembled themselves over
against the others on the great sea, a mighty firebrand lightened
before them, in front of the mouths of the river. A wall of iron
shut them in upon the lake. They were driven away, dashed to the
ground, hewn down on the bank of the water. They were slain by
hundreds of heaps of corpses. The end was a new beginning. Their
ships and all their possessions lay strewn on the mirror of the
water. Thus have I taken from the nations the desire to direct
their thoughts against Egypt. They exalt my name in their country ;
yea, their heart is on fire for me so long as I shall sit on the throne
of Horemkhu.

A trembling seized the inhabitants of the northern regions in
their body, because of the Purosatha and the Zakkar, because they
plundered their land. If they went out to meet them, their spirit
failed. Some were brave people by land, others on the sea. Those who
came by way of the land, Amen-Ra pursued them and annihilated
them. Those who entered into the mouths of the Nile were caught
like birds in nets. They were made prisoners.

It came to pass that the people of the northern regions, who
reside in their islands and on their coasts, shuddered in their bodies.
They entered into the lakes of the mouths of the Nile. Their noses
snuffed the wind : their desire was to breathe a soft air. The king
broke forth like a whirlwind upon them, to fight them in the battle-
field, like all his heroes. Their spirit was annihilated where they
stood, their soul was taken from them ; a stronger than they came
upon them.

In the 11th year of Rhampsinitus, a new struggle

<hr />

[1] See p. 138.

threatened the safety of the country from the West. The Maxyes attacked Egypt under the leadership of their king Mashashal (Massala), a son of Kapur, in great force, in order to obtain possession of the rich districts on the banks of the Canopic mouth of the Nile. A great battle was fought about the month of Mesori in the same year, and the enemy were utterly defeated. The list of the killed was very considerable, and not less was the number of the prisoners and the amount of spoil, of which a list is here subjoined :—

Total number of hands (cut off) . . .		2175
Prisoners of war of Pharaoh belonging to the nation of the Maxyes :		
Commander-in-chief . .	1	
Commanders	5	
Maxyes : Men . . .	1205	
Youths . . .	152	
Boys . . .	131	
Total .	——	1494
Their wives	342	
Girls	65	
Maid-servants . . .	151	
Total .	——	558
Total number of prisoners of war of Pharaoh, without distinction, heads .		2052
Maxyes, whom the king killed on the spot		2175
Other things (as spoil) :		
Cattle—bulls		$119+x$
Swords, 5 cubits long		115
Swords, 3 cubits long		124
Bows		603
Chariots of war		93
Quivers		2310
Spears		92
Horses and asses of the Maxyes . .		183

We know that the king also conquered the negroes (Nahasu), the Thiraui, and the Amarai, and that, besides the Purosatha, the 'Tuirsha of the sea' were numbered among his enemies, and that the Khar (Phœnicians) and the Amorites received a severe chastisement from him.

Of special value are the effigies of the conquered kings, which Ramses III. caused to be sculptured in his palace by the side of the temple of Amen at Medînet Habû.

1. The king of the miserable land of Cush (Ethiopia).
2–3. Destroyed.
4. The king of the Libu (Libya).
5. The king of Turses (land of the Negroes).
6. The king of the Mashauasha (Maxyes).
7. The king of Taraua (land of the Negroes).
8. The miserable king of Kheta (Hethites) as a living prisoner.
9. The miserable king of the Amori (Amorites).
10. The leader of the hostile bands of the Zakkari (Zygritæ).
11. The people of the sea of Shardana (Chartani).
12. The leader of the hostile bands of the Shasu (Edomites).
13. The people of the sea of Tuirsha (Taurus).
14. The leader of the hostile bands of the Pu[rosatha] (Prosoditæ).

Ramses III. conducted a campaign of vengeance against several of the above-named nations. The names of the conquered cities and countries cover one side of the pylon of the temple at Medînet Habû.

1. Ma . . .
2. Poro . . .
3. Puther . . . . (Patara ? in Lycia).
4. Zizi . . .
5. Tharshka (Tarus in Cilicia).
6. Khareb.
7. Salomaski (Salamis in Cyprus).
8. Kathian (Citium in Cyprus).
9. Aimar (Marion in Cyprus).
10. Sali (Soli in Cyprus).
11. Ithal (Idalium in Cyprus).
12. (M)aquas (Acamas in Cyprus ?).
13. Tarshebi.
14. Bizar.
15. A . . . si.
16. Aman (Mons Amanus).
17. Alikan.
18. Pikaz.
19. . . . ubai.
20. Kerena, Kelena (Cerynia in Cyprus)
21. Kir . . . (Curium in Cyprus).

22. Aburoth.

23. Kabur (Cibyra in Cilicia).

24. Aimal (Myle in Cilicia).

25. U . . . lu (Ale in Cilicia).

26. Kushpita   (Casyponis   in Cilicia).

27. Kanu (comp. Caunus in Caria).

28. L . . . aros (Larissa).

29. Arrapikha.

30. Shabi.

31. Zaur (Zor-Tyrus in Cilicia).

32. Kilsenen   (Colossæ ?   in Phrygia).

33. Maulnus (Mallus in Cilicia).

34. Samai (Syme,   a   Carian island).

35. Thasakha.

36. Me . . . ari.

37. I-bir-, I-bil.

38. Athena (Adana in Cilicia).

39. Karkamash (Coracesium in Cilicia).

Even if some of the parallel names should receive rectification hereafter, yet still the fact remains certain, that in this list places on the coast and islands of Asia Minor were intended by the Egyptians.

In the case before us we may assume as certain that the places enumerated were the seats of Carian peoples in Asia Minor and in the neighbouring islands, but especially in Cilicia and Cyprus. The presents and buildings for which the gods were indebted to their grateful son Ramses III. are all set forth in detail in the great Harris Papyrus.

The Ramessea, or buildings raised for the glorification of Rhampsinitus, are found in various parts of the country. Thebes possesses the lion's share, and next to it Heliopolis and Memphis. With regard to other places, new temples of Ramses III. are named in a summary, in their succession from south to north :—

A Ramesseum in Thinis in honour of the Egyptian Mars, Anhur.

A Ramesseum in Abydos for the god Osiris.

A Ramesseum in Coptos.

A Ramesseum in Apu.

Two Ramessea in Lycopolis.

Two Ramessea in Hermopolis.

A Ramesseum in the temple-town of Sutekh, in the city of Pa-Ramses Meri-Amen.

The temple of Amen at Medînet Habû, on Neb-ankh, the holy mountain of the dead, still remains the most beautiful and remarkable monument of this king. The reliefs, which cover the interior and exterior walls, represent in a lifelike and artistic style various detached episodes in his campaigns, even to an occasional lion-hunt. The appended inscriptions give an instructive explanation of the scenes. Others give an insight into the order of the feasts, as then observed, inclusive of the sacrifices, and into the fixed holidays of the old Egyptian calendar, according to the latest arrangement. We find here a ' heavenly ' calendar, expressly distinguished from the ' earthly ' one. Among the general holidays were the 29th, 30th, 1st, 2nd, 4th, 6th, 8th, and 15th days of each month. The days are set forth in this order, according to the Egyptian assumption that the 29th day is that on which the conjunction of the sun and moon takes place, and on which the world was created :—

1	Tehuti.	Rising of the Sothis-star (Sirius), a sacrifice for Amen.
17	„	Eve of the Uaga feast.
18	„	Uaga feast.
19	„	Feast of Tehuti.
22	„	Feast of the great manifestation of Osiris.
17	Paophi.	Eve of the Amen-feast of Hapi.
19–23	„	The first five days of the Amen-feast of Hapi.
12	Athyr.	Last day of the festival of Hapi.
17	„	Special feast after the festival of Hapi.
1	Khoiak.	Feast of Hathor.
20	„	Feast of sacrifice.
21	„	Opening of the Tomb (of Osiris).
22	„	Feast of the hoeing of the earth.
23	„	Preparation of the sacrificial altar in the Tomb (of Osiris).
24	„	Exhibition of [the corpse] of Sekar (Osiris) in the midst of the sacrifice.

25	Khoiak.	Feast of the (mourning) goddesses.
26	,,	Feast of Sekar (Osiris).
27	,,	Feast (of the father) of the palms.
28	,,	Feast of the procession of the obelisk.
30	,,	Feast of the setting up of the image of Did.
1	Tybi.	Feast of the coronation of Horus, which served also for that of King Ramses III.
6	,,	A new Amen-feast founded by Ramses III.
22	,,	Heri-feast.
29 (?)	,,	Day of the exhibition of the meadow.

The feasts which follow these are unfortunately obliterated. To the special feast-days must be added the 26th of Pakhons, in commemoration of the king's accession to the throne.

On the eastern side of Thebes, Ramses III. laid the foundation-stone of an oracle-giving temple of the god Khonsu, the son of Amen and the goddess Mut. He likewise founded a new Ramesseum, which adjoined the great forecourt of the temple of Amen at Thebes. It is still well preserved, but is almost worthless from an artistic point of view. An inscription on its eastern side records as a fact that Ramses III., in the 16th year of his reign, in the month Payni, appointed special sacrifices for the god. The altar dedicated to this purpose was an artistic work of silver.

In foreign countries also temples were built, and according to the Harris Papyrus the king erected a Ramesseum to Amen in the city of Kanaan. The statue of the god was set up in its holy of holies, and obligation was laid on the tribes of the Ruthen to provide this temple with all necessaries. That Ramses III. did not enjoy his throne without cares and alarms is proved by a harem conspiracy which aimed at his overthrow. It was discovered, and the king immediately summoned a court of justice and himself named the judges who were to try and sentence the guilty. The names of the judges and the judgments which were delivered have been handed down to us nearly complete in the Judicial Papyrus of Turin, which has been translated by M. Le Page Renouf :—

PAGE 2. (1) 'And the commission was given to the treasurer Mentu-em-taui, the treasurer Paif-roui, (2) the fan-bearer Karo, the councillor Pa-besat, the councillor Kedenden, the councillor Baal-mahar, (3) the councillor Pa-aru-sunu, the councillor Tehuti-rekh-nefer, the royal interpreter Pen-rennu, the scribe Mai, (4) the scribe Pra-em-heb of the chancery, the colour-bearer Hor-a, of the garrison ; to this effect :—

(5) 'Regarding the speeches which people have uttered, and which are unknown, you shall institute an enquiry about them. (6) They shall be brought to a trial to see if they deserve death. Then they shall put themselves to death with their own hand.'

Ramses III. warns the judges to conduct the affair conscientiously, and concludes with these words :—

PAGE 3. (1) 'If all that has happened was such that it was actually done by them, (2) let their doing be upon their own heads. (3) I am the guardian and protector for ever, and (4) bearer of the royal insignia of justice in presence of the god-king (5) Amen-Ra, and in presence of the prince of eternity, Osiris.'

This is followed by a second and longer section, which enables us to understand very clearly the result of the trial :—

PAGE 4. (1) 'These are the persons who were brought up on account of their great crimes before the judgment-seat, to be judged by the treasurer Mentu-em-taui, by the treasurer Paif-roui, by the fan-bearer Karo, by the councillor Pa-besat, by the scribe Mai of the chancery, and by the standard-bearer Hor-a, and who were judged and found guilty, and to whom punishment was awarded, that their offence might be expiated.

(2) 'The chief culprit Beka-kamen. He was house-steward. He was brought up because of actual participation in the doings of the wife Thi and the women of the harem. He had conspired with them, and had carried abroad their commission given by word of mouth to their mothers and sisters there, to stir up the people, and to assemble the malcontents, to commit a crime against their lord. They set him before the elders of the judgment-seat. They judged his offence, and found him guilty of having done so, and he was fully convicted of his crime. The judges awarded him his punishment.

(3) 'The chief culprit Mestu-su-Ra. He was a councillor. He was brought up because of his actual participation in the doings of Beka-kamen, the house-steward. He had conspired with the women to stir up the malcontents, to commit a crime against their lord. They set him before the elders of the judgment-seat. They judged his offence. They found him guilty, and awarded him his punishment.

(4) 'The chief culprit Panauk. He was the royal secretary of the harem, for the service of the women's house. He was brought up on account of his actual participation in the conspiracy of Beka-kamen and Mestu-su-Ra, to commit a crime against their lord. They set him before the elders of the judgment-seat. They judged his offence. They found him guilty, and awarded him his punishment.

(5) 'The chief culprit Pen-tuauu. He was the royal secretary of the harem, for the service of the women's house. He was brought up on account of his actual participation in the conspiracy of Beka-kamen and Mestu-su-Ra and the other chief culprit, who was the overseer of the harem of the women in the women's house, to increase the number of the malcontents who had conspired to commit a crime against their lord. They set him before the elders of the judgment-seat. They judged his offence. They found him guilty, and awarded him his punishment.

(6) 'The chief culprit Pa-nef-emtu-Amen. He was a land-surveyor, for the service of the women's house. He was brought up because he had listened to the speeches which the conspirators and the women of the women's house had indulged in, without giving information of them. He was set before the elders of the judgment-seat. They judged his offence, and found him guilty, and awarded him his punishment.

(7) 'The chief culprit Karpusa. He was a land-surveyor, for the service of the women's house. He was brought up on account of the talk which he had heard, but had kept silence. He was set before the elders of the judgment-seat, and they judged his offence, and found him guilty, and awarded him his punishment.

(8) 'The chief culprit Kha-m-apet. He was a land-surveyor, for the service of the women's house. He was brought up on account of the talk which he had heard, but had kept silence. He was set before the elders of the judgment-seat, and they judged his offence, and found him guilty, and awarded him his punishment.

(9) 'The chief culprit Kha-em-maanro. He was a land-surveyor, for the service of the women's house. He was brought up because of the talk which he had heard, but had kept silence. He was set before the elders of the judgment-seat, and they judged his offence, and found him guilty, and awarded him his punishment.

(10) 'The chief culprit Seti-em-pa-Tehuti. He was a land-surveyor, for the service of the women's house. He was brought up on account of the talk which he had heard, but had kept silence. He was set before the elders of the judgment-seat, and they judged his offence, and found him guilty, and awarded him his punishment.

(11) 'The chief culprit Seti-em-pa-Amen. He was a land-surveyor, for the service of the women's house. He was brought up on account of the talk which he had heard, but had kept silence. He was set before the elders of the judgment-seat, and they judged his offence, and found him guilty, and awarded him his punishment.

(12) 'The chief culprit Ua-ro-maat. He was a councillor. He was brought up because he had been an ear-witness of the communications of the overseer of the house, and had held his tongue and kept silence, without giving any information thereof. He was set before the elders of the judgment-seat, and they found him guilty, and awarded him his punishment.

(13) 'The chief culprit Akh-heb-set. He was the accomplice of Beka-kamen. He was brought up because he had been an ear-witness of the communications of Beka-kamen. He had been his confidant, without having reported it. He was set before the elders of the judgment-seat, and they found him guilty, and awarded him his punishment.

(14) 'The chief culprit Pa-lo-ka. He was a councillor, and scribe of the treasury. He was brought up on account of his actual participation with Beka-kamen. He had also heard his communications, without having made report of them. He was set before the elders of the judgment-seat. They found him guilty, and awarded him his punishment.

(15) 'The chief culprit, the Libyan Inini. He was a councillor. He was brought up because of his actual participation with Beka-kamen. He had listened to his communications without having made report of them. He was set before the elders of the judgment-seat. They found him guilty, and awarded him his punishment.

PAGE 5. (1) 'The wives of the people of the gate of the women's house, who had joined the conspirators, were brought before the elders of the judgment-seat. They found them guilty, and awarded them their punishment. Six women.

(2) 'The chief culprit Pa-keti, a son of Lema. He was treasurer. He was brought up on account of his actual participation with the chief accused, Pen-heban. He had conspired with him to assemble the malcontents, to commit a crime against their lord. He was

brought before the elders of the judgment-seat. They found him guilty, and awarded him his punishment.

(3) 'The chief culprit Ban-em-us. He was the captain of the foreign legion of the Cushi. He was brought up on account of a message, which his sister, who was in the service of the women's house, had sent to him, to stir up the people who were malcontent (saying), "Come, accomplish the crime against thy lord." He was set before Kedenden, Baal-mahar, Pa-aru-sunu, and Tehuti-rekh-nefer. They judged him, and found him guilty, and awarded him his punishment.

(4) 'Persons who were brought up on account of their crime, and on account of their actual participation with Beka-kamen (namely), Pa-as and Pen-ta-ur. They were set before the elders of the judgment-seat to be tried. They found them guilty, laid them down by their arms (i.e. by force) at the judgment-seat, and they died by their own hand [1] without their expiation being completed.

(5) 'The chief accused Pa-as : he was a captain of the soldiers. The chief accused Mes-sui : he was a scribe of the treasury. The chief accused Kamen : he was an overseer. The chief accused I-ri : he was a priest of the goddess Sekhet. The chief accused Nebt'efau : he was a councillor. The chief accused Shat-setem : he was a scribe of the treasury. Making together, 6.

(6) 'These are the persons who were brought up, on account of their crime, to the judgment-seat, before Kedenden, Baal-mahar, Pa-aru-sunu, Tehuti-rekh-nefer, and Meri-usi-Amen. They judged them for their crime, they found them guilty. They laid them down before the tribunal. They died by their own hand.

(7) 'Pen-ta-ur, so is called the second of this name. He was brought up because of his actual participation with Thi, his mother, when they hatched the conspiracy with the women of the women's house, and because of the crime which was to have been committed against their lord. He was set before the councillors to be judged. They found him guilty, they laid him down where he stood. He died by his own hand.

(8) 'The chief accused Han-uten-Amen. He was a councillor. He was brought up because of the crime of the women of the women's house. He had been an ear-witness in the midst of them, without having given information. They set him before the councillors to judge him. They found him guilty. They laid him down where he stood. He died by his own hand.

(9) 'The chief accused Amen-khau. He was Adon for the service

[1] M. Le Page Renouf observes :— 'The expression au-f mutnef t'esef is a very remarkable one. The pronoun t'esef has a reflexive force and emphatically marks the agent of the deed. As kheper t'esef signifies self-existent so mut t'esef means dying by one's own hand.'

of the women's house. He was brought up because of the crime of the women of the women's house. He had been an ear-witness among them, without having given information. They set him before the councillors to be judged. They found him guilty. They laid him down where he stood. He died by his own hand.

(10) 'The chief accused Pa-ari. He was a royal scribe of the harem, for the service of the women's house. He was brought up because of the crime of the women of the women's house. He had been an ear-witness in the midst of them, without having given information of it. They set him before the councillors to be judged. They found him guilty. They laid him down where he stood. He died by his own hand.

PAGE 6. (1) 'These are the persons who received their punishment, and had their noses and their ears cut off, because they had in fact neglected to give full evidence in their depositions. The women had arrived and had reached the place where these were. They kept a beer-house there, and they were in league with Pa-as. Their crime was thus expiated.

(2) 'The chief culprit Pa-bast. He was a councillor. His punishment was accomplished on him. He died by his own hand.

(3) 'The chief culprit Mai. He was scribe in the chancery.

(4) 'The chief culprit Tai-nekht-tha. He was commander of the garrison.

(5) 'The chief culprit Nanai. He was the overseer of the Sakht (?).

(6) 'Persons, about whom it was doubtful if they had conspired with them with thoroughly evil intentions.

(7) 'They laid down, without completing his expiation, the chief culprit Hor-a. He was the standard-bearer of the garrison.'

Here ends the Turin Papyrus. The following extracts, which belong to the same trial, are found in two separate fragments of the Lee and Rollin Papyrus.

The translation of the first fragment is as follows :—

. . . . to all the people of this place, in which I am staying, and to all inhabitants of the country. Thus then spake Penhi, who was superintendent of the herds of cattle, to him : 'If I only possessed a writing, which would give me power and strength !'

Then he gave him a writing from the rolls of the books of Ramses III., the great god, his lord. Then there came upon him a divine magic, an enchantment for men. He reached (thereby ?) to the side | of the women's house, and into that other great and deep place. He formed human figures of wax, with the intention

of having them carried in by the hand of the land-surveyor Adi-
roma ; | to alienate the mind of one of the girls, and to bewitch the
others.   Some of the discourses were carried in, others were brought
out.   Now, however, he was brought to trial | on account of them,
and there was found in them incitation to all kinds of wickedness,
and all kinds of villany, which it was his intention to have done.
It was true, that he had done all this in conjunction with | the
other chief culprits, who, like him, were without a god or a goddess.
They inflicted upon him the great punishment of death, such as the
holy writings pronounced against him.

In a second fragment of the same papyrus the following words can be further made out :—

[He had committed this offence and was judged] for it.   They
found in it the material for all kinds of wickedness and all kinds of
villany which his heart had imagined to do.   It was true, (namely)
[all that he had done in conjunction with] the other chief culprits,
who, like him, were without a god or a goddess.   Such were
the grievous crimes, worthy of death, and the grievous sins [in the
country], which he had done.   But now he was convicted on
account of those grievous offences worthy of death, which he had
committed.   He died by his own hand.   For the elders, who were
before him, had given sentence that he should die by his own
hand | [with the other chief culprits, who, like him,] were without
the sun-god Ra, according as the holy writings declared what should
be done to him.

The contents of the Rollin Papyrus, and likewise a
fragment of a greater papyrus, are confined to the
following official statement :—

He had made some magical writings to ward off ill luck ;
he had made some gods of wax, and some human figures, to paralyse
the limbs of a man ; | and he had put these into the hand of Beka-
kamen, though the sun-god Ra did not permit that he should
accomplish this, either he or the superintendent of the house, or
the other chief culprits, because he (the god) said, ' Let them go forward with it, that they may furnish grounds for proceeding against
them.'   Thus had he attempted to complete the shameful deeds
which he had prepared, without the sun-god Ra having granted
them actual success.   He was brought to trial, and they found out the
real facts, consisting in all kinds of crime and | all sorts of villany,
which his heart had imagined to do.   It was true that he had
purposed to do all this in concert with all the chief culprits, who
were like him.   This was | a grievous crime, worthy of death, and

grievous wickedness for the land, which he had committed. But they found out the grievous crime, worthy of death, which he had committed. He died by his own hand.

The wife of Ramses bore, besides her Egyptian appellation Isis, the foreign name of Hema-rozath. Her father's name, Hebuan-rozenath, has nothing of an Egyptian sound, so that it is possible the Pharaoh brought home a foreign princess as his wife. The subjoined list of his sons is from the temple of victory at Medînet Habû :—

1. Prince Ra-messu I., commander of the infantry, afterwards King Ra-messu IV.
2. Prince Ra-messu II., afterwards King Ra-messu VI.
3. Prince Ra-messu III., royal master of the horse, afterwards King Ra-messu VII.
4. Prince Ra-messu IV., Set-her-khopeshef, royal master of the horse, afterwards King Ra-messu VIII.
5. Prince Pra-her-unamef, first captain of the chariots of war.
6. Prince Mentu-her-khopeshef, chief marshal of the army.
7. Prince Ra-messu V., Meri-atmu, high priest of the Sun in Heliopolis, afterwards King Meri-atmu.
8. Prince Ra-messu VI., Khamuas, high priest of Ptah-Sekar in Memphis.
9. Prince Ra-messu VII., Amen-her-khopeshef.
10. Prince Ra-messu VIII., Meri-Amen.

Of eight other princes and fourteen princesses we do not know the names. Their portraits have no explanatory inscriptions appended.

Among the contemporaries of the king was Meribast, the Theban chief priest of Amen.

After the example of his predecessors, Ramses III. prepared his sepulchre in the valley of the royal tombs. It is remarkable only for a range of side-chambers, in which, among other things, the possessions of the king, such as weapons, household furniture, and so forth, are represented in coloured pictures.

After the death of Rhampsinitus, the eldest of his sons,

RA-MESSU IV. HAQ-MAAT (CIR. B.C. 1166),

ascended the throne. According to the rock inscriptions in the valleys of Hammamât, this Ramses took especial pleasure in the exploration of the desert mountain valleys on the Arabian side of Egypt. Under the pretext of searching there for stone suitable for monuments, the most distinguished Egyptians were sent away to those gloomy regions. Subjoined is a literal translation of the historical contents of a rock-tablet of the third year of his reign, which will give an idea of the number of officials and workmen who, in the twelfth century before our era, gave life to these wild valleys.

The memorial tablet begins with the date of the 27th Payni in the third year of the reign of King Ra-messu IV.

After the usual official flatteries ' for that the king had laid waste the lands and plundered the inhabitants in their valleys,' it continues :—

Good times were in Egypt, as in those of the Sun-god Ra, in his kingdom, for this divine benefactor was like the god Tehuti, on account of the keeping of the laws.

. . . .

Crimes had increased, but the lies were put down, and the land was restored to a peaceful state in the time of his reign.

He prepared joy for Egypt a hundred-thousandfold.

His heart watched to seek out something good for his father (Hor of Coptos), the creator of his body. He caused to be opened for him (9) an entrance to the Holy Land, which was not known before, because the (existing) road to it was too distant for all the people, and their memory was not sufficient to discover it. Then the king considered in his mind, like his father Horus, the son of Isis, how he might lay down a road, to reach the place at his pleasure. (10) He made a circuit through this splendid mountain land, for the creation of monuments of granite for his father and for his ancestors, and for the gods and goddesses, who are the lords of Egypt. He set up a memorial-tablet on the summit of this mountain, inscribed with the full name of King Ra-messu.

(11) Then did the king give directions to the scribe of the holy sciences, Ra-messu-akhtu-heb, and to the scribe of Pharaoh, Hora, and to the seer, User-maat-Ra-nekhtu, of the temple of Amsu-Hor, and of Isis in Coptos, to seek a suitable site for (12) a temple on the mountain of Bukhan. When they had gone (thither) [they found a fit place], which was very good. There were great quarries of granite.

And the king issued a command, and gave directions to the chief priest of Amen, and the chief architect (13) Ramessu-nekhtu, to bring such (monuments) to Egypt.

These are the distinguished councillors, who were in his company (namely) :

The royal councillor User-maat-Ra-se-kheper,

The royal councillor Nekhtu-Amen,

And the Adon Kha-m-thir of the warriors,

The treasurer Kha-m-thir,

(14) The superintendent of the quarry, Prince Amen-mas of the city (Thebes),

The superintendent of the quarry and overseer of the (holy) herds, Bek-en-Khonsu, of the temple of User-maat-Ra-meri-Amen,

The colonel of the war chariots, Nekhtu-Amen of the court,

The scribe of the enlistment of the warriors, Suanar,

(15) The scribe of the Adon of the warriors, Ramessu-nekhtu,

20 scribes of the warriors,

20 superior officials of the court administration,

The colonel of the marshal's-men of the warriors, Kha-m-maat-anar,

20 marshal's-men of the warriors,

(16) 50 captains of the two-horse chariots,

50 superiors of the seers, superintendents of the (holy) animals, seers, scribes, and land surveyors,

5,000 people of the warriors,

(17) 200 foremen of the guild of the fishermen,

800 redskins (Erythræans, *Aperiu*) from the tribes of Ain (between the Red Sea and the Nile),

2,000 house servants of the house of Pharaoh,

1 Adon as chief overseer (of these),

50 men of the police (*Mazai*),

The superintendent of the works of art, Nekhtu-Amen,

3 architects for the workmen of the (18) quarries,

130 quarrymen and masons,

2 draftsmen,

4 sculptors ;

900 of the number had died in consequence of the long journey, making together 8,368 men.

(19) And the necessaries for them were carried on ten carts. Six pair of oxen drew each cart which was brought from Egypt to the mountains of Bukhan.   (20) [There were also] many runners, who were laden with bread, flesh, and vegetables, for they had not placed them thereon (i.e. on the waggons) ; and there were also brought the expiatory offerings for the gods of heaven and of the earth from the capital city of Patoris (Thebes) in great purity.

After some unintelligible and half-obliterated words, the conclusion of the inscription follows :—

(21) And the priests made a proper offering, the oxen were slain, the calves were killed, the incense steamed heavenward, wine flowed as if in rivers, and there was no end of the mead, in that place.   The singers raised their song.   Then was made the holy offering to Amsu, to Horus, to Isis, [to Amen, to Mut, to Khonsu,] and to the divinities, the lords of these mountains.   Their heart was joyful, they received the gifts, which may they requite with millions of 30-years' feasts of jubilee to their dear son, King Ra-messu, the dispenser of life for ever !

With the exception of some additions to the temple erected by his father, to Khonsu of Thebes, and some insignificant sculptures on the walls and columns of the great temple of Amen at Apet, the memory of this king has not been preserved in any remarkable manner.

That his rule over Egypt was contested by a claimant to the throne, who was beyond the immediate family of Ramses III., is proved by the name of his successor,

RA-MESSU V.,

whose sepulchral chamber, in the valley of Bibân-el-Molûk, was appropriated by Ramses VI., after he had substituted his own names for those of his hated rival. What this Ramses V. thought of himself, is proved by the contents of his rock-tablet at Silsilis, which contains absolutely nothing of historic value.

Of the sons of Ramses III., who followed next in order, two seem to have reigned simultaneously. One of these was the seventh son,

RA-MESSU · MERI-ATMU,

a son of the queen Mut-nefer-ari, whose cartouche, with the name Meri-Amen Meri-Atmu, was discovered many years ago, at Heliopolis, on one of the stones lying in the road. It led to the conjecture, that Meri-Atmu reigned as viceroy in Lower Egypt in his brother's name. The Theban monuments give us the names of this brother with perfect distinctness. He was called

RA-NEB-MAAT. RA-MESSU VI.

The few inscriptions which have survived the ravages of time speak of his monuments dedicated to the gods. The most important edifice is his splendid tomb in the valley of Bibân-el-Molûk. The tables of the hours, with the times of the risings of the stars, which formed the houses of the sun's course in the 36 or 37 weeks of the Egyptian year, will be for all times the most valuable contribution to astronomical science in the 12th century before our era. According to Biot, whose labours in order to fix certain epochs of Egyptian history are almost the only ones which have treated the subject with scientific accuracy, the drawing up of these tables of stars would fall in the reign of Ra-messu VI., in the year 1240 B.C. Professor Lepsius has, however, from his own point of view, sought to prove that herein lay an error, and that, on the authority of the already cited table of hours in the grave of this king, the year 1194 B.C. is indicated as the only proper date. This last view does not differ very much from our calculation of 1166 B.C., deduced from the number of successive generations.

An interesting record of this time has faithfully preserved the king's name :—

Land (which is devoted to the maintenance of the holy service) of the statue of King Ra-messu VI., which is dedicated to the city of Ama (consisting of the following districts) :

I. The district to the north of Pa-Ra (that is, the temple of the sun), and of the town in the midst of the temple of Ra, the lord of this earth, and to the east and south of the fields of the land of the (statue) of Queen Nefer-tera, which is dedicated to the city of Ama. (The position of this district is as follows) : (it is bounded)

    on the east by the great mountain,
    on the north by the papyrus-field of Pharaoh,
    on the west is the river. Size, 3 × 100 cubits.

II. The district at the commencement (*lesha-t*, 'head') of the land of Ma-iu, opposite to the field of the Adon of Ua-ua-t,

    on the south by the land of the statue of the king, which is
      under the administration of the chief priest Amenemape,
    on the east by the great mountain,
    on the north by the papyrus-field of Pharaoh, which is set
      apart as a field for the Adon of Ua-ua-t,
    on the west by the river. Size, 2 × 100 cubits.

III. The district of the overseers of the temple of the goddess, east of the field just described :

    on the east by the great mountain,
    on the south by the field of the estate of the king's statue,
      which is under the administration of the Adon Meri of
      the land of Ua-ua-t, east of the great mountain,
    on the north by the field of the keeper of the herds (?) Bih,
    on the west by the river. Size, 4 × 100 cubits.

IV. The district at the commencement of the land of Thuhen at the extreme west boundary of the basin of Thuhen, in the direction of the papyrus-field of Pharaoh, and behind the field that has been described :

    east by the great mountain,
    south by the papyrus-field of Pharaoh, which lies east of the
      great mountain,
    north by the field of the land of Airos,
    west by the river. Size, 6 × 100 cubits.

Total superficies of the fields, which belong to him (the statue), 15 × 100 cubits.

V. With regard to the high-lying field (of) Nef-ti, the Adon Penni, the son of Heru-nefer, has written and set up his proprietorship of the land of Ua-ua-t as an estate, which he has chosen to furnish him with (sustenance) for each ox, which is yearly slaughtered in his honour.

The circuit of the superficies of the fields of the potters' earth, which are in the possession of the (former) Adon of Ua-ua-t, is not included in the roll.

> Its west is at the gravelly land of the Adon Penni,
> its south is at the gravelly fields of the Adon Penni,
> on the north are the fields with potters' earth, which are the
>   property of Pharaoh,
> the east is at the gravelly fields of the Adon Penni.
> Size of the whole, 4 × 200, and 2 × 200 cubits.

Any one who will not observe these demarcations, to him will Amen-Ra be an avenger, from one avenging to (another) avenging; Mut will take vengeance on his wife, Khonsu will take vengeance on his children; he shall hunger, he shall thirst, he shall be miserable, he shall vanish away.

The inscription is in a rock-tomb at Anibe, on the western bank of the Nile, opposite to the village of Ibrîm, about thirty-one miles north of Abû Simbel. The owner of the tomb was an official named Penni, who as governor of the land of the Ua-ua-t died and was buried in this lonely region. What makes it particularly valuable is the designation of lands in those parts, and the offices connected with them. An Adon is mentioned by the name of Meri. The sun-city of Pa-Ra is the ancient designation of the modern place called Derr. The city mentioned by the name of Ama, in which a Nubian Horus enjoyed an especial worship, is very often named in the inscriptions, and seems to have been the ancient appellation of Ibrîm. At Derr, in all probability, was the seat of the administration of the whole country of Ua-ua-t. The districts of Ahi and the gold land of Akita belonged to it, the revenues of which Penni had to collect and pay over to Pharaoh. For his diligence in the fulfilment of his service he was most warmly commended by the 'King's son of Cush' of that time, whose name is passed over in silence. On a royal visit, the king appears accompanied by the above-named Meri, who is also called 'the superintendent of the temple,' to recommend his officials to the grace of Pharaoh. The statue of the royal lord, which had been set up, plays here an important part. His Majesty appears to have been much pleased with the services of his faithful servant, since he presented Penni with two silver vessels filled with precious ointments.

Penni was certainly an artist, as is shown by the statue of Pharaoh, and by the sculptures in his own rock-tomb, but especially by his office, mentioned in the inscriptions, of 'master of the quarry,' besides that of a 'superintendent of the temple of Horus, the lord of the town of Ama.' Several members of his family appear to have all held during their lifetime various offices in the Horus-city of Ama. Among them is a chief priest of Isis whose son was the Amenemape named in the inscription; also two treasurers of the king in Ama, a captain of the city of Ama, a priest and a scribe, while the women are mostly named as female singers of Amen or of Horus the lord of the town of Ama.

Passing over in silence the two insignificant successors and brothers of this king, who perhaps reigned simultaneously as Pharaohs, and of whom the monuments have merely handed down the names,

RA-MESSU VII. and RA-MESSU VIII.,

we come to the last Ramessides of the Twentieth Dynasty,

NEFER-KA-RA-SOTEP-EN-RA. RA-MESSU IX.   CIR. B.C. 1133.

It is not his deeds, about which the monuments tell us next to nothing, nor his buildings, which are extremely few in number, but his relations to the priests of Amen at Thebes at this time that call for attention. It is a very evident fact that from the time of Ramses III. the

holy fathers who bore the dignity of chief priest in the
temple-city of Amen come more and more into the
foreground of Egyptian history. Their influence with
the kings assumes gradually an increasing importance.
As formerly it was the priests who expressed in the
name of the gods their thanks to the kings for the
temple-buildings in Thebes, so now it is the kings who
begin to testify their gratitude to the chief priest of
Amen for the care bestowed on his temple by the erection of new buildings, and by the improvement and
maintenance of the older ones.

On the eastern wall and the adjoining buildings,
which connect the third and fourth pylons with the
southern part of the temple of Amen at Karnak, we
see the ' hereditary prince and chief priest of Amen-Ra,
the king of the gods, Amenhotep, standing opposite to
King Ra-messu IX., and the meaning of his presence
in this place is made quite clear by the inscription
annexed :—

The king in person, he speaks to the princes and companions
by his . 'de : Give rich reward and much recompense in good gold
and silver, and in a hundred-thousandfold of good things, to the
high priest of Amen-Ra, the king of the gods, Amenhotep, on
account of these many splendid buildings [which he has erected] at
the temple of Amen-Ra to the great name of the divine benefactor,
the king Ra-messu IX.

In the 10th year, the month Athyr, the 19th day, in the temple
of Amen-Ra, the king of the gods. The chief priest of Amen-Ra, the
king of the gods, Amenhotep, was conducted to the great forecourt
of the temple of Amen.   His (the king's) words uttered his reward,
to honour him by good and choice discourses.

These are the princes, who had come to reward him, namely :
the treasurer of Pharaoh and the royal councillor, Amenhotep ; the
royal councillor, Nes-Amen ; the secretary of Pharaoh and the
royal councillor, Neferka-Ra-em-pa-Amen, who is the interpreter of
Pharaoh.

The discourses which were addressed to him related to the
rewards for his services on this day in the great forecourt of
Amen-Ra, the king of the gods. They were of this import :

Mentu was invoked as a witness :

As witness is invoked the name of Amen-Ra, the king of the gods, that of the god Horemkhu, of Ptah of Memphis, of Tehuti, the lord of the holy speech, of the gods of heaven, of the gods of the earth :

As witness is invoked the name of Ra-messu IX., the great king of Egypt, the son and friend of all the gods, for levying all services. Let the taxing and the usufruct of the labours of the inhabitants for the temple of Amen-Ra, the king of the gods, be placed under thy administration. Let the full revenues be given over to thee, according to their number. Thou shalt collect the duties. Thou shalt undertake the interior administration (literally, side) of the treasuries, of the store-houses, and of the granaries of the temple of Amen-Ra, the king of the gods ; so that the income of the heads and hands for the maintenance of Amen-Ra, the king of the gods, may be applied to the service. [Thus does] Pharaoh, thy lord, [reward] the deeds of a good and distinguished servant of Pharaoh, his lord. He shall be strengthened to do the best for Amen-Ra, the king of the gods, the great and glorious god, and to do the best for Pharaoh, his lord, who has seen and admired what thou hast done. This is for explanation of the commission to these (present) treasurers and the two councillors of Pharaoh concerning the gold, silver, [and all other gifts, which are given to thee as a reward].

The accompanying representation shows that the words of the king were exactly fulfilled, for the two councillors of Pharaoh who are named adorn the priest with necklaces and jewels.

What the high priest did for the temple of his god is related in his own words :—

Thus has the teacher of the king, the chief priest of Amen-Ra, the king of the gods, Amenhotep, done, namely :

I found this holy house of the chief priests of Amen of old time, which is in the temple of Amen-Ra, the king of the gods, hastening to decay. What was done to it dates since the time of King Usertsen I. I took the building in hand, and restored it anew in good work, and in a work pleasant to look at. I strengthened its walls behind, around, and in front. I built it anew. I made its columns, which were bound together with great stones in skilful work. I inserted in the gates great folding doors of acacia wood, for closing them up. I built out on its great stone wall, which is seen at the . . . .   I built my high new house for the chief priest of Amen, who dwells in the temple of Amen.   I inserted the whole gate of [acacia wood].   The bolts in it are of bronze ; the engraved pictures are of the finest gold and [silver].   I built a great forecourt of stone, which opens on the southern temple-lake, [to serve for] the purification of the temple of Amen.   I chased [the whole with . . . .] of Seb.   I set up its great blocks of carved stone in the connecting hall. The valves of the doors are of acacia wood.   I [caused to be erected one ?] of great carved blocks of stone.   The outlines of the carved work were drawn in red chalk. . . .   The whole was inscribed with the full name of Pharaoh.—Also a new treasury was built on the ground within the great hall which bears the name : . . . . The columns are of stone, the doors of acacia wood, painted with . . . . [Also I built a chamber for] the king.   It lies behind the store-chamber for the necessaries of the temple of Amen.   [It is constructed] of stone, the doors and door-valves are of acacia wood . . . . [I made and set up statues in] the great splendid forecourt for each chief priest of Amen-Ra [the king of the gods.   I laid out gardens behind] Asheru.   They were planted with trees.

Towards the end, the architect declares that he had done all this, ' to glorify my lord Amen-Ra, the king of the gods, whose greatness, doctrine, and [power ?] I acknowledge.'   To this is appended the usual prayer for life, welfare, health, and a long enjoyment of existence for the king and—for himself.

Emphatically as Amenhotep speaks of ' his lord the Pharaoh,' the power of the latter was already broken. For with Amenhotep the chief priests began to play that double part which at last raised them to the royal throne.

To the time of this king belong the burglaries in the tombs of the earlier kings, about which a whole series of judicial papyri affords information.   There existed in Thebes a regularly constituted thieves' society, for the secret robbing of the royal tombs, in which even sacerdotal persons took a part.   It required extensive enquiries to follow the track of the offenders, and among the persons entrusted by the king with the conduct of this official enquiry are some whose acquaintance we have

already made—viz. Amenhotep, the chief priest of
Amen; Khamuas and Ra-neb-Maat-nekht, governors of
Thebes; the royal councillor and scribe of Pharaoh,
Nes-su-Amen; the royal councillor and interpreter of
Pharaoh, Neferka-Ra-em-pa-Amen; Pharaoh's councillor
and secretary, Pai-net'em; the leader of the Mazai
(police), Mentu-khopeshef; and some other persons.
The tombs, which were broken open and partly plun-
dered, contained the kings and queens of the XIth,
XIIIth, XVIIth, and XVIIIth Dynasties.[1]

According to the arrangement of Lepsius, the following are to be ranked as the Pharaohs following
Ramessu IX. :—

RA-MESSU X., RA-MESSU XI., RA-MESSU XII.

Their names are found only here and there on the
monuments, most frequently in the small oracle-temple
of Khonsu in Thebes, which their forefather Ra-messu
III. had founded, and which since that time had received the particular attention of the kings of the
Twentieth Dynasty.

Khonsu, the young son of Amen and of the goddess
Mut, was worshipped in this temple in his particular
character as Khonsu-em-us Nefer-hotep, that is, ' Khonsu
of Thebes, the good and friendly,' and a special importance was attached to his oracles on all grave occasions.

The following inscription is on a stone now in the
Bibliothèque Nationale in Paris :—

(4) When Pharaoh was in the river-land of Naharain, as his
custom was every year, the kings of all the nations came with
humility and friendship to the person of Pharaoh. From the
extremest ends (of their countries) they brought the gifts of gold,
silver, blue and (5) green stones ; and all sorts of (sweet smelling)
woods of the holy land were upon their shoulders ; and each one
endeavoured to outdo his neighbour.

[1] See p. 359 *et seq.*

Then the king of Bakhtan brought his tribute, and placed at the head of it his eldest daughter, to honour Pharaoh and to beg for his friendship. And the woman (6) was much more beautiful to please Pharaoh than all other things. Then was the king's name written upon her, as the king's wife, Neferu-Ra. When the Pharaoh had come to Egypt, everything was done for her which a queen required to use.

It happened in the year 15, in the month Payni, on the 22nd day. Then Pharaoh was in Thebes, the strong, the queen of cities, in order to thank (7) his father Amen-Ra, the lord of Thebes, at his beautiful feast of Apet of the south, the seat of his desire from the beginning. They came to announce to Pharaoh : A messenger of the king of Bakhtan has arrived with rich gifts for the queen. Then was he brought (8) before Pharaoh, together with his gifts. He spoke in honour of Pharaoh : 'Greeting to thee, thou sun of the nations, let us live before thee !' Thus he spake, while he fell down before Pharaoh, and repeated the message to Pharaoh : 'I am come to thee, the great lord, on account of Bint-resh, the youngest sister of the queen Neferu-Ra. (9) She is suffering in her body. May thy Majesty send a learned expert to see her.' Then spake Pharaoh : 'Let them bring to me the learned men from the places of the holy sciences, and the knowers of the most intimate secrets.' (10) They brought them to him forthwith. Then spake Pharaoh after a time : 'Ye have been assembled here to hear these words. Now, then, bring to me a man of a clever mind, and a finger skilful in writing, out of your company.' When the royal scribe, (11) Tehuti-em-heb, had come before Pharaoh, Pharaoh bade him, that he should start for Bakhtan with the envoy, who was present. When the expert had reached the city of the land of Bakhtan, in which Bint-resh dwelt after the manner of one possessed with a spirit, then he found himself (12) unable to contend with him (the spirit).

And the king again sent to Pharaoh, speaking thus : 'Great lord and ruler ! May thy Majesty order that the god may be sent [Khonsu, the administrator, of Thebes, to the youngest sister of the queen.' (13) And the messenger remained with] Pharaoh till the 26th year. In the month Pakhons (of that year), at the time of the feast of Amen, Pharaoh abode in Thebes, and Pharaoh stood again before the god Khonsu of Thebes, the kind and friendly, while he spake thus : 'O thou good lord ! I present myself again before thee on account of the daughter of the king of Bakhtan.' (14) Then went from thence the god Khonsu of Thebes, the kind and friendly ; Khonsu, the administrator, the great god, the driver away of evil. Then spake Pharaoh in presence of Khonsu of Thebes, the kind and friendly, 'Thou good lord, shouldest thou not

charge Khonsu (15), the administrator, the great god, the driver
away of evil, that he may betake himself to Bakhtan?' To that
there was a very gracious consent. Then spake Pharaoh, 'Give
him thy talisman to take with him. I will let his Holiness be
drawn to Bakhtan, to release the daughter of the king of Bakhtan.
(16) Thereupon a very gracious consent of Khonsu of Thebes, the
kind and friendly. Then he gave the talisman to Khonsu, administrator, of Thebes, at four different times. And Pharaoh gave command, to cause Khonsu, the administrator, of Thebes, to embark on
the great ship. Five barks and many (17) carriages and horses
were on his right and on his left.

That god reached the city of the land of Bakhtan after the
space of a year and five months. Then the king of Bakhtan
and his people and his princes went to meet Khonsu, the administrator. And he threw himself (18) prostrate, and spake thus:
' Come to us, be friendly to us, according to the commands of the
king of Upper and Lower Egypt, Ra-messu Meri-Amen.' Then
that god went to the place where Bint-resh dwelt. Then he caused
the talisman to work upon the daughter of the king of Bakhtan. She became well (19) on the spot. Then spake that spirit,
which possessed her, before Khonsu, the administrator, of Thebes:
' Welcome as a friend, thou great god, driver away of evil. Thine
is the city of Bakhtan. Thy servants are its inhabitants. I am
thy servant. (20) I will return whence I came, to make thy
heart satisfied about the object for which thou wast brought hither.
May I request thy Holiness, that there may be a feast celebrated in
my company and in the company of the king of Bakhtan?' Then
this god assented graciously to his prophet, and he said : (21) ' Let
the king of Bakhtan prepare a great sacrifice for this spirit.
When that has been done, then will Khonsu, the administrator, unite
himself with the spirit.' And the king of Bakhtan stood there,
together with his people, and was very much afraid. Then (22) he
prepared a great sacrifice for Khonsu, the administrator, of Thebes,
and for this spirit. The king of Bakhtan celebrated a feast for
them. Then the glorious spirit went thence, whither it pleased him,
as Khonsu, the administrator, of Thebes, had commanded. (23) And
the king of Bakhtan was delighted beyond measure, together with
all the men who dwelt in Bakhtan. Then he considered in his
heart, and he spake to them thus : 'Might it be so that this god
should remain in the city of the land of Bakhtan ? I will not
let him return to Egypt.' Then (24) this god remained three
years and nine months in Bakhtan. Then the king of Bakhtan rested on his bed, and he saw as if this god stepped out from
his holy shrine, as in the form of a golden sparrow-hawk he took

his flight heavenwards towards Egypt. (25) When he awoke he was lame. Then spake he to the prophet of Khonsu, the administrator, of Thebes : ' This god he staid among us, and now he withdraws to Egypt. His carriage must return to Egypt.' (26) Then the king of Bakhtan had the god drawn back to Egypt, and gave him very many presents of all sorts of good things, and they arrived safely at Thebes. Then went Khonsu, the administrator, of Thebes, (27) into the temple of Khonsu of Thebes, the kind and friendly, and he laid down the presents just as the king of Bakhtan had presented them to him, namely, all kinds of good things, before Khonsu of Thebes, the kind and friendly ; he kept nothing of them for his house. But Khonsu, the administrator, of Thebes, (28) returned happily to his house in the 33rd year, in the month of Mekhir, on the 13th day, of King Ra-messu Meri Amen. Such was what happened to him ; to him, the dispenser of life to-day and for ever.[1]

It is difficult to say where the land of Bakhtan should be sought. A journey of seventeen months from Thebes to the foreign city shows that it was very distant. The (doubtful ?) stay of Ra-messu XII. in the riverland of Naharain suggests a Syrian town. Probably the town referred to may be Bakhi or Bakh, which is mentioned in the lists of the victories of Ra-messu III. and earlier kings as a conquered place.

With his successor,

MEN-MAAT-RA-SOTEP-EN RA, RA-MESSU (XIII.) MERI-AMEN (CIR. B.C. 1100),

we seem to have arrived at the end of this Dynasty, although it is proved by the monuments that some Ramessides, as petty kings, put forward their claim to the throne, even in the time of the foreign conqueror, Shashanq I. They did so with little success, for the chief priests of the god Amen had already placed the

[1] This story has long been known as that of 'The Possessed Princess of Bakhtan,' and until lately was considered authentic. It has now been shown to be a legend of the Egyptian priests, and written for the purpose of the glorification of Khonsu. It is of much later date than the period to which it purports to belong.

crown on their own heads, and being the lords of
Thebes they behaved as lords also of the whole kingdom.

The temple of Khonsu at Thebes had been finished
under Ra-messu XIII., as far as the open forecourt with
the small colonnade round it. The king prides himself
on having erected these last buildings 'as a memorial
to his father Khonsu,' who promises him as a reward
'the kingdom of Tmu.' In other parts of the first hall
the king insists in a still more earnest manner on his
own importance as a builder :—

Splendid things has he made, many and wonderful monuments :
all his schemes were carried out immediately like those of his
father, the Memphite Ptah. He has embellished Thebes with
great monuments. No other king has done the like.

In the collection of papyri in the Turin Museum, as
published by M. Pleyte, there exists what is possibly an
autograph letter of Ra-messu XIII. dated the 17th year,
the month Khoiakh, the 25th day.

The following is a translation of it :—

A royal order is issued to the King's son of Cush, the royal
scribe of the warriors, the superintendent of the granaries, the
commander of Pharaoh's foreigners, Painehas, to the following
effect :—The king's order will be brought to thee, making the
communication, that Jani, the Major-domo and counsellor (Ab)
of Pharaoh, has set out on his journey. His departure has been
caused by commissions from Pharaoh, his lord, which he has started
to execute in the land of the South. As soon as this letter of
Pharaoh, thy lord, reaches thee, do thou act in the fullest accord
with him, for he is to execute the commissions of Pharaoh, his
lord, on account of which he has departed from hence.

Thou art to look up the hand-barrows of the great goddess, to
load them and put them on board the ship. Thou art to have
them brought into his presence, where the statue is appointed to
stand.

Thou art to have the precious stones (here follows a list of unknown sorts of stones) brought together to the same place where
the statue stands, to deliver them into the hands of the artists.
Let no delay be interposed in the execution of this commission, or

else I should degrade thee. Behold ! I expect thy best attention to this message. Such is the message which is made known to thee.

The conclusion of the letter is clear and explicit, evidently on the assumption that the viceroy of Ethiopia might prove a negligent servant.

THE ROYAL MUMMIES OF DEIR-EL-BAHARI.

[THE year 1881 was signalised by one of the most remarkable 'finds' ever recorded in the annals of Egyptology, and which, judged from an historical standpoint, is invaluable. It brought to light nothing less than the bodies of many of the great Pharaohs and other royal personages, together with their coffins and funerary furniture. The history of it may be briefly related thus :—

Ever since 1876 M. Maspero—then the director-general of the Bûlaq Museum in Cairo—had strong suspicions that the Theban Arabs had come upon some royal tombs, which they were gradually despoiling, and the contents of which they were dispersing and selling in different parts of the country. Early in that year General Campbell, an English officer, bought a hieratic papyrus at Thebes, for which he paid 400*l.* On being unrolled and examined it proved to be that of Painet'em II., one of the priestly usurpers of the Twenty-first Dynasty. In 1877 M. de Saulcy sent to M. Maspero photographs of a papyrus which had belonged to Queen Net'emet, the mother of Her-Hor, who was the founder of the line of priest-kings. This papyrus is torn in two, part of it being in the British Museum, the rest in the Louvre. At the same time there constantly appeared in the market at Cairo *ushabtiu* figures of Painet'em, some being fine and well made, while others were very coarse. In 1879 Rogers Bey showed to M. Maspero a tablet which had belonged to one of the Her-Hor family, and which was then in his possession. This caused the French savant to feel quite convinced that his surmise concerning the royal tombs could not be far wrong. In March 1881 he started up the river, determined to leave no means untried which should lead to the capture of the Arabs and their treasures. The only clue M. Maspero possessed was the names of those who had sold the objects; they were Mustapha Agha, the consul for Great Britain and Belgium at Luqsor, and Abd-er-Rassûl Ahmad of Gûrnah. The former, in consequence of his diplomatic position, escaped, but the latter was ordered by the Mudîr of Keneh to be arrested at once. After a most searching examination nothing could be elicited from him but that he was a most honest Arab, who would never dream of breaking open a tomb, far less of selling the contents. Bribes, threats, imprisonment—some say even tortures—were tried, but all in vain; he and his friends still maintained that he was the most truthful of men and of unimpeachable honesty. In the face of such universal testimony to his good character M. Maspero could only oppose that of absent foreigners. Ahmad was, therefore, provisionally released. But a quarrel appears to have broken out immediately upon his return home between himself and his three brothers, which resulted in Muhammed Abd-er-Rassûl travelling secretly to Keneh and divulging the whole secret to the Mudîr. A telegram was despatched to the Minister of the Interior, who proceeded to convey the intelligence without further delay to the Khedive. Thereupon M. Émil Brugsch—the director-general having just left for Europe—set out for Thebes, where he was met by Muhammed Abd-er-Rassûl, who conducted him to the cleft in the mountain at Deir-el-Bahari which has since become historic. Here was the opening of the tomb-shaft down which M. Brugsch and his companions had to be lowered to a depth of nearly 40 feet. On reaching the bottom they found themselves in a corridor about 225 feet in length, along which they had to grope their way, and which finally led them to a large chamber about 25 feet long and nearly rect-angular in shape. This was found to be quite full of mummies, coffins, canopic vases, *ushabtiu* figures, boxes, bronze objects, funerary furniture, &c., while care-lessly thrown aside at a sharp turn in the corridor was the beautiful funeral canopy of the Princess Isi-em-kheb. It is a marvellous piece of leather patch-work, for which the skins of hundreds of gazelles must have been used. It has been most carefully restored by M. Brugsch, and is now in the Gîzeh Palace. Notwithstanding the intense heat—July 11—it was resolved to remove the contents of the chamber to Cairo, and for forty-eight hours a gang of workmen was occupied in bringing them to the mouth of the tomb, while M. Brugsch and Ahmad Effendi Kamal stood superintending the work. In less than a fortnight the whole 'find' was sent across the river to Luqsor, and was thence conveyed by the Khedive's steamer to Cairo.

The arranging of the mummies and the sorting of their respective cases was no easy task, as it was found that the coffins often contained a body other than that of the real owner. For instance, in the mummy-case of Queen Nefertari was found the body of Ramses III., while the coffin of the nurse of Queen Nefertari Raa contained the mummy of Queen An-Hapi; and Painet'em was found to have taken possession of the coffin of Tehuti-mes I. Four dynasties of the ancient Egyptian Empire are represented by these mummies, the most important personages among them being :—

King Seqenen-Ra of the Seventeenth Dynasty;

Kings Aahmes and Amen-hotep I., Prince Se-hotep, Princess Set-Amen, the royal scribe Senu of the household of Queen Nefertari, the royal wife Set-Kames, the royal daughter Meshent-themhu, Tehuti-mes II., and Tehuti-mes III. of the Eighteenth Dynasty;

Seti I. and Ramses II. of the Nineteenth; and

Ramses III. of the Twentieth.

Among the priestly representatives of the Twenty-first dynasty are Queen Net'emet, Masahertha and Painet'em III., high-priests of Amen, Queen Maat-ka-Ra, and the Princesses Isi-em-kheb and Nesi-Khonsu.

In 1883 it was found necessary to bury certain of the mummies; but before doing so M. Maspero decided to unroll them. Since then the whole collection has been undone. In 1885 Queen Nefertari's was examined, and was found to contain the body of a middle-aged woman, of average height and belonging to the white and not black race of mankind. It will be remembered that this queen is often represented on the monuments with a black complexion, although some of them depict her as very fair; hence, doubtless, arose those innumerable discussions as to her nationality. During her lifetime she was immensely beloved, and after her death her worship was very popular at Thebes. She is there deified under one of the many forms of Hathor, the black goddess of death and the 'divine hidden land.' This may possibly account for the queen's face being so often painted black; while the opening of the mummy settles once and for all the historical question of her nationality. Later on the bodies of Seqenen-Ra, Seti I., and Ramses II. and III. were unrolled, and are now exhibited in the galleries of the Gîzeh Palace.[1]

.   .   .   .   .

[While these sheets were going through the press

---

[1] *Les Momies Royales de Deir-el-Bahari.* By G. Maspero and É. Brugsch.

information was received from Luqsor that a large collection of mummies—supposed to be those of the high-priests of Amen—and a considerable number of papyri had been discovered at Deir-el-Bahari, in a secluded spot east of the great Stage-temple of Queen Hatshepsu. The mortuary chamber, when first entered, was found to be in exactly the same state of hopeless confusion as was that of the Royal Mummies when discovered in 1881. Sarcophagi, baskets containing funeral wreaths, statuettes, boxes, funerary offerings, and small cases crammed with papyri all lay about as if hurriedly thrust away for purposes of concealment. Some of the sarcophagi bore the date of the Eleventh Dynasty, and it was for a few hours fondly hoped that the explorers might have come upon an unbroken sequence of the high-priests from that period onwards. But the majority of the 163 mummies appear to belong to the Twenty-first Dynasty, and, though called 'high-priests of Amen,' are thought to be the corpses of generals and other dignitaries who bore priestly as well as official titles. It is as yet difficult to form any estimate as to their archæological value, for many of the sarcophagi bear totally different names on the outer and inner casings, while others contain mummies which obviously do not belong to them. From some of the sarcophagi the name of the rightful occupant has been deliberately effaced. The whole 'find,' including 75 papyri, has now been safely moved to the Gîzeh Palace, near Cairo; but M. Grébaut, the director, thinks that, owing to the size and importance of the collection, some time must elapse before any definite scientific information can be given.]

CHAPTER XV.

DYNASTIES XXI.-XXIV.[1]

THE PRIEST HER-HOR AND HIS SUCCESSORS.
1100–966 CIR. B.C.

'THE king of Upper and Lower Egypt, the chief priest of Amen, SE-AMEN (SON OF AMEN) HER-HOR':—

Thus did the ambitious priest of Amen, the head of the Theban clergy, style himself officially, when he took possession of the Thebaïd. Ra-messu XIII. had, before his own fall, honoured the first servant of the god Amen in a distinguished manner, inasmuch as he had entrusted him with the most important offices of the government. Her-Hor calls himself on the monuments an 'hereditary prince, the fan-bearer on the right of the king, King's son of Cush, chief architect of the king, chief general of the army in Upper and Lower Egypt, administrator of the granaries,' as Joseph was of old at the court of Pharaoh. Such high dignities, which in the course of time were held by one and the same person, either together or in succession, must have essentially facilitated his project of overthrowing the sovereign. His position as the chief priest of Amen secured to Her-Hor no inconsiderable following among the most powerful of all the priestly societies in the whole country. As in Upper Egypt it was the inhabitants of the Theban nome and the priests of Amen who took part with the new king, so, on the

[1] For Table of Kings see pp. xxv.–vi.

other hand, in Lower Egypt he had won over a moderate number of the holy fathers of the Ramses-city of Zoan-Tanis, who stood in close connection with the imperial city of Thebes, owing to their common worship of Amen. The letters and documents of the Ramessides which have come down to us leave not the slightest doubt upon this point. And yet the plans of Her-Hor were not destined to attain complete success. While Ra-messu XIII. and his successors, according to all probability, were banished to the Great Oasis, they had raised up in silence an enemy to the priest-kings, whose power and importance might be brought in to aid their cause.

On the east of Mesopotamia the great empire of the Kheta had been succeeded by a new race of rulers, to whom the Egyptian monuments of the time give the short name of *Mā*,[1] and whose ruler they designate as 'the great king of kings.' Even though, in a style which is rather pompous than historically true, Her-Hor conferred on himself the honorary title of conqueror of the Ruthen, to which in all probability he had no right, it may be assumed that the power of these Mā had reached a strength which must at any rate have restrained the priest-king from thinking of conquests in the East.

His successors, whom the reader will find named in the Genealogical Table opposite p. 325, were far from securing a firm position in the country. Their most

---

[1] Since the year 1876, when Dr. Brugsch first brought out his history, his opinions concerning these Mā, whom he then designated as Assyrians, have undergone considerable modification. It is no longer possible to regard them as Assyrians, though to define their nationality would be too bold a venture. They were certainly foreigners, as the determinative sign placed after their name when written in hieroglyphs clearly indicates. Mr. Renouf believes that they should be considered Elamites, Shashanq being the equivalent of a Susan word—Sesonqu, meaning 'the man of Susa.' Professor Oppert says that all the names of the Twenty-second Dynasty are Susan. The Libyan origin of this dynasty is generally admitted by Egyptologists on insufficient grounds.

determined enemies were the banished race of the
Ramessides, who succeeded in forming alliances with
these foreigners, for a great-grandson of that Ra-
messu XIII. who was overthrown by Her-Hor married
an unnamed daughter of 'the general of the Mā.' The
consequences of such a connection quickly appeared.
The Mā marched against Egypt.

In the twenty-fifth year of the reign of Painet'em I.,
a grandson of Her-Hor, disturbances broke out in the
Thebaïd in favour of the Ramessides. Meantime
Painet'em, who had to await the attack of Nimrod (the
son of that Shashanq who had married a Ramesside
princess), remained at Tanis, while his son Men-
kheper-Ra was sent to Thebes, with full powers to quell
the insurrection. After he had succeeded in doing
this, he was named as his father's successor in the
office of high-priest of Amen. His first act was to
recall the Egyptians banished into the Oasis and their
adherents. This was apparently done with the consent
of Amen, whose oracle had approved Men-kheper-Ra's
proposal. We learn this from the following inscription
at Thebes :—

(1) In the year 25, the month Epiphi, the 29th day, at the same
time as the feast of the god Amen-Ra, the king of the gods, at his
[beautiful] monthly feast of Apet [of the south]. . . . . (2) Nes-
her-Hor in their multitude. The Majesty of this noble god Amen-
[Ra, the king of the gods,] was . . . . (3) Thebes. He showed
the way to the scribes, the land-surveyors, and people. . . . .
(4) In the year 25, in the first month of the year . . . . Amen-Ra,
the lord of Thebes. . . . (5) . . . the high-priest of Amen-Ra, the
king of the gods, the general in chief of the army, Men-kheper-Ra,
the son of the king . . . Meri-Amen Painet'em . . . (6) at his feet.

Their heart was joyfully moved on account of his design. He
had come to Patoris (to the south land) in victorious power, to
restore order in the land and to chastise the opponents. He gave
to them [the punishment they deserved, and established the old
order of things, just as] (7) it had been in the times of the reign of
the sun-god Ra. He entered the city (of Thebes) with a contented

soul. The families of Thebes received him with songs of joy. Messengers had been sent before him. The Majesty of this noble god, the lord of the gods, Amen-Ra, the lord of Thebes, was brought out in procession. He (8) rewarded (?) him very much. He placed him in the seat of his father as chief priest of Amen-Ra, the king of the gods, and as general in chief of the army of Upper and Lower Egypt. He dedicated to him numerous and splendid wonderful works, such as had never been seen before.

Now [had reached its end] (9) the month Mesori. On the 4th intercalary day, the day of the birthday feast of Isis, at the same time as the feast of Amen on the new year, the Majesty of this glorious god, the lord of the gods, Amen-Ra, the king of the gods, was brought out in procession. He came to the great hall of the temple of Amen, and rested before the pylon of Amen. And (10) the general in chief of the army, Men-kheper-Ra, went in to Amen-Ra, the king of the gods. He worshipped him much with many prayers, and set before him an offering of all sorts of good things. Then the high-priest of Amen-Ra, Men-kheper-Ra, added the words : ' O thou, my good lord ! There is a talk and it is repeated [by the people.]' (11) Then the god gave full assent to him. Then he again went to the god, and spake thus : ' O thou, my good lord ! This talk of the people is a complaint, on account of thy anger against those who are in the Oasis, in the land which thou hast appointed for them.' Then the god gave full assent (12) to him. Therefore this chief captain lifted up his hands praying, in order to worship his lord. As the moon changes with the sun, thus he spake : ' Hail to thee ! thou creator of all [being, thou bringer forth] of all being which exists, father of the gods, creator of the goddesses, as they remain in the cities and in the villages, begetter (13) of men, bearer of women, who dispenses life to all men, for he is a skilful master of work . . . . the life . . . . of the great god Ptah, (the fashioner) . . . . . [who creates provisions] in abundance, who brings forth sustenance for gods and men, sunshine by day, moonlight by night, who traverses the heaven in peace, (14) without rest, as the greatest among the spirits, powerful as the goddess Sekhet, resembling the sun . . . . [be again friendly disposed to the banished ones, against whom thy command went out]. Do thou recall it, to heal what is diseased ; look [graciously upon] this people, who do not stand before thy countenance, for there are (15) a hundred thousand of them. Is any one able to appease thee, if thou at all turnest thyself away ? [Hail to thee] thou shining beam ! [Listen to] my words on this very day. Mayest thou [feel a pity for] the servants, whom thou hast banished (16) to the Oasis, that they may be brought back to Egypt.' Then

the great god gave full assent to him.   Then went in the captain of
the army again to the great god, speaking thus : ' O thou, my good
lord !   Since thou hast assented] to their return, let it be published
abroad, that thou [art] friendly [disposed] to [the banished ones.']
Then the great god gave full assent to him.   Then went he in
again (17) to the great god, and spake thus : ' O thou, my good
lord !   Give forth a valid command in thy name, that no inhabitant
of the land shall be banished to the far distance of the Oasis, that
no one . . . . from this very day for ever.'   (18) Then the great
god gave full assent to him.   Then he spake again to him : 'Speak
that it may be done thus according to thy command, which shall [be
written down] on a memorial stone [in writing], and set up in thy
cities, to last and to remain for ever.'   Then the great god gave full
assent to him.

Then spake again the chief priest (19) of Amen, Men-kheper-Ra :
' O thou, my good lord !   Now am I contented (?) a hundred thousand times ; this was my intention, that all families should hear it.
All (their) words express contentment with me.   I am thy servant
in truth, [for I am thy likeness] (20) in youthful form for thy city.
I was created as originator of all riches according to thy [word],
when I was yet in my mother's womb.   Thou didst fashion me in
the egg.   Thou didst bring me to the light to the great joy of thy
people.   Give me a beautiful duration of life (21) in the service of
thy [being], and purity and protection from all thy plagues (?).   Let
my feet walk in thy ways, and make thy path straight for me.   May
my heart be friendly towards (thy ?) house, to do [what thy commands enjoin].   (22) Give me consideration with the great god, in
peace, that I may abide and live in thy glorious house.   In like
manner may all reward be mine from . . .'   (23) Then did the high
priest of Amen, Men-kheper-Ra, go in to the great god, and spake
thus : ' If any one of the people should in thy presence contradict,
saying that he has done great things for the people, that the land
may gain life,—then destroy him, kill him.'   Then the great god
gave full assent to him.

The distracted state of the empire could not have
been more clearly exhibited than in this inscription.
Even if we reject ' the 100,000 banished ones,' of whom
the high-priest speaks, the whole proceeding throws a
sad light on the state of things then prevailing in
Egypt.   Persecutions and banishments form, in every
age, a measure of the internal condition of an empire.
That the recall of the exiles from the Oasis, proposed by

the priest-king Men-kheper-Ra, did not spring from any special goodness of heart, but was a politic measure, to quiet the agitation fermenting in the country, can hardly require further proof.

While the events were taking place, which the inscription sets forth in such an ambiguous manner, it appears that Na-ro-math (Nimrod), who had been associated on the throne by his father Shashanq, had advanced into Egypt with an army, not only to render help and support to the Ramessides, but also with the intention of conquering the country. Here in Egypt death surprised him. His mother, Mehet-en-usekh, was an Egyptian, in all probability a daughter of the 14th Ra-messu. According to her desire, her son was buried in Abydos, and the feasts of the dead were instituted in his honour, the cost of which was to be defrayed from the income of certain estates. At the same time men and women were appointed for the preservation of his tomb, herds of cattle were purchased, and all other things provided, which could serve for a worthy establishment in honour of the dead.

When Egypt had thus become subjected to Shashanq I., Pasebkhanu, the brother of Men-kheper-Ra, was left as sub-king at Tanis, while the conqueror fixed his capital at Bubastis. Meanwhile Men-kheper-Ra carried on his functions as chief priest of Amen in Thebes, where, as we have reason to suppose, Ra-messu XVI. was for some time, in name at least, recognised as king.

These measures were evidently taken during the presence of the elder Shashanq (grandfather of the above-mentioned prince who afterwards became Shashanq I.) in Egypt. He visited Thebes, and did not fail, on his journey to the city of Amen, to pay a visit to the grave of his beloved son at Abydos. He was bitterly chagrined at its neglected state. The Egyptian

officials, who probably had little inclination to honour
the remains of a foreign king, had plundered, as far as
they could, the temple-revenues which had been appointed for keeping up the grave.   They were brought
to an account by Shashanq, and with the approval of
Amen they were all punished with death.   These circumstances have been handed down in a lengthy inscription on a granite block at Abydos.   Even though
the upper half of the stone is wanting, the under part
is well preserved, so far at least that the contents can be
read without misapprehension.   Here is the translation :—

[To Amen-Ra spake the general of the Mā, when] the generalissimo, Shashanq, [had visited] his son, at his beautiful burial-place with
his father Osiris, where his body had been laid on his bed of rest in
the city of Nifur (Abydos), in sight of [the temple of Osiris] : 'Thou
hast freed him from attaining to an infirm old age, while he remained
on earth.   Thou hast granted him his rest.   My feasts will consist
in this, to receive the undivided victory.'   Very, very much did the
great god give assent to him.

Then spake his Majesty anew to the great god thus : 'O thou
good lord, put to death [the captains] of the army, the . . . . secretary, the land-surveyor, and all . . . ?   whom [I] sent [with a com-
mission] to this estate, and who plundered [the property] of the altar
of the Osirian general of the Mā, Na-ro-math (Nimrod), the son of
Mehet-en-usekh, who is buried in Abydos, and all the people who
have robbed his holy property, his people, his herds of cattle, his
gardens, his offerings, and all that was dedicated for his honour.   Act
according to thy great spirit in its whole extent, to replace them
again, and to replace the women and their children.'   The great god
assented to this most graciously.

Then his Majesty threw himself on the ground before him, and
his Majesty spake thus : 'Grant triumph to Shashanq, the general
of the Mā, the great generalissimo, the glorious . . . . and all
those who are with him, and all warriors, and all [his people]
together.'

Then [spake to him] Amen-Ra, the king of the gods : 'I will do
[according to thy wish].   Thou shalt receive (the blessing of) a great
age and remain on earth, and thy heir shall sit on thy throne for
ever.'

Then his Majesty had the statue, in the form of a walking man, of the Osirian general of the Mā, the great generalissimo, Na-ro-math, brought up the river to Abydos. There were in attendance on it a large body of soldiers in many ships, no man knows their number, together with the ambassadors of the general of the Mā. And it was set down in the splendid royal chamber of the holy of holies of the right eye of the sun, to carry the offerings on the altar-table of Nifur. According to the directions of the holy anointing, the dedication was accomplished.

The incense was burnt in the room of the star-chamber for three days. This was set up for the temple-ordinances in the form of a written record, according to the contents of the ordinances for the feasts of the gods. A memorial tablet was erected in the language of the land of Bab[el], containing the command [of the great lord] in his name. And it (the memorial tablet) was laid up in the holy of holies of the gods for ever and ever.

[This is the catalogue] of that which was appointed for the altar of the Osirian general, Na-ro-math, the son of Mehet-en-usekh, who is buried at Abydos. There were allotted (to it) the people who had been [bought ?] out of [the countries ?] of the general of the Mā, namely: Aïromapatut, of the people of the Phœnicians, and obedient at call: Khu-Amen . . . . and . . . . a Phœnician (called) Bek-Ptah. (The price of) their purchase makes in silver money 15 lbs. His Majesty had given for them in silver money 20 lbs., making together 35 lbs. This is the number of that which they cost. The 50 aruræ of land, which are situated in the region of the heights to the south of Abydos, which is called 'permanent duration of the kingdom (*Heh-suteni*),' cost 5 lbs. of silver money. The (fields) which are situated by the side (?) of the canal which is at Abydos, an estate of 50 aruræ, for these there was paid 5 lbs. in silver money. This makes together an estate [of 100 aruræ] in these two places in the region of the heights to the south of Abydos, and in the region of the heights to the north of Abydos. For this estate of 100 aruræ there was also paid 10 lbs. in silver.

[Catalogue of the servants for the estate]: His servant Pa-uer, his servant . . . . , his servant Ari-bek, his servant Bu-pa-Amen-kha, his servant Nai-shennu, his servant Pesh-en-Hor. Making a total of 6 servants, for whom there was paid, for each 3 lbs. and 1 ounce of silver money, making in all 1[8] pounds 6 ounces of silver money. [His boy (?) . . . . and his boy (?)] . . . . son of Hor-se-Ise, for these was paid $4\frac{2}{3}$ ounces of silver money.

The garden, which is situated in the district of the northern heights of Abydos, cost 2 lbs. of silver money; the gardener, Hor-mes, the son of Pen-mer, $x + \frac{2}{3}$ ounces of silver money, the water-carrier . . . . , the son of . . . . for $6\frac{2}{3}$ ounces of silver money.

Catalogue of maid-servants : Nes-ta-tep, whose mother is Tat-mut ; the maiden Tat-Ise, the daughter of Nebt-hepet, whose mother is Ariamakh ; the maiden Tat-Amen, the daughter of Pinehas [the maiden . . . . , the daughter of . . . .], each one for $5\frac{2}{3}$ ounces of silver money.

The outlay for [the purchase of honey] is to amount to $3\frac{2}{3}$ lbs. of silver money, and is charged upon the treasury of Osiris, so that a hin-measure of honey shall be given by the treasury of Osiris [for the daily supply of honey of the Osirian] general of the Mā, Na-ro-math, whose father is the great generalissimo, [Shashanq, and whose mother is Mehet-en-usekh, for all eternity]. The treasury of Osiris is charged with the money for this, neither more nor less. [The out-lay for the purchase] of balsam shall amount to $4\frac{2}{3}$ lbs. of silver money, and is charged on the treasury of Osiris, so that 4 ounces of balsam shall be delivered from the treasury of Osiris every day for the offering of the Osirian general of the Mā, Na-ro-math, whose mother is Mehet-en-usekh, to all eternity. [For the provision] of the balsam the treasury of Osiris is thus charged with the money neither more nor less. [The outlay for the purchase of] incense shall amount to $5\frac{2}{3}$ ounces of silver money, and is charged on the treasury of Osiris, so that a hin of $x + \frac{2}{3}$ ounces shall be delivered from the treasury of Osiris every day for the [keeping up] of the burning of incense for the Osirian general of the Mā, Na-ro-math, whose mother is Mehet-en-usekh, to all times. For the procuring of the incense the treasury of Osiris is thus charged with the money, neither more nor less. [The outlay for the different persons of the spice-kitchen, and for the persons of the labours of the harvest, shall amount to for each] $x + 3$ ounces, and for each 1 ounce of silver money, and these are charged on the treasury of Osiris, so that there shall be delivered [. . . . the spice-cakes] each day from the trea-sury of Osiris, and [that there shall be delivered . . . .] from the treasury of Osiris, and that there shall be delivered . . . . from the treasury of Osiris for the altars of the Osirian general of the Mā, Na-ro-math, whose mother is Mehet-en-usekh, to all eternity. For the support of the workmen of his spice-kitchen, the money for it also is charged on the treasury of Osiris. [Also for the] harvest workers in the upper fields, [the payments for these] are charged on the treasury of Osiris, to the amount of . . . . in silver money, neither more nor less. This is the sum total of the silver money for the people, which is charged on the treasury of Osiris, [so that all payments shall be made from it] which are to be borne by [the treasury of Osiris] for the altars of the Osirian general of the Mā, Na-ro-math, the son of the generalissimo of the Mā, Shashanq, whose mother is Mehet-en-usekh. It is assigned for the Osirian

general of the Mā, Na-ro-math, the son of Mehet-en-usekh, who ⌊is
buried⌋ in Abydos, for the estate of 100 aruræ of land, for the 25
men and women, for the gardens, and it amounts in silver money to
100 + x lbs., x ounces . . . . . .

The statue of Na-ro-math in red granite is now in the
museum in Florence. A son of that general Nimrod
was raised to the Egyptian throne. He is that Shashanq of whom, as the founder of the Twenty-second
Dynasty, we have to speak in the next chapter.

At about the same time, by direction of this Shashanq, the affair of the inheritance of the princess
Ka-Ra-maat (for thus, and not Maat-ka-Ra or Ra-maat-ka,
ought the name to be read) was regulated by express
royal command, in the name of the Theban circle of
gods. This lady was the offspring of the marriage of
King Pasebkhanu I. with a Theban (Ramesside ?), and,
according to a frequent Egyptian custom, she had been
robbed of her patrimony situated in Upper Egypt. By
her marriage with King Shashanq I. (for this Ka-Ra-maat
was his wife), her position was completely changed.
The ordinance, which relates to the agreement for
placing the princess in her full hereditary right, is
engraved in large letters on the north wall of the third
pylon on the south of the great temple of Amen at
Karnak. The upper half of this wall is completely
destroyed; and in this case also the first lines of the
inscription, which contained the date and the name of
the king, are unfortunately wanting. We give the
complete literal translation of this stone document, so
important historically, and leave it to our readers
themselves to draw all the conclusions which follow
from it:—

Thus spake Amen-Ra, the king of the gods, the great god of the
beginning of all being, and Mut and Khonsu, and the great gods :
With regard to any object of any kind, which Ka-Ra-maat, the
daughter of the king of Upper Egypt, Meri-Amen Pasebkhanu,

has brought with her, of the hereditary possession which had descended to her in the southern district of the country, and with regard to each object of any kind whatever, which (1) (the people) of the land have presented to her, which they have at any time taken from the (royal) lady, we hereby restore it to her. Any object of any kind whatsoever [which] belongs [as an inheritance to the children], that [we hereby restore] to her children for all time. Thus speaks Amen-Ra, the king of the gods, the great king of the beginning of all being, Mut, Khonsu, and the great gods : (2) 'Every king, every chief priest of Amen, every general, every captain, and the people of every condition, whether male or female, who had great designs, and they who carried out their designs later, they shall restore the property of all kinds, which Ka-Ra-maat, the daughter of the king of Upper Egypt, Meri-Amen Pasebkhanu, brought with her as her inherited estate in the southern district (3) of the country, together with all possessions of all kinds, which the inhabitants of the country have given her, and what they have at any time taken from the lady, it shall be restored into her hand, we restore it into the hand of her son and of her grandson, and to her daughter and to her grand-daughter, the child of the child of her daughter. It shall be preserved to the latest times.'

Again [spake Amen-Ra], the king of the gods, the great god of the beginning (4) of all being, and Mut, and Khonsu, and the great gods : 'Slain shall be all people of every condition of the whole land, whether male or female, who shall claim any object of any kind whatsoever, which Ka-Ra-maat, the daughter of the king, and lord of the land, Meri-Amen Pasebkhanu, brought with her, as inherited estate of the south land, and any object of any kind whatsoever, which the inhabitants (5) of the land have given her, which they have at any time taken from the lady as property. They who shall keep back any object thereof one morning after (another) morning, upon them shall our great spirits fall heavily, we will not be a helper (?) to them. They shall be full, full of [snares ?] on the part of the great god, of Mut, of Khonsu, and of the great gods.'

Then spake Amen-Ra, the king of the gods, the great god [of the beginning of all being, and Mut, and Khonsu, and the great gods :] (6) 'We will slay every inhabitant of every condition in the whole land, whether male or female, who shall claim any object of any sort whatsoever, which Ka-Ra-maat, the daughter of the king of Upper Egypt, and the lord of the land, Meri-Amen Pasebkhanu, brought with her, as inherited estate of the south land, and any object of any kind whatsoever, which the inhabitants of the country have presented to her, and which they have at any time taken away from the [lady as their possession. They who shall keep back any object thereof] (7) one morning after the (other) morning, to them shall our great spirits be heavy. We will not be any help to them, we will sink (their) noses into the earth, we will . . . . .'

DYNASTY XXII.[1]

SHASHANQ I.   CIR. B.C. 966.

We have seen that Shashanq had set up his throne at Bubastis, and it appears that he seldom extended his visits to the upper country of Patoris, though he followed the traditions of his family by living on the best of terms with the Ramessides. He became a conspicuous person in the history of Egypt through his expedition against the kingdom of Judah. It is well known how Jeroboam, the servant of King Solomon, rebelled against his master. After the prophet Ahijah had publicly designated him beforehand, as the man best qualified to be the future sovereign, Jeroboam was obliged to save himself from the anger of the king, and fled to Egypt, to the court of Shashanq I.[2] Recalled after the death of Solomon, he was elected king of Israel, while the crown of Judah fell to Solomon's son, Rehoboam.[3] In the fifth year of this latter king's reign, and probably at the instigation of his former guest (Jeroboam), Shashanq made his expedition against the kingdom of Judah, which ended in the capture and sack of Jerusalem.[4]

The story of this campaign has been related on the walls of the temple of Amen at Karnak. On the south external wall, behind the picture of the victories of King Ramses II., to the east of the room called the Hall of the Bubastites, the spectator beholds the colossal image of the Egyptian sovereign dealing heavy blows upon

---

[1] For Table of Kings see p. xxv.

[2] 1 Kings xi. 26-40.   [3] 1 Kings xii.   [4] 1 Kings xiv. 25-28.

the captive Jews. The names of the conquered towns and districts are paraded in long rows, in their Egyptian forms of writing, and frequently with considerable repetitions, each name being enclosed in an embattled shield.

We subjoin, so far as is possible, a list of them :—

Ra-bi-tha (Rabbith)

Ta-an-kau (Taanach)

She-n-mau (Shunem)

Beith-Shanlau (Beth-shean ?)

Re-ha-bau (Rehob)

Ha-pu-re-mau (Hapharaïm)

A-dul-ma (Adullam)

She-ua-di . . .

Ma-ha-ne-ma (Mahanaïm)

Qe-be-a-na (Gibeon)

Beith-Huaron (Beth-horon)

Qa-de-moth (Kedemoth)

A-ju-lon (Ajalon)

Ma-ke-thu (Megiddo)

A-dir

Judah-malek

Ha-an-ma

Aa-le-na (Eglon ?)

Bi-le-ma (Bileam)

Zad-poth-el

A . . ha . . ma

Beith-a-l-moth (Allemeth)

Ke-qa-li

Shau-ke (Socho)

Beith-tapuh (Beth-tappuah)

A-bi-lau (Abel)

Beith-zab . .

Nu-p-a-l

P . . d-shath

Pa-(shel)-keteth

A-do-maa (EDOM)

Za-le-ma (Zalmonah ?)

. . . . lela

. . . . lzau

. . . . apen

Pa-Amaq, 'the valley-plain' (Emek)

A-au-za-maa (Azmon)

A-na-la

Pa-Ha-qa-laa, 'the stone of'

Fe-thiu-shaa

A-ro-ha-lel (Aroër ?)

Pa-Ha-qa-laa, 'the stone of'

A-bi-ro-ma

She-bi-leth

Na-ga-bi-li

She-bi-leth

Ua-ro-kith

Pa-Ha-qa-laa, 'the stone of'

Ne-a-baith

A-de-de-maa

Za-pe-qe-qa

Ma . . . . a

Ta . . . .

Ga-naa-t, 'the garden'

Pa-Na-ga-bu, 'the Negeb (i.e. south) of'

A-za-m . . . th

Ta-shed-na

Pa-Ha-ga-le-(t), 'the stone of'

She-nai-aa

Ha-qa

Pa-Na-ga-bu, 'the Negeb of'

Ua-hath-lu-ka

A-sha-ha-tha-t

Pa-Ha-ga-li, 'the stone of'

Ha-ni-ni-au

Pa-Ha-ga-lau, 'the stone of'

A-le-qad

A-do-mam-t

Ha-ni-ni

A-do-rau

Pa-Ha-ga-l

Thel-uan

Ha-i-do-baa	. . ariuk
Sha-li-n-laa	Freth-maa
Ha-i-do-baa	A-bi-r
Di-ua-thi	Bal-ro-za
Ha-qe-le-ma	Beith-A-n-th (Beth-anoth)
A-l-daa-(t)	Sha-r (?)-ha-tau
Ri-bith	A-ro-ma-then (Ramah ?)
A-l-daai	Ga-le-naa
Neb-tath	A-ro-ma . . .
Jur-he-ma	. . . . r-hath
Ari . . . m	. . . . raa
A-d-raa	Ma . . .
Pa-Ba-aa	A-li . . . .
Ma-he-gaa	Jula . . . .

The speech, with which the divine Amen accompanies his delivery of the conquered cities to Shashanq I., contains not the slightest indication from which we might construct a background of facts for the names of the conquered peoples, or for the historical events connected with them.

This king built a sort of entrance hall which leads from the south, close by the east wall of the sanctuary of Ramses III., into the great front court of the temple. Seeing that the family names of the line of Shashanq have been perpetuated from the builder of this modest hall down to several of his successors, we have a right to regard it as the memorial hall of the Bubastites. Respecting the architect and also the erection of this edifice an inscription at Silsilis gives the following information :—

In the year 21, in the month Payni, at that time his Majesty was in his capital city, the abode of the great presence of the god Horemkhu. And his Majesty gave command and issued an order to the priest of the god Amen, the privy councillor of the city of Horemkhu, and the architect of the monuments of the lord of the land—Hor-em-saf—whose skill was great in all manner of work, to hew the best stone of Silsilis, in order to make many and great monuments for the temple of his glorious father, Amen-Ra, the lord of Thebes.

His Majesty issued the order to build a great temple-gate of wrought stones, in order to glorify the city (Thebes), to set up its doors several cubits in height, to build a festival-hall for his father Amen-Ra, the king of the gods, and to enclose the house of the god with a thick wall.

And Hor-em-saf, the priest of Amen-Ra the king of the gods, the privy councillor of the city of Horemkhu, the architect over the house of King Shashanq I. at Thebes, had a prosperous journey back to the city of Patoris (Thebes), to the place where his Majesty resided ; and his love was great towards his master, the lord of might, the lord of the land, for he spake thus :—

'All thy words shall be accomplished, O my good lord ! I will not sleep by night, I will not slumber by day. The building shall go on uninterruptedly, without rest or pause.'

And he was received graciously by the king, who gave him rich presents in silver and gold.

The quarries of Silsilis have also furnished this architect with the fit opportunity of immortalising his royal master's memory. On a memorial tablet the king is seen with his son Auputh in the act of being presented by the goddess Mut to the three principal divinities of Egypt—Amen of Thebes, Horemkhu-Tmu of Heliopolis, and Ptah of Memphis. The inscription states—

This is the divine benefactor. The sun-god Ra has his form. He is the image of Horemkhu. Amen has placed him on his throne to make good what he had begun in taking possession of Egypt for the second time. This is King Shashanq. He caused a new quarry to be opened, in order to begin a building, the work of King Shashanq I. Of such a nature is the service which he has done to his father, the Theban Amen-Ra. May he grant him the thirty years' jubilee-feasts of Ra, and the years of the god Tmu ! May the king live for ever !

To this the king replies :—

My gracious lord ! Grant that my words may live for hundreds of thousands of years. It is a high privilege to work for Amen. Grant me, in recompense for what I have done, a lasting kingdom. I have caused a new quarry to be opened for him for the beginning of a work. It has been carried out by Auputh—the high-priest of Amen, the king of the gods, and the commander-in-chief of the most excellent soldiery, the head of the whole body of

warriors of Patoris, the son of King Shashanq I.—for his lord
Amen-Ra, the king of the gods. May he grant life, welfare, health,
a long term of life, power, and strength, an old age in prosperity!
My gracious lord! Grant that my words may live for hundreds of
thousands of years! It is a high privilege to work for Amen.
Grant me power, in recompense for what I have done!

Auputh, the king's eldest son, died before his father.
Already he had been invested with the title of chief
priest of Amen, to which was joined the position of
commander-in-chief of the military force in the South.
In a side inscription in the same place he thus recalls
himself to posterity :—

This was made by the chief priest of Amen-Ra, the king of the
gods, the commander-in-chief and general, Auputh, who stands at
the head of the whole body of the great warriors of Patoris, the
son of King Shashanq. I.

In the Hall of the Bubastites at Karnak, also, the
name of this high-priest of the god Amen appears
beside the name of his father.

UASARKEN I.   CIR. B.C. 933.

Save for a passing mention of his name the monuments relate nothing about this son of Shashanq. Of
his two wives who are mentioned one—Tashed-Khonsu
—bore him a son called Takeleth, who was his successor.
His second son, Shashanq, born of his marriage with the
daughter of Pasebkhanu II. of Tanis, and thus of royal
descent, became high-priest of Amen with the same rank
as that held by his uncle Auputh, viz. commander-in-
chief, but with this difference, that the whole Egyptian
army was placed under his control, and not only that
part stationed in Patoris.

There seems to have been a contest between the
brothers for the crown. The inheritance which was
assured to the first by his right as first-born was
disputed by the second as the son of a royal princess.

The claim, which was not admitted in his person, seems, however, to have been conceded to his descendants, the younger line of kings of the race of Shashanq.

TAKELETH I. CIR. B.C. 900.

The monuments pass over the history of his time in silence. His son by his wife Karos was his successor.

UASARKEN II. CIR. B.C. 866.

According to the monuments he had two wives. The first had the name, already well known to us, of Ka-Ra-maat. She was the mother of his first-born son, Shashanq, who as crown prince was at once invested with the dignity of a chief priest of Ptah of Memphis. In this character he conducted the burial of the Apis-bull, which died in the 23rd year of the reign of Uasarken II.

His younger brother Na-ro-math (Nimrod), a son of the second wife, Mut-ut-ankhes, was next appointed overseer of the prophets and commander of the soldiery of Khinensu (Akhnas), that is, Heracleopolis Magna; but the office was also conferred on him of a governor of Patoris and a chief priest of Amen of Thebes. His descendants succeeded their father in the hereditary office of priests of Khnem in Heracleopolis Magna; while the descendants of Prince Shashanq, who was the high-priest of Ptah at Memphis, inherited in like manner their father's office, and appear as officiating high-priests at the burial of several Apis-bulls. With Uasarken II. the direct line of the kings died out and a younger branch succeeded.

SHASHANQ II. CIR. B.C. 833.

This king was the grandson of Shashanq the high-priest of Amen, and thus belonged to a junior branch of the same royal family. The monuments are absolutely silent concerning his history. He was followed by

TAKELETH II. CIR. B.C. 800.

Takeleth II. married Mer-mut Keromama Set-Amen Mut-em-hat, a daughter of Na-ro-math, high-priest of Amen. Their eldest son is designated in the inscriptions as high-priest of the Theban Amen, and commander-in-chief of the military force of the whole land, and he was at the same time a petty king. He is the Uasarken of whom so much is related on a long memorial tablet in the interior of the Hall of the Bubastites. This account begins with the date of the 9th of the month Tehuti in the 12th regnal year of his father. From it we learn that the prince Uasarken went to Thebes in his character of high-priest of Amen, to enter on his office of subjecting the Theban temple and its territory to a careful examination and restoring the offerings to the god :—

When now had arrived the 15th year, the month Mesori, the 25th day, under the reign of his father, the lordly Horus, the god-like prince of Thebes, *the heaven could not be distinguished, the moon was eclipsed* (literally, *was horrible*), for a sign of the (coming) events in this land ; as it also happened, for enemies (*literally*, the children of revolt) invaded with war the southern and northern districts (of Egypt).

I have not the slightest doubt that the foregoing words have reference to the irruptions of the Ethiopians from the South and to the attack of the Assyrian power from the North. The rest of the inscription supposes the return, however temporary, of a period of rest for Egypt. The priest-king Uasarken used this respite to evince his devotion to Amen and to his temple. The sacrifices were established in such a manner that certain sums of money were put aside for the maintenance of the offerings, as had been done before in the case of Abydos.

The last descendants of the line of Shashanq had meanwhile subsided into the position of petty kings in the divided realm. Their names are

SHASHANQ III. CIR. B.C. 766.
PA-MAI. CIR. B.C. 733.
SHASHANQ IV. CIR. B.C. 700.

We owe our knowledge of these monarchs chiefly to the Apis-stêlæ upon which are inscribed references to their reigns and the locality of their kingdom. If they no longer possessed Bubastis, Memphis still remained in their hands. It was here that the sacred bull lived in the temple of Ptah-Sekar-Osiris, and hence it was that the solemn translation of the deceased Apis was made on a car fitted with heavy wooden wheels to the Serapeum in the desert between the Arab villages of Abusîr and Saqqarah.

Subjoined is a literal translation of the Apis memorial stones brought to light in 1850, in so far as they relate to the kings of the Twenty-Second Dynasty.

I. MEMORIAL STONE OF THE PRIEST AND SEER OF THE APIS-BULL, SENEBEF, SON OF SHED-NEFER-TMU, AND OF HIS SON, THE MEMPHITE PRIEST HOR-HEB.

In the year [2], the month [Mekhir,] on the [1st] day, under the reign of King Pa-mai, the friend of the Apis-god in the West. This is the day on which this (deceased) god was carried to the beautiful region of the West, and was laid at rest in the grave, at rest with the great god, with Osiris, with Anpu, and with the goddesses of the nether world, in the West. His introduction into the temple of Ptah beside his father, the Memphite god Ptah, had taken place in the year 29, in the month Paophi, in the time of King Shashanq III.

II. MEMORIAL STONE OF THE HIGH-PRIEST OF MEMPHIS, PET-ISE.

In the year 2, the month Mekhir, on the 1st day, under the reign of King Pa-mai, the friend of the great god Apis in the West.—This is the day on which the god was carried to his rest, in the beautiful region of the West, and was laid in the grave, and on which he was deposited in his everlasting house and in his eternal abode. He was born in the year 28, in the times of the deceased king Shashanq III. His glory was sought for in all places of Patomit (that is, Lower Egypt). He was found, after (some) months, in the city of Ha-shed-abot. They had searched through the lakes of Natho and all the islands of Patomit. He had been solemnly introduced into the temple of Ptah, beside his father, the Memphite god Ptah of the south wall, by the high-priest in the temple of Ptah, the general of the Mashuasha, Pet-Ise, the son of the high-priest [of Memphis and the great chief of the] Mashuasha, Takeleth, and of the princess of royal race, Thes-Bast-per, in the year 28, in the month Paophi, on the 1st day. The full lifetime of this god amounted to 26 years.

III. Memorial Stone of the Memphite Priest Hor-se-Ise.

In the year 2, the month Mekhir, the 1st day, under the reign of Kìng Pa-mai, the friend of the great god Apis in the West, the god was carried to his rest in the beautiful region of the West. He had been solemnly introduced into the temple of Ptah beside his father, the Memphite god Ptah of the south wall, in the year . . . . . under the reign of King Shashanq . . . [in the year] 5 [+ x] after he had shown his   ?   , after they had sought for [his glory . . .]. The full lifetime of this god amounted to 26 years. (This tablet is dedicated) by the hereditary [prince] (here follows a string of titles in the priestly style) Hor-se-Ise, the son of the high-priest] of Memphis and chief of the] Mashuasha, Pet-Ise, and of the eldest of the wives . . . . [and by the . . .] Takeleth, whose mother Ta-ti-Hor . . . . is.

IV. Memorial Stone of the Satrap Pet-Ise, and his Sons Pef-tot-Bast and Takeleth.

In the 28th year of King Shashanq.

Then follows a sculpture, in which three men are seen before the bull-headed god, Apis-Tmu. The first of them has on his head the fillet of a general of the Mashuasha ; the last is adorned with the youth-locks worn by royal and princely persons. Above and beside these persons are the following inscriptions :—

May he grant health, life, prosperity, to the general of the

Mashuasha, Pet-Ise, the son of the general Takeleth—his mother is Thes-Bast-per—the son of the first and greatest of the princely heirs of his Majesty Shashanq, the son of the king and lord of the land, Uasarken II.,—

And to his venerator and friend, the high-priest of Ptah, Pef-tot-Bast, the son of the general Pet-Ise, whose mother is Ta-ari, a daughter of the general Takeleth,—

And to his venerator and friend, the priest of Ptah, Takeleth, the son of the general Pet-Ise and of (his wife) Hor-set.

From these four inscriptions it follows, with certainty, that, under the reign of Shashanq III., Pet-Ise and his son Pef-tot-Bast ascribe to themselves the title of 'generals of the Mā (Mashuasha).' The new Apis is sought for in all *Lower Egypt*. As to *Upper Egypt*— where Uasarken, the king and high-priest of Amen, maintained the kingdom, until the time when the Ethiopian Piankhi broke his power—the inscription is completely silent.

With regard to the Apis himself, the following results are obtained from the four memorial tablets now cited :—He was born in the 28th year of the reign of King Shashanq III., at the city of Ha-shed-abot in Lower Egypt. Months passed by before he was discovered. On the 1st of Paophi, in the 29th regnal year of the king, he was solemnly introduced into the temple of Ptah of Memphis. After a life of 26 years, he was buried in the Serapeum of Memphis on the 1st of Mekhir in the 2nd year of the reign of King Pa-mai. His death must therefore have happened 70 days earlier, that is, on the 20th of Athyr. Supposing him to have lived 26 *complete* years, as the inscription expressly testifies, his birth must have fallen on the 20th of Athyr in the 28th regnal year of King Shashanq III. In that case about ten months and a half would have elapsed until his introduction into Memphis on the 1st of Paophi in the 29th year of the reign of Shashanq III.

DYNASTY XXIII., OF TANIS.

Under this title, the priest Manetho, in his Book of
the Kings, sets down the reigns of the three kings :—

PETA-SE-BAST, with 40 years;
UASARKEN III., with 9 years;
PSAMUS, with 10 years.

All three disappear in the struggle waged against
Egypt, with varying success, by Ethiopia from the South
and Assyria from the North. Hence their names emerge
but occasionally in the historical records of this time.
Judging from the elements contained in their titles, Peta-
se-Bast seems to have had his royal seat in Bubastis,
Uasarken in Thebes or Tanis, Psamus in Memphis. The
last we shall have to recognise again under his Assyrian
name of Is-pi-ma-tu, as a contemporary of King Taharaqa about 700 B.C.

DYNASTY XXIV.

BAK-EN-RAN-F, the Bocchoris of Manetho, stands alone
in this dynasty, and appears to have belonged to a
number of petty kings who formed a connection with
the younger contemporaries of Taharaqa. The Ethiopian tradition says that he was taken prisoner by
Shabakh and burnt alive.

Mariette has recognised in this king the UAH-KA-RA
BAK-EN-RAN-F, whose Apis-sarcophagus (of the 6th year
of the king) was placed in the same chamber of the
Serapeum, in which the deceased Apis of the 37th year
of King Shashanq IV. was deposited. Here then we
have brought to light a new connection in time between
Bocchoris and Shashanq IV.

This same Bak-en-ran-f appears again in the Assyrian list of the Egyptian petty kings, under the name

of Bu-kur-ni-ni-ip, as *sar* of Pa-ah-nu-ti. The name of the city must not be confused with the Assyrian transcription of Saïs, the city from which Bocchoris had his origin, as it is evident that some other place in Egypt is intended.

CHAPTER XVI.

DYNASTY XXV.[1]

THE ETHIOPIANS.

TOWARDS the end of the ninth century Egypt had far too much to do in defending herself to trouble about her supremacy in the South, which she had heretofore so carefully guarded. The 'Viceroys of the South' and 'King's sons of Cush' are now struck out of the official list of court dignitaries, and the 'Kings of Cush' take their place. The whole South, from the boundary line at the city of Syene, recovered its freedom, and the Ethiopians began to enjoy a state of independence. Meanwhile, if the power of Egypt was no longer felt, Egyptian civilization had survived. All that was wanting was a leader. Nothing could have appeared more opportune for the priests of Amen than this state of things in Nubia and Ethiopia, where the minds of an imperfectly developed people must needs, under skilful guidance, soon show themselves pliable and submissive to the dominant priestly caste. Mount Barkal, where Amen-hotep III. had already raised a sanctuary for the great Amen of Thebes in the form of a strongly fortified temple-city, was the site chosen by the newly arrived priests for the seat of their future royalty. The capital of this kingdom of Cush was Napata, which is so often mentioned in the inscriptions of Ethiopian origin.

[1] For Table of Kings see p. xxvi.

It is difficult to say who it was of the race of Her-Hor that first made preparations for the foundation of that Ethiopian kingdom which became afterwards so dangerous to the Egyptians. The Ethiopian monuments, from which the cartouches have been carefully erased by a later Egyptian dynasty, give not the slightest information on this point. So much the more important, therefore, is the circumstance, that several successors of this priest—among whom was the son and successor of Her-Hor—bore the same name, namely, that of the priest-king Piankhi, an Egyptian word, which signifies 'the living one.' The sovereign enthroned at Napata, 'the City of the Holy Mountain,' called himself 'King of the land of Cush.' The Theban Amen-Ra was reverenced as the supreme god of the country. The king's full name was formed exactly according to the Egyptian pattern. The Egyptian language and writing, divisions of time, and everything else relating to manners and customs were preserved. A distinguished position was assigned to the mother, daughters, and sisters of the king; each of whom bore the title of 'Queen of Cush.'

In the course of time the power of the Ethiopians increased, until at last the whole of Patoris came into their possession, and the 'great city' of Niaa, that is, Thebes, became their capital. While the Assyrians regarded Lower Egypt—the Muzur so often mentioned in the cuneiform inscriptions—as their permanent fief, the districts of Patoris were virtually an Ethiopian province. Middle Egypt formed a 'march,' contested on both sides between the two kingdoms, and at the same time a barrier which tended to hinder the outbreak of open hostilities between the one and the other.

Thus the old priestly race succeeded in again ac-

quiring full possession of Thebes, the city out of which
Shashanq I. had chased them so ignominiously. The
loss of the city of Amen was to them equivalent to
suffering a conquest.

As in Lower Egypt the foreign rulers were content
with drawing a tribute from the petty kings, so in
Patoris and Middle Egypt petty kings or vassals were
set up by the Ethiopians, whose supremacy these
princes had to recognise, and to pay their taxes.

Thus the great kingdom of Kamit was split up into
little dependent states, which leant, now on Ethiopia,
now on Assyria as each foreign master gained prepon-
derance for the time.

About the year 766 B.C. a revolt broke out under
an enterprising petty king of Saïs and Memphis, by
name TEFNEKHT, the Technactis or Tnephachthus of
classic writers. Profiting by the momentary weakness of
the Assyrian Empire, he prevailed on the other princes
of Lower Egypt to join him, and made an inroad with his
whole force upon Middle Egypt, where the Egyptian
vassals of Piankhi at once submitted to him. The
tidings having reached Piankhi, he forthwith sent orders
to his generals to check the advance of Tefnekht, and
so to force the bold petty king to beat a retreat.

Subjoined is a translation of the memorial stone of
Piankhi, discovered several years ago at Mount Barkal.
This monument, a granite block covered with writing,
was set up there by the Ethiopian king Piankhi, in
remembrance of his conquest of Middle and Lower
Egypt, and will show, far better than any description,
the several stages of the Ethiopian expedition, and the
peculiar position of the Egyptian petty kings. Of these
we give a list according to the account furnished by
the stone :—

King and General TEFNEKHT, Prince of Saïs and Memphis ;

King NIMROD, lord of Hermopolis Magna ;

King AUPUTH, of the nome of Clysma ;

General SHASHANQ, of the city of Busiris ;

General T'A-AMEN-AUF-ANKH, of the city of Mendes ;

His eldest son ANKH-HOR, commander of the city of Hermopolis, in Lower Egypt.

The hereditary lord, BEK-EN-ISI ;

General NES-NA-AI (or NES-NA-KETI), of the nome of Xoïs ;

King UASARKEN, of the city of Bubastis ;

Prince PEF-TOT-BAST, of the city of Heracleopolis Magna ;

The hereditary lord, PET-ISE, of the city of Athribis ;

General PA-THENEF, of Pa-Saptu (the Arabian nome) ;

General PA-MAI, of the (second) city (named) Busiris ;

General NEKHT-HOR-NA-SHENNU, of Phagroriopolis ;

General of Tanis (not named, being a native Assyrian) ;

General of Ostracine (not named, for the same reason) ;

Prophet of Horus, PET-HOR-SAM-TAUI, of the city of Letopolis ;

Prince HE-RO-BI-SA, of the cities of Sa and Hesaui ;

Prince T'A-KHI-AU, of Khent-nefer ;

Prince PA-BI-SA, of Babylon and Nilopolis (in the Heliopolitan nome).

By the term 'vassals' is meant the princes subject to Piankhi.

In the 21st year, in the month Tehuti, under the reign of the king of Upper and Lower Egypt, Amen Meri-Piankhi—may he live for ever !—My Royal Majesty issued the command that men should be informed of what I have done more than all my predecessors. I the king am a part of God, a living image of Tmu. As soon as I came out of my mother's womb I was chosen to be ruler, before whom the great men were afraid, knowing that I [was to be a powerful lord].

(2) His mother well knew that he was destined for a ruler in his mother's womb, he, the god-like benefactor, the friend of the gods, the son of Ra, who had formed him with his hands, Amen Meri-Piankhi.

Messengers came to inform the king : 'The lord of the West country (that is, the Western part of the Delta), the great prince in the holy city (Saïs), Tefnekht, has established himself in the nome [name wanting], in the nome of Xoïs, in the city of Hapu (Nilopolis), in the city [. . . .], (3) in the city of Ain, in the city of Pa-Nub (Momemphis), and in the city of Memphis. He has taken possession of the whole West country, from the Mediterranean coast (of

Buto) up to the boundary city (between Upper and Lower Egypt).
He is advancing up the river with many warriors.   The inhabitants of both parts of Egypt have joined themselves to him.
The princes and lords of the cities are like dogs at his feet.   The
fortresses are not shut (against him) (4) of the nomes of the South.
The cities of Meri-Tmu (Meidûm), Pa-Sekhem-kheper-Ra (Crocodilopolis, the city of Uasarken I., at the entrance to the Fayûm), Pa-Mas
(Oxyrhynchus), Thekanath, and all the (other) cities of the West,
have opened their gates to him, through fear of him.   He turns
himself to the nomes of the East.   They open their gates to him,
namely, the following : Ha-Bennu (the Phœnix-city, Hipponon),
Tai-ut'ai, and Aphroditopolis.   He is preparing (5) to beleaguer
the city of Heracleopolis Magna.   He has surrounded it as with
a ring.   None who would go out can go out, none who would go in
can go in, because of the uninterrupted assaults.   He has girt it
round on every side.   All the princes who acknowledge his power,
he lets them abide every one in his own district, as princes and
kings of the cities.   And they [do homage to him] (6) as to one
who is distinguished through his wise mind ; his heart is joyful.'

And the lords and the princes and the chiefs of the warriors,
every one according to his city, sent continual messages to his
Majesty (i.e. Piankhi) to this effect : ' Art thou then silent, so as
not to wish to have any knowledge of the South country and of
the inland regions ?   Tefnekht is winning them to himself, and
finds no one that withstands him.   Nimrod, the [lord of Hermopolis Magna] (7) and prince of Ha-Uer (Megalopolis), has demo-
lished the fortress of Nofrus, and has razed his city with his
own hands, through fear that he (Tefnekht) should take it from
him, in order to cut it off after the manner of the other cities.   Now
he has departed, to throw himself at his feet, and he has renounced
allegiance to his Majesty.   He is leagued with him like any [of
the other princes.   The lord] (8) of the nome of Oxyrhynchus has
offered him gifts according to his heart's desire, of everything that
he could find.'

Then his Majesty sent orders to the princes and captains of
the army, who were set over the land of Egypt, (namely) the
captain Pa-ua-ro-ma, and the captain La-mis-ke-ni, and to all his
Majesty's captains, who were set over the land of Egypt, that they
should hasten to prevent the arming (of the rebels) for war, to invest
[the city of Hermopolis], (9) to take captive its inhabitants, their
cattle, and their vessels on the river, to let no labourer go out to
the field, nor suffer any ploughman to plough, and to blockade all
that were in the city of Hermopolis, and to fight against it without
ceasing.   And they did so.

Then his Majesty sent his warriors to Egypt, enjoining upon them very very strictly : 'Take [care, watch, do not pass] (10) the night in the enjoyment of play. Be on the alert against the attack (of the enemy), and be armed for the battle even afar off. If any (of the commanders) says, " The army and the chariots are to turn to another city : why will ye delay to go against its army ? "—ye shall fight as he has said. If any (of the enemy) attempts to fetch his defenders from another city, (11) turn about to meet them. If any of these princes should have brought with him, for his protection, warriors from Marmarica, or combatants from those faithful (to him), arm yourselves to fight against them. As an old hero says, " It avails not to gather together the warriors and numerous chariots with the best horses out of the stable, but, (12) when going into the battle, to confess that Amen, the divine, is he who sends us." When you have arrived at Thebes, in sight of (the temple of) Apet, go into the water, wash yourselves in the river, draw yourselves up at the chief canal, unstring your bows and lay aside your weapons before (13) the king (of the gods), as the Almighty. No strength shall the man have who despises him ; he makes the weak strong, and however many there be of them (the strong), they must turn their back before the few, and be one (ever so weak) ; he copes with a thousand. Sprinkle yourselves with the water from his altars of sacrifice, fall down before him on your faces, and speak (14) to him thus : " Show us the way to fight in the shadow of thy mighty arm. The peoples that go forth for thee shall beat down the enemy in many defeats." '

Then they threw themselves prostrate before his Majesty, (saying) : 'Is it not thy name that makes our arm strong ? Is it not thy wisdom that gives firmness to thy warriors ? Thy bread is in our bodies during all our march, and thy mead (15) quenches our thirst. Does not thy power give us strength and manly courage at the thought of thee ? An army is naught, whose commander is a coward. And who is like unto thee ? Thou art the king whose hands create victory, a master in the work of war.'

When they had gone (16) down the river, they reached the city of Thebes, and did all that his Majesty had commanded. Proceeding down the stream upon the river, they met a number of vessels sailing up the stream with soldiers, sailors, and captains, of the best warriors of Upper Egypt, equipped with all munitions, (17) for the war against the army of his Majesty. Then they inflicted on them a great overthrow. No one knows the number of their prisoners, together with their ships, who were brought as living prisoners to the place where his Majesty resided. When they had advanced further to the city of Heracleopolis Magna, they arrayed themselves for the battle.

(18) The following is the list of the princes and kings of Lower Egypt :

The king NIMROD, and

The king AUPUTH :

The general SHASHANQ, of the city of Busiris ; and

The general T'A-AMEN-AUF-ANKH, of the city of Mendes ; and

His eldest son, who was military commander of the city of Hermopolis Parva :

The warriors of the hereditary lord BEK-EN-ISI ; and

His eldest son, the general (19) NES-NA-AI of the nome of Xoïs :

The grand-master of the fan-bearers in Lower Egypt ; and

The king UASARKEN, who resides in the city of Bubastis and in the city of Uu-n-Ra-nefer :

and all the princes and kings of the cities on the West side, on the East side, and on the islands between. They had gathered themselves together at the bidding of that one, and they sat thus at the feet of the great lord of the West country, the prince of the cities of Lower Egypt, the prophet of Nit, the Lady of Saïs, (20) and the high-priest of Ptah (of Memphis), TEFNEKHT.

When they had advanced further, they inflicted on them a great defeat, greater than ever, and captured their ships upon the river. When the survivors had fled, they landed on the West side, in the territory of the city of Pa-Pek. When the earth had become light in the early morning (of the next day), the warriors of his Majesty advanced (21) against them, and army joined in battle with army. Then they slew much people of them, as well as their horses. No one knows the number of the slain. Those that were left alive fled to Lower Egypt, because of the tremendous overthrow, for it was more terrible than ever.

List of the people of them that were killed: Men [. . . . .]

(22) The king Nimrod (advanced) up the river to Upper Egypt, because the news had been brought to him that the city of Hermopolis Magna had fallen into the power of the enemy—meaning the warriors of his Majesty—who had captured its inhabitants and their cattle. Then he came before Hermopolis. But the army of his Majesty was on the river at the harbour (23) of the Hermopolitan nome. When they heard that the king (Nimrod) had surrounded them on all four sides, so that none could go either out or in, they sent a messenger to his Majesty Amen Meri-Piankhi, the dispenser of life, (to tell him) of the complete over-throw which had been prepared for them by all the forces of his Majesty (King Nimrod).

Then was his Majesty furious against them, like a panther, (and

said) : 'Then did they leave (24) a remnant of the army of Lower
Egypt surviving, and suffer to escape from them whosoever would
escape in order to give information, that he might advance, so that
they should not suffer death, (but) make their escape ? I swear,
as truly as I love the god Ra, as truly as I hallow the god Amen,
I will myself go down the river ; I will frustrate (25) what
that man has done ; I will drive him back, even should the struggle
last long ; after performing the solemnity of the customary rites of
the new year's feast. I will offer a sacrifice to my father Amen at
his beautiful feast ; he shall celebrate his procession on the beautiful day of the new year. I will go in peace to behold Amen on his
beautiful feast of the Theban month (Paophi). I will cause his
image to go forth (26) to Apet of the south on his beautiful feast of
the Theban month (Paophi), in the night of the feast which is established for Thebes, and which the Sun-god Ra first instituted
for him. I will conduct him back to his temple, where he sits on
his throne. But on the day of the god's return, on the second of
the month Athyr, I will let the people of Lower Egypt feel the
weight of my finger.'

(27) Then the king's warriors remained in Egypt. They had
heard of the wrath which his Majesty had conceived against them.
Then they fought against the city of Pa-Mas, in the Oxyrhynchite
nome, and they took it like a flood of water. And they sent a
message to his Majesty ; but his heart was not appeased thereby.

Then they fought against the very strong city of Ta-tehan
(now Tehneh), and they found it filled (28) with soldiers, of
the best warriors of Lower Egypt. Then they made the batter-
ing-ram play against it, which threw down its walls. They inflicted on them a great overthrow—no one knows the numbers—
among them (the slain) was also the son of the satrap Tefnekht.
Then they sent a message to his Majesty ; but his heart was not
appeased thereby.

(29) Then they fought against the city of Ha-Bennu and
broke it open, and the warriors of his Majesty entered. Then they
sent a message to his Majesty ; but his heart was not appeased
thereby.

In the month Tehuti, on the 9th day of the month, when his
Majesty had gone down to Thebes, he celebrated the feast of Amen
in the Theban month Paophi. When his Majesty had sailed
(30) down the river to the city of Hermopolis Magna, he came
forth out of the cabin of his ship, caused the horses to be harnessed,
and mounted his war-chariots, the names of which were, 'The fear
of his Majesty reaches to the Asiatics,' and 'The hearts of all men
fear him.' When his Majesty had marched on, he threw himself

upon the (31) haters of his warriors, full of wrath against them, like the panther, (saying) : 'Are they not standing there ? Fight, I tell you ! This is loitering over my business ! The time is at length come once for all to make the land of Lower Egypt respect me.' A mighty overthrow was inflicted upon them, frightful for the slaughter which they suffered.

His tent was pitched on the south-west of Hermopolis Magna. The city remained cut off (32) continually. A rampart was thrown up, to overtop the high wall of the fortress. When the wooden structure (raised) against it was high enough, the archers shot in (their arrows), and the catapults (*lit.* slinging machines) threw stones, so as continually to kill the people. This lasted three days. Then those in Hermopolis had become stinking, and had lost their sweet savour. (33) Then Hermopolis surrendered and supplicated the king of Lower Egypt, and ambassadors came out of it and presented themselves with all things good to behold —gold, precious stones, garments of cotton—(before his Majesty), who had put on the serpent-diadem, in order to inspire respect for his presence. But several days passed before they dared to supplicate his Uræus. Then (Nimrod) sent forth (34) his wife, the queen and daughter of a king, Nes-thent-nes, to supplicate the queens and the royal concubines and the king's daughters and sisters. And she threw herself prostrate in the women's house before the queens (saying) : 'Pray come to me, ye queens, king's daughters, and king's sisters ! Appease Horus, the ruler of the palace. Exalted is his person, great his triumph. Cause (35) his [anger to be appeased before] my [prayer] ; else he will give [over to death the king, my husband, but] (36) he is brought low.' When she had finished [her speech, her Majesty] (37) was moved in her heart at the supplication of the queen . . . . . (38–50) (*This part of the inscription is entirely erased*) . . . . . (51) before (?) thee. Who is leader ? Who is leader ? Who, when he is led, who is led . . . . (52) to thee the boon of living. Is not the swollen stream like an arrow ? I am . . . .

(53) The inhabitants of the South bowed down ; the people of the North said, 'Let us be under thy shadow ! If any one has done wrong, let him [come] to [thee] (54) with his peace-offerings. This is the helm which turns about (like a ship) its governor towards him who belongs (henceforth) to the divine person. He has seen the fire in . . . . (55) Worth naught is the great man, who is admired for his father's sake. Thy fields are full of little men.'

Then he (Nimrod) threw himself prostrate before his Majesty [speaking thus : 'Thou art] (56) Horus, the lord of the palace

Wilt thou not grant me to become one of the king's servants, and to pay tribute of my productions for the treasury [like those who pay contributions] (57) of their productions? I will furnish thee more than they do.'

Then he offered silver, gold, blue and green stones, iron, and many jewels. (58) Then was the treasury filled with these gifts. He led forward a horse with his right hand, in his left was a sistrum, and the striking-plate was of gold and blue stones. Then the king went forth out of (59) his palace, and betook himself to the temple of Tehuti, the lord of the city of the eight (gods) (Akhmun, Hermopolis Magna). He sacrificed oxen, calves, and birds, to his father Tehuti, the lord of the city of the eight (gods), and to the eight deities in the (60) temple of the eight deities. And the people of Hermopolis played a hymn, and they sang : ' Beautiful is Horus, who abides in (61) his city, the son of the Sun, Piankhi ! Thou makest festival for us, as if thou wert the tutelar lord of the nome of Hermopolis.'

When the king had entered into (62) the house of King Nimrod, he visited all the chambers of the king, his treasury and his storerooms. And he was content.

Then came (63) to him the king's wives and the king's daughters, and they praised his Majesty after the manner of women, but his Majesty did not turn his countenance upon (64) them.

When his Majesty visited the stables and the studs of foals, he observed that [they had] (65) let them starve. He said : ' I swear, as surely as the youthful Sun-god Ra loves me, as surely as I breathe in life, it is a viler thing to my heart (66) to let the horses starve, than all the other faults that thou hast committed. That thou hast laid thy heart bare through this, evidence is furnished me of thy habitual views (!). (67) Hast thou forgotten that the shadow of God rests upon me? The proof thereof shall not be wanting to him on my part ! (68) Would that another had done such a thing to me, an ignorant man, not a haughty one, as he is ! I was born out of my mother's womb, and created out of the egg of a divine essence. I was begotten (69) by a god. By his name ! I will not forget him in what he has commanded me to do.' Then he ordered his (Nimrod's) possessions to be assigned to the treasury, (70) and his granaries to the property of the god Amen of Apet.

When the prince of Heracleopolis Magna, Pef-tot-Bast, had come with his presents (71) to the great house of the god-like one (Piankhi), with gold, silver, fine precious stones, horses from the best of his stable, then he threw himself prostrate before his Majesty, and spake thus : 'Hail to thee, Horus, (72) mighty king ! Bull

that wardest off the bulls ! The abyss has swallowed me up ; I am
sunk in darkness ; give me light (73) for my countenance. I have
not found a friend in the day of adversity, nor one that could stand
in the day of battle save thee, O king ! (74) Chase away the darkness from before my face. I will be a servant (to thee), together
with my subjects of Heracleopolis Magna, who will pay tribute
(75) to thy house ; for thou art like the god Horemkhu, the prince
of the planets. He is what thou art as king. He does not pass
away, (76) thou dost not pass away, O king of Upper and Lower
Egypt, Piankhi, the ever-living.'

When his Majesty had sailed downwards to the point of the
lake region (the Fayûm), to the place of the sluice (77) of the canal,
he came to the city of Pa-Sekhem-kheper-Ra (the capital of Uasarken I.), whose walls were high and its citadel close shut, filled with
the best troops of the land of Lower Egypt. Then he sent a
summons to it, saying : 'To live in dying is dreadful : (78) thy life
shall be [rescued] from death, if (the gates) are at once opened. If
you do not open to me, you are counted in the number of my fallen
foes. It is an affront to a king, to shut him out before the gates.
Your life will be good for the high court of justice, good will be this
day, from him who loves death to him who hates life. (79) [Make
your decision] in the face of the whole land.'

Then they sent an embassy to his Majesty, to address him thus:
'The shadow of God rests upon thee, thou son of the goddess
Nut. He lends thee his hand. What thy heart wishes, that
forthwith happens. As the word is uttered from the mouth of
God, so it comes to pass. Thou art born of God, to behold us in
thy hand. Safe is the city which is thine, and the possessions in
its houses.'

(80) Then they threw open all that was shut. Whoever would
go in went in, and whoever would come out came out ; his Majesty
did as it pleased him. Then they came out with a son of the
prince Tefnekht. When the warriors of his Majesty had entered,
they did not kill one of the inhabitants. He found (81) [the
people of the prince busy] with the officers of the court in putting
seals on his property. But his treasuries were assigned to the
(king's) treasury, and his granaries to the property of his father,
the Theban Amen-Ra.

When his Majesty had sailed down the river, he reached the
city of Meri-Tmu (Meidûm), the city of Sekar, the lord of enlightenment. It was shut and not to be entered, for their intention was
to fight, and [they had] (82) gathered [many warriors, but] they
were afraid of his power, and they (the people of the city) had
shut their mouth. Then his Majesty sent them a message, to this

effect : 'Two ways lie before you ; it is for you to choose.   Decide
to open, then you shall live ; to shut, then you are doomed to death.
My Majesty does not pass by any shut-up city.'   Then they opened
forthwith.   His Majesty entered.   He offered (83) [a sacrifice to
the] goddess Men-hi,[1] the author of enlightenment.   He assigned
his treasury (to his own), and his granaries to the property of the
god Amen of Apet.

When his Majesty had sailed down the river to the city of Thi-
taui (on the borders of Upper and Lower Egypt), he found the fortress shut and the walls full of warriors of Lower Egypt.   Then
they opened the bolts and threw themselves prostrate (84) [saying
to] his Majesty : 'Thy father hath given thee the charge of his inheritance.   Thou art the world ; thou art that which is in it ; thou
art the lord of all that is upon the earth.'   When his Majesty had
set out, a great sacrifice was offered to the gods in this city, of oxen,
calves, birds, and all things good and clean.   Then his treasury was
assigned to the treasury, and his granaries to the property (85) [of
the god Amen of Apet].

When his Majesty had reached the city of Memphis, he sent it
a summons to this effect : 'Shut not ; fight not ; thou seat of the
god Shu from the beginning of all things !   Whoever will go in,
let him go in ; and whoever will come out, let him come out.   No
traveller shall be molested.   I wish to celebrate a sacrifice to the
god Ptah, and to the gods of Memphis.   I wish to do homage to
the god Sekar in his crypt.   I wish to behold the god Anbu-res-ef.
Then I will proceed down the river in peace.   (86) [No harm shall
befall the inhabitants] of Memphis ; let them prosper and be in
health ; the children shall not weep.   Look at each several district of the South country.   No one was killed, except the impious
who blasphemed the gods.   None but felons were delivered up to
execution.'

But they shut up their fortress, and sent out warriors to some
of the warriors of his Majesty (disguised) as workmen, master-
masons, and sailors, (87) [who approached] the harbour of Memphis.
For at the same time the prince of Saïs had arrived at the city of
Memphis towards evening, having given directions to his warriors,
his sailors, and all the captains of his warriors, 8,000 men.   And
he had very very urgently given them (the following) directions :
'Memphis is full of warriors, of the best of Lower Egypt.   There
is in it wheat, durra, and all manner of corn of the granaries, in
abundant measure ;[2] all sorts of implements (88) [of war are pre-
pared].   The citadel [is well fortified] ; the battlements are strong,

---

[1] A form of Sekhet, the lion-headed goddess.
[2] Lit. 'in the measure of an inundation.'

where the work is planned with reference to the river which surrounds it on the East. At that part no assault is possible. The
cattle-layers are full of oxen. The treasury is provided with all
that is needful, of silver, gold, bronze, woven stuffs, balsam, honey,
butter. I am advancing, I will give up their possessions to the
under-kings of the South country. I am (again) opening their
territories ; I will be (89) [their deliverer. Only wait during] the
days till my return.'

When he had mounted his horse—for he did not desire his
war-chariot—and when he had gone down the river through fear
of his Majesty, the earth grew light on (the next) morning very
early. Then his Majesty came to the city of Memphis, and he
landed on its north side, and he found the water reaching up to
the walls. The vessels came to land (90) at the harbour of Memphis. Then his Majesty saw how strong the city was. The walls
were high, quite newly built, the battlements were formed strongly,
so that there was no means of assaulting it. Among the warriors of his Majesty every one spoke in conversation of all possible modes of attack, and every one said : 'Come now ! Let
us blockade (91) [the city.' Whereupon the king said :] 'The
soldiers must not make too many words about the passage to
it. We will raise the earth up to its wall ; we will fasten wood-
works together ; we will set up masts ; we will make a bridge
of the yard-arms, we will reach by help of them to all its parts
by means of the ladders and (92) [bridges] against its north side,
so as to raise up the earth to its wall. So shall we find a way
for our feet.

Then was his Majesty furious against them, like a panther. He
said : 'I swear, as truly as I love the Sun-god Ra, as truly as I
reverence my father Amen, I have found that all this happens
according to the will of Amen. But this comes from the fact that
the people say : (93) "[The king had an easy task] with the districts
of the South. They opened to him even from afar." They do not
regard Amen in their heart ; they do not know that what he has
ordained must happen, in order that his presence may show itself,
and that his power may be manifest. I will come upon them like
a flood of water. What he commands me (94) [that shall happen].'

Then he ordered his ships and his warriors to advance, to fight
against the harbour of Memphis. They brought to him all the
vessels, all the barges, all the passenger-vessels and ships of burthen,
as many as there were of them. The landing took place at the
harbour of Memphis. The foremost landed at the houses [of the
port. (95) The inhabitants of it, great and] small, wept because
of all the army of his Majesty. Then came his Majesty in person,

to lead on the ships, as many as there were. Then his Majesty ordered his warriors : ' Take heed in encircling the walls and entering the dwelling-houses from the river. Each of you, when he has set foot on the wall, let him not remain standing in his place. (96) [Go forwards], do not press the commanders back ; that would be miserable to bear. Our fortress is the South country ; let our landing-place be the North country ; we will establish ourselves in the city of Maki-taui (a quarter of Memphis).'

Then was Memphis taken, like an inundation, and many people in it were killed or were brought alive as prisoners to the king. When (97) [the earth] grew light, on the second day, his Majesty sent people to the city, to guard the temples of God. For it was of great moment with him, on account of the supreme holiness of the gods, to offer libations of water to the chief gods of Memphis, and to purify Memphis with salt, balsam, and frankincense, and to set the priests in their place upon their feet. His Majesty went into the house (98) [of Ptah], purifying himself with the holy water in the star chamber. He performed all that is prescribed for the king. He entered the house of the god, where a great sacrifice was prepared to his father Ptah of his south wall, of bulls, calves, birds, and of all good things.

When his Majesty had entered his house, the inhabitants heard thereof in all the districts that lie round about Memphis (namely), Heri the town, Peni- (99) na-auaa, the tower of Bui, and the village of Biu. They opened their gates, and they fled all at once, without any one's knowing whither they were gone.

Upon the arrival of Auputh, and the general A-ka-neshu, and the hereditary lord Pet-Ise, (100) and all the princes of Lower Egypt, with their presents, to behold the grace of his Majesty, the treasuries and the granaries of the city of Memphis were assigned to the possession of Amen, of Ptah, and of the company of divinities in the city of Ptah.

When the earth grew light, at the dawn of the next morning, his Majesty proceeded eastward. A libation of holy water was poured out to the god Tmu of Khar-kharan (Babylon), (101) and to the host of divinities in the temple of Pa-Paut, a grotto, and to the gods there, of bulls, calves, and birds, in order that they might grant life, prosperity, and health, to the king of Upper and Lower Egypt, Piankhi, the ever-living.

His Majesty proceeded to On, over the hill of Babylon, along the road of the god Sep to Babylon. His Majesty entered the tent, which (was pitched) on the west side of the canal of Ao. He performed his purification by bathing in the middle (102) of the lake Kebhu, and he washed his face with the milk of the Nun (i.e.

with the water of the rising Nile), where Ra is wont to wash his face. His Majesty went to the sand-hill in On, and offered a great sacrifice on the sand-hill in On, before the Sun-god Ra at his rising, of white cows, milk, balsam, and frankincense, of the best and (103) the most fragrant woods.

Returning and on his way to the temple of the Sun, he was greeted most warmly by the overseer of the house of the god, and the leader of the prayers pronounced the formula 'of the keeping away of evil spirits from the king.' The arrangement of the house of stars was completed, the fillets were put on, he was purified with balsam and holy water, and the flowers were presented to him for the house of the obelisk (Ha-Benben). He took the flowers, ascended (104) the stairs to the great window, to look upon the Sun-god Ra in the house of the obelisk. Thus the king himself stood there. The prince was alone. He drew back the bolt and opened the doors, and beheld his father Ra in the exalted house of the obelisk, and the morning-bark of Ra and the evening-bark of Tmu. The doors were (then) shut, the sealing-clay was laid (105) on, and the king himself impressed his seal. He commanded the priests (as follows) : 'I have satisfied myself of the secure closing ; none other of all the kings shall enter any more.' As he stood there, they threw themselves prostrate before his Majesty, while they spake thus : 'May Horus, the friend of the city of On, endure and increase and never vanish away !' On his return, as he entered the temple of Tmu, the statue of (106) his father, the god Tmu, the creator, the king of On, was brought in (in procession).

Then came the king Uasarken to behold the grace of his Majesty.

When the earth grew light, at the dawn of the next morning, the king took the road to the harbour, and the foremost of his ships sailed to the harbour of the nome of Athribis. There a tent was pitched for his Majesty on the south of the place (called) Ka-hani on the east side of the (107) nome of Athribis.

When the kings of Upper Egypt, and the princes of Lower Egypt, all the grand-masters of the whole body of fan-bearers, all the grand-masters of the whole body of the king's grandsons, had arrived from the West country and from the East country and from the islands between, with the purpose of beholding the grace of his Majesty, the hereditary lord Pet-Ise laid himself prostrate (108) before his Majesty, saying thus : 'Come to the nome of Athribis ; look upon the god Khent-Khethi of the cities ; honour the goddess Khui ; offer a sacrifice to Horus in his temple, of bulls, calves, and birds ; enter into my house, I lay open to thee my treasury, with the possessions inherited from my father. I give thee gold after the desire of thy heart, (109) green stones, heaped up before thy face, and numerous horses of the noblest breed out of the stalls, the best from the prince's stable.'

When his Majesty had gone into the temple of Horus Khent-Khethi a sacrifice was offered of bulls, calves, and birds to his father, Horus-Khent-Khethi, the lord of Kem-ur (Athribis). (Then) his Majesty went into the house of the hereditary lord Pet-Ise, who made him a present of silver, gold, (110) blue and green stones, a great abundance of every sort, woven stuffs, cloths of byssus in great number, beds covered with linen, frankincense, oil in anointing-vials, stallions and mares, of the best of his stable. He took an oath of expurgation before God, in the presence of those kings of Upper Egypt and of the great princes of the land of (111) Lower Egypt—(for) every one of them (had said that) he had hidden away his horses and had concealed his riches, because they desired that he might die the death of his father—(and he spake thus) : 'An abhorrence to me is this, that ye desire to crush a servant (of the king). Be well assured, that the sovereign is on my side. Your talk is an abhorrence to me, that I have hidden from his Majesty the whole inheritance (112) of the house of my father. The gold, the golden objects (set) with precious stones, in all manner of vessels and rings for the hands, the golden neckchains, the breast ornaments composed of precious stones, the talismans for every part of the body, the head-bands, the earrings, and all other royal array, all the vessels of gold and jewels for the king's ablutions,—all these (113) I here openly present. The stuffs of byssus and the woven cloths by thousands, are of the best from my house. I know now that thou art content with them. Go into the prince's stable, choose according to thy pleasure of all the horses whichever thou desirest.' And his Majesty did so.

And the kings and the princes said to his Majesty : 'Let us go (each) to our city; we will open (114) our treasuries ; we will select whatever thy heart loveth : we will bring to thee the best of our stable, the most excellent of our horses.' Then his Majesty did so.

This is the list of them : namely :

King UASARKEN of Bubastis and Uu-n-Ra-nefer ;

King AUPUTH of the city of Thent-ram and Ta-ain-ta ;

(115) Prince T'A-AMEN-AUF-ANKH of Mendes and Ta-ap-Ra ;

His eldest son, a lord, captain of Hermopolis Parva, ANKH HOR ;

Prince A-KA-NESHU of Sebennytus, of Hebi (Iseum), and of Samhud (Diospolis Parva) ;

Prince and General PA-THENEF, of Pa-Saptu and in Ap-en-An-buhat ;

(116) Prince and General PA-MA of Busiris ;

Prince and General NES-NA-KETI of Xoïs ;

Prince and General NEKHT-HOR-NA-SHENNU of Pa-Garer (Phagroriopolis) ;

Prince and General (unnamed) of Ta-Ur (Tanis) ;

Prince and General (unnamed) of Bekhen (Ostracine) ;

(117) Prophet of Horus, the lord of Letopolis, PET-HOR-SAM-TAUI ;

Prince HE-RO-BISA of the city of the goddess Sekhet, the lady of Sa, and of the city of Sekhet, the lady of Hesani ;

Prince T'A-KHI-AU of Khent-nefer ;

Prince PA-BI-SA of Babylon and Nilopolis (in the Heliopolitan nome).

They brought to him their presents of all good things ; (118) of gold, silver, [blue and green stones], of [stuffs, beds] covered with linen, of frankincense, of (119) anointing-vials, of . . . . trappings (?) well adapted for the horses, (120) of . . . . .

After this (messengers) came to his Majesty saying : (121) ['The king and general Tefnekht of] the city of [Saïs] has assembled his [warriors]. He has razed the walls (122) [of his city,] he has set fire to [his] treasury, [he has fled to the islands] in the midst of the river, he has strengthened the city of Mas-di (123) with his warriors. Whatever [he needs] is brought to him.'

Then his Majesty ordered his soldiers to go forth (124) and see what had happened, and his body-guards were entrusted to the hereditary lord Pet-Ise. Then they came to report to (125) his Majesty as follows : ' We have killed all the people that we found there.' Then his Majesty gave rewards to (126) the hereditary lord Pet-Ise. When the king and general Tefnekht heard this, he sent (127) an ambassador to the place where his Majesty was staying, to supplicate his grace thus : ' Be of friendly mind ! I have not beheld thy face in (128) the days of disgrace. I cannot stand before thy fire. My manhood is in thy power, for thou art the god Nub in the land of the South, (thou art) Mentu, (129) the powerful bull. If thou settest thy face towards anything, thou findest no servant (able) to resist thee, so that I betook myself to the islands of the great river. (130) I am full of anguish before thy presence on account of the sentence, that the flaming fire is preparing enmity for me. (131) Is not your Majesty's heart softened by all that you have done to me ? If I have been a despiser of the truth, punish me not after the measure of my guilt. (132) Measured with the balance is the produce in ounces. Thou hast dealt it to me threefold. The seed is sown for thee, which was (sown) for me. Is it then proper to cut down (133) the fruit-trees, instead of gathering them (i.e. the fruit) ? By thy name !

The fear of thee is in my body, and distress before thee in my bones. I sit not in (134) the festive hall (*lit.* the chamber of mead), nor do I take down the harp. I eat bread for hunger, and I drink water for (135) thirst every day, since thou hast heard of my name. A shivering is in my bones, my head is shorn, my garments (136) are old, in order that I may appease the goddess Nit. Long is the race which has brought thee to me. Turn thy (face from) above on me who am below. Is it well to (137) torment my existence? Purify thy servant from his haughtiness. Come! receive my property for thy treasury : (138) gold and jewels, also the most excellent of the horses. They may pay for all. (139) Let a messenger straightway come to me. Let him chase away the anguish from my heart. My desire is to go up into a sanctuary before him : I will purify myself by an oath (140) before God.'

Then his Majesty sent the leader of the prayers, Pet-Amen-nestaui, and the general Pa-ur-Maat. He (i.e. Tefnekht) presented (141) them with silver and gold, with robes and jewels. He went up into a sanctuary. He prayed to God, he (142) purified himself by an oath before God, speaking thus : 'I will not transgress the king's command, nor will I neglect (143) the words of his Majesty. I will not compass harm to any prince without thy knowledge. I will behave according to the words (144) of the king, and will not transgress what he has commanded.' With this his Majesty was satisfied.

Tidings were brought to (145) his Majesty : 'The city of Crocodilopolis has opened its fortress and the city of Matennu has surrendered.'

(146) Thus no district was shut against his Majesty, of the nomes of the South and of the North. The West and the East and the islands in the midst had submitted through fear before him, and (147) brought their presents to the place where his Majesty resided, as subjects of the palace.

When the earth grew light, in the morning, (148) very early, there came the two kings of the South and two kings of the North, with their royal serpent-diadems, to worship before the presence (149) of his Majesty. With them also the kings of Upper Egypt and the princes of Lower Egypt, who came to behold the grace of his Majesty. (150) Their legs were the legs of women. They did not enter the king's house, because they were unclean, (151) and besides they ate fish, which is an abomination to the king. But as for King Nimrod, he went (152) into the king's house, because he was clean and ate no fish. They stood there (153) upon their legs, every one at the entrance of the king s house.

Then were the ships laden with silver, gold, bronze, (154) stuffs, and all the good things of Lower Egypt, and with all the products of Phœnicia and with all the woods of the Holy Land.

When his Majesty sailed up (155) the river, his heart was glad. All its banks resounded with music. The inhabitants in the West and East took their drums (156) to make music at his Majesty's approach. To the notes of the music they sang, 'O King, thou conqueror! (157) Piankhi! O thou conquering king! Thou hast come and thou hast smitten Lower Egypt. Thou madest the men (158) as women. The heart of thy mother rejoices, who bore (such) a son, for he who begat thee dwells in the valley (of the dead). Happiness to thee, the cow, (159) who hast borne the bull! Thou shalt live for ever in after ages! Thy victory shall endure, thou king and friend of Thebes!'

Piankhi does not seem to have enjoyed his success for long. Whether it was that the Assyrians again got the upper hand or that Tefnekht or his sons rose up afresh and, supported by the petty kings of the lower country, threw off the Ethiopian sovereignty, is unknown, but Nut, the successor of Piankhi, was left in possession of Patoris only, with its capital, Thebes. The war which he undertook against Lower Egypt was in consequence of a dream, and seems to have had some temporary success, rather from special circumstances than through the bravery of his army. But he dedicated to the fame of this passing victory a memorial stone, which was found several years ago on the site of the ruins of Napata. The inscription engraved thereon is accompanied by a sculptured representation, consisting of a double relief, on the right side of which the king testifies his devotion for the Theban Amen-Ra. To the name of the king is appended a cartouche on which he is designated as Ba-ka-Ra. Behind him is seen 'the king's sister and wife, the queen of Egypt Ge-ro-a-ro-pi.' She must have been married a second time to an Egyptian of high rank, named Usa-Hor, and have borne a son, to whom the inscriptions assign the title of a 'royal grandson.' The monuments name him Pet-Amen.

On the left hand, King Nut himself offers a breast-plate with chains, as a talisman, to the Theban Amen 'of the holy mountain' (that is, Noph or Napata), who is here represented with a ram's head. He is accompanied by 'the king's sister, the queen of Ta-Khent (Nubia).' While this sister of the king is designated as 'Queen of Nubia,' another, who was also a wife of Meri-Amen Nut, is called 'Queen of Egypt.' We have here an example of the distinguished position which the women of the Ethiopian court must have occupied.

The inscription begins with titles of honour; and the Oriental pomp of rhetoric without a background of facts is here conspicuous. It runs thus :—

On the day on which he was brought forth to light, he became as a god Tmu for mankind. He is the lord of the two horns, a prince of the living, a great king, who has taken possession of the whole world. Of a victorious arm in the day of slaughter, of piercing look on the day [of battle], a slayer and lord of the strong, like the god Mentu, powerful like a raging lion, prudent as the god Hiser (i.e. Tehuti), beautiful as he sets forth upon the river as pursuer and achiever of his purpose, bringing back what he has won. He gained possession of this land without fighting : no one had the power to resist him.

.   .   .   .

(3) In the first year, which was that of his coronation as king, (4) his Majesty had a dream in the night. There were two serpents, the one on his right hand, the other on his left. When his Majesty woke, he did not find them. Then spake his Majesty [to the interpreters of dreams] : (5) 'Why has such a thing happened to me ?' Then they explained it to him, speaking as follows :—'The land of Upper Egypt is thine. Thou shalt take possession of the land of Lower Egypt. The double crown shall adorn thy head. The land is given to thee in its length and in its breadth. Amen, besides whom (6) there is no other god, will be with thee.'

His Majesty held a court, sitting on the throne of Horus, in this year. When his Majesty had come out from the place where he had been staying, as Horus came out of his marsh, then he went forth : in [his suite were] (7) a hundred thousand, who marched near him.

His Majesty said : 'So may the dream come true.' For this was indeed a thing that coincided with his purpose ; and it would have fallen out ill, if he had desisted from it.

When his Majesty had repaired to the city of Noph (Napata), no one was [with him] (8) when he entered it. After his Majesty had visited the temple of Amen of Noph, on the holy mountain, his heart was strengthened when he had seen the Theban god Amen-Ra on the holy mountain. They presented him with garlands for the god. (9) Then his Majesty caused Amen to be brought out (in procession) from Noph. He prepared for him a rich sacrifice, for he offered to him what [was acceptable to] his heart : 36 bulls, 40 jars of mead, 100 asses.

When his Majesty had sailed down the river to the land of Upper Egypt, he wished to behold the god (10) whose being is more hidden than that of all the gods (i.e. the god Amen).

When he arrived at Elephantiné, his Majesty put in at Elephantiné. When he had come into the temple of Khnem-Ra, the lord of the city of the new water (i.e. the inundation), (11) he caused the god to be brought out (in procession). A rich sacrifice was prepared for him. He offered bread and mead to the gods of the two sources. He propitiated the river in its hidden cave.

When his Majesty had sailed down the river towards [the territory of the city of] Thebes, which belongs to Amen, then his Majesty landed (12) before Thebes. When his Majesty had entered the temple of the Theban Amen-Ra, there came to him the chief priest and the ministers of the temple of Amen-Ra, (13) the Theban god, and they brought him flowers for him whose being is hidden. And his Majesty's heart was glad, when he beheld this house of the god. He caused the Theban Amen-Ra to be brought out (in procession), and a great feast was celebrated in all the land.

(14) When his Majesty sailed down the river towards Lower Egypt, then the inhabitants on the right and on the left bank were jubilant, great was the rejoicing. They said : 'Go onward in the peace of thy name, in the peace of thy name ! Dispense life (15) through all the land ; that the temples may be restored, which are hastening to ruin ; that their statues of the gods may be set up after their manner ; that the revenues may be given to the gods and the goddesses, and the offerings for the dead to the deceased ; (16) that the priest may be established in his place ; and that all may be fulfilled according to the holy learning' (i.e. of the ritual). Even those, whose intention it was to fight, were moved with joy.

When his Majesty had come to Memphis, and (17) the rebels

(*lit.* the sons of revolt) had made a sally, to fight against his Majesty, then his Majesty inflicted on them a great slaughter, without number. And his Majesty took Memphis, and entered into the temple of (18) Ptah of his south wall. He prepared a sacrifice to Ptah-Sekar, he adored Sekhet, whose love is so great. For the heart of his Majesty was joyful for what his father Amen of Noph had done for him.

And he issued an ordinance, (19) to enlarge [the temple of Ptah], and that a new hall should be built for him. No such building was seen in the times of his predecessors. His Majesty caused it to be built of stones which were inlaid with gold. (20) Its panelling was made of acacia-wood, (21) which was impregnated with frankincense of the land of Punt. Its doors were of white brass, and (22) their frames of iron. He built for him a second hall as an outbuilding behind, wherein to milk his milk (23) from a numerous herd of 116 goats. No one can count the number of young calves (24) with their mothers.

When all this was done, his Majesty sailed downwards, to fight with the princes of (25) Lower Egypt, for they had retired within their walls in order [to avoid battle] near their towns. Before these his Majesty spent many days, but none of them came out (26) to fight with his Majesty.

After his Majesty had sailed up to Memphis, he rested in his palace, and meditated a resolution (27) with himself, to send his warriors to seek them.

[Before the army set out], tidings were brought to him, saying : 'The great princes have come to (28) the place where his Majesty resides. [What does] our lord [decide] ? ' His Majesty said, ' Are they come to fight ? Or are they come to serve me ? In that case they shall live from this hour.' (29) Then spake they to his Majesty, 'They are come to serve the great lord, our governor.' The king said : ' My governor is that glorious god, the Theban Amen on the holy mountain. The great god is gracious to him who confesses his name ; he watches (30) over him who loves him ; he grants strength to him who does his will, and transgresses not his bidding. He who walks according to his commandments will not stagger, for he leads him and guides him. It is he that speaks to me in the night (31) of that which I shall see in the day.'

His Majesty said : ' What they wish cannot be transacted at this hour.' They spake before the king : 'They are without, they stand near the king's house.'

When his Majesty had gone forth (32) out of his [palace], then he beheld these princes, who learned to know the god Ra on the horizon. He found them lying prostrate, in order to supplicate before his face. The king speaks : 'Since that is the truth, which Amen decrees, (33) I will act according to the [command that he shall reveal to me]. Lo ! to know what will happen means this— what God ordains, that shall come to pass. I swear, as truly as the Sun-god Ra loves me, as truly as I hallow Amen in his house, I will [enquire of] this glorious god (34) of Noph on the holy mountain whether he stands against me. Whatever he shall say to me, to that let effect be given by all means and in every way. Good for naught is the saying : " O that I had waited with my resolution till the next morning which shall arise ! " (35) I am as a servant [mindful of his master's] interest, and every workman must know what tends to the interest of his Majesty. [Say not, Why] should I wait for the morning, which comes later ? Had I only thy power ! '

Then they answered him and spake thus : 'May this glorious god (36) be thy guide and leader ! May he give what is good into thy hand ! Turn thyself not away from that which shall come out of his mouth, O great king, our lord ! '

When Pi-qe-ro-ro, the hereditary lord and prince of the city of Pa-Saptu, had stood up to speak as follows : (37) 'Kill whom thou wilt ; let live whom thou wilt ; there shall be no r proach against our lord on account of that which is just ;'—then they responded to him all together, speaking thus : ' Grant us the breath of life, for none can live without (38) it. We will serve him (i.e. Amen) as his dependents, just as thou hast said from the beginning, from the day when thou wast made king.'

Then was the heart of his Majesty glad, when he had heard these words. He entertained (39) them with food and drink and all good things.

After many days had passed in this manner, and he had imparted to them all good things, notwithstanding their great number, then they said : 'Shall we stay longer? Is such the will of the great lord, our governor ?' Then spake (40) his Majesty, saying thus : 'Why ?' They speak before his Majesty : 'We would return home to our cities ; we would care for our inhabitants and our servants according to the need of the city.' Then his Majesty let them depart thence (41) (each) to his city, and they remained in life.

Then the inhabitants of the South sailed down the river, and those of the North up the river, to the place where his Majesty resided, and brought all the good things of Upper Egypt and all the riches (42) of Lower Egypt, to propitiate the heart of his Majesty.

May the king of Upper and Lower Egypt, Ba-ka-Ra, the son

of the Sun, Meri-Amen Nut—to him be health, prosperity, life !—
sit enthroned upon the seat of Horus for ever !'

What gives an especial value to this inscription is
the mention of Pi-qe-ro-ro, the prince of the city of
Pa-Saptu, who here comes forward and treats direct
with the Ethiopian. His name appears again in the
Assyrian account of the campaign of Assurbanipal
the son of Esarhaddon against Taharaqa.

King Nut was not permitted to enjoy for long the
crown of Lower Egypt. In Ethiopia as in Egypt a schism
appears to have broken out in the reigning family
which could only be decided by arms. The statement
that Nut 'had gained possession of this land (Ethiopia)
without fighting' clearly alludes to some such circumstances.

With Taharaqa, king of Ethiopia, begins the latest
period of the history of Ancient Egypt. From this
time the classical writers contribute authentic data
respecting the fortunes of their contemporaries the
Egyptian kings. The sovereign just mentioned bore
the title of

NEFER-ATMU-KHU-RA. TAHARAQA I. B.C. 693–666.

According to the Apis-stêlæ this king reigned more
than twenty-six years. To him belonged Patoris with
its capital, Thebes, in which several monuments, mostly
in the form of dedicatory inscriptions, are memorials
of his dominion and presence. He was well known
in antiquity as a conqueror. In the Bible he appears
under the name of Tirhakah ; in the classic writers
as Tearko, Etearchus, Tarakus, and Tarkus : the
Egyptian inscriptions know him simply as the lord of
Kamit, Tesherit, and Kipkip—i.e. Egypt, the red land,
and Ethiopia.

It is to the cuneiform records that historical science

owes the most important elucidation of the reign of this king in Egypt, and of his wars against the great kings of Assyria.   Jules Oppert was the first who deciphered the fragments relating to these wars, and brought out the connection of their contents with the events in Egypt.   The subjoined important text is taken from his work entitled ' Mémoire sur les rapports de l'Égypte et de l'Assyrie dans l'antiquité éclaircis par l'étude des textes cunéiformes' (Paris, 1869) :—

RECORD OF ASSURBANIPAL.

(I.) In my first expedition I went against Muzur (Egypt) and Meluhha (Meroë). Tarquu, the king of Muzur and Ku-u-si (Ethiopia), whom Asur-ah-idin (Assarhaddon), the father who begat me, had subdued, returned out of his land. Trusting in his strength (*lit*. hands) he despised the commandments of Assur and Istar, the great gods, my lords. His heart was hardened, and he sinned of his own will (*lit*. of himself). The kings, satraps, and generals, whom Assarhaddon, my father, had set over the kingdom of Egypt, were driven out by him.

(II.) They betook themselves to Ninua (Nineveh). Against such deeds my heart was moved and my bile (*lit*. liver) was stirred up. I numbered my army and my whole forces, with which the great gods had filled my hands, to bring help to the kings, satraps, generals, and servants, who were expecting my presence (*lit*. face). I set forth speedily and came to the city Karbanit (Canopus). When Tarquu, the king of Egypt and Ethiopia, in the city of Memphis, heard of the arrival of my expedition, he prepared for battle his munitions of war, and counted the host of his warriors.

(III.) Tarquu, king of Egypt and Ethiopia, despised the gods. He put in motion his strength to take possession of Egypt. He disregarded the commandments of the great god Assur, my lord. He trusted in his own strength, and did not observe his own treaties, which my father who begat me had made (with him).   He came from Ethiopia and entered Memphis, and took that city for himself. Upon the Assyrians (*lit*. men of Assur), who were servants in Egypt expecting my presence, whom Assarhaddon, my father, had set over the kingdom in it (Egypt), he ordered his army to inflict death, imprisonment, and plunder.

A messenger came in haste to Nineveh and . . . . . . On account of such deeds my heart was moved and my bile was stirred. I was incensed, and I ordered, by an imperative decree, the Tartan (general), the satraps, with the men of their hands (?), and my chief guards, to start on an expedition to the help . . . . . of the kings, satraps, and servants.   I ordered an expedition to be made to Egypt . . . . (they) went down quickly, and came to Karbanit. Tarquu, (the king of) Kuusi, when he had heard in the city of Memphis of the approach of my army, numbered his host to make war and battle, and drew up his army opposite to my army.

With invocations to Assur, Sin (the Moon-god), the great gods, my lords, I ordered the onslaught of my forces.   In a fierce battle they put them to flight, and conquered with arms the men who served him (lit. of his service).   Fear and terror seized him, and he turned back.   He escaped from Memphis, the city of his kingdom, the place of his honour, and he fled away in ships to save his life (lit. soul).   He left his tent standing and withdrew himself alone and came to Ni (the 'great city,' i.e. Thebes), and gave orders to his men of battle to embark on all the ships and barks (?) that were with him, and he commanded the man set over the barks (?) . . . . .

I gathered together the commander of the satraps of the cities beyond the river, the servants faithful before me, them and their garrisons, their ships, the kings of Egypt, the servants faithful before me, and their garrisons and their ships, in order to drive out Tarquu from Egypt and Ethiopia.   There were more of them than before.   I sent them against Thebes, the city of the empire of Tarquu, the king of Ethiopia.   They went a journey of a month and ten days.   Tarquu, when he heard of the approach of my army, left Thebes, the city of his empire, and went up the river.   My soldiers made a slaughter in that city.

Nikuu (Necho), Sarludari, Paakruru, whom my father had made satraps, sinned against the commandments of Assur and the great gods, my lords, and did not keep to their treaties (with him). They despised the glory of my father, and hardened their hearts to enmity ; they devised a plan of rebellion, and sinned wilfully (lit. of themselves) against their flesh, speaking thus : 'Tarquu will not go back from his designs upon Egypt ; he is afraid, and do ye all watch over your safety (?)'   They sent their envoys to Tarquu, king of Ethiopia, to make peace and friendship (speaking) thus : 'Let peace be made in our league, and let us be friendly to each other.   On this side (i.e. on our part) we pledge our faith ; from no other quarter shall there be a breach in our alliance, O our Lord.   They tried to entice into their league the whole army of Assur, the guards of my dominion ; they prepared what their revenge desired. . . . . .

My judges heard of their designs, and derided their cunning.

They intercepted their envoys with the letters, and perceived the work of their treason. They bound those kings hand and foot in fetters. The justice of Assur, king of the gods, reached them, because they had sinned against the commandments of the great gods. At their hands they found what my will had devised for them. Memphis, Saïs, Mendes, Tanis—all the cities which they had enticed to themselves and which had formed intrigues in the desire of revenge,—I subdued with arms, male and female, small and great ; they did not leave in them one, ... they brought into my presence. Thus (I spake) : 'I am Assur-ban-habal . . . . performing glorious deeds . . . . . they delivered up in the city Karbelmate ("of the great mother," i.e. Saïs).'

(IV.) About 20 kings, satraps, commanders of the cities, who in Egypt had obeyed my father before me—all those kings I gave over to the hand of Nabu-sezibanni, who waited in my presence (Some lines are wanting) . . . . . of Assur, of Istar, of the gods my lords . . . . . I made a great slaughter of his army . . . . . over his army Nabu . . . . .

Nikuu (Necho) was seized with great terror of my Majesty. He left his gods in the city of Memphis, and fled, to save his life, to the middle city, Ni (Thebes). I took that city, and placed my army in it.

Ni-ku-u, king of Memphis and Saïs,

Sar-lu-da-ri, king of Tanis,

Pi-sa-an-hu-ru (Pa-sen-Hor), king of Na-athu-u (Na-athu, Natho),

Pa-ak-ru-ru (Pa-qror), king of Pa-Sa-ptu (Pasapt, in the Arabian nome),

Pu-uk-ku-na-an-ni-pi (Bok-en-nifi), king of Ha-at-hi-ri-bi (Ha-ta hir-ab, Athribis),

Na-ah-ki-e, king of Hi-ni-in-si (Khinensu, Heracleopolis),

Pu-tu-bas-ti (Pef-tot-Bast), king of Zanu (T'aan, Zoan-Tanis),

U-na-mu-nu, king of Na-at-hu-u (Natho),

Har-si-e-su (Hor-se-Ise), king of Zab-an-nuti (Thebnuti, Sebennytus),

Pu-u-iu-ma (Pamai), king of Bi-in-di (Bindid, Mendes),

Shu-shi-in-qu (Shashanq, Sesonchis), king of Pu-si-ru (Pa-Usiri, Busiris),

Tap-na-akh-ti (Tefnekht, Tnephachthus), king of Pu-nu . . . (Pa-Nub, Momemphis ?),

Bu-uk-ku-na-an-ni-pi (Bok-en-nifi), king of Ahnir (On ?),

Ipti-har-si-e-su (Pet-Hor-se-Ise), king of Pi-za-at-ti-hu-ru-un-pi (Pa . . . Hor-en-pa),

Na-ah-ti-hu-ru-an-shi-ni (Nekht-Hor-na-shennu), king of Pa-Sap-ti-nu-ti),

Bu-kur-ni-ni-ip (Bak-en-ran-f, Bocchoris), king of Pa-Ah-nu-ti,
Si-ha-a (Zichiau, Tachos), king of Si-ya-a-tu (Siaut, Lycopolis),
La-mi-in-tu (Na-li-moth, Li-ma-noth = Nimrod), king of Hi-mu-ni
  (Khmunu, Hermopolis Magna),
Is-pi-ma-tu (Psamut), king of Ta-i-ni (Tini, Thinis),
Ma-an-ti-mi-au-hi-e (Mentu-em-ha), king of Ni (Niaa, Thebes) ; —

these (are the) kings, commanders, satraps, who in Egypt had
obeyed my father, (but) who on account of the arms of Tarquu had
forgotten their allegiance. I brought them back to their state of
obedience. I recovered (or, restored) Egypt and Ethiopia, which
my father had conquered, I strengthened the garrisons more than
in former days ; I surrounded them with ditches. With a great
treasure and splendid booty I returned safe to Nineveh.

Afterwards those kings, whom I had subdued, sinned against me
and broke the commandments of the great gods. . . . . . They
revolted, and their heart was hardened in wickedness ; they plotted
the artifices of rebellion ; they sinned wilfully, (saying) : ' Tarquu
will not go back from his designs upon Egypt ; he is afraid. Do
ye all watch over your own safety.' They sent envoys to Tarquu,
king of Ethiopia, to make peace and friendship, saying : ' Let there
be peace in our alliance, and let us be friendly to one another.
On our part we pledge our faith, and we give as security the land
. . . . . the city. . . . . . Never shall there be a desertion in our
alliance to any other party, O our lord.' The army of Assyria, the
support of my dominion, they tried to seduce to their league ; they
prepared for their desired revenge.

My judges heard of their purpose. They intercepted their
envoys and their letters, and perceived the works of their treason.
They seized these kings, and bound them hand and foot in iron
fetters and iron chains. The vengeance of Assur, king of the
gods, reached them, and, because they had sinned against the commandments of the great gods, they experienced at their hands what
my will had devised for them. [The city of Memphis], the city
of Saïs, Mendes, Tanis, and all the cities which they had led away
with them [I took by storm], (putting to death) both great and
small.

According to Oppert's view, here followed the
account of the conquest of Egypt, the return of Taharaqa, his death, and the first exploits of his successor,
Urdamaneh, who succeeded in re-conquering Kamit,
while he advanced as far as Lower Egypt. Thebes
was still his capital. Sardanapalus marched against

Egypt the second time, and defeated the army of Urda-maneh.

[M. Oppert's comments upon this are too interesting to be omitted; he says (p. 72):—

The thirteen lines which follow relate the first campaign of Sardanapalus to the end. This part is, in general, too much muti-lated to enable us to give the text; but we find that Taharaqa comes to Thebes, and conquers it again. Necho, now a prisoner in Assyria, obtains his pardon from Sardanapalus, and returns to Egypt; the Ninevite king giving him presents with the view of detaching him from the Ethiopian. Necho makes his entry into Saïs, and changes its name to Kar-Bel-mate (lord of the two regions). But an Asiatic governor watches over the Egyptian. Meanwhile a son of Necho, who also receives an Assyrian name, Nabu-sezibani, is raised to the kingdom over the city of Mahariba, which is likewise honoured with an Assyrian name, Limir-patisi-Asur, i.e. 'which the lieutenant of Asur governs.' The name of Nabuse-zibani is found in Jeremiah xxxix. 13, נבושזבן Nebo, deliver me!'

This inscription gives the complete sequence of the historical events. It alone gives an account of the first capture of Thebes by the Assyrians. This event, which the cylinder doubtless set forth with fuller details, was the result of the Ethiopian intrigues after the death of Assar-haddon. Taharaqa, in violation of the treaty, had killed, imprisoned, and spoiled the Assyrians who were left in Egypt. Sardanapalus marches against him, and joins in battle with him near the city of Karbanit. The Ethiopian, who had established his residence at Memphis, retreats on Thebes, whither the Assyrians pursue him. The Assyrians, after a forty days' march, reach Thebes and massacre its inhabitants.

This part of the first campaign was contained in the lost portion of the cylinder. After the retreat of Taharaqa, Sardanapalus defeats Necho, and then follow the events forming the narrative which is preserved.

The great document (No. II. above) tells us nothing about the sequel of this campaign. Then the document a (No. III.) continues the war of Sardanapalus against Urdamaneh, which we shall relate presently. Scarcely is Egypt pacified, when Taharaqa dies, and his step-son (his wife's son) Urdamaneh succeeds him. This king invades Egypt, and forces the Ninevite king to try the fortune of war a second time. Urdamaneh had penetrated as far as Memphis, whither Sardanapalus marches to attack him. Here is the sequel of the inscription, after a chasm of about 30 lines :—

'In . . . of my expedition I directed . . . my march. Urdamaneh heard of the advance of my expedition ' - and so forth, as in the text, No. IV.]

RECORD OF ASSURBANIPAL CONTINUED.

(V.) Urdamaneh heard of the advance of my expedition. He [lost?] Me-luhha (Meroë) and Egypt, abandoned Memphis, and fled to Thebes to save his life. The kings, commanders, and satraps, whom I had established in Egypt, came to me and kissed my feet. I directed my march in pursuit of (*lit.* after) Urdamaneh. I came to Thebes, the city of his dominion. He saw the strength of my army, and left Thebes (and) fled to the city of Kipkip. Of that whole city, with thanksgiving to (*lit.* in adoration of) Assur and Istar, my hands took the complete possession. Silver, gold, metals, stones, all the treasures of its palace whatsoever, dyed garments of berom and linen, great horses (elephants? Oppert), men and women, great and small, works of zahali (basalt?) and marble, their kelal and manzas, the gates of their palace, their . . . I tore away and carried to Assyria. I made spoil of [the animals of the land] without number, and [carried them forth] in the midst out of Thebes. . . . of my weapons . . . I caused a catalogue to be made [of the spoil]. I returned in safety to Nineveh, the city of my dominion.

The first lines of another document, which stand in immediate connection with the inscription No. III., present unfortunately great gaps through obliteration. According to Oppert's researches, they contained the enumeration of the tributes and the booty, which the king of Assyria had carried away out of Egypt, as well as the account of the end of the campaign. Sardanapalus increased the tribute imposed by his father, and set up Necho's son, Nabu-sezi-banni, as governor of the western districts of Mahariba (?) and Limirpatesi-Assur. Then the death of Tirhakah is touched upon, and the king continues his record as follows:—

(VI.) The fear of the terror of Assur my lord carried off Tarquu, king of Ethiopia, and his destined night came. Urdamaneh, the son of his wife, sat upon the throne, and ruled the land. He brought Ni (Thebes) under his power, and collected his strength. He led out his forces to make war and battle against my army, and

he marched forth (*lit.* directed his step). With the invocation of
Assur, Sin, and the great gods, my lords, (my warriors) routed him
in a great and victorious battle, and broke his pride. Urdamaneh
fled alone, and entered Thebes, the city of his kingdom.

In a march of a month and ten days through intricate roads
(my warriors) pursued him up to Thebes. They attacked that city
and razed it to its foundations, like a thunderbolt. Gold, silver,
the treasure of the land, metals, precious stones, stuffs of berom and
linen, great horses, men male and female . . . huge apes, the race
of their mountains—without number (even for skilful counters)—
they took out of the midst of the city, and treated as spoil. They
brought it entire to Nineveh, the city of my dominion, and they
kissed my feet.

We have here set before us a remarkable portion
of the history of Egypt, in this case not according to
an Egyptian version, but in the contemporaneous
description of her enemy. In the year B.C. 680
(according to Oppert) Sennacherib, king of Assyria, died
and Esarhaddon reigned in his stead. Towards the
end of his reign (cir. 670) Esarhaddon attacked Egypt,
defeated the reigning king of Ethiopia and Egypt,
Taharaqa, and set up petty kings and satraps in the
land from the northern sea-board to the city of Thebes.
The king on his return out of Egypt had an immense
memorial tablet constructed on the surface of the rock
at the mouth of the Nahr-el-Kelb, near Beyrût, as a
monument of his victory over Tarquu. Henceforth
Esarhaddon styles himself king of Upper and Lower
Egypt and Nubia.

Scarcely had this king died (B.C. 668) when Taharaqa
broke the treaties, seized Memphis, and made a league
with several of the under-kings who had been acknowledged or set up by Esarhaddon for driving the
Assyrians out of Egypt. At the head of the petty kings
stood Nikuu of Memphis and Saïs, Sar-lu-da-ri of Zi'nu,
and Pa-ak-ru-ru of Pa-Saptu. The Assyrian satraps and
other adherents of the late king were driven out, and

fled to Nineveh for protection and help to punish King
Taharaqa. Assurbanipal, the son of Esarhaddon, who
had meanwhile been crowned king, marched against
Egypt with a large army. The further details are
placed before us with all needful clearness in the dupli-
cate records of the cuneiform inscriptions.

In these events a conspicuous part was played by
the king Nikuu, or Neku (Nechao, Necho, Neco), of
Saïs and Memphis, the son of that Tefnekht who had
opposed so long and obstinate a resistance to the Ethiopian king Piankhi. Carried in fetters to Nineveh, he
succeeded in obtaining pardon from Sardanapalus and
his renewed establishment as petty king of Saïs and
Memphis. Of his violent end, according to the Greek
accounts, the inscriptions give us no information.

A thick veil covers the ensuing times, in which the
Ethiopians occupy the foreground of Egyptian history.
Taharaqa, Piankhi (with his oft-named wife, Ameniritis), Shabak and Shabatak—all appear as contemporary, and are frequently introduced in connection
with each other. Their family relationships are set
forth with all exactness in the Genealogical Table facing
p. 325. If we might give credit to the lists of Manetho,
they would seem to have reigned in succession over
Patoris, whose capital, Thebes, retains manifold evi-
dences of their presence; but we are unable to find
anything in the monuments to confirm this succession.

Upon a mutilated statue of King Shabatakh at
Memphis, a brief inscription calls the Pharaoh thus
represented Miptah Shabatak. But the latter name
has already in ancient times been rendered half illegible
by chisel-strokes, obliterating the name of a usurper of
the throne.

At Thebes, the memorials of King Taharaqa and of
an Egyptian under-king have lasted the longest. The

former had given liberal tokens of his regard for the sanctuary of Apis by buildings and presents. The latter had re-established the festivals of the gods after the ancient usage; provided the needful sacrifices; set up statues of the gods (after the Assyrian model), and built the sacred barques; renewed the parts that had fallen into ruin, even to the enclosing wall; and caused the sacred pool and the canals to be lined with stone from the bottom. He also served Taharaqa as his faithful counsellor and helper.

This man was the eminent Egyptian Mentu-em-ha, a son of Nes-Ptah, priest of Amen, and his wife Nes-Khonsu. Mentu-em-ha was fourth prophet, and finally second prophet of the Theban Amen, and, like his father, a governor of Niaa (Thebes). At the same time he is mentioned in the inscriptions as the 'chief of the governors of Patoris.' There must have been some special reason for his high distinction in the Thebaïd, since he himself relates how '[he] had smitten the enemy in the nomes of Patoris.' I recognise in him (as I have said) a faithful ally and friend of Taharaqa, who invested him with the government of the country named above.

He is introduced into the list of the petty kings, as Ma-an-ti-mi-an-hi-e, Sar of Niaa (Thebes)—a tolerably faithful transcription of the Egyptian name, Mentu-em-ha.

In the son of Taharaqa's wife, Urdamaneh, as the Assyrian text calls him, is certainly preserved the name of the king, Rudamen, who is referred to on the Egyptian monuments.

In the Genealogical Table facing p. 325 he is inserted as the second king of this name, inasmuch as his grandfather, Rudamen I., is described as the father-in-law of Pef-tot-Bast, the 'general' and afterwards 'vassal' of

Piankhi, and hence he belongs to a considerably earlier generation.

At length Psamthek I.—the great-grandson of Tefnekht, the opponent of Piankhi—comes to the forefront of the history, as the deliverer of his country from the condition of the Dodecarchy—the name which the Greeks chose to describe that period. His marriage with the Ethiopian heiress, Shep-en-apet—a daughter of King Piankhi, and his beautiful queen Ameniritis—restored peace to the distracted relations of the royal succession. Regarded in this light, the founder of the Twenty-sixth Dynasty appears practically as the reconciler of all rival claims. The daughter of the renowned queen of Cush and Patoris, in giving her hand to the petty king of Saïs, brought Patoris as a wedding-gift to her husband; and thus Egypt was again united into a great kingdom.

The splendid alabaster statue of Ameniritis, which was found at Karnak and now adorns the rooms of the Egyptian Museum in the Gîzeh Palace, near Cairo, is a most important memorial of that age.

Upon it are inscribed these words :—

This is an offering for the Theban Amen-Ra, of Apet, to the god Mentu-Ra, the lord of Thebes.

May he grant everything that is good and pure, by which the divine (nature) lives, all that the heaven bestows and the earth brings forth, to the princess, the most pleasant, the most gracious, the kindest and most amiable queen of Upper and Lower Egypt, the sister of the king [Sabaco] the ever-living, the daughter of the deceased king [Kashta], the wife of the divine one—AMENIRITIS. May she live !

Upon the back she is represented as saying among other things :—

I was the wife of the divine one, a benefactress to her city (Thebes), a bounteous giver for her land. I gave food to the hungry, drink to the thirsty, clothes to the naked.

CHAPTER XVII.

DYNASTIES XXVI.-XXX.[1]

B.C. 666—358.

DYNASTY XXVI.

THE monuments now become more and more silent. The beautiful old capitals Memphis and Thebes were at this time in ruins, or at all events depopulated and deserted, and the strong bulwark of the 'white citadel' of Memphis alone served as a refuge for the persecuted native kings and their warriors in times of need. The Persian satraps dwelt in the old royal halls of the city, and they, after a short interval, took up the part played by the Assyrians, and gave Egypt her final death-blow. Although, by his sage measures, Psamthek I. succeeded in gaining the throne as sole king, for himself and his descendants, and though the monuments, from the ruins of Saïs to the weather-worn rocks of Elephantiné, show traces of the rule of the Pharaohs of the Twenty-sixth Dynasty, the old splendour was gone.

The city of Saïs, at this period the capital of Egypt, in whose temples the goddess Nit was invoked, stood near the sea, and was easily accessible to the Greek and Persian foreigners. When Alexander the Great entered Egypt Saïs in its turn became deserted and forlorn. The new capital of Alexandria—which is called 'the fortress of the king of Upper and Lower Egypt, Alexander, on the shore of the great sea of

[1] For Table of Kings see p. xxvii.

the Ionians (Racotis)'—succeeded to the inheritance of
Thebes, Memphis, and Saïs, assuredly not for the welfare of the Egyptians. All that they lost, all they were
doomed to lose, turned to the profit of the young and
energetic world in the North. The city grew with
incredible speed; her foundations were laid from the
destroyed temples and monuments of Saïs, which found
a new destination in the construction of the royal
palaces, temples, fountains, canals, and other public
works. In short, Alexandria became one of the capitals
of the world.

From this epoch the monuments are absolutely silent,
and there are only isolated inscriptions to be found here
and there, containing perpetual songs of woe. Henceforth the source of our knowledge is the inquisitive
Greek, who, travelling in the Nile valley, gathered his
information from ignorant interpreters.

The art of this period is distinguished by a peculiar
beauty, in which we cannot fail to recognise Greek
influence. An extreme neatness of manipulation in
the drawing and lines, in imitation of the best epochs
of art in earlier times, serves for the instant recognition
of the work of this age, the fineness of which often
reminds one of that of the seal-engraver. The little
statues holding a shrine of the Saïte dignitary Pa-Tebhu,
the monument of Ut'a-Hor-resenet in the Vatican, and
many small objects which now enrich the collection in
the Gîzeh Palace, besides numberless statuettes in
bronze, furnish specimens of the refinement and delicacy of the artists' work during the period now in
question. The return to the good old times is proved
by monuments, not few in number, upon which the
representations, both of lifeless objects and of living
creatures, standing out in relief upon a flat surface, call
to remembrance the masterpieces of the old kingdom.

The stone door-posts of the date of Psamthek-nefer-
sem found in the *débris* at Mitraheny reveal the ancient
Memphite style revived after a lapse of 4,000 years.

To the old Egyptian theology and the esoteric traditions of the priestly schools a new contribution appears to have been made, modelled closely after the
Græco-Asiatic pattern, which was far from harmonising
with the time-honoured wisdom taught in the temples.
Besides the established pantheon there now appear
upon the monuments monstrous forms, demons and
genii, of whom the earlier age with its pure doctrine
had scarcely an idea. Exorcisms of the demons formed
henceforth a special science, which was destined to
supersede the old and half-lost traditional lore of past
ages. The demon-song of 'The aged man who re-
gained his youth, the hoary one who became young,'
the exorcisms of Tehuti and the powers of witchcraft
in league with him, are the favourite themes which
cover the monuments of this remarkable time of tran-
sition. A priest Ankh-Psamthek, a son of the lady
Thent-nub, finds an ancient writing in the temple of
the Mnevis-bull of Heliopolis, in the time of King
Nekht-Hor-heb, and forthwith a whole stone is adorned
with indescribably fine inscriptions and figures—a
unique work of art, which now forms the most remarkable ornament of Prince Metternich's collections at
Königswerth in Bohemia.

All the walls of the sanctuary in the temple of Amen,
founded by Darius I. in the Great Oasis of El-Khargeh
(the ancient Hibis), are covered with demoniacal representations, the explanation of which is little aided by
the annexed inscriptions. Their origin goes back to the
same king, Nekht-Hor-heb. The last Egyptian king,
Nekht-neb-ef, earned the cheap reputation of an exor-
cist. He was a famous magician, who left Egypt and

fled into Ethiopia, laden with rich treasures—never to return!

A flood of light has been thrown on the chronological relations—to the very day as well as year—of the several reigns of the Twenty-sixth Dynasty, since the discovery of the Apis-stêlæ in the Serapeum at Memphis.

Subjoined is a translation of the most important of them:—

TABLET I.

Year 20, month Mesori, day 20, under the reign of King Psamthek I., the Majesty of the living Apis departed to heaven. This god was carried in peace (to his burial) to the beautiful land of the West, in the year 21, month Paophi, day 25; having been born in the 26th year of the king of Upper Egypt, Taharaqa; and after having been inaugurated at Memphis in the month Pharmuthi, on day 9. (The total) makes 21 years.

TABLET II.

After the full name of King Psamthek I., we read :—

In the year 52, under the reign of this god, information was brought to his Majesty : 'The temple of thy father Osiris-Apis, with what is therein, is in no choice condition. Look at the sacred corpses (the bulls), in what a state they are ! Decay has usurped its place in their chambers.' Then his Majesty gave orders to make a renovation in his temple. It was made more beautiful than it had been before.

His Majesty caused all that is due to a god to be performed for him (the deceased bull) on the day of his burial. All the dignitaries took the oversight of what had to be overseen. The sacred corpse was embalmed with spices, and the cere-cloths were of byssus, the fabric becoming for all the gods. His chambers were panelled with ket-wood, sycomore-wood, acacia-wood, and the best sorts of wood. Their carvings were the likenesses of men in a chamber of state. A courtier of the king was appointed specially for the office of imposing a contribution for the work on the inner country and the lower country of Egypt.

As Mariette has already proved, Psamthek I. was the founder of a new gallery and new sepulchral chambers (with panelled woodwork, as the inscription informs us) in the subterranean necropolis of the sacred Apis-bulls. This was done, according to the above inscription, in the 52nd year of his reign, on the occasion of the burial of a bull who died at that time.

TABLET III.

Year 16, month Khoiakh, day 16, under the reign of King Neku, the ever-living, the friend of Apis-Osiris. This is the day of the burial of this god, and of the arrival of this god in peace into the nether world. His interment was accomplished at his burial-place in his holy house in the Libyan Desert near Memphis, after they had fulfilled for him all that is customary in the chambers of purification, as has been done from early times.

He was born in the year 53, in the month Mekhir, on the 19th day, under the reign of King Psamthek I. He was brought into the temple of Ptah (of Memphis) in the year 54, in the month Athyr, on the 12th day. His union with life took place [in the year 16,] month Paophi, day 6. The whole duration of his life amounted to 16 years, 7 months, 17 days.

His Majesty King Neku II. supplied all the costs and everything else in splendour and glory for this sublime god. He built his subterranean tomb of fine white limestone in well-wrought workmanship. The like of it was never done before.

TABLET IV.

Year 12, month Payni, day 21, under the reign of the king Uah-ab-Ra (Hophra), the friend of Apis-Osiris, the god was carried in peace to the good region of the West. His interment was accomplished in the West of the Libyan Desert near Memphis, after they had fulfilled for him all that is customary in the chambers of purification. The like was never done since the early times.

This god departed to heaven in the year 12, month Pharmuthi, day 12. He was born in the year 16, month Paophi, day 7, under the reign of King Neku II., the ever-living. His introduction into the temple of Ptah took place in the year 1, month Epiphi, day 9, under the reign of King Psamthek II. The full life-time of this god was 17 years, 6 months, 5 days.

The god-like benefactor Uah-ab-Ra supplied all the costs and everything else in splendour and glory for this sublime god. Thus has he done for him, who bestows life and prosperity for ever.

TABLET V.

Year 23, month Pakhons, day 15, under the reign of King Khnum-ab-Ra (Amasis), who bestows life for ever, the god was carried in peace to the good region of the West. His interment in the nether-world was accomplished, in the place which his Majesty had prepared—never had the like been done since early times—after they had fulfilled for him all that is customary, in the chambers of purification ; for his Majesty bore in mind what Horus had done for his father Osiris. He had a great sarcophagus of rose granite made for him, because his Majesty approved the custom, that all the kings in every age had caused it (the sarcophagus of each Apis-bull) to be made out of costly stone. He caused curtains of woven stuffs to be made as coverings for the south side and the north side (of the sarcophagus). He had his talismans put therein, and all his ornaments of gold and costly precious stones. They were prepared more splendidly than ever before, for his Majesty had loved the living Apis better than all (the other) kings.

The holiness of this god went to heaven in the year 23, month Phamenoth, day 6. His birth took place in the year 5, month Tehuti, day 7 ; his inauguration at Memphis in the month Payni, day 8. The full lifetime of this god amounted to 18 years, 6 months. 'This is what was done for him by Aahmes-se-Nit, who bestows pure life for ever.'

The granite sarcophagus of this bull stands to this day *in situ* in the Serapeum. On the cover are inscribed the words :—

The king Amasis. He has caused this to be made for his memorial of the living Apis, (namely) this huge sarcophagus of red granite, for his Majesty approved the custom, that all the kings in all ages had had such made of costly stones. This did he, the bestower of life for ever.

Besides the embalming and the funeral pomp, the kings were put to great expense for the restoration of the subterranean tombs, which were each of them hewn out of the rock during the lifetime of the Apis for which they were destined. Besides, the construction of the sepulchral vault required some time.

A memorial tablet of the time of Ptolemy II. is inscribed with the following data :—

	Working Time		Holidays
	Months	Days	
From the year 32, 21st Payni, to the year 33, 1st Paophi, excavating the chamber	3	15	17
From the year 33, 4th Paophi, to [the year 33, 9th Pharmuthi], finishing the same	6	5	33
In the year 37, 8th Mesori, transport of sarcophagus ; time	1	5	7
In the year 38, 17th Athyr, the completion of the whole edifice ; time . . .	2	9	12

In the reign of Cambyses there occurred the death of one Apis, and the birth of another. This latter was born in the 5th year of the king, on the 28th day of the month Tybi ; he died in the 4th year of Darius I., on the third day of the month Pakhons ; and seventy days later he was buried according to the prescribed usages. The whole length of his life amounted to seven years, three months, five days. His predecessor was the very Apis whom, according to the accounts of the Greek writers, Cambyses is said to have slain with the sword, immediately after his return from his disastrous expedition against Ethiopia ; —a story on which little reliance can be placed. According to an inscription, this Apis was buried in the Serapeum ' in the 4th year ' of the king's reign, ' in the month of Epiphi ' (the day not being specified). On the same stone we see Cambyses represented, under his regal name of Sam-taui Mastu-Ra, *in a kneeling posture, distinctly as a worshipper of the Apis-bull.* Underneath is a long inscription, of which only the following words are legible :—

Year 4, month Epiphi, under the reign [of King Cambyses] the bestower of life for ever, [this] god was carried to his burial [in peace to the Libyan Desert near Memphis, to be interred] in his place, which his Majesty had already caused to be prepared for him . . .

Under Amasis, the Apis died in the 23rd year of the king's reign, on the sixth day of the month Phamenoth, that is to say, about the year 550. His successor, as usual, was not long waited for. Supposing this to be the same that Cambyses caused to be buried in the year 526 B.C., the bull had reached an age of about 24 to 25 years, which is in perfect accord with the average lifetime of the sacred bulls, derived from other examples.

A special inscription on a monument of the time of King Darius I. states that this sovereign was pleased to show marked honour to the Apis-bulls.

In the year 31 under the Majesty of the king and lord of the land, Nthariush—may he live for ever!—behold a living Apis appeared | in the city of Memphis. This (his future) sepulchre was opened, and his chamber was built for an endless duration of years.

This record also agrees most precisely with the age of his predecessor, who in his turn had been born not long after the burial of the bull before him (in the 4th year of Darius I.), and must have died shortly before the appearance of the one now in question, and therefore in the 31st or 30th year of Darius ; whence again we deduce for him a lifetime of 24 or 25 years.

The monuments enable us to pursue still further the traces of the Apis-bulls.

As King Darius I. still enjoyed about five years more of life, after the manifestation of the Apis in his 31st year, so, if we continue to assume a lifetime of 25 years, the new bull must have died about the 20th regnal year of Xerxes I., and therefore about

466 B.C. Now, in place of this Xerxes, we find mention of a King Khabbash, whom the monuments designate as the *Egyptian rival king* to Xerxes. This rival must have succeeded in establishing himself at Memphis, where he provided a solemn burial for the Apis which was just deceased. But unexpected events occurred to frustrate his intention. The proof of this is furnished by the place in the subterranean galleries, where have stood, from ancient times down to the present day, the lid and base of the stone sarcophagus, with the dedicatory inscription of King Khabbash. · The sarcophagus itself stands in the *northern* gallery leading to the Apis-tombs, and almost bars the approach, while the lid lies on the ground in the *southern* gallery. The two were never brought together to enclose the deceased bull. The lid itself bears the following inscription :—

Year 2, month Athyr, under the Majesty of King Khabbash, the friend of Apis-Osiris, of Horus 'of Kakem' (a name for the locality of the Apis tombs).

The latest authentic inscription, proving the death of an Apis under the Pharaohs, is a memorial-stone of the 3rd year of King Nekht-neb-ef, in which the bull died, that is, about 356 B.C. With this we conclude our review of the Apis tablets, and turn to other inscriptions, which belong to the times of the Persian kings.

THE PERSIANS IN EGYPT.

We can hardly award to the Egyptian nobles, who lived in the neighbourhood of the royal court at Saïs, the praise of loyalty to their masters. As soon as the Persians made good their footing in Egypt and honoured Saïs especially by their visits, there were found many descendants of the former royal houses, who did not think it beneath their dignity to prove themselves submissive to the Great King of Persia, and to enter his service.

There was, in particular, a Suten-rekh (i.e. 'King's-grandson'), named Ut'a-Hor-resenet, a son of Pef-tot-Nit (the high-priest of the goddess Nit) and his wife Tmu-iritis, probably a daughter of King Apries (Uah-ab-Ra). To this nobleman the command of the royal fleet had been entrusted under the kings Amasis and Psamthek III. When Cambyses conquered Egypt, Ut'a-Hor-resenet passed at once into the service of the Persian king. On the famous shrine-bearing statue of this eminent nobleman, in the Vatican at Rome, he relates quite unaffectedly the history of his life, from which we have derived the foregoing account of his family.

(I.) When the great lord of all nations, Kambathet (Cambyses), came to Egypt,—at that time the people of all lands were with him,—he ruled this land as king in its whole extent. They settled in it, inasmuch as he was a great king of Egypt and the great lord of all lands. He committed to me the office of a president of the physicians, and kept me beside him as friend and temple-master. His official name was assigned to him as 'King Mastu-Ra.' I made known to him the greatness of the city of Saïs, as the city of Nit, the great mother, who gave birth to the Sun-god Ra—he was the first-born, no (other) being was yet born :—moreover (I informed him) also of the high consequence of the habitation of Nit—it is such as a heaven—in all its quarters :—moreover also of the high import-ance of the chambers of Nit, which are the abodes of Nit and of all the gods in them ; as well as the high consequence of the temple Hakheb, in which the great king and lord of the heaven resides ;—moreover also of the high importance of the south-chamber, of the north-chamber, of the chamber of the morning-sun Ra, and of the chamber of the evening-sun Tmu. These are the mysterious abodes of all the gods.

(II.) And I made my complaint to King Kambathet concerning all the foreigners, who had taken up their quarters in the temple of Nit, that they might be driven out, that so the temple of Nit might be established in its full splendour, as was the case formerly. Then the king gave command to drive out all foreigners, who had taken up their quarters in the temple of Nit, and to pull down all their huts and all their chattels in this temple, and they themselves were forced to remove out of the precincts of this temple. The king gave command to purify this temple of Nit, and to restore to it all its inhabitants, and to acknowledge the people as servants of the temple. He gave command to replace the sacred property of Nit, the great mother, and of all the gods in Saïs, as it had been formerly. He gave command to re-establish the order of all their festivals and of all their processions, as they were formerly. All this did the king, because I had made him acquainted with the high consequence of Saïs, for it is the city of all the gods. May they remain on their thrones in her for ever!

(III.) When King Kambathet came to Saïs, he entered the temple of Nit in person. He testified in every good way his reverence for the great exalted holy goddess, Nit, the great mother, and for the great gods in Saïs, as all the pious kings had done. He did this, because I had made him acquainted with the high importance of the holy goddess, for she is the mother of the Sun-god Ra himself.

(IV.) The king bestowed all that was good upon the temple of Nit. He caused the libations to be offered to the Everlasting One in the house of Nit, as all the kings of former times had done. He did this because I had informed him of all the good that should be done for this temple.

(V.) I established the property of Nit, the great mother, as the king had ordered, for the duration of eternity. I caused the monuments of Nit, the lady of Saïs, to be set up in every proper way, as an able servant of his master ought to do. I was a good man before his face. I protected the people under the very heavy misfortune which had befallen the whole land, such as this country had never experienced before. I was a shield to the weak against the powerful; I protected him who honoured me, and he found it best for him. I did all good for them, when the time had come to do it.

(VI.) I entrusted to them the prophetic offices; I gave them the best land, as the king had commanded, to endure for ever. I made a present of proper burial to such as (died) without a coffin; I nourished all their children and built up again all their houses; I did for them all that is good, as a father does for his son, then when the calamity fell upon this nome, at the time when the grievous calamity befell the whole land.

(VII.) Now King Nthariush (Darius)—may he live for ever!— commanded me to go to Egypt, while he was in the land of Elam,—for he also was the great lord of all lands and a great king of Egypt,— in order that I might re-instate the number of the sacred scribes of the temples, and might revive whatever had fallen into ruin. The foreigners escorted me from land to land, and brought me safe to Egypt, according to the command of the lord of the land. I did according to what he had commanded. I chose of the sons of the inhabitants from all their (schools ?)—to the great sorrow of those who were childless—and I placed them under expert masters,—skilful in all kinds of learning, that they might perform all their works. And the king ordered that all favour should be shown them, because of the pleasure with which they performed all their works. I supplied all those who distinguished themselves with whatever they needed for the scribe's profession, according to their progress. The king did all this because he knew that such a work was the best means of awakening to new life all that was falling into ruin, in order to uphold the name of all the gods, their temples, their revenues, and the ordinance of their feasts for ever.

(VIII.) I was honoured by each of my masters, so long as I sojourned on the earth. Therefore they gave me decorations of gold, and showed me all favour.

(IX.) O ye gods who are in Saïs ! Remember all the good that has been done by the president of the physicians, Ut'a-Hor-resenet. In all that ye are willing to requite him for all his benefits, establish for him a great name in this land for ever.

(X.) O Osiris ! thou Eternal one ! The president of the physicians, Ut'a-Hor-resenet, throws his arms around thee, to guard thy image. Do for him all good according to what he has done, (as the protector of thy shrine for ever.

No further comment on the foregoing text is necessary, for its historical value can hardly be overrated as giving an entirely new aspect of the character of Cambyses. Darius I. took great delight also in rescuing the Egyptian temple-learning from its threatened extinction. He provided for the training of the youth in the priestly schools and built new sanctuaries. There is a temple in the great Oasis at El-Khargeh which is still in a good state of preservation, and whose walls are covered with the name of Nthariush, the Egyptian form of Darius. But the variation in the official coronation names leads to the inference that Darius II. also took part in the building and decorating of this temple. It was dedicated

to the Theban Amen, under his special surname of
Us-khopesh ('the strong-armed'). The record of the
works executed by Darius II., on the northern outer
wall, runs as follows :—

He did this in remembrance of his father, the great god Amen-
Ra, the lord of Hebi, with the Strong Arm, and his associated
gods, inasmuch as he built this new house of good white stone in
the form of a Mesket. Its doors were formed of the Libyan
acacia-wood, which is called Pir-shennu, and covered with Asiatic
bronze in well-wrought lasting work. His (the god's) monument
was renewed according to its original plan. May the gods preserve him among living men for hundreds of thousands of thirty
years' jubilee-feasts on the throne [of Horus], to-day and for ever
and eternally !

The building and decoration of the temple was
continued to the times of King Nekht-Hor-heb (378–
360 B.C.) No royal names of subsequent date appear
there.

The buildings erected here and elsewhere by Darius
were entrusted to an Egyptian architect, whose pedigree
—up to his forefathers of the times of the Third
Dynasty—is given on p. 434.

Some lesser inscriptions of this same Khnum-ab-Ra
inform us that he held his office during the years 27 to
30 of King Darius I. The inscription of the 30th year
runs thus :—

On the 15th day of the month Pharmuthi, in the 30th year of
the king of Upper and Lower Egypt and lord of the land, Nthariush (Darius I.), the ever-living, the friend of all the gods, (this was
written by order of) the master of works in the whole land, the
architect of Upper and Lower Egypt, Khnum-ab-Ra, son of the
architect of Upper and Lower Egypt, Aahmes-se-Nit.

It is well known that Darius I. conceived the bold
plan of connecting the Red Sea with the Nile by a
canal. The remains of a statue of the king, as well
as several memorial stones covered with cuneiform
inscriptions and Egyptian hieroglyphs, which have been

THE PEDIGREE OF THE ARCHITECTS.

IMHOTEP:
Architect of S. and N. Egypt; chief burgomaster; a high functionary of King T'a-sar; (lived in the time of the Third Dyansty).

RA-HOTEP:
Prophet of Amen-Ra, king of the gods; secret-seer of Heliopolis; Architect of Upper and Lower Egypt; chief burgomaster.

BEK-EN-KHONSU:
Chief burgomaster.

UT'A-KHONSU:
Architect; chief burgomaster.

NEFER-MENNU:
Architect; chief burgomaster.

MI (OR AI?)
Architect; chief burgomaster.

SE-UER-NENEN-HEB:
Architect.

PEPI:
Architect; chief burgomaster.

AMEN-HER-PA-MESHA:
2nd, 3rd, and 4th prophet and high-priest of Amen, king of the gods; chief burgomaster.

HOR-EM-SAF:
Architect; chief burgomaster.

MERMER:
Architect; commander.

HOR-EM-SAF:
Architect; commander.

T'A-HEB:
Architect; commander.

NAS-SHUNU:
Architect; commander.

T'A-HEB:
Architect; commander.

NAS-SHUNU:
Architect; commander.

T'A-HEB:
Architect; commander.

NAS-SHUNU:
Architect; commander.

T'A-N-HEBU:
Architect of Upper and Lower Egypt; chief burgo-master.

NAS-SHUNU:
Architect.

UAH-AB-RA RAN-UER:
Architect.

ANKH-PSAMTHEK:
Architect of Upper and Lower Egypt.

AAHMES-SE-NIT:
(*m.* SET-NEFER-TMU)
Architect of Upper and Lower Egypt.

KHNUM-AB-RA:
Chief minister of works for the whole country; architect of Upper and Lower Egypt, in the 27th to 30th years of King Darius I. (about 490 B.C.)

found near the line of the canal (North of Suez), place the fact beyond all doubt. Below is a translation by Jules Oppert of the best preserved of these inscriptions :—

A great god is Auramazda, who created this heaven, who created this earth, who created man, who gave to man a will, who established Darius as king, who committed to King Darius so great, so [glorious] an empire.

I am Darius, king of kings, king of lands of many tongues, king of this great earth, far and near, the son of Hystaspes, the Achæmenid.

Says Darius the king : 'I am a Persian ; with (the power of) Persia I conquered Egypt (Mudrâya). I ordered this canal to be dug, from the river called Pirâva (the Nile), which flows in Egypt, to the sea which comes out of Persia (Erythræan Sea). This canal was afterwards dug there, as I had commanded, and I said : "Go, and destroy half of the canal from Bira to the coast. For such was my will."'

According to Strabo's statement (bk. xvii. p. 804), Darius left off constructing the canal, because some had assured him that Egypt lay below the level of the Red Sea, and so there was danger of the whole land being laid under water.

The city of Coptos—at the western terminus of the caravan route which led through the desert valleys of Hammamât from the Red Sea to the Nile—was for years the residence of two eminent Persians who were invested with the office of Erpa (governor) under the kings just named. They were two brothers named Ataiuhi and Aliurta, sons of a certain Arthames and his Persian wife Qanzu. Both are designated as Seres (i.e. eunuchs) of Parse (Persia). Posted at Coptos—in which city the god of the mountaineers, Amsu, was held in the highest honour—the two brothers had frequent occasion to visit the valleys of Hammamât, in order to have stones quarried for the materials of the royal buildings. Through their long residence in the country

they seem to have adopted Egyptian manners and
customs, and so they did not disdain to perpetuate their
names on hieroglyphic memorial-tablets in that valley.
The representations of the god Amsu of Coptos are
accompanied by hieroglyphs, in which the names of
the 'eunuchs of Persia' are preceded, whenever they
occur, by chronological data. In stating these, however, they departed from the old Egyptian rule, inasmuch as, instead of the current regnal year of the
sovereigns in question, they chose to exhibit the full
sum of the years of their reigns, and also the full
sum of their own years of service under one or more
kings, with the addition of *ar en*, 'has made,' i.e. lived
during, (so many years): just as in the case of the
name of Taharaqa on the Apis-stêlæ.[1] Some examples
of these inscriptions will illustrate this mode of dating:—

FIRST INSCRIPTION.

The sum of the 6 years of the lord of the land Kanbuza
(Cambyses), the sum of the 36 years of the sovereign Nthariush
(Darius I.), and the sum of the 12 years of the sovereign Khshiarsh
(Xerxes I.), has the eunuch of Persia (*seres . en Parse*) Ataiuhi
lived, remaining in the presence of the god Amsu, the chief of the
city.

SECOND INSCRIPTION.

The sum of the 36 years of the godlike benefactor and sovereign, the son of the Sun and wearer of the crown, Nthariush
(Darius I.)—may he live to-day and evermore !—and | the sum of
the 13 years of his son, the sovereign, the son of the Sun and
wearer of the crown, Khshiarsh (Xerxes I.)—may he live to-day
and evermore !—has lived the eunuch of Persia and governor of the
city of Coptos, Ataiuhi.

THIRD INSCRIPTION.

The 5 years of the king of Upper and Lower Egypt, the sove-
reign, Arta-khshesesh (Artaxerxes), and | the 16 years of the god-
like benefactor Arta-khshesesh (Artaxerxes) | has lived the eunuch

---

[1] See p. 424.

of Persia Aliurta, the son of Arthames and the child of his wife Qanzu, remaining before the face of the [god Amsu of Coptos].

A comparison of all these rock-inscriptions gives the following determination of the regnal years of the kings, in their relation to the years of service of the two Persians.

Ataiuhi lived—

(1)　6 full years under the reign of Kanbuza (Cambyses) ;

(2) 36　„　　„　　„　　„　　„　Nthariush (Darius I.) ;

(3)　2 „　　„

(4)　6 „　　„

(5) 10 „　　„ ⎫under the reign of Khshiarsh (Xerxes I.).

(6) 12 „　　„

(7) 16 „　　„

Aliurta lived—

(1)　5 full years │ under the reign of Arta-khshesesh

(2) 16 „　　„　│ (Artaxerxes).

That the phrase ' he lived ' referred, not to the whole lifetime of the person from his birth, but to his actual years of service spent in Egypt, is proved by the dates given in the two inscriptions of Aliurta, who expressed the five years, besides the sixteen years, in order to show his service under Artaxerxes. If Cambyses reigned six years as king of Egypt, the conquest of Egypt must be placed, not in the year 525, but in 527, as before stated.

Xerxes I.—or, as he is named in the Egyptian inscriptions, Khshiarsh or Khsherish—did not enjoy the best reputation among the Egyptians, who had learnt to esteem his predecessor, Darius I., as a benignant and well-disposed ruler. After Xerxes had by force of arms crushed the insurrection made by the Egyptians to throw off the Persian yoke, the foreign rule pressed more severely than ever on the land, over which Achæmenes, the king's brother, was placed as satrap.

The defeats which the Persians soon after suffered

from the Greeks roused anew the desire of the Egyptians for liberty, and an anti-king Khabbash, with the coronation name of Senen-Tanen Sotep-en-Ptah, boldly made head against the Persian sovereign. The memorial inscription of the satrap Ptolemy relates that

the sea-board, which bears the name of Patanut (in Greek, Phthenotes), had been assigned by the king Khabbash to the gods of the city of Buto, when his Majesty had gone to Buto to examine the sea-board, which lies in their whole domain, with the purpose of penetrating into the interior of the marsh-land of Natho, to inspect that arm of the Nile, which flows into the sea, in order that the Asiatic fleet might be kept at a distance from Egypt.

This lake-district, called Patanut, belonged to the deities of Buto from early times. But the hereditary foe Xerxes had alienated it. He kept none of it for the gods of the city of Buto.

Thus the hereditary foe Xerxes had shown an evil example against the city of Buto. But the great king, our lord, the god Horus, the son of Isis and the son of Osiris, the prince of the princes, the king of the kings of Upper and Lower Egypt, the avenger of his father, the lord of Buto, the beginning of the gods and he who came after, after whom no (god) was king, he drove out the hereditary enemy Xerxes out of his palace together with his eldest son, and so he made himself famous in Saïs, the city of the goddess Nit, on that day by the side of the Mother of the Gods.

THE LAST PHARAOHS.

After the retreat of the Persians, a ray of hope for freedom dawned upon the Egyptians. During a period of about sixty years, two dynasties (the Twenty-ninth and Thirtieth) established themselves, at Mendes and Sebennytus, to venture on the last effort to re-conquer their lost independence. The monuments, on which the names of the kings of these dynasties can only be deciphered with difficulty, are silent as to their deeds. As the most remarkable monument of their times we may point to the sarcophagus of King Nectanebo I., now in the British Museum, and also to that of a descendant of the last kings of the Thirtieth Dynasty,

now at Berlin. The inscriptions have accurately preserved the pedigree of the latter.

KING NEKHT-HOR-HEB.

?

T'e-her (Tachos)

Nes-bi-n-didi, = Mertuhap*   KING NEKHT-NEB-EF
a military | (*the last Pharaoh*).
commander,   Thakebes* = Pet-Amen, hereditary prince and
nomarch of | military commander.
Sebennytus.   NEKHT-NEB-EF,
nomarch of the district of Buto, Sebennytus and Tanis,
commander-in-chief of the king.

* *The names thus marked are those of women.*

Nekht-neb-ef, ' the chief captain of his Majesty,' the
grandson of the last Pharaoh, Nekht-neb-ef, had his last
resting-place in that Berlin sarcophagus of stone. But
who was ' his Majesty,' to whom he gave his service as
commander ? The question can only be answered approximately. As grandson of King Nekht-neb-ef, who
reigned over the land from 358 to 340 B.C., the end of his
life falls about sixty years after his grandfather's death,
and therefore about 280 B.C., that is, about fifty years
after the conquest of Egypt by Alexander the Great.
He could not therefore have served either him or his
immediate successors, Philip Arrhidæus and Alexander II., as commander. We must rather reckon
Ptolemy I. Soter, or Ptolemy II. Philadelphus, as his
contemporary.

The translation of the following inscription of a
priest who was contemporary with Darius III. and
Alexander of Macedon will form a fit conclusion to the
History of Egypt according to the Monuments :—

(1) The hereditary prince, the noble, one of the friends ; the
seer of Horus, the lord of Hibonu (Hipponon) ; the seer of the gods
of the nome of Hibonu ; the seer of the god Samtaui, of the city of

(2) A-hehu : the chief seer of the goddess and the president of the priests of Sekhet in the whole land—SAMTAUI-TEF-NEKHT—the son of the temple-master and (3) seer of the god Amen-Ra, the lord of the city Pa-Sha, Nes-samtaui-auf-ankh, and the child of his wife Ankhet : he speaks as follows :—

O thou lord of the gods, Khnem, thou king of Upper and Lower Egypt, (4) thou prince of the land, at whose rising the world is enlightened, whose right eye is the sun's disk, whose left eye is the moon, whose spirit (5) is the beam of light, and out of whose nostrils comes the North wind, to give life to all.

I was thy servant, who did according to thy will, and whose heart was replenished by thee. (6) I have not let any city be higher than thy city, I have not failed to impart of thy spirit to all the children of men among hundreds of thousands, which (spirit) is the most wonderful in all houses, (7) day by day. Thou hast for this recompensed me good a hundred-thousandfold. Thus wast thou diffused everywhere, and (wast made) a leader for the king's house. The heart of the divine benefactor was moved to clemency (8) at my speech. I was exalted to be the first among hundreds of thousands. *When thou turnedst thy back upon the land of Egypt, thou didst incline thyself in thy heart to the master of Asia.* His (9) twice five friends loved me. He conferred on me the office of president of the priests of the goddess Sekhet on the seat of my mother's brother, the president of the goddess Sekhet (10) in Upper and Lower Egypt, Ser-henb. Thou didst protect me *in the battle of the Ionians* (i.e. the army of Alexander) *when thou didst rout the Asiatic* (Darius III.).

(11) They slew a hundred thousand at my side, (but) none lifted up his hand against me. When what befell had befallen, there was peace (12) afterwards. Thy Holiness spake to me : 'Proceed to Khinensu (Heracleopolis Magna) ; I will be with thee ; I will be thy guide among the foreign people.'

(13) I was alone, I sailed up the great stream ; I was not afraid, for I thought of thee. Since I did not transgress thy commandment, I reached the city of Khinensu (14) without having a hair of my head rumpled. And as was the beginning, only by the one appointment of thy decree, so also was the end, for thou gavest me a long life in peace of heart.

(15) O all ye priests, who serve this glorious god Khnem, the king of both worlds, the (god) Horemkhu, the lord of the universe, the good spirit in the city of Khinensu, (16) the (god) Tmu in the city of Tanis, the king of the rams, the primordial male power, the Majesty of the ram, the male, the begetter, the last king of the kings of the land ;— 17) the son who loved the king of Upper and

Lower Egypt, has departed to the heavenly kingdom, to see what is there : (to see) the god Khnem, the king of Upper and Lower Egypt, the god Tmu in his shrine, Khnem, (18) the great god in his hall, the king Unnefer.

May your name remain for ever upon the earth, reaping the reward of honour from Khnem, the king of both worlds ! And sing ye praise and laud to the kingly gods of Khinensu, and praise ye the image of the godlike, who was reverenced in his nome, SAM-TAUI-TEF-NEKHT : so shall all that is best be your portion, and another will praise your name in turn in years to come.

TOMB AT SAQQARAH, INSCRIBED WITH THE NAME OF PSAMTHEK.

SUPPLEMENTARY NOTE ON THE LAST PHARAOHS.

DYNASTY XXVI.

[WITH the Twenty-fifth Dynasty Dr. Brugsch's history practically ends, for it was his special object to write the story of the kingdom of Ancient Egypt from the evidence of the monuments alone. At this point their information becomes but very scanty; while in the fragments of Manetho and among the Greek and Roman authors there is to be found an abundance of material which, even if some of it must be accepted with caution, furnishes us with ample means for laying down the broad outlines of the history of Egypt from the Twenty-sixth Dynasty until its close.

The national historian of this period was Manetho, an Egyptian, who was well acquainted with the Greek tongue, and was ordered by Ptolemy Philadelphus to write in that language the history of his native land. He appears to have been both a scribe and a high-priest, and thoroughly well versed in the language and literature of his country, as the monuments often afford confirmation of many of his statements. If only the Book of Manetho were yet extant, the writing of a history of Ancient Egypt would be, comparatively speaking, a light task; but the manuscript itself perished, along with other priceless documents, in the burning of the great library at Alexandria. All that is left of it are the Lists of the Kings, and some fragments which are quoted by Josephus in his 'Treatise against Apion.' Syncellus and Eusebius have also preserved small portions of it in their writings; but it is evident that many are incorrect transcriptions, even if they are not absolutely spurious. The most important classic writer upon this subject is Herodotus, who devotes the whole of the second and the beginning of the third book of his celebrated history to Egypt and the Egyptians. Notwithstanding the many attacks which have of late years been made upon the veracity of the ancient historian, modern excavations and the deciphering of texts prove that his statements from his own personal knowledge are, on the whole, to be trusted. Next to him in rank, but greatly his inferiors, are Diodorus Siculus, Strabo, Josephus, and Plutarch.

PSAMTHEK I., B.C. 666–612. — After the Assyrian defeat of Urdamen, the son-in-law and successor of Taharaqa, which was followed by the sack of Thebes, the country seems to have settled down for a time under the rule of several petty princes. At last one of them, named Psamthek, the son of that Neku who was put to death by Shabak (p. 418), succeeded in gaining the supremacy in Lower Egypt. The means he adopted for attaining his object are so mixed up with tradition and popular fable that it is impossible to do more than assume that it was chiefly through the aid of the Greek mercenaries in the Delta that he gained the throne. To further secure the sovereignty, he married Shep-en-apet, an Ethiopian princess, the niece of Shabak, thus rendering his line legitimate. The ruins near Sâ-el-Hagar mark the site of Saïs, his capital. According to Herodotus, this town became one of the most flourishing in the kingdom, and was the centre of that great revival of art which is one of the distinguishing features of the Twenty-sixth Dynasty.

True it is that it was wanting in that boldness and vigour which characterised the work of the Ancient Empire; but the ideas were the same, though the results showed the touch of Hellenic influence.

Psamthek spent his long reign of fifty-four years in restoring the temples which had fallen into decay in the troublous times which preceded him, in fostering art, and in strengthening the kingdom. He made a successful expedition into Ethiopia, and re-conquered part of Nubia. Then turning his attention to the internal affairs of the country, he made a treaty of commerce with the Greeks, by which their merchants were to be allowed to settle in the Delta. He enlisted also a large body of mercenaries from among the Carians and Ionians, through whom he had gained his crown; but this so enraged his Egyptian and Libyan soldiers that 200,000 of them deserted and went over to the king of Ethiopia. This information is gained from Herodotus, the truth of which is confirmed by a Greek inscription on one of the colossal figures at Abû Simbel. With the help of the Phœnicians Psamthek built a fleet, and attempted the recovery of the Egyptian power in Western Asia; but he was only successful in re-conquering Ashdod, after a siege which lasted twenty-nine years.

NEKU II., B.C. 612–596. — Psamthek I. was succeeded by his son Neku, a king full of energy, and very brave, but wanting in prudence. The fleet established by his father was maintained, and ships were stationed both on the Red Sea and at the mouths of the Nile; and by his orders Phœnician sailors successfully circumnavigated Africa. Neku also endeavoured to re-construct the canal from the Nile to the Red Sea, which had been attempted by both Seti I. and Ramses II. It was cut from the eastern side of the

Pelusiac arm of the Nile, a little north of Bubastis, in the direction of Lake Timsah, and from thence proceeded in a southerly direction, past the western side of the Bitter Lakes, straight to the Gulf of Suez. 120,000 Egyptians are said to have lost their lives in this undertaking.

Neku then attempted to assert the Egyptian supremacy in Asia. The Assyrian army encountered the king of Egypt at Carchemish, the key to the Euphrates, and was completely defeated there. It was on this occasion that Josiah, the king of Judah, interfering, was slain in battle at Megiddo. Three years later Nabopolassar, king of Babylon, sent Nebuchadnezzar, his son, to eject the Egyptians from Carchemish, and thus finally destroyed their rule in Asia.

PSAMTHEK II., B.C. 596–591.—There is nothing to be recorded of the reign of this king, except an expedition into Napata.

UAH-AB-RA, called also APRIES and PHARAOH HOPHRA, B.C. 591–572.—This king inherited both the bravery and the ambition of his predecessors, as well as their love of art. He built at Saïs a very beautiful temple, with a wonderful portico, before which were erected colossal statues and sphinxes; and for which his successor caused a monolithic shrine to be quarried at Elephantiné. Two thousand boatmen, working in relays, took three months to convey it to Saïs; but it was never set up in its proper place, and remained at the entrance of the temple. Its external dimensions were 39 feet × 22 feet × 12 feet, and when hollowed out it weighed over 428 tons. At his accession Pharaoh Hophra made a league with Zedekiah against Nebuchadnezzar, king of Babylon, which was unsuccessful, Jerusalem being taken and the Jewish king sent in chains to Babylon. However Pharaoh's fleet was successful against that of Nebuchadnezzar, and with his help Tyre held out against that monarch for thirteen years. Uah-ab-Ra next went to war with the Greeks of Cyrene, and was there completely defeated. His soldiers afterwards broke out into open revolt, and elected Aahmes as their king, who in his turn defeated the followers of Uah-ab-Ra, took their king prisoner, and shut him up in his own capital. Herodotus (bk. ii. 169) says that after this 'the Egyptians took him (Uah-ab-Ra) and strangled him; but having done so, they buried him in the sepulchre of his fathers.'

AAHMES (or AMASIS) II., B.C. 572–528, was of extremely low origin, but, marrying the princess Ankhs-en-Ra-nefert, the daughter of Psamthek II., he thus made his family to belong to the true royal line. He appears to have been a brave and energetic king, and withal prudent. One of his first acts was to remove the Carian and Ionian mercenaries from the Delta to Memphis, where he established them as his body guard. He encouraged commercial enterprise, and granted Naukratis as a free port to Greek merchants, permitting them at the same time to settle there. He maintained the old friendship with Phœnicia and conquered Cyprus. He appears to have been on an amicable footing with the Greek states, for when the temple at Delphi was burnt down in B.C. 548 Aahmes sent gifts for its re-building. Instead of continuing hostilities with Babylon, or attempting by himself to stem the tide of Persian invasion, then rapidly setting in, he became an ally of Crœsus, king of Lydia, and promised him a contingent against Cyrus. On the death of the Persian monarch Cambyses immediately attacked Egypt; but Aahmes died at the beginning of the invasion.

PSAMTHEK III., B.C. 525.—It was to a lost inheritance that the son of Aahmes succeeded; for, after a gallant resistance—first at Pelusium and then at Memphis—Cambyses took him prisoner. He treated him at first with kindness, but afterwards, on a suspicion of conspiracy, put to death the unfortunate young prince within six months of his accession.

DYNASTY XXVII.

THE PERSIANS IN EGYPT.

KAMBATHET, or CAMBYSES, B.C. 527–514 (?).—The first years of this king's reign appear to have been peaceful. From the inscription on the statue of a Saïte priest, named Ut'a-Hor-resenet, in the Vatican, Cambyses appears to have tolerated the Egyptian gods, if he did not actually worship them, and he caused himself to be taught those sciences for which the Egyptian priests were so celebrated; he maintained and beautified the temples, and was initiated into the mysteries of Nit of Saïs.[1] He appears to have adopted the style of a true Pharaoh, and to have done all in his power to conciliate the people. After five years Cambyses left Egypt, placing it in the charge of Aryandes, the first of a line of Persian satraps who governed the country. Then came a series of reverses. An expedition was sent to the Oasis of Amen, but, being badly provisioned and betrayed by treacherous guides, it wandered into the desert, never to return, and not one soldier came back to tell by what catastrophe an entire army perished. Then another force was equipped, and went against Napata, headed by Cambyses himself, but this too was unsuccessful. Thereupon the king vented all his rage and disappointment on the temples, monuments, statues, and other objects of worship in Egypt, and a wholesale de-

[1] See p. 430.

struction of them was ordered throughout the kingdom. Cambyses died in Syria, it is thought by his
own hand.

NTHARIUSH (DARIUS) I., B.C. 521-486. — Cambyses
was succeeded by the son of Hystaspes, whose chief
desire seems to have been to conciliate his people and
efface from their minds the cruelties and wanton destruction caused by his predecessor. He respected
their gods, supported their religion, and promoted
education; he encouraged commerce, re-opened the
canal from the Nile to the Red Sea, and restored the old
caravan route from Coptos through the Hammamât
valley to the sea-board. He also erected a magnificent
temple to Amen in the Oasis. In the 35th year of the
reign of Darius the Egyptians revolted, expelled the
Persians, and set up a native ruler, Khabbash. This
prince succeeded for three years in holding his own
against the conquerors.

XERXES I., B.C. 485-465.—Egypt was again conquered by this king, who appointed his brother Achæmenes governor. It is evident that in the meantime
the Egyptians in the Delta were preparing for another
revolt.

ARTAXERXES I., B.C. 465-425.—In the fifth year of the
reign of Artaxerxes, Inaros, king of Libya, together with
an Athenian fleet of 200 ships, aided the Egyptians to rise
against the Persian domination. A desperate battle en-
sued at Papremis, when Inaros slew Achæmenes with his
own hand; and shortly afterwards a Phœnician fleet sent
to help the Persians was destroyed by the Athenians.
The allies moved up the river to Memphis, and re-captured
the old capital of the empire except the fortification
called ' Anbu-hat ' (' the white wall '). Here the Persians
held out so long that reinforcements under Megabyzus
being sent to their aid, they pushed the Egyptians

into the island of Prosopitis, which they besieged for eighteen months, at the end of which time Megabyzus diverted the river and stranded their ships. The Athenians fled to Cyrene, and Inaros, betrayed by his own people, was taken prisoner, sent to Persia, and there crucified. Amyrtæus of Saïs, the Egyptian leader, managed to escape to the marshes, and there maintain his independence.

XERXES II., B.C. 425-4, and DARIUS II., B.C. 424-405. — There is nothing to record of the reigns of these kings except the gradual endeavour on the part of the Egyptians to throw off the Persian yoke.

DYNASTY XXVIII.

AMEN-RUT (AMYRTÆUS), B.C. 405-399.—This king was probably the son of Pausiris and grandson of Amyrtæus the friend and ally of Inaros, king of Libya. He revolted against Persia, and on the death of Darius II. Egypt became practically independent. He is the only king of this dynasty, for at his death the government passed into the hands of the princes of Mendes.

DYNASTY XXIX.

NIAFAAURUT I., B.C. 399-393.—At the time of this king's accession Sparta was at war with Persia; he therefore sent a fleet of 100 ships, laden with corn and arms, to the Lacedæmonians. Unfortunately it was intercepted at Rhodes by Conon, who commanded the Athenian fleet, and dispersed.

HAKER, B.C. 393-380; PSA-MUT, B.C. 380; NIA-FAAURUT II., B.C. 379.—There is but little to relate of these kings, and they are chiefly known for their alliances with the enemies of Persia.

DYNASTY XXX.

With NEKHT-HOR-HEB (NECTANEBO) I., B.C. 378-360, commenced the last dynasty of native kings of Egypt : his capital was Sebennytus. The Egyptians at this time possessed a large army of mercenaries, commanded by Chabrias, an Athenian. The Persians, who were now planning an invasion of the Delta, managed to persuade the Athenians to recall both Chabrias and the mercenary troops, and also to send Iphicrates, with 20,000 men, to the help of their general Pharnabazus. It took two years to equip this invading army, which numbered, when complete, 200,000 barbarians, under the Persian command, and 20,000 Greeks, under that of Iphicrates. They arrived at the Mendesian mouth of the Nile, and at once scattered the Egyptians placed there to guard the frontier. The Greek commander then wished to push on without delay to Memphis, but Pharnabazus refused ; this gave the Egyptians time to collect their forces and win a pitched battle near Mendes. The Persians re-embarked their soldiers and departed forthwith, and Iphicrates fled. This victory secured peace and independence to Egypt for some years, during which time art revived and temples and monuments were both erected and restored.

T'E-HER (TACHOS), B.C. 364-361.—The short reign of this king was chiefly occupied with wars against Persia. Tachos first of all made an alliance with Agesilaus, king of Sparta, and secured the help of a Greek fleet, commanded by Chabrias. Contrary to the advice of the former, Tachos insisted upon going into Phœnicia in person, leaving his brother to take the government of the country. During the king's absence his brother stirred up a revolt in Egypt, in which the son of the latter, then serving as a soldier with the army in Phœnicia, joined, and Agesilaus with his Greek mercenaries, going over to the side of the pretender, overthrew Tachos, who sought refuge first at Sidon and then at the court of Artaxerxes, who received him kindly, and under whose protection he ended his days.

NEKHT-NEB-EF (NECTANEBO) II., B.C. 361–340.—This king's first act was to defend himself against a rival prince of Mendes, who opposed him with an immense force of townsmen and artificers. Owing to the skill of Agesilaus Nectanebo was victorious. The monuments of this period testify to the king's love of art; and it is evident that he preferred to encourage art and sciences rather than secure his crown. The Persians again and again invaded Egypt, and at first unsuccessfully, owing to the skill of the Greek generals in the pay of the Egyptian monarch. But at last Ochus in person appeared before Pelusium with an army of 340,000 soldiers, and on the first repulse Nectanebo shut himself up in Memphis, and from thence fled into Napata. So fell the empire of the Pharaohs after the unparalleled duration of nearly 4,000 years.—M. B.]

THE NOMES OF EGYPT ACCORDING TO THE LISTS OF THE MONUMENTS.

A. PATORIS (UPPER EGYPT).

NOMES		CAPITALS		DIVINITIES
		Egyptian Names	Greek Names	
I.	TA-KENS	Abu	*Elephantiné*	Khnem
II.	TES-HOR	Teb	*Apollinopolis Magna*	Horus and Hathor
III.	TEN	Nekheb	*Eileithyia, Latopolis*	Nekheb
IV.	UAST	Uast	*Thebes, Hermonthis*	Amen-Ra and Mut
V.	HIRUI	Qobti	*Coptos*	Amsu
VI.	AATI	Tanterer	*Denderah*	Hathor
VII.	SEKHEM	Ha	*Diospolis Parva*	Hathor
VIII.	ABT	Abtu	*Abydos, Tini*	Anhur
IX.	AMSU	Apu	*Panopolis*	Amsu
X.	UAT'ET	Tebu	*Aphroditopolis*	Hathor
XI.	SET	Shas-hotep	*Hypsele*	Khnem
XII.	TUF	Nen-ent-bak	*Antæopolis*	Horus
XIII.	ATEF-KHENT	Saiut	*Lycopolis*	Ap-uat
XIV.	ATEF-PEH	Qos	*Cusæ*	Hathor
XV.	UN	Khmennu	*Hermopolis*	Tehuti
XVI.	MEH-MAHET	Hebennu	*Hipponon*	Horus
XVII.	. . . . . .	Qasa	*Cynonpolis*	Anpu
XVIII.	SAPET	Ha-suten	*Alabastrônpolis*	Anpu
XIX.	UAB	Pa-mat'et	*Oxyrhynchos*	Set
XX.	AM-KHENT	Khinensu	*Heracleopolis Magna*	Hor-shefi
XXI.	AM-PEH	Smen-Hor	—	Khnem
XXII.	MATEN	Tep-ahet	*Aphroditopolis*	Hathor

B. PATOMIT (LOWER EGYPT).

NOMES		CAPITALS		DIVINITIES
		Egyptian Names	Greek Names	
I.	ANUB-HET'	Mennefer	*Memphis*	Ptah and Sekhet
II.	AA	Sekhem	*Letopolis*	Hor-ur
III.	AMENT	Menten-Hapi	*Apis*	Hathor-nub
IV.	SEPI-RES	T'eka	*Canopus*	Amen-Ra and Nit
V.	SEPI-EMHET	Sa	*Sais*	Nit
VI.	KASET	Khesun	*Xois*	Amen-Ra
VII.	. . . . AMENT	Sent-nefer	*Metelis*	Hu
VIII.	. . . . ABTET	T'ukot	*Sethroë*	Atmu
IX.	AT'I	Pa-Ausar	*Busiris*	Osiris
X.	KAKEM	Hataherab	*Athribis*	Horus-khenti-khati
XI.	KAHEBES	Kahebes	*Kabasos*	Isis
XII.	KAT'EB	T'ebneter	*Sebennytos*	Anhur
XIII.	HAKAT	Annu	*Heliopolis*	Ra
XIV.	KHENT-ABET	T'an	*Tanis*	Horus
XV.	TEHUTI	Pa-Tehuti	*Hermopolis*	Tehuti
XVI.	KHAR	Pabaneb-tet	*Mendes*	Ba-neb-tet
XVII.	SAM-BEHUTET	Pa-khen-en-Amen	*Diospolis*	Amen-Ra
XVIII.	AMKHENT	Pa-Bast	*Bubastis*	Bast
XIX.	AMPEH	Pa-Uat'	*Buto*	Uat'
XX.	SEPT	Qesem	*Phacussa*	Sept

LIST OF VALUES AND PRICES, ABOUT B.C. 1000.

1 *Ten* = 10 *Ket.*
1 *Ket* =   9·0959 grammes = 154 grains nearly (or $\frac{1}{3}$ oz. Troy).
1 *Ten* = 90·959   „   = 1537 grains (above $\frac{1}{4}$ lb. Troy).

Table of the Estimated Value of Ancient Egyptian Uncoined Silver and Copper Money.   Ratio of silver to copper, 1 : 80.

Egyptian Weights	Weight in Grammes	Silver (1 Mark = 1 Shilling)		Copper	
		Mark	Pfennige	Mark	Pfennige
$\frac{1}{3}$ Ket	3·0319	—	$53\frac{1}{3}$	—	$\frac{2}{3}$
$\frac{1}{2}$ „	4·5479	—	80	—	1
$\frac{2}{3}$ „	6·0638	1	$6\frac{2}{3}$	—	$1\frac{1}{3}$
1 „	9·0959	1	60	—	2
2 „	18·1918	3	20	—	4
3 „	27·2877	4	80	—	6
4 „	36·3836	6	40	—	8
5 „	45·4795	8	—	—	10
6 „	54·5754	9	60	—	12
7 „	63·6713	11	20	—	14
8 „	72·7672	12	80	—	16
9 „	81·8631	14	40	—	18
1 Ten	90·959	16	—	—	20
2 „	181·918	32	—	—	40
3 „	272·877	48	—	—	60
4 „	363·836	64	—	—	80
5 „	454·795	80	—	1	—
6 „	636·713	96	—	1	20
7 „	727·672	112	—	1	40
8 „	818·631	128	—	1	60

By the help of this Table the reader will find it easy to form a correct idea of the values and prices in the following List.

The *Ket of Silver* corresponds to the Greek *Didrachmon* or *Stater*, and the *Ket of Copper* to the *Chalcus* (= $\frac{1}{8}$th of the Obolus). Accordingly the Copts translate the Greek didrachmon by *Kiti* or *Kite.*

1 Slave cost 3 Ten, 1 Ket, silver.
1 Ox   „   1 Ket, silver (= 8 Ten, copper).
1 Goat cost 2 Ten, copper.
1 Pair of Fowls (Geese ?) cost $\frac{1}{3}$ Ten, copper.

500 Fish, of a particular kind, cost 1 Ket, silver (= 8 Ten, copper).

800 Fish, of another kind, cost 1 Ket, silver.

100 Fish, of a third kind, „ 1 „ „

1 Tena of Corn of Upper Egypt cost 5–7 Ten, copper.

1 Hotep of Wheat cost 2 Ten, copper.

1 „ „ Spelt „ 2 „ „

5 Hin of Honey „ 4 „ „

(Hence 1 Hin of Honey cost 8 Ket, copper.)

365 Hin of Honey cost $3\frac{2}{3}$ Ten, silver.

(Hence 1 Hin of Honey cost $\frac{1}{10}$ Ket, silver.)

11 Hin of Oil cost 17 Ten, copper.

50 Acres (Set) of arable land cost 5 Ten, silver.

1 Garden land cost 2 Ten, silver.

1 Knife cost 3 Ten, copper.

1 Razor „ 1 „ „

1 Metal Vessel, weighing 20 Ten, cost 40 Ten, copper.

1   Ditto   „   6 „   „ 18 „   „

1   Ditto   „   1 „   „ 3 „   „

1 Apron of fine stuff cost 3 Ten, copper.

The month's wages of an ordinary workman amounted to 5 Ten of copper.

The above values are derived from inscriptions, and there can be no doubt as to the accuracy of their interpretation.

TABLE OF THE ANCIENT EGYPTIAN CALENDAR,

IN ITS NORMAL FORM, COMPARED WITH THE JULIAN YEAR.

SACRED SOTHIC YEAR			ALEXANDRIAN YEAR		JULIAN YEAR		ANCIENT EGYPTIAN SEASONS
Days	Day	Month	Day	Month	Day	Month	
1	1	Tehuti (I)	26	Epiphi	20	July	
6	6	„	1	Mesori (XII)	25	„	
31	1	Paophi (II)	26	„	19	August	
36	6	„	1		24		
				Intercalary Days		„	
40	10		5		28		I. The Inundation
41	11	„	1	Tehuti (I)	29	„	
61	1	Athyr (III)	21	„	18	September	
71	11	„	1	Paophi (II)	28	„	
91	1	Khoiakh (IV)	21	„	18	October	
101	11	„	1	Athyr (III)	28	„	
121	1	Tybi (V)	21	„	17	November	
131	11	„	1	Khoiakh (IV)	27	„	
151	1	Mekhir (VI)	21	„	17	December	
161	11	„	1	Tybi (V)	27	„	II. Winter
181	1	Phamenoth (VII)	21	„	16	January	
191	11	„	1	Mechir (VI)	26	„	
211	1	Pharmuthi (VIII)	21	„	15	February	
221	11	„	1	Phamenoth (VII)	25	„	
241	1	Pakhons (IX)	21	„	17	March	
251	11	„	1	Pharmuthi (VII)	27	„	
271	1	Panoi (X)	21	„	16	April	
281	11	(Payni)	1	Pakhons (IX)	26	„	
301	1	Epiphi (XI)	21	„	16	May	
311	11	„	1	Payni (X)	26	„	III. Summer.
331	1	Mesori (XII)	21	„	15	June	
341	11	„	1	Epiphi (XI)	25	„	
361	1		21	„	15		
		Intercalary Days				July	
365	5		25		19		

INDEX.

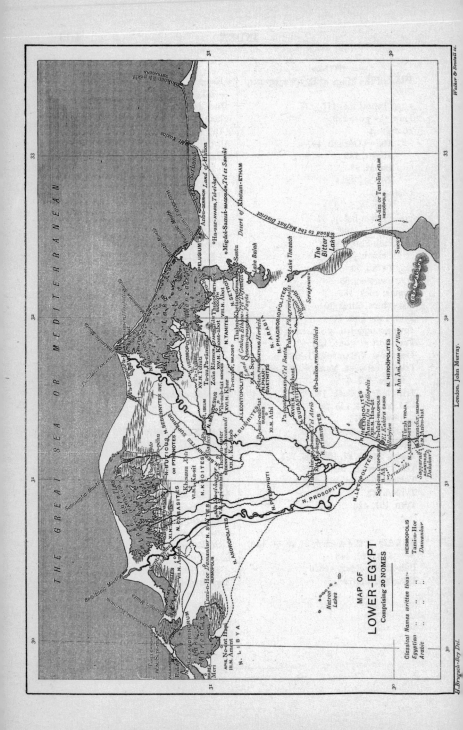

MAP OF
LOWER-EGYPT
Comprising 20 NOMES

London, John Murray.

H. Brugsch-Bey Del.

Walker & Boutall sc.

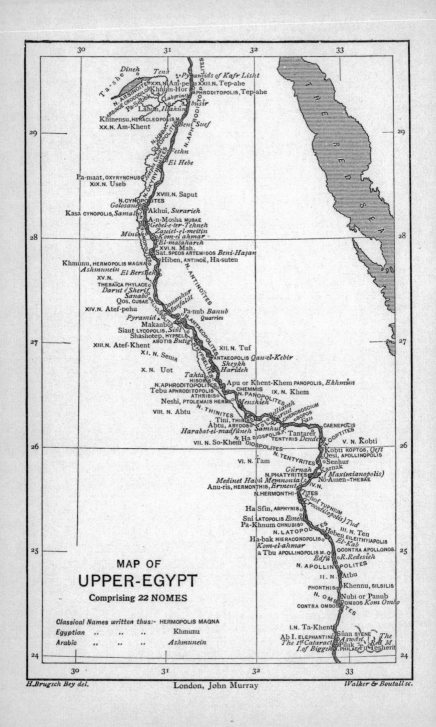

MAP OF
UPPER-EGYPT
Comprising 22 NOMES

Classical Names written thus:- HERMOPOLIS MAGNA

Egyptian .. .. .. Khmunu

Arabic .. .. .. *Ashmunein*

H.Brugsch Bey del.   London, John Murray   Walker & Boutall sc.

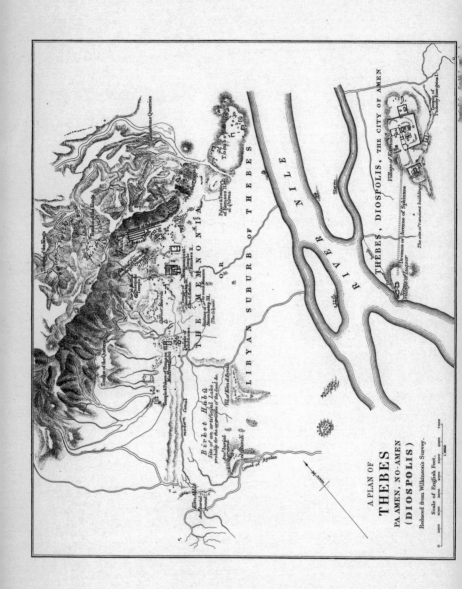

A PLAN OF

THEBES

PA AMEN, NO AMEN
(DIOSPOLIS)

Reduced from Wilkinson's Survey.

Scale of English Feet.

THEBES, DIOSPOLIS, THE CITY OF AMEN

RIVER NILE

THE MEMNONIA

LIBYAN SUBURB OF THEBES

OR